ALASTAIR SAWDAY'S
SPECIAL PLACES TO STAY

BRITISH
BED AND
BREAKFAST

Simply the best, all 664 of them.
Whether for the people, houses
or settings – it's a glittering collection.

EDITED BY JACKIE KING

Cover Design:	The Bridgewater Book Company
Design:	Caroline King
Maps & Mapping:	Bartholomew Mapping, a division of HarperCollins, Glasgow
Printing:	Canale, Italy
UK Distribution:	Portfolio, Greenford, Middlesex
US Distribution:	The Globe Pequot Press, Guilford, Connecticut

Published in September 2002

Alastair Sawday Publishing Co. Ltd
The Home Farm Stables, Barrow Gurney, Bristol BS48 3RW
Tel: +44 (0)1275 464891 Fax: +44 (0)1275 464887
E-mail: info@specialplacestostay.com   Web: www.specialplacestostay.com

The Globe Pequot Press
P. O. Box 480, Guilford, Connecticut 06437, USA
Tel: +1 203 458 4500 Fax: +1 203 458 4601
E-mail: info@globe-pequot.com   Web: www.globe-pequot.com

Seventh edition

ISBN 1-901970-28-0 in the UK
ISBN 0-7627-2460-9 in the US

Printed in Italy

ALASTAIR SAWDAY'S
SPECIAL PLACES TO STAY

BRITISH
BED AND
BREAKFAST

"He who is outside of his door already has the hard part of his journey behind him."

Dutch proverb

The
Globe
Pequot
Press

Guilford
Connecticut, USA

ALASTAIR
SAWDAY
PUBLISHING

Alastair Sawday Publishing
Bristol, UK

CONTENTS

Acknowledgements • A word from Alastair Sawday •
• Introduction • General map • Maps

england

CONTENTS

CONTENTS

wales

CONTENTS

scotland

See back of the book for:

• What is Alastair Sawday Publishing? •

• www.specialplacestostay.com •

• Alastair Sawday's Special Places to Stay series •

• The Little Earth Book • Report Form • Quick Reference Indices •

• Index by Surname • Index by Place name •

• Exchange Rates • Explanation of symbols •

ACKNOWLEDGEMENTS

This is our most complex book, not least because most owners are, once consulted about their entry, anxious to make changes. Others are slow to respond. Most have strong opinions. Jackie King would love to please everybody – clearly impossible. But her skill and patience are ineffable and for every feather ruffled there is a 'frippery' of them smoothed. She is a wonderful editor and we owe her more than she would admit.

Laura Kinch has provided solid and immensely kind support, supported in her turn by the superb team named below. This book is a mammoth 'oeuvre', demanding in its need for accuracy, even more so in its greed for reliable good taste and judgement. Jackie keeps that great ball rolling and Laura gives it a judicious push. But nothing would be possible without the deep support of a great many owners and the tireless labours of them all.

Belated thanks, too, to the calm genius of Russell Wilkinson. This is only our second in-house production and to him is owed its success. With him, fingers dancing on the keyboard, was Tom Dalton, Rachel Coe in key support. We are still impressed that they 'cracked' it.

Alastair Sawday

Series Editor:	Alastair Sawday
Editor:	Jackie King
Editorial Director:	Annie Shillito
Production Manager:	Julia Richardson
Web Producer:	Russell Wilkinson
Editorial Assistants:	Laura Kinch, Jo Boissevain
Production Assistants:	Rachel Coe, Tom Dalton, Paul Groom
Accounts:	Bridget Bishop
Additional writing:	Jo Boissevain
Photo of Alastair Sawday:	Mark Bolton
Country photos:	Michael Busselle
Inspections:	David Ashby, Lindy Ball, Tom Bell, Fredena Burns, Gillian Charlton Meyrick, Annie Coates, Trish Dugmore, Sorrel Everton, Jonathan Goodall, Deborah Jacobs, Alastair Langland, Joanne MacInnes, Auriol Marson, Tom Pinsent, Caroline Portway, James & Petrina Pugh, Eva van Eeghan

A special thank you, too, to the other inspectors who saw just one or two houses for us – often at short notice.

A WORD FROM ALASTAIR SAWDAY

I feel slightly fraudulent – rather like those who write about bird life, describing beautiful and fascinating creatures in whose creation they have taken no part at all.

Yet without them we would know so much less about the incredible range of birds we have, about their beauty and their strange ways. We learn how subtly but crucially they differ, how they sing and fly, feed and hunt. We are told how their habitats are threatened, how they build their nests. And we learn to wonder at their ingenuity and instincts for survival. We want to protect them.

So it is with us – and with these houses and their remarkable owners. We owe them much, and we celebrate them and their survival, for the world around them is going slowly, slightly mad. And in a country which is losing its regional variety – apparent in so many ways – it is no surprise to find conformity everywhere. People even share a shrinking vocabulary to describe their shrinking cultural experience. In our own field, many hotels sink into deep sameness and banality; most B&Bs display few signs of character.

A word about our new cover design: we hope that it is fresher and more contemporary than those lovely water-colours – which we are sad to lose. They have always set us apart but we feel that our style is now well-entrenched and respected and we are free to branch out with a new design. Fingers crossed that the change pleases many and seduces even more.

Most of the houses and owners in this book have been chosen because they stand (like King Canute?) against the rising tide of standardisation. We have no rules about how they do their work; we just admire them and like them for doing things well, even brilliantly, and for being themselves. Some of them may be eccentric, some are conventional; others will overwhelm you with kindness, others are shy. All of them are intensely human. (Sounds an odd thing to say, but it cannot be said of everybody running a B&B, or of those who run most hotels.) They are a threatened species so if you use this book you are helping them (and us, of course) to survive and prosper.

Alastair Sawday

INTRODUCTION

How do we choose our Special Places?

The simplest answer is that we look for people and places that we like. But the reality is more complicated. It would be silly of us to look for just one type of house or one type of person that pleases us for, while pleasing ourselves, we would leave a whole army of you disappointed. We nevertheless look for specialness: in the owner's personality, in architecture, furniture, decoration, history, food, surroundings, garden or peace. Each B&B in this book is a fascinating cocktail of those things.

At the heart of our choice is the owner. We have turned down the finest and most comfortable houses because the owner is grumpy or aloof, or the atmosphere cold. Equally we have less-than-perfect houses – some even slightly dusty or chaotic or crumbling – but with owners to whom we have felt so drawn that the minor negatives were immediately forgotten.

There are many near-perfect mixes of magical architecture, enviable garden, handsome furniture, beautiful art and wonderfully comfortable beds and bathrooms to rave about. Good taste, generosity and kindness excite us, whether in our castles, cottages, farmhouses or bungalows.

We like owners who are generous: a drink before dinner, the offer of a lift to a pub, a simple, early supper for your children, help with planning your day. Many of them will go out of their way to be flexible. We know that an encounter with genuine kindness and an easy welcome live longer in the memory than any amount of five starred 'facilities'.

How we go about it

The process we go through to find entries is very different from that of other books.

We have visited every place here – most of them several times. If other books or organisations do inspect – and many don't – there is often no evaluation of friendliness, taste, authenticity or style. Often there is only form filling; we admit to a little of that, but only to get the facts right.

The real value of our visits lies in a personal account of the meeting, the detail that can't be gleaned during a phone call. We like to know what the owners were like, how they were with guests, what the house felt like, what was memorable.

Writing each entry is the most challenging part of putting the book together. Why do we do the writing ourselves? We want a lively, vibrant book that avoids the estate agents' language and cliché that often litters other accommodation guides.

Gaining the owner's approval of the text can be difficult! We need to draw attention to drawbacks or quirks of taste or personality. It is often quite contentious, but we have to do it.

There are cheaper and quicker ways of producing a book like this and corners that could be cut. Initially, you'd be none the wiser. However, if we didn't do all that research you'd soon come across places that we shouldn't have included. You'd stop trusting us.

So we have screened out the B&Bs that offer more 'facilities' than you should ever hope for but are simply missing out on old-fashioned generosity, or have become jaded. Not for us, either, are those who feel that if they have the 'right' number of hooks on the backs of doors, the 'right' curtain rails and the 'right' hospitality trays no one could fail to be impressed.

We like to include people who are relaxed, who enjoy sharing their family life and their home with you. We are not keen on those who want you to feel privileged to be staying in their historic, beautiful home, or those who have succumbed to 'C.G.H.S.' (see below).

Creeping Guest House Syndrome

We first mentioned this in 2001 and expected brickbats, but many owners saw it as a deft summing up of what separates our B&Bs from guest houses. What confirms the diagnosis? 'Private' signs on doors leading to 'their' part of the house, tourist pamphlets in the hallway, a surfeit of Fire Exits, laminated information, large exterior B&B signs, strict timetables for meals or arrivals or departures, separate dining tables…

We call it 'Creeping' because of the gradual change from the house being a home first and B&B second, to being first and foremost a business. Some of the above may be sensible measures, but C.G.H.S. is a subtle shift away from 'looking after' to 'processing' guests.

We hope you will be enriched by the whole experience of staying in someone's home. Your hosts are 'real' people who have families, sometimes other jobs, pets, friends, gardens or farms to look after. We choose them all because we know that they will look after you, too, in spite of any other commitments.

INTRODUCTION

What to expect

Most houses run on well-oiled wheels but occasionally there will be a spanner in the works. Most of you are tolerant but if your needs aren't being met please do say so – your host wants you to be happy.

Our favourite owners are un-selfconsciously easy about having guests around. Some need to set rules about arrivals and departures and, if such things bother you, discuss it all beforehand. You are embarking on a B&B 'contract' and anything extra is a bonus; time in the garden or pool, or early or late breakfasts, need to be negotiated.

We have masses of feedback from owners expressing delight at their Sawday guests who clearly understand that these houses are homes, not hotels. You don't expect your bags to be carried, wet towels to be picked up or snacks brought to your room. By the same token, you are right to expect to feel more like a 'human being' than a 'hotel guest'.

Do read between the lines and be canny about interpreting our descriptions. Let us know if a house isn't what we led you to expect. We have only 100 words to tell a story, but a phone call to the owner before booking can fill the gaps. If traffic noise, walks, bedding, bathing, meal times or other guests matter to you, check.

Finding the right place for you

Quick reference indices

At the back of the book we list those owners:

* with single rooms or those who charge no single supplement

* willing to let your pet sleep in your room

* that accept children of any age

* willing to collect you from local train or bus stations

* with houses suitable for wheelchair users or for those of limited mobility.

How to use this book

Map

Look at the map in the front of the book first, find the area you want to visit and look for the nearest houses: just focusing on counties can be misleading. In cities, check individual entries for their position. www.multimap.com is a useful site – just type in the postcode of the property and print off a detailed map of the area.

INTRODUCTION

Rooms

We tell you if rooms are double, twin, family or single. Most owners are flexible and can juggle things to suit you – just ask.

Bathrooms

The words 'en suite' no longer appear.

If a room does have an en suite bathroom, we now say 'with' bathroom or shower room.

If it is not en suite, we state if the bathroom is shared (maybe with others guests or the owners) or private, ie, just for you.

Prices

Please note that we now give prices PER ROOM. Afterwards we usually tell you the single occupancy rate, i.e., the amount one person has to pay to stay in a double room.

Breakfasts

Unless we say otherwise, a full, cooked breakfast is included. Some owners – particularly in London – will give you a prodigious continental breakfast instead.

Some owners vary their prices during the year. Double check if any supplements or discounts apply.

Symbols

On the very last page we explain our symbols. Use them as a guide, not as a statement of fact. Owners may occasionally bend their own rules.

Types of houses

We hope you'll find value for money in all of our houses – including the most expensive ones.

If you are staying in a sprawling, old, country house, go prepared for the odd draught. Townhouses or working farms may be noisy at times, so light sleepers should pack ear plugs. Some houses have rooms in converted stables, annexes or garden cottages. If you have strong preferences for being either in or out of the thrub, check where your bedroom is.

Meals

Apart from breakfast, no meals should be expected unless you have arranged it – all our owners need advance notice.

INTRODUCTION

When booking discuss your diet and mealtimes; prices are quoted per person.

You'll find some wonderful cooks in this book, so eat in if you can – at the end of a long day it is good to amble downstairs to a table set for you rather than climb in the car again.

Very few of our houses are licensed, so do ask the owner if you may bring wine; some entries state B.Y.O. (Bring Your Own).

Seasons and public holidays

We have tried to give a price bracket for each B&B that covers high and low season but many owners offer discounts for longer stays or for winter weekends. Others may charge supplements at certain times (houses in Edinburgh at festival time, for example). Book early for popular holidays or specific rooms.

Bookings

There are various ways of booking, but phoning enables you to 'get the feel' of people and place. Do, if you can, get written confirmation of the room booked and the price for B&B and for meals. Say roughly what time you will arrive as most hosts want to welcome you personally.

Be on time if you have booked dinner; delays happen, but a phone call to explain averts burnt dinners and boiled tempers.

Requests for deposits vary, too; some are non-refundable, especially in our London homes, and some homes may charge you for the whole of the booked stay in advance (see below).

Cancellations

If you have to cancel your booking, please phone the owner as soon as possible. You may lose your deposit or have to pay part of the cost of your booking. Some owners will charge you the total cost if you cancel at short notice.

We have steered clear of suggesting a cancellation policy; it's a hornets' nest! The contract is between you and your host.

If an owner holds your credit card details he/she may deduct a (widely varying) cancellation fee from it and not contact you to discuss this. This is rare, but be aware of the legalities of this in the eyes of your credit or debit card company.

Payment

All our owners take cash and cheques with a cheque card.

INTRODUCTION

If they also take credit cards, we have given them the appropriate symbol. If you have an obscure card, check that it is acceptable.

Children

The 'Child Welcome' (teddy bear) symbol is given to houses that accept children of any age. They may or not have all the 'paraphernalia'.

If an owner welcomes children, but only those of certain ages, we have put the lowest age limit on their entry. These houses do not have the teddy symbol.

It can be difficult for owners to balance the needs of mixed age groups. Nevertheless, many owners love having children to stay, particularly if parents encourage 'best' behaviour.

Dogs

The 'Pets Welcome' (dog collar) symbol is given to places where your pet can sleep in the bedroom (but not the bed) with you. A section at the back of the book tells you where your pet can sleep in the house but not in your room. Please be honest about your pet – if it is an excitable Rottweiler, then say so.

Smoking

A 'No-Smoking' symbol means no smoking anywhere. Even at houses without the symbol you should still ask the owner where you may smoke and ask other people if they mind. (Owners and non-smoking guests usually can't stand the smell of cigarette smoke in bedrooms; they spot it at twenty paces, even if the window has been opened!)

Tippings

Owners do not expect tips. If you have been treated with extraordinary kindness, write to them, or leave a present. (We love to hear about it, too.)

Environment

We try to reduce our impact on the environment by:

* planting trees. We are officially Carbon Neutral®. The emissions directly related to our office, paper production, printing and distribution of this book have been 'neutralised' through the planting of indigenous woodlands with Future Forests.

* re-using paper, recycling stationery, tins, bottles, etc.

* encouraging staff use of bicycles (they're loaned free) and encouraging car sharing.

INTRODUCTION

- celebrating the use of organic, home-grown and locally-produced food.

- publishing books that support, in however small a way, the rural economy and small-scale businesses.

- running an Environmental Benefit Trust to stimulate business interest in the environment.

- working to establish an organic standard for B&B's. (Watch this space).

- We publish The Little Earth Book (www.thelittleearth.co.uk), a collection of essays on environmental issues. We also have a new title in production called The Little Food Book, another hard-hitting analysis – this time of the food industry.

Subscriptions Owners pay to appear in this guide. Their fee goes towards the huge costs of a sophisticated inspection system and the high costs of an all-colour book.

We only include places and owners that we find positively special. It is not possible for anyone to buy their way into our guides, whatever our competitors may suggest!

Internet Our web site www.specialplacestostay.com has online pages for all the places featured here and many from our other books. In 2003, every house will have a web entry. For more detail see the back of the book.

Disclaimer We make no claims to pure objectivity in choosing our Special Places to Stay. They are here because we like them. Our opinions and tastes are ours alone and this book is a statement of them; we hope that you will share them.

We have done our utmost to get our facts right but apologise unreservedly for any mistakes that may have crept in. We would be grateful to hear of any errors that you find. Feedback from you is invaluable and we always act upon comments. With your help and our own inspections we can maintain our reputation for dependability.

Finally We hope this book is a trumpet blast for all that is best about Britain. We take you to the moors, the dales, the coast, the wolds, the mountains and the lakes and link you with the people that live there. They, in turn, can take you deeper into their bit of Britain – the bits that only the locals know.

Happy travels.   *Jackie King*

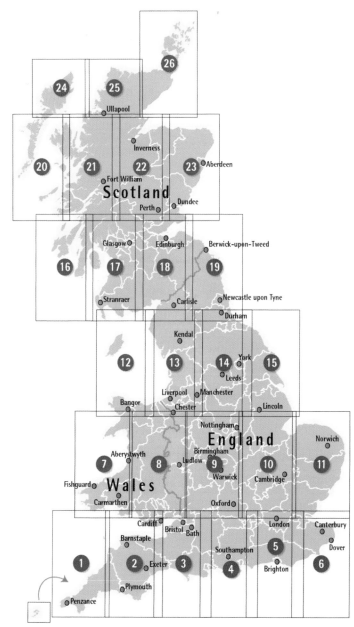

24

25

26

Ullapool

Inverness

20   21   22   23   Aberdeen

Fort William

Scotland

Perth   Dundee

Glasgow   Edinburgh   Berwick-upon-Tweed

16   17   18   19

Stranraer   Carlisle   Newcastle upon Tyne

Durham

Kendal

12   13   14   York   15

Leeds

Liverpool   Manchester

Bangor   Chester   Lincoln

Nottingham

England

Norwich

Aberystwyth   Birmingham

7   8   Ludlow   9   10   11

Warwick   Cambridge

Fishguard   Wales   Oxford

Carmarthen

Cardiff   Bristol   Bath   London   Canterbury

Barnstaple   Southampton   Dover

1   2   Exeter   3   5

4   Brighton   6

Plymouth

Penzance

© Bartholomew Ltd 2002

A guide to our map page numbers

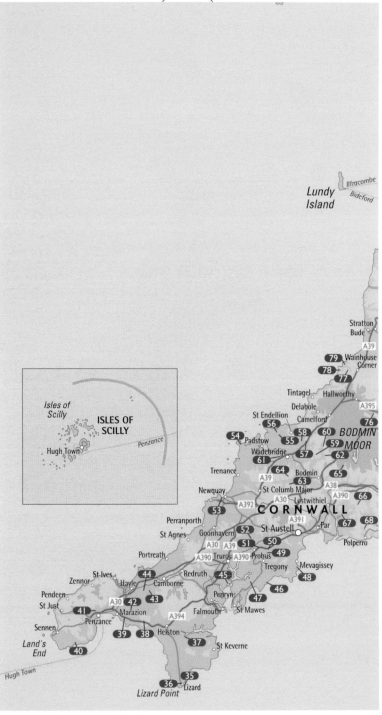

© Bartholomew Ltd 2002

Map 1

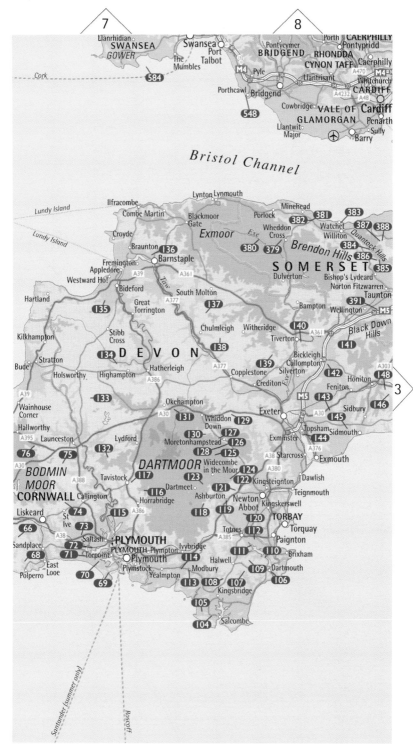

Map 2

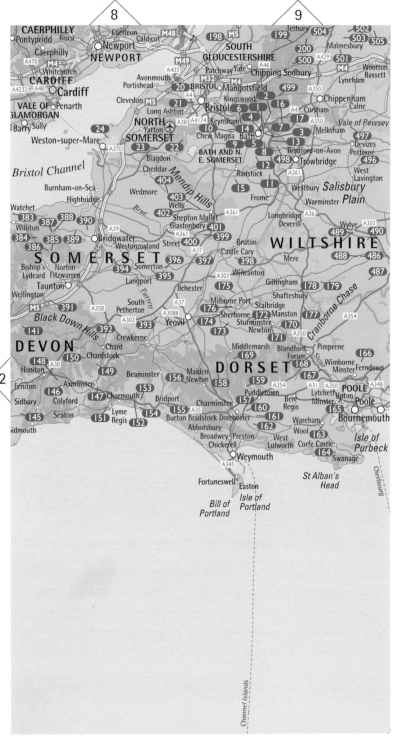

Map 3

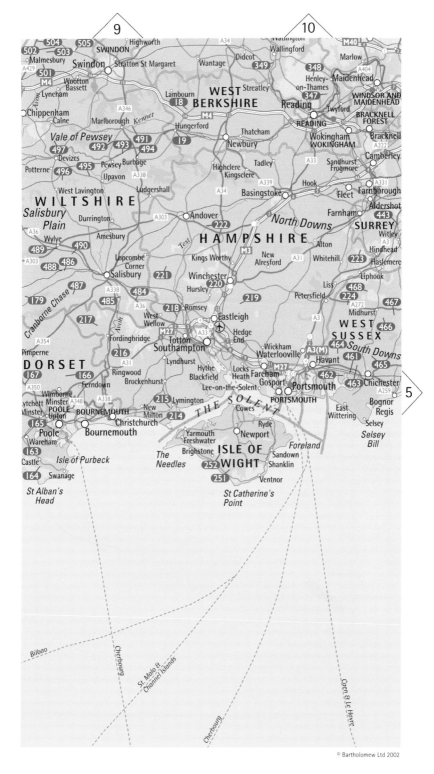

Map 4

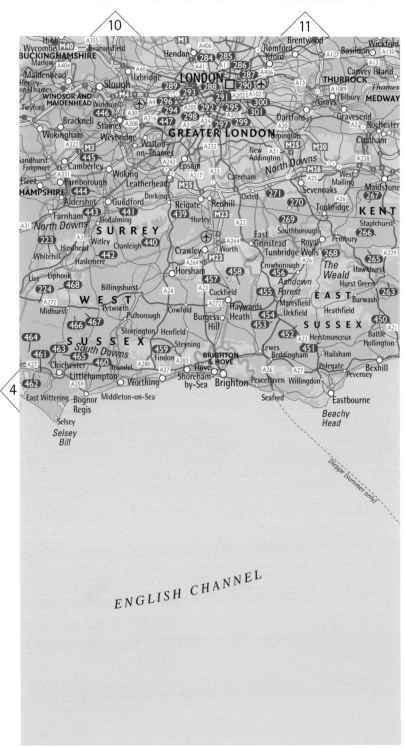

Map 5

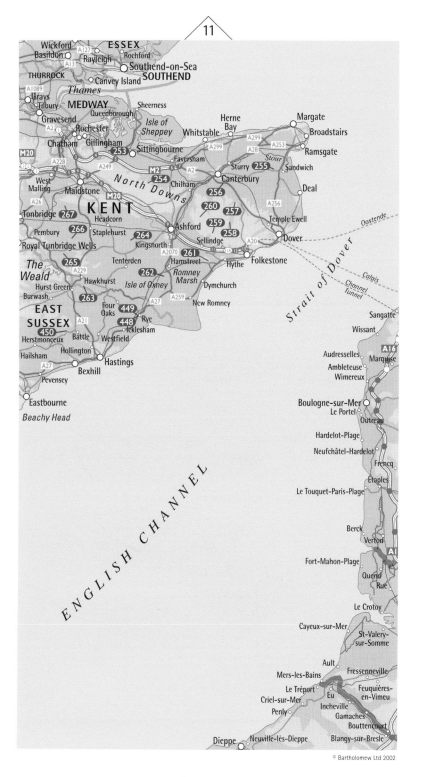

Map 6

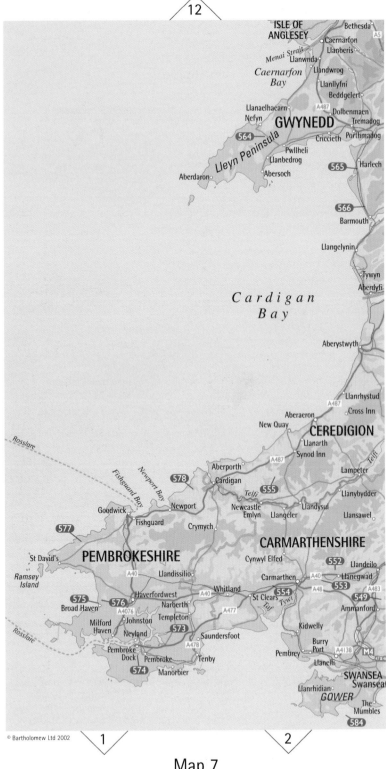

ISLE OF
ANGLESEY
Bethesda
A5
Caernarfon
Menai Strait Llanberis
Caernarfon Llanwnda
Bay Llandwrog
Llanllyfni
Beddgelert
Llanaelhaearn Dolbenmaen
Nefyn GWYNEDD Tremadog
564 Criccieth Porthmadog
Lleyn Peninsula Pwllheli
Llanbedrog 565 Harlech
Aberdaron Abersoch
566
Barmouth

Llangelynin

Cardigan Tywyn
Bay Aberdyfi

Aberystwyth

Llanrhystud
A487
Cross Inn
Aberaeron
Rosslare New Quay CEREDIGION
Llanarth Teifi
Synod Inn
Aberporth Lampeter
Newport Bay 578 A487
Fishguard Bay Cardigan Llanybydder
Teifi 555
Newport Newcastle Llandysul Llansawel
Goodwick Emlyn Llangeler
577 Fishguard Crymych
CARMARTHENSHIRE
St David's PEMBROKESHIRE Cynwyl Elfed
Ramsey A40 552 Llandeilo
Island Llandissilio Carmarthen A40 Llanegwad
575 576 Haverfordwest A40 Whitland A48 553
Broad Haven A4076 Narberth St Clears 554 549 A483
Milford Johnston Templeton A477 Taf Tywi Ammanford
Haven Neyland 573 Kidwelly
Pembroke Saundersfoot Burry M4
Dock A478 Pembrey Port A4138
574 Pembroke Tenby Llanelli
Manorbier SWANSEA
Swansea
Llanrhidian GOWER The
Mumbles
584

© Bartholomew Ltd 2002

Map 7

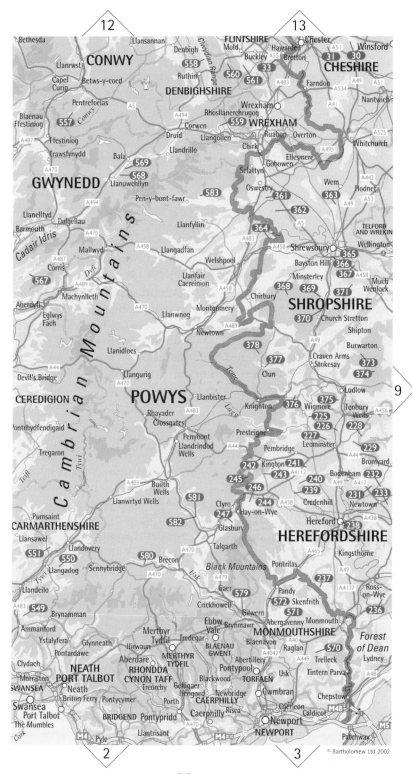

Map 8

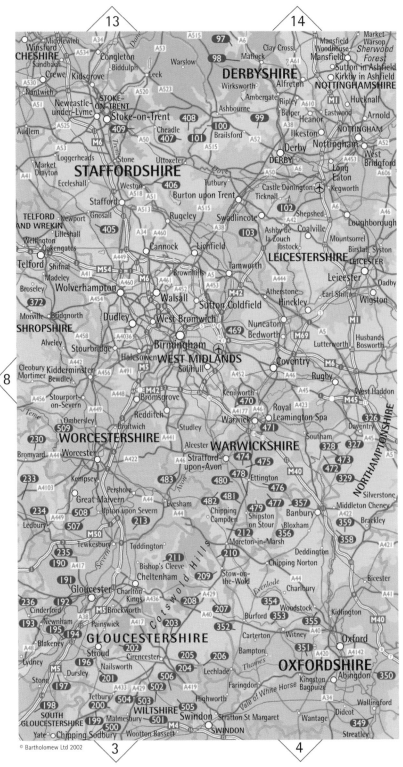

Map 9

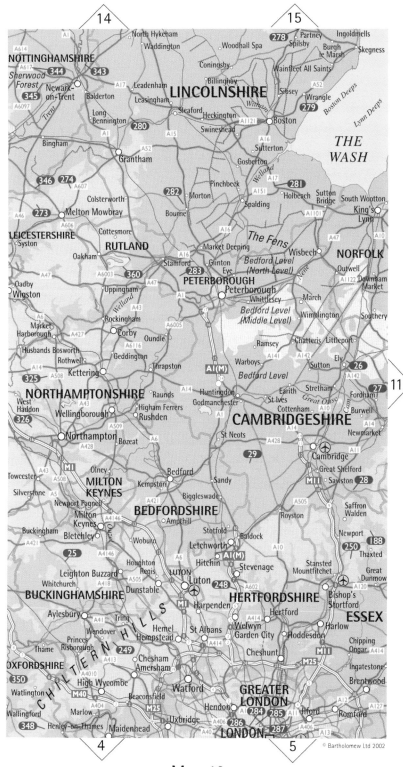

Map 10

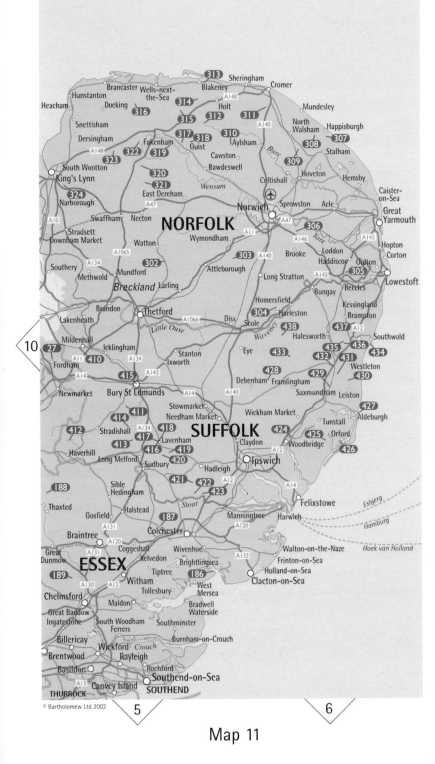

Map 11

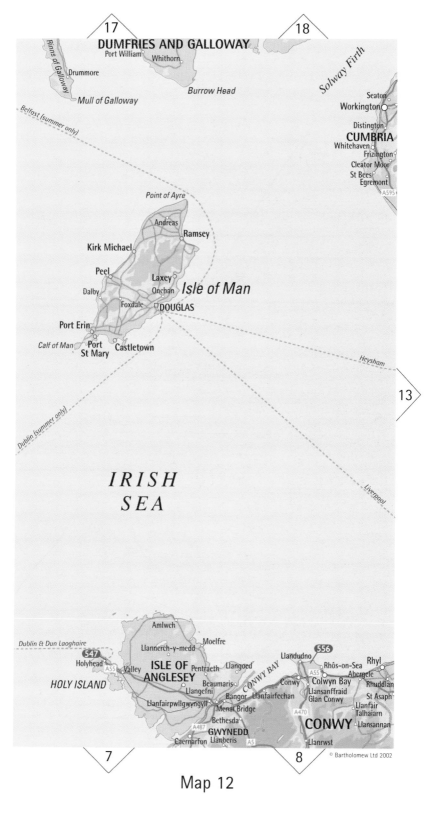

Map 12

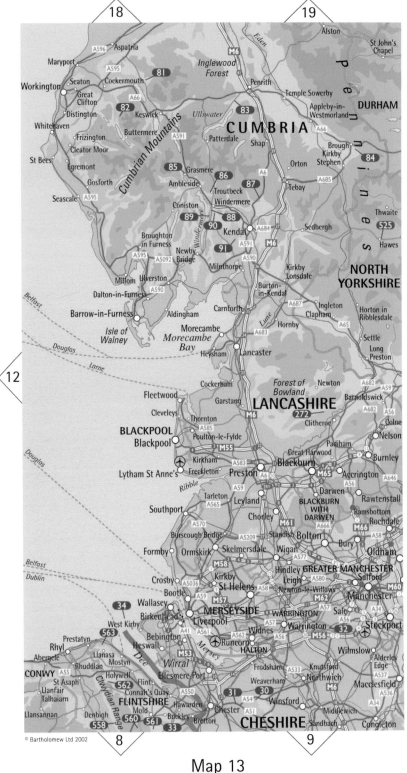

Map 13

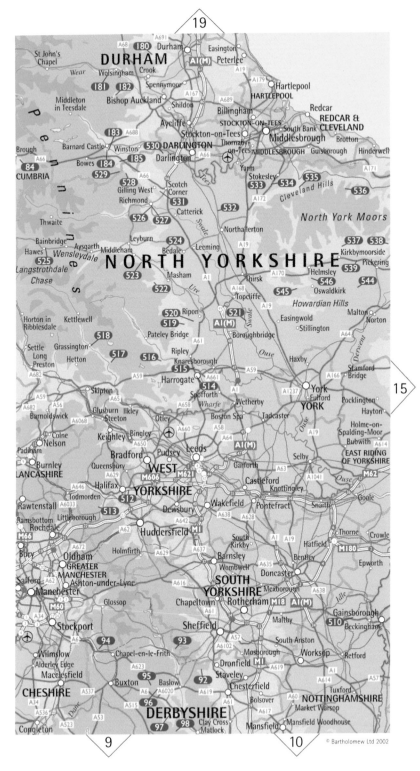

Map 14

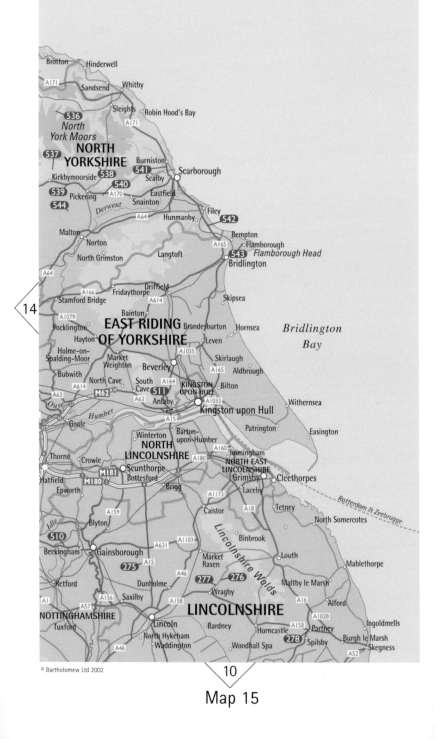

Map 15

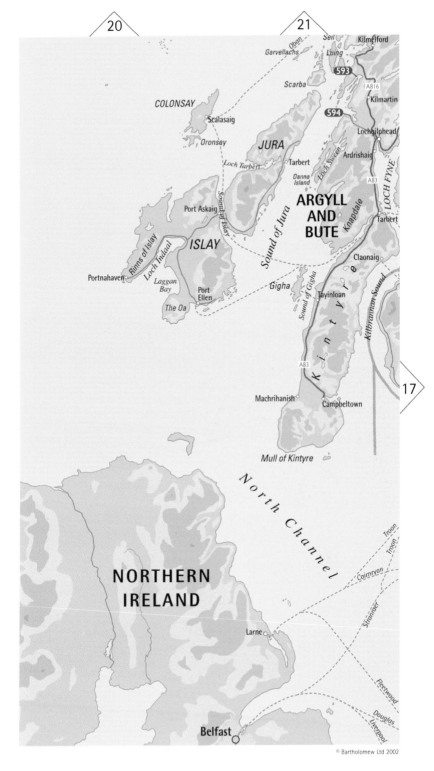

Kilmelford

Seil

Oban

Garvellachs

Luing

A816

593

Scarba

Kilmartin

COLONSAY

594

Scalasaig

Lochgilphead

JURA

Oronsay

Loch Tarbert

Tarbert

Ardrishaig

Danna
Island

ARGYLL
AND
BUTE

Port Askaig

LOCH FYNE

A83

Knapdale

Tarbert

ISLAY

Rims of Islay

Loch Indaal

Sound of Islay

Sound of Jura

Claonaig

Portnahaven

Gigha

Tayinloan

Laggan
Bay

Sound of Gigha

Kilbrannan Sound

Port
Ellen

The Oa

Kintyre

A83

Machrihanish

Campbeltown

Mull of Kintyre

North Channel

Troon

Troon

NORTHERN
IRELAND

Cairnryan

Stranraer

Larne

Fleetwood

Douglas

Liverpool

Belfast

© Bartholomew Ltd 2002

Map 16

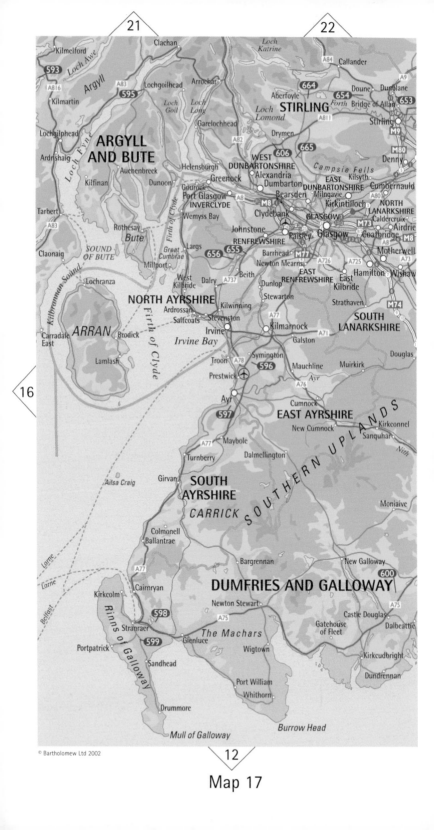

Kilmelford   Clachan   *Loch Katrine*   Callander

Loch Awe   A84   Doune   Dunblane

593   *Argyll*   A83   Lochgoilhead   Arrochar   Aberfoyle   664   654   Bridge of Allan   A9   653

A816   595

Kilmartin   *Loch Goil*   *Loch Long*   **STIRLING**   Stirling   M9

Lochgilphead   Garelochhead   *Loch Lomond*   AB11   M80

Ardrishaig   A82   Drymen   *Forth*   Denny

ARGYLL   Helensburgh   *Campsie Fells*

AND BUTE   **WEST**   606   665   Kilsyth   Cumbernauld

Tarbert   A83   *Loch Fyne*   Auchenbreck   **DUNBARTONSHIRE**   Alexandria   **EAST**   A80

Kilfinan   Dunoon   Greenock   Dumbarton   **DUNBARTONSHIRE**   Kirkintilloch   **NORTH**

Gourock   Bearsden   Milngavie   **LANARKSHIRE**

Rothesay   Port Glasgow   M8   Clydebank   Calderruix

Bute   **INVERCLYDE**   **GLASGOW**   Airdrie

Claonaig   Wemyss Bay   Johnstone   Glasgow   Coatbridge   M8

SOUND   **RENFREWSHIRE**   Paisley   M73   A8

OF BUTE   *Great Cumbrae*   656   655   Barrhead   M77   A725   Motherwell

Lochranza   Millport   Largs   Newton Mearns   **EAST**   Hamilton   Wishaw

Kilbrannan Sound   West   Dalry   A737   **RENFREWSHIRE**   East   M74

Carradale   *ARRAN*   Brodick   Kilbride   Beith   Dunlop   Kilbride   Strathaven   **SOUTH**

East   *Firth of Clyde*   **NORTH AYRSHIRE**   Stewarton   **LANARKSHIRE**

Lamlash   Kilwinning   A77

Ardrossan   Stevenston   Kilmarnock   A71   Douglas

Saltcoats   Irvine   Galston

Irvine Bay   Symington   Mauchline   Muirkirk

Troon   A78   596   *Ayr*

Prestwick   A76

Ayr   Cumnock   **EAST AYRSHIRE**   Kirkconnel

Ailsa Craig   597   New Cumnock   Sanquhar   *Nith*

Maybole   *SOUTHERN UPLANDS*

Turnberry   Dalmellington

Girvan   **SOUTH**   Moniaive

AYRSHIRE   *CARRICK*

Colmonell   Ballantrae   Bargrennan   New Galloway   600

Lorne   A77   Cairnryan   Newton Stewart   **DUMFRIES AND GALLOWAY**   A75

Lorne   Kirkcolm   598   A75   Castle Douglas

Belfast   Stranraer   Glenluce   *The Machars*   Gatehouse of Fleet   Dalbeattie

Portpatrick   599   Wigtown   Kirkcudbright

Rinns of Galloway   Sandhead   Dundrennan

Drummore   Port William   Whithorn

Mull of Galloway   *Burrow Head*

Map 17

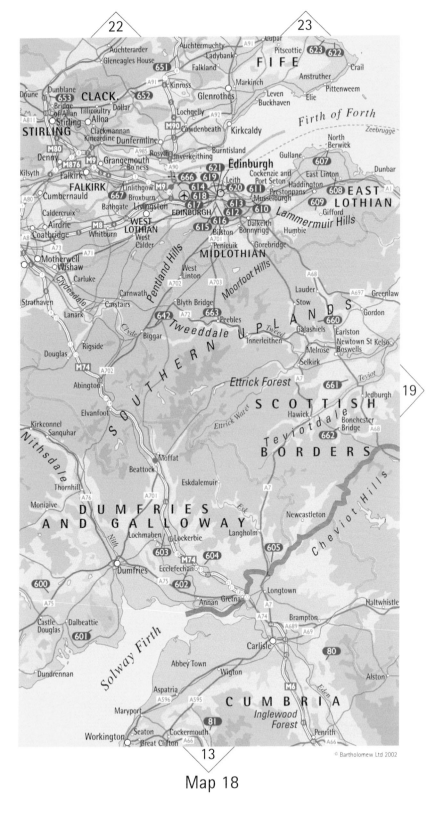

Map 18

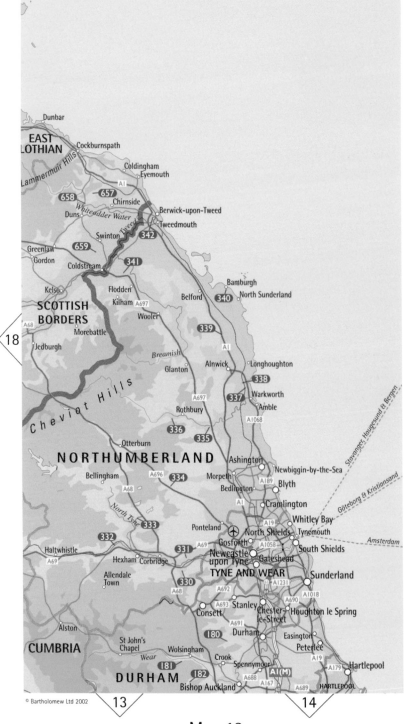

Dunbar

EAST LOTHIAN
Cockburnspath

Lammermuir Hills

Coldingham
Eyemouth

A1

658 657

Whiteadder Water
Chirnside

Berwick-upon-Tweed

Duns

Tweedmouth

Swinton 342

Greenlaw 659
Gordon

Coldstream 341

Kelso

Flodden
Kilham A697

Belford 340

Bamburgh
North Sunderland

**SCOTTISH
BORDERS**

A68

Wooler

18

Morebattle

Jedburgh

Breamish

339

A1

Glanton

Alnwick

Longhoughton

338

Warkworth
337 Amble

A1068

Rothbury

336 335

Cheviot Hills

Otterburn

NORTHUMBERLAND

Ashington

Newbiggin-by-the-Sea

Bellingham

A696 334

Morpeth

Bedlington

A189 Blyth

A68

North Tyne

333

A1

Cramlington

Whitley Bay

A19 Tynemouth

Stavanger, Haugesund & Bergen

Göteborg & Kristiansand

Ponteland

332

Haltwhistle

A69

Hexham Corbridge

331 A69
Gosforth
A1058
North Shields

Newcastle
upon Tyne Gateshead

South Shields

Amsterdam

Allendale
Town

330

TYNE AND WEAR

Sunderland

A1231

Alston

A68

A692

A693 Stanley

A690 A1018

Houghton le Spring

CUMBRIA

St John's
Chapel

Consett

A691

Chester-
le-Street

Wolsingham

Wear

181

Crook

Durham

Easington

Peterlee

A19

182

Spennymoor

A1(M)

A179 Hartlepool

DURHAM

A688 A167

Bishop Auckland

A689 **HARTLEPOOL**

© Bartholomew Ltd 2002

Map 19

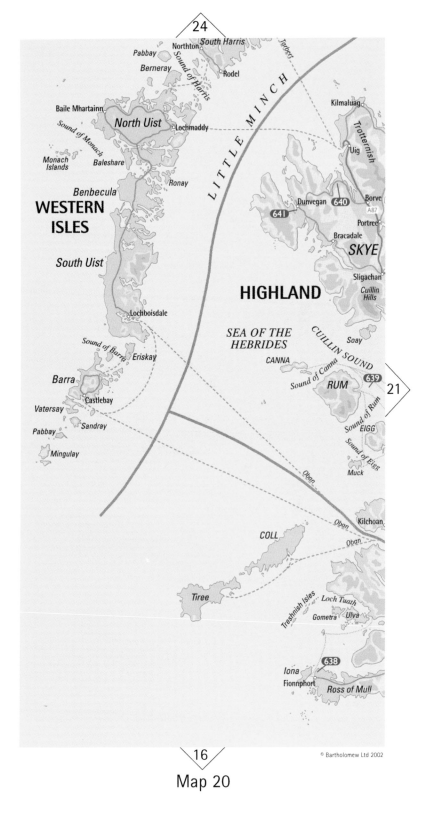

Pabbay
Northton *South Harris*
Berneray
Sound of Harris
Rodel

Tarbert

Kilmaluag

Baile Mhartainn
North Uist
Lochmaddy

Sound of Monach

Monach
Islands
Baleshare

Ronay

Uig

Trotternish

Benbecula

**WESTERN
ISLES**

Dunvegan `640` Borve
A87
`641`

Portree

Bracadale

SKYE

South Uist

HIGHLAND

Sligachan
*Cuillin
Hills*

Lochboisdale

**SEA OF THE
HEBRIDES**

Sound of Barra
Eriskay

CANNA

CUILLIN SOUND

Soay

Sound of Canna
RUM `639`

Barra
Castlebay

Sound of Rum

Vatersay
Sandray
Pabbay

EIGG

Sound of Eigg

Mingulay

Oban

Muck

Oban
Kilchoan

Oban

COLL

Tiree

Treshnish Isles
Loch Tuath
Gometra Ulva

`638`
Iona
Fionnphort *Ross of Mull*

Map 20

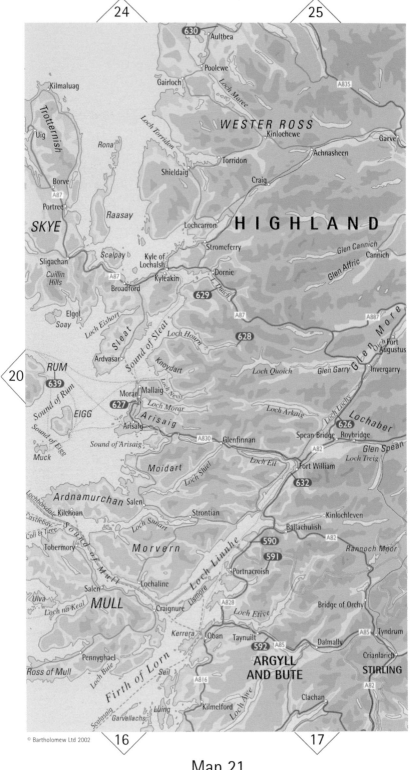

Map 21

© Bartholomew Ltd 2002

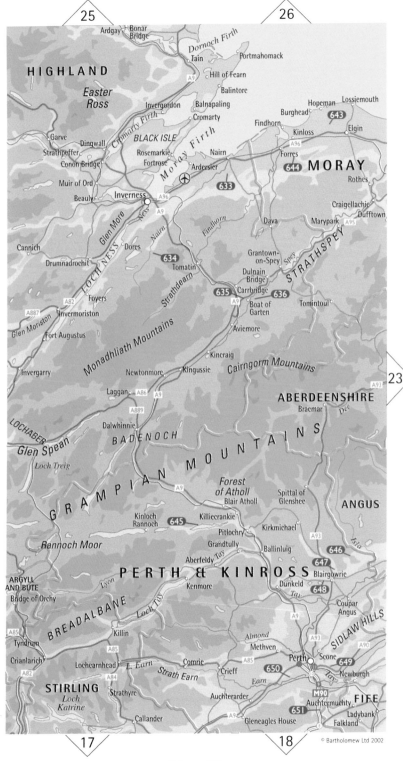

Map 22

© Bartholomew Ltd 2002

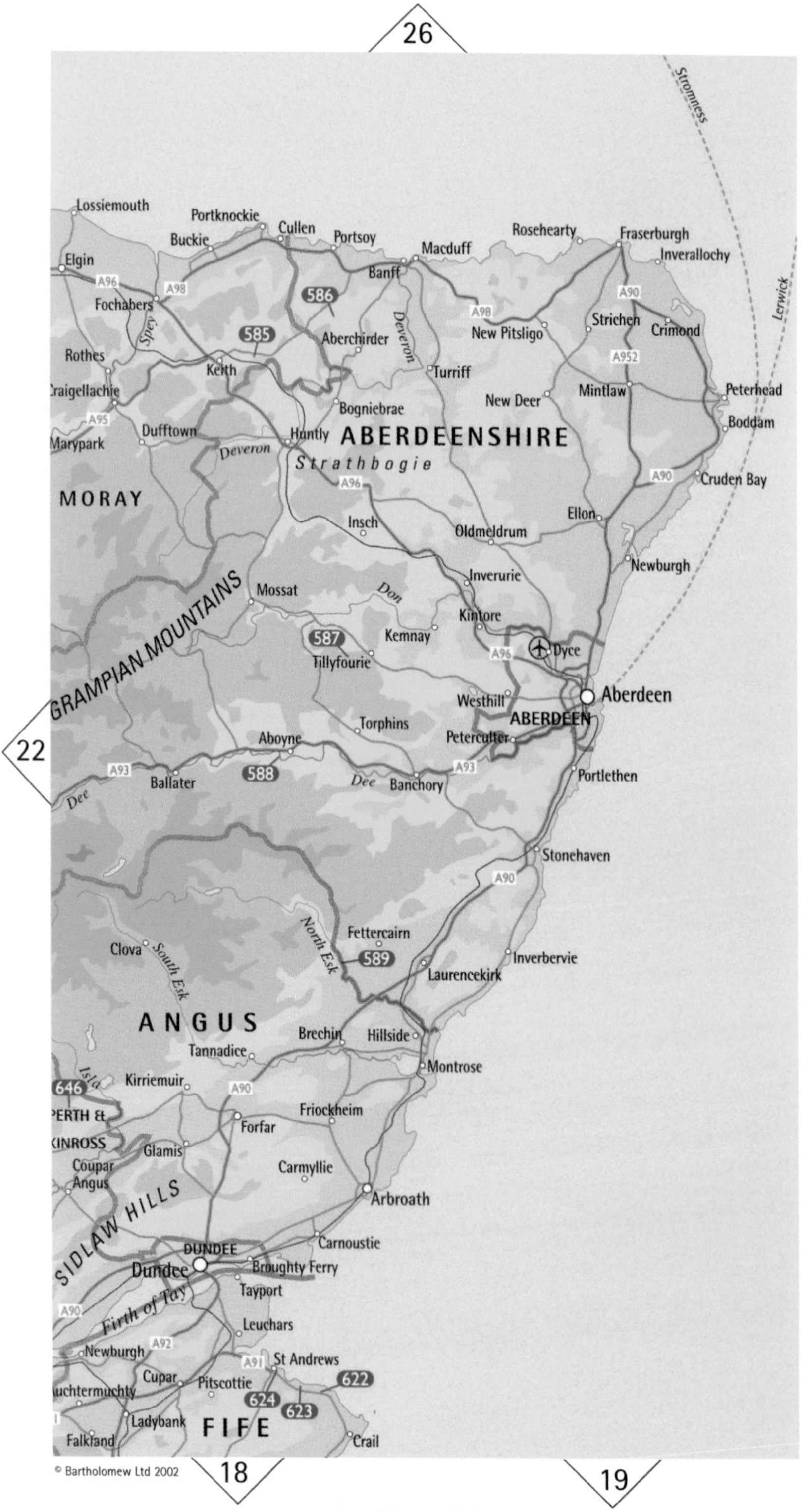

Stromness

Lossiemouth
Portknockie
Cullen
Portsoy
Macduff
Rosehearty
Fraserburgh
Elgin
Buckie
Banff
Inverallochy
A96
A98
Fochabers
A98
New Pitsligo
Strichen
Crimond
Spey
A585
A586
Aberchirder
A90
Rothes
Keith
A952
Craigellachie
Turriff
Peterhead
A95
Dufftown
Bogniebrae
New Deer
Mintlaw
Boddam
Marypark
Deveron
Huntly
ABERDEENSHIRE
Strathbogie
Cruden Bay
MORAY
A96
Insch
Oldmeldrum
Ellon
Inverurie
Newburgh
Mossat
Don
Kintore
A587
Kemnay
Dyce
Tillyfourie
A96
Aberdeen
Westhill
Torphins
ABERDEEN
Aboyne
Peterculter
A588
Ballater
Dee
Banchory
A93
Portlethen
A93
Stonehaven
A90
Clova
Fettercairn
Inverbervie
A589
Laurencekirk
ANGUS
Brechin
Hillside
Tannadice
Montrose
Kirriemuir
A90
Friockheim
PERTH &
Forfar
KINROSS
Glamis
Carmyllie
Coupar
Angus
Arbroath
SIDLAW HILLS
Carnoustie
DUNDEE
Dundee
Broughty Ferry
Tayport
A90
Firth of Tay
Leuchars
Newburgh
A92
A91
St Andrews
uchtermuchty
Cupar
A622
Pitscottie
Ladybank
A624
A623
Falkland
FIFE
Crail

Lerwick
North Esk
South Esk
Isla
A646
Deveron
Grampian Mountains
Dee
A93
A22

© Bartholomew Ltd 2002

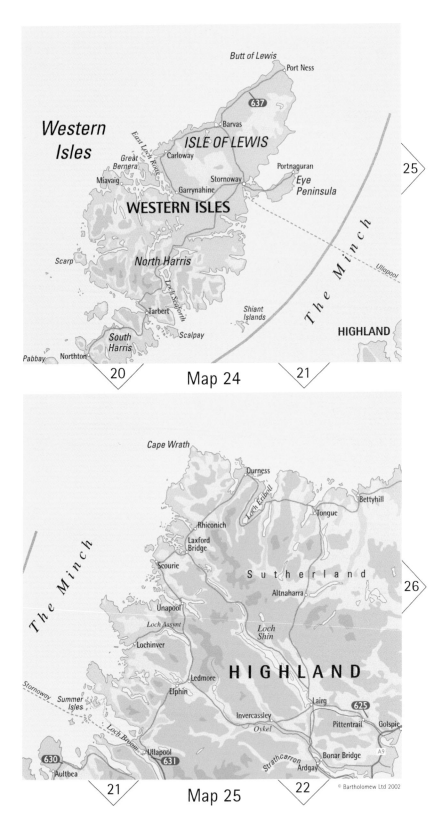

Map 24

Western Isles

Butt of Lewis
Port Ness

637

Barvas

East Loch Roag

ISLE OF LEWIS

Carloway

Great Bernera

Miavaig

Stornoway

Portnaguran

Eye Peninsula

Garrynahine

WESTERN ISLES

Scarp

North Harris

Loch Seaforth

The Minch

Ullapool

Shiant Islands

Tarbert

Scalpay

HIGHLAND

Pabbay
Northton

South Harris

20

21

25

Map 25

Cape Wrath

Durness

Loch Eriboll

Bettyhill

Tongue

Rhiconich

Laxford Bridge

Scourie

The Minch

Sutherland

26

Altnaharra

Unapool

Loch Assynt

Loch Shin

Lochinver

Stornoway

HIGHLAND

Summer Isles

Ledmore

Elphin

Lairg

625

Invercassley

Pittentrail

Golspie

Loch Broom

Oykel

A9

630

Ullapool

631

Bonar Bridge

Aultbea

Strathcarron

Ardgay

21

22

© Bartholomew Ltd 2002

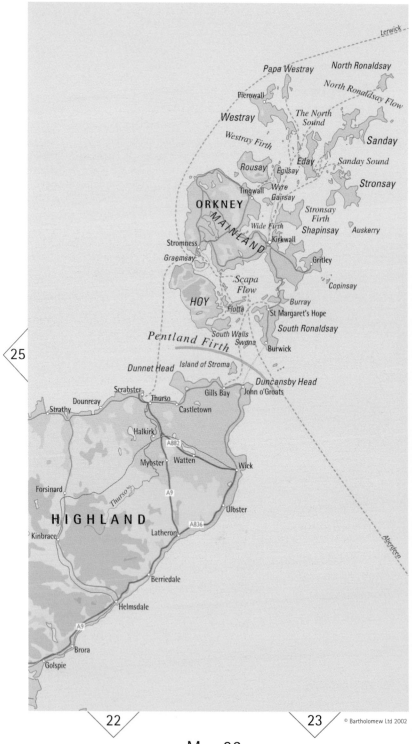

Lerwick

Papa Westray
North Ronaldsay
Pierowall
North Ronaldsay Flow
Westray
The North
Sound
Sanday
Westray Firth
Sanday Sound
Rousay
Eday
Egilsay
Stronsay
Tingwall
Wyre
ORKNEY
Gairsay
Stronsay
Firth
MAINLAND
Shapinsay
Auskerry
Wide Firth
Stromness
Kirkwall
Graemsay
Gritley
Scapa
Copinsay
Flow
HOY
Burray
Flotta
St Margaret's Hope
South Walls
South Ronaldsay
Pentland Firth
Swona
Burwick
Dunnet Head
Island of Stroma
Duncansby Head
Scrabster
Gills Bay
John o'Groats
Dounreay
Thurso
Strathy
Castletown
Halkirk
A882
Mybster
Watten
Forsinard
Wick
Thurso
A9
Kinbrace
Ulbster
HIGHLAND
Latheron
A836
Berriedale
Helmsdale
A9
Brora
Golspie
Aberdeen

© Bartholomew Ltd 2002

Map 26

HOW TO USE THIS BOOK

sample entry

CORNWALL

Watch the surfers hug the waves, schools of them, all year. Watch the sun, the sand and, it seems, the world. The vastness of the view astonishes. At high tide you are on an island of granite – but not marooned. The bridge, a breathtaking entry, is the only privately owned suspension bridge in the country – not for those with vertigo. High seas can, spectacularly, wet the house. But all is elegance within: good furniture, deep carpets, family portraits, tradition and luxury with a modern touch. Decking all round for sun bathing, and views to the south, north, east and west. A great escape.

rooms	1 double with private shower room.
room price	£96-£114. Single occ. £48-£57.
meals	Sandwiches & coffee, £5. Excellent pubs/restaurants short walk away.
closed	Very occasionally.
directions	From Treloggen r'bout before Newquay right at Safeways, down hill. Across double r'bout. Left at lights; 1st right Grovesnor Ave. Straight across main road down narrow road, over bridge; 1st left, 1st right down Island Crescent.

	Lady Long
	The Island,
	Newquay,
	Cornwall TR7 1EA
tel	01637 879754
e-mail	helen@towanisland.fsnet.co.uk

---

❻

❼ map: 1 entry: 53

explanations

❶ rooms

We do not use the words 'en suite'. If a bathroom is 'en suite' we say **with bath** or **with shower**.

If a room is not 'en suite' we say **with private bathroom** or **with shared bathroom**: the former you will have to yourself, the latter may be shared with other guests or family members; both will have a wc, basin and either a bath or a shower.

❷ room price

The price shown is for B&B for two people sharing a room. A price range incorporates room/seasonal differences. We also give single occupancy rates – the amount payable by one person staying in a room for two.

❸ meals

Prices are per person. All meals must be booked in advance. Ask the owner if you may bring your own wine. Some entries say B.Y.O.

❹ closed

When given in months, this means for the whole of the named months and the time in between.

❺ directions

Use as a guide; the owner can give more details.

❻ symbols

see the last page of the book for fuller explanation:

 all children welcome

 wheelchair facilities for one bedroom/bathroom

 step-free access to bathroom/bedroom

 no smoking anywhere

 smoking restrictions exist.

 this house has pets

 pets can sleep in your bedroom

 credit cards accepted

 vegetarians catered for with advance warning

mostly home-grown/local/organic produce used

licensed premises

working farm

bike

walk

❼ Map page number; entry number.

Photography by Michael Busselle

ENGLAND

"There is no pillow so soft as a clear conscience."

Built in 1820 and with lovely views over the city, this is a fine Bath stone 'residence'. Beautifully furnished with pieces accumulated over the years, it feels evolved rather than designed. Mrs Bowman gives her guests the freedom to come and go and the run of the large living room with French windows. Open these and step out onto an exceptional walled garden that she largely manages herself. In one bedroom there are a bow-fronted mahogany chest, a bureau, and an arched alcove bookshelf; its bathroom is across the hall. The second looks over the north lawn. *Children over 12 welcome.*

Need a lift to/from the station? Maria or Derek will oblige with memorable good humour and kindness. They love their 1778 Georgian city home and have decorated the rooms with colours authentic to the era, restored the veranda at the front to its former glory and collected period furniture. There is road noise in the two front bedrooms, but there is also a quiet room overlooking the rear garden and many guests have stayed here happily. A 20-minute canal-side stroll takes you to the centre of Bath and all its wonders. *Minimum stay two nights. Children over 10 welcome. Secure parking.*

rooms	2 twins, both with private bathroom.
room price	£50. Single occ. £28.
meals	Breakfast 7.30-9.30am. Dinner within 15 minutes' walk.
closed	Christmas & New Year.
directions	From Bath centre, 15-minute walk. Quarter way up Bathwick Hill. Pass Cleveland Walk on left, house one of big ones on right.

rooms	3: 2 doubles, both with shower; 1 twin with private bathroom.
room price	£70-£75. Single occ. £45-£55.
meals	Breakfast 7.30-8.45am. Pub/restaurant 200 yds.
closed	Sometimes at Christmas.
directions	On A4 (London Rd), for city centre, near junc. of A46. Opposite Bath Rugby Club training ground. Locked car park on premises.

Mrs Elspeth Bowman
9 Bathwick Hill,
Bath,
Bath & N. E. Somerset BA2 6EW
tel   01225 460812

Derek & Maria Beckett
Cedar Lodge,
13 Lambridge, London Road, Bath,
Bath & N. E. Somerset BA1 6BJ
tel   01225 423468

map: 3 entry: 1

map: 3 entry: 2

Simone has a natural sense of hospitality. Hers is a French-Caribbean welcome and she spoils you with cross-cultural colour: breakfasts of fruit, yogurt and cereals, as well as traditional English; the décor and even the pretty crockery have an exotic flavour. Bedrooms feel luxurious with embroidered cotton, fluffy towels and thick curtains in beautiful fabrics. The garden looks French and formal, with box parterre, lavender and roses. You are less than 10 minutes' walk from the city centre and there are views to the floodlit Abbey and National Trust land. *Babies and children over 10 welcome.*

rooms	3: 1 double with bath/shower; 1 twin, 1 single, both with private bathroom.
room price	£65. Single occ. £45.
meals	Breakfast 7.30-9am. Dinner available close by.
closed	Christmas Day.
directions	From Bath centre follow signs to American Museum. Pass Mercedes garage (300 yds up Bathwick Hill on right). 1st road on right after garage. On right, 300 yds down.

Mrs S. Johnson
47 Sydney Buildings,
Bathwick Hill, Bath,
Bath & N. E. Somerset BA2 6DB
tel   01225 463033
fax   01225 463033
e-mail   sydneybuildings@bigfoot.com
web   www.sydneybuildings.co.uk

map: 3 entry: 3

Step inside and forget the bustle of the city – serenity pervades the Smiths' Grade I-listed Bath apartment. A Chinese lantern with hand-painted silk, a fascinating mix of furniture and pottery, framed embroideries and pictures from all over the world hint at their life of travel; he was with the British Council, both are charming and multi-lingual. The calm bedroom – pale walls, Delft chandelier, cream counterpanes – has a collection of books on art/tea/opera; choose one and wander into the courtyard garden where the colourful pots are arranged as artfully as the treasures in the house.

rooms	1 twin/double with bath.
room price	£60. Single occ. £45.
meals	Breakfast until 8.45am. Good restaurants within walking distance.
closed	Christmas & New Year.
directions	A46 to Bath, then A4 for city centre. Left onto A36 over Cleveland Bridge; follow signs to Holburne Museum. Gt Pulteney St opp. museum. Down steps to basement. Parking £1 per day.

Chan Loo Smith
Apartment One,
60 Great Pulteney Street, Bath,
Bath & N. E. Somerset BA2 4DN
tel   01225 464134
fax   01225 483663
e-mail   chanloosmith@aptone.fsnet.co.uk

map: 3 entry: 4

The Bath stone of this Georgian replica will soon be swathed in rambling roses and who wouldn't have chosen this spot to build? It is close to the centre of Bath, yet wonderfully secluded in its elevated grounds and the views are tremendous. The house, named after one of Andrew's illustrious forbears, is pristine with handsome furniture and family portraits in gilt frames. Your lovely hosts enjoy entertaining and will spoil you with an excellent dinner from the Aga – Philippa is an experienced *Cordon Bleu* cook. *Children over 12 welcome.*

Such a gorgeous, mullion-windowed, rambler-rose-strewn home. It sits in 450 acres with views to Bristol on a clear day. Graham runs the farm (converting to organic status, and he makes Bath soft cheese – "delicious", said our inspector), and helps the sweet, sunny Gabrielle run the B&B. Quiet guest bedrooms are in their own wing; they overlook the village gardens and are carpeted, cottagey and decorated in soft colours. You can breakfast beside the inglenook fireplace, or in the garden on a warm summer's day. The guest book overflows with praise for Gabrielle's cooking – and her welcome.

rooms	2: 1 twin/double with bath/shower; 1 twin/double with basin & private shower room.
room price	£70. Single occ. £45.
meals	Breakfast until 9.30am. Dinner £25.
closed	Occasionally.
directions	A4/A46 Bath, then ring-road clockwise, signed A4, for Bristol. Left for Claverton Down just before White Hart. 0.5 miles up Widcombe Hill on left.

rooms	2: 1 double with bath/shower; 1 double with shower.
room price	£60. Single occ. £45.
meals	Good pubs in village.
closed	Occasionally.
directions	A431 out of Bath (Upper Bristol Rd), signed Bitton. Kelston 2.5 miles. 1st left into 1st turning in village by cul-de-sac sign. House 1st on right.

Philippa & Andrew Gordon-Duff
Blantyre House,
Widcombe Hill, Bath,
Bath & N. E. Somerset BA2 6AE

tel	01225 480682
fax	01225 789543
e-mail	blantyrebath@aol.com

G. P. Padfield
Park Farm,
Kelston, Bath,
Bath & N. E. Somerset BA1 9AG

tel	01225 424139
fax	01225 331601
e-mail	parkfarm.b.b@amserve.net
web	www.parkfarm.co.uk

map: 3 entry: 5

map: 3 entry: 6

Stroll easily into Bath or stay above the fray – with fine mature trees all around you, a croquet lawn and summer house. Your very affable, well-travelled hosts' Victorian family home is smartly decorated: pale fitted carpets, ruched curtains, Regency stripes. Peaceful, big-windowed bedrooms are comfortable, with space to sit, original fireplaces and cosy touches. 'Albert' has views of Bath Abbey – wonderful illuminated at night; 'Palmerston' has its own baby grand, which you're welcome to play. Dining room breakfasts include fresh fruit served on family china.
Children over 12 welcome.

You are in a conservation area, yet just five minutes from the centre of Bath. And the views: breathtaking from wherever you stand. The steep valley rolls out ahead of you from most of the rooms and from the garden comes a confusion and a profusion of scents and colours – it's a glory in its own right. The friendly and likeable Sticklands are conservationists too and have a Green Certificate to prove it. Breakfasts are a feast: bacon and eggs, cereals, home-grown jam, kedgeree. Jane will tell you all about excellent local gardens to visit.

rooms	3: 1 twin/double, 1 double, both with shower room; 1 double with private bath/shower.
room price	£60-£75. Single occ. £50-£65.
meals	Breakfast 7.30-9am. Excellent choice of restaurants in Bath.
closed	Christmas.
directions	A36 (Warminster road) from Bath. At boundary Bath/Bathampton, right on to North Rd, pass Golf Club entrance on left, house 200 yds further on right.

rooms	3: 2 twins/doubles, 1 family, all with shower.
room price	From £60. Single occ. £35.
meals	Breakfast 7-9.30am. Pub/restaurant 2 miles.
closed	Very occasionally.
directions	From A36 about 3 miles out of Bath on Warminster road, take uphill road by lights & Viaduct Inn. 1st left (approx. 100 yds) signed Monkton Combe. After village (0.5 miles on) house 1st on left.

Patrick & Hilary Bryan
Ravenscroft,
North Road, Bathwick, Bath,
Bath & N. E. Somerset BA2 6HZ

tel   01225 461919
fax   01225 461919
e-mail   patrick@ravenscroftbandb.co.uk
web   www.ravenscroftbandb.co.uk

Jane & Anthony Stickland
Grey Lodge,
Summer Lane, Combe Down, Bath,
Bath & N. E. Somerset BA2 7EU

tel   01225 832069
fax   01225 830161
e-mail   greylodge@freenet.co.uk
web   www.greylodge.co.uk

map: 3 entry: 7

map: 3 entry: 8

Duchy of Cornwall farmland stretches as far as the eye can see – the views from this neatly-converted, open-plan barn are magnificent by any standards, but remarkable considering you are so close to Bath. There's much wildlife, too: sparrowhawks nest in the gable end and Giles 'converses' with owls. Spruce guest rooms with houseplants and excellent beds are painted in pale colours. For breakfast, Sue, competent and kind, offers kippers or croissants on the terrace if it's fine. And the glories of Bath are just a short ride away – by bus or car.

The Addicotts have given over a generous swathe of their farm to the creation of a natural habitat for indigenous wildlife and have a Gold Award under the Duke of Cornwall's Habitat Award 2002 scheme to boot. Utterly committed to the environment, they use flax from the vibrant blue linseed crops to heat their sturdy listed house. There are stone mullion windows, dressers with old china, Chinese rugs on wooden floors, open fires, a smattering of Africana and big bedrooms with all mod cons. Your affable hosts manage the mix of B&B-ing and farming with easy-going humour and a passion for Bath rugby.

rooms	2: 1 twin with bath; 1 double with private shower.
room price	£55-£60. Single occ. £37.50-£40.
meals	Excellent restaurants nearby.
closed	Christmas & New Year.
directions	South from Bath, A367 (Wells Rd). At Odd Down r'bout right (Bristol A4). Straight on, past Culverhay School on left. After 100 yards left to Englishcombe. There, right after postbox to church, fork right, follow rd; last on right.

rooms	4: 1 double with bathroom; 2 doubles sharing bath/shower; 1 twin with bathroom.
room price	From £52. Single occ. £32.
meals	Pub 300 yds.
closed	Christmas & New Year.
directions	From A4 west of Bath, A39 through Corston. 1 mile on, just before Wheatsheaf Pub (on right), right. Signed 200 yds along lane on right.

Sue & Giles Barber
Manor Farm Barn,
Englishcombe, Bath,
Bath & N. E. Somerset BA2 9DU

tel	01225 424195
fax	01225 427434
e-mail	info@manorfarmbarn.com
web	www.manorfarmbarn.com

Gerald & Rosaline Addicott
Corston Fields Farm,
Corston, Bath,
Bath & N. E. Somerset BA2 9EZ

tel	01225 873305
fax	01225 874421
e-mail	corston.fields@btinternet.com
web	www.corstonfields.com

map: 3 entry: 9

map: 3 entry: 10

Meandering lanes lead you to this quintessentially English 17th-century cottage, with roses round the door, a grandfather clock in the hall and an air of genteel tranquillity. The cottage charm has been updated with Regency mahogany and sumptuous sofas. Bedrooms have long views over farmland and undulating countryside; behind is a conservatory and sloping, south-facing garden with pond and seats. Bath is 20 minutes away and Julia knows the city well.

Our inspector loved the way this place manages to combine elegance with cosiness. Logs burn in the fireplace, the colours are warm, the dresser is Welsh, the stones are flagged. The kitchen – with Aga and terracotta tiles – is beamed and easy around the cherrywood refectory table. There is peace and comfort among the quirky internal touches, the winding stairs and old bread oven. Angharad is an aromatherapist (treatment available). The bedroom is "pure magic", with gorgeous furniture. *Children over five welcome.*

rooms	4: 2 doubles, sharing bath & shower, let only to members of same party; 1 twin, 1 single four-poster, both with bath/shower.
room price	£60; family suite (2 rooms) from £80; single occ. £30.
meals	Dinner, 3 courses, £20.
closed	Christmas Day.
directions	From Bath, A36 to Woolverton. Just past Red Lion, turn for Laverton. A mile to x-roads, & on towards Faukland. Downhill for 80 yds. House on left, just above farm entrance on right.

rooms	2: 1 double with shower room, 1 single with bathroom.
room price	£50. Single occ. £30.
meals	Light supper, from £10. Good pub 2 doors away.
closed	Very occasionally.
directions	From Bath A367 Exeter road. After 3 miles, left opp. Strydes Inn, signed 'Wellow 3 miles'. Park in square by Fox & Badger pub. House 2 doors down in Railway Lane.

Mrs Julia Naismith
Hollytree Cottage,
Laverton, Bath,
Bath & N. E. Somerset BA2 7QZ
tel   01373 830786
fax   01373 830786

Angharad Rhys-Roberts
Honey Batch Cottage,
Railway Lane, Wellow, Bath,
Bath & N. E. Somerset BA2 8QG
tel   01225 833107
e-mail   angharad@waitrose.com

BATH & N. E. SOMERSET

There's city convenience (Bath's only five miles), but this feels a world away from... most places! There's an other worldliness about the Lock Cottage and its pretty, rose-filled garden: narrow boats drift lazily up the old Somerset Coal Canal and it feels as if blissful idling is compulsory. There's a peaceful towpath walk to the local pub and to a café/restaurant. You can hire an electric launch for a day's pootling, or a bike; the Wheeldons will set you off on a safe, scenic route. Bedrooms are cottagey with watery views.
Self-contained apartment with canal views available for B&B or self-catering.

On warm summer mornings you can come to, peacefully, on the terrace – it's sheer bliss with amazing views over the Mendips' rolling hills. Views from the bedroom are of the walled garden and you're sure to want to explore it... immaculate lawns, deep herbaceous borders, croquet lawn, masses of roses and clematis and a burgeoning fruit and vegetable garden. The Stevens have poured a huge amount of love into it all. There are home-made biscuits on the bedroom tea tray and you have exclusive use of the drawing room. You are minutes from Bath and Bristol and Julia has deep local knowledge. *Children over 12 welcome.*

rooms	2: 1 double, 1 twin/double, both with private bath/shower.
room price	£50-£55. Single occ. by arrangement.
meals	Breakfast until 9am. Pub 1 mile.
closed	Christmas & New Year.
directions	5 miles south of Bath just off A36, 50 yds north of BP garage. Entrance at an oblique angle, so turn into garage & approach entrance from south.

rooms	1 twin/double with extra single bed, bath & shower.
room price	£60. Single occ. £35.
meals	Dinner £15-£20. Excellent pubs/restaurants nearby.
closed	Mid-December-mid-January.
directions	From Bath, A4 west. At r'bout by Globe Inn, left onto A39 for Wells. Through Corston, after 0.5 miles take B3116, sharp right. After 1 mile left for Burnett & next right. House 100 yds on left.

Tim & Wendy Wheeldon
Dundas Lock Cottage,
Monkton Combe, Bath,
Bath & N. E. Somerset BA2 7BN
tel   01225 723890
fax   01225 723890
e-mail dundaslockcottage@freenet.co.uk

Patrick & Julia Stevens
Brooklands,
Burnett, Keynsham, Bath,
Bath & N. E. Somerset BS31 2TF
tel   0117 986 8794
fax   0117 986 8794
e-mail patrick@micamail.com

map: 3 entry: 13

map: 3 entry: 14

Interesting, child-friendly hosts who are entirely natural and un-businesslike make this place special – and it's excellent value, too. The large old Mendip-style 'long cottage' with mullioned windows and beams made of ships' timbers is fronted by a vineyard and temptingly close to Babington House, the treasures of Bath and Wells, the gardens and concerts at Stourhead and Gregorian chant in Downside Abbey. Fresh, simple bedrooms have sloping ceilings and fresh flowers; jams and marmalades are home-made. No sitting room, but tea in the beautiful walled garden is rich compensation. *Children over five welcome.*

rooms	2: 1 small double/single with bathroom, sometimes shared; 1 twin/family with shower room.
room price	£34-£44. Single occ. £22.50.
meals	Pub 2 miles.
closed	Very occasionally.
directions	From Bath A367, Wells road, through Radstock. After 3 miles, at large r'bout, B3139 for Trowbridge. 1.1 miles on, right up drive. House at top, visible from road.

Virginia & Hugh Pountney
Melon Cottage Vineyard,
Charlton, Radstock, Nr. Bath,
Bath & N. E. Somerset BA3 5TN

tel 01761 435090

Owl House has the best of both worlds: a rural setting yet only three miles from Bath. Breakfast on the terrace and gaze over the honey-coloured collage of the city below – a stunning spectacle from this lofty vantage point. Old Cotswold stone outside, modernity within; there are good beds in comfortable rooms, a striking selection of art and a décor spiced with a touch of the orient. Anne has spent many years in the East and rooms are bedecked with batiks and other Malaysian memorabilia; she enjoys welcoming guests to her home.

rooms	3: 1 twin/family with shower; 1 double with bath & shower; 1 double/single with private shower room.
room price	£52-£65. Single occ. £38.
meals	Breakfast 8.30-9.30am. Excellent pub within walking distance.
closed	Occasionally.
directions	M4 exit 18, A46. A46 joins A4, left for Chippenham. At r'bout, A363. Under bridge, bear left at Crown pub into Bathford. 1.5 miles uphill, left after Swan pub (Lower Kingsdown Rd). Bear right at bottom, house 300 yds on left.

Anne Venus
Owl House,
Kingsdown, Nr. Box, Bath,
Bath & N. E. Somerset SN13 8BB

tel 01225 743883
fax 01225 744450
e-mail venus@zetnet.co.uk
web www.owlhouse.co.uk

BATH & N.E. SOMERSET

Wellington the parrot will sing you the Archers' signature tune if he's in the mood. The 16th-century farmhouse, with its charming mêlée of comfy sofas, books, pets and pretty china, breathes an air of warmth and easy fun. The heart and soul of it all is Julia, painter, gilder, fine-flapjack-maker and all round excellent cook – and Edward, who cycles to work (they have a picture-framing business) whatever the weather. Your bedroom, reached via the studio-cum-library, gives you field views and perfect peace. A home that arty types especially will love – and so close to Bath. *Children over 10 welcome.*

rooms	1 double with private bathroom.
room price	£60. Single occ. £35.
meals	Breakfast until 9.30am. Packed lunch £4. Supper £12.
closed	Occasionally.
directions	A4 from Bath to Chippenham. Right for Bradford-on-Avon & left through Bathford to Kingsdown. Right to South Wraxall & follow road for about a mile. Left at stone cottage. Farm on right.

Julia Rooth
Mount Pleasant Farm,
South Wraxall, Bradford-on-Avon,
Bath & N. E. Somerset BA15 2SD
tel   01225 864580
fax   01225 868440
e-mail juliarooth@rooths.co.uk

map: 3 entry: 17

BERKSHIRE

If you want to swim, there's an indoor heated pool; if you want to walk, there are 650 acres of farmland and a dog to keep you company. Both hosts are multilingual and enjoy their guests: Henry works less on the farm now and has turned his hand to breakfasts; Mary cooks the evening meals which include home-grown produce. Some of the guest rooms date back to the 16th century and are bright, airy, simply and attractively decorated and have views of garden and fields. There are books and a fire for you in the sitting room.

rooms	3: 2 twin/doubles, both with bath/shower; 1 twin/double with private bathroom.
room price	£52-£60. Single occ. £35-£50.
meals	Breakfast 7.30-9am; continental until 10am. Dinner (for 4 or more) £18. Good pub 0.5 miles.
closed	Very occasionally.
directions	From M4 junc. 14, A338 north for Wantage. After 0.5 miles, 1st left (B4000). House 1st farm road on right after Pheasant Inn.

Mary & Henry Wilson
Fishers Farm,
Shefford Woodlands, Hungerford,
Berkshire RG17 7AB
tel   01488 648466
fax   01488 648706
e-mail mail@fishersfarm.co.uk
web   www.fishersfarm.co.uk

map: 4 entry: 18

BERKSHIRE

The welcome is the same, the house is new – and what a place! The Welfares moved here from another *Special Place* and Pevsner has described this as "the most ambitious house in Hungerford". It is a classic townhouse with a Queen Anne façade and, inside, wood panelling and beams, wonky floors, period furniture and family portraits. Bedrooms are just right, and so is breakfast in the 18th-century dining room; the Welfares give a terrific welcome. Antique shops to the front and a walled garden with cordon-trained fruit trees behind. *Children over eight welcome.*

rooms	2: 1 double, 1 twin/double, both with bathroom.
room price	£58. Single occ. £39.
meals	Breakfast until 9am (Mon-Fri); flexible Sat-Sun. Packed lunch £5. Dinner within walking distance.
closed	Christmas.
directions	Junc. 14 from M4. Follow A338 to A4; right for Marlborough. Turn off A4 at Bear Hotel onto Salisbury road (A338). Over canal bridge into High St. House 200 yds past Town Hall on right.

Deborah & Jonathan Welfare
Wilton House,
33 High Street, Hungerford,
Berkshire RG17 0NF

tel	01488 684228
fax	01488 685037
e-mail	welfares@hotmail.com
web	www.wiltonhouse.freeserve.co.uk

map: 4 entry: 19

BRISTOL

Unabashedly 1920s mock-Tudor with an oak-panelled hall and a great engraved fireplace. This is a generous house on the edge of the Bristol Downs, perfectly placed for country quiet in the evening after city bustle in the daytime. Light from the garden floods in and Philippa, with long experience of five-star hotels, does an efficient, professional job. The breakfast menu is mouthwatering and the morning papers come with it. The guest rooms – some in the house and some in the annexe – are 'fully-equipped', pastel-decorated and eminently comfortable. *Children over seven welcome.*

rooms	6: 4 doubles, all with shower room & private wc; 1 twin with bathroom; 1 single with private bathroom.
room price	£64-£69. Single occ. £45-£49.
meals	Dinner within 10 minutes' walk.
closed	Christmas & New Year.
directions	From M5, exit 17 onto A4018. At 4th r'bout 3rd exit into Parry's Lane. Left into Saville Rd. 3rd right into Hollybush Lane. 1st left immed. after 2nd road hump into Downs Edge. Drive to end.

Alan & Philippa Tasker
Downs Edge,
Saville Road, Stoke Bishop,
Bristol BS9 1JA

tel	0117 968 3264
fax	0117 968 3264
e-mail	welcome@downsedge.com

map: 3 entry: 20

An easy-going family house and hostess; you'll feel at home in the city and have enough privacy to ensure a peaceful stay. Anne has furnished the freshly-painted bedrooms with modern paintings, stunning wall hangings, antiques, pretty china and comfy sofas. They all have luxurious bathrooms, large mirrors, fluffy towels and seriously strong showers. Light and airy, the sky blue room with white muslin curtains and white linen is a delight. Breakfast (as organic as possible) is served on the raspberry silk tablecloth, on white china. It's a short walk to Clifton village, the Suspension Bridge and the thriving harbourside.

rooms	3: 2 doubles, 1 twin, all with shower.
room price	From £60. Single occ. from £42.
meals	Breakfast from 7.30am. Places to eat within a 10-minute walk.
closed	Very occasionally.
directions	From M5 SW, junc. 18. Follow A4 signs to Bristol West & airport. Under Suspension Bridge & follow city sign on road. Follow lane for Clifton. Left into Clifton Vale before church. 1st right into Camden Terrace. On right.

Anne Malindine
14 Camden Terrace,
Clifton Vale,
Bristol BS8 4PU

tel	0117 914 9508
fax	0117 914 9508
e-mail	anne@amalindine.freeserve.co.uk
web	www.roseberyhouse.net

map: 3 entry: 21

Smothered in clematis, jasmine, roses and honeysuckle – the scent wafts delectably through the bedroom window; it's hard to believe that Spring Farm, with its colourful walled garden and lush meadow of wild flowers, is only a few miles from Bristol and close to Bath and Wells, too. Plump beds and lovely linen in light, cottagey bedrooms decorated with country simplicity. Laze in the garden, lulled by the sound of summer bees. In winter, breakfast by an open fire, enveloped by the friendly, generous atmosphere of the Gallannaughs' charming English farmhouse, with its Aga, terracotta tiles and antique pine.

rooms	2: 1 double with bath; 1 double with private bathroom.
room price	£45-£55. Single occ. by arrangement.
meals	Packed lunch £5.
closed	Christmas.
directions	From Bristol A38 for airport. 5 miles out, left on B3130 for Winford. On leaving village, bear right up Regil Lane. After the Crown pub, farm 5th on right.

Judy & Roger Gallannaugh
Spring Farm,
Regil, Nr. Winford,
Bristol BS40 8BB

tel	01275 472735
fax	01275 474445
e-mail	springfarm@ic24.net

map: 3 entry: 22

Cool and uncluttered, with wooden floors, a piano and open fires. They are interesting people, he ex-business in Africa, she an English (EFL) teacher. The house is Grade II-listed and has lovely views across the Vale of Wrington. The bedrooms are in a wooden-floored wing (built long and low, around 1760, for rope-making); it looks onto a paddock and a copse. You feel very private here. The bed, made for them in Africa, is huge and has the best linen and a large bathroom with an old pine dresser comes stacked with books. *Only 5 minutes from Bristol airport.*

Fresh strawberries on Villeroy & Boch plates at breakfast, Egyptian cotton on beds with goose down duvets as soft as a cloud – just a taste of the perfect attention to detail at this Victorian/Georgian rectory. All is pristine, sparkling, fresh and light and each bedroom has a harmonious blend of furniture, be it rattan, Provençal or classic. Walls are mostly cream: a perfect backdrop for pretty fabrics. Bathrooms have double power showers and the same stylish feel. There is the odd caravan visible but this is a world away from Weston, and with far-reaching views. Jane and Tony are delightful.

rooms	1 double with bath.
room price	£50. Single occ. £35.
meals	Supper from £12.50. Pub 2 miles.
closed	Christmas & New Year.
directions	From Bristol A38. 4 miles past airport, right to Lower Langford. 200 yds on, 5th, pink, house on left.

rooms	5: 2 doubles, both with shower room; 2 doubles, 1 twin, both with bath/shower.
room price	£65. Single occ. £50.
meals	Good pubs 400 yds.
closed	Very occasionally.
directions	M5, junc. 21 then follow signs for Kewstoke. After Old Manor Inn on right, left up Anson Rd. At T-junc. right into Kewstoke Road. Follow road for 1 mile; see church on right; drive between church and church hall.

Rebecca Wimshurst
Dring Cottage,
Lower Langford,
Bristol BS40 5BW
tel   01934 862243
fax   01934 862670
e-mail   wimshurst@dringcottage.fsnet.co.uk

Mr A. C. Chapman
Church House,
27 Kewstoke Road, Kewstoke,
Weston-Super-Mare,
North Somerset BS22 9YD
tel   01934 633185
fax   01934 633185
e-mail   chapman1@euphony.net

map: 3 entry: 23

map: 3 entry: 24

BUCKINGHAMSHIRE

This is a one-off. Sarah's conversion, architectural rather than religious, has turned a fascinating church into a fascinating home, complete with tower and spiral staircase, original stained glass and stone mullion windows. It has a charm all of its own – the Winnie the Pooh mural in one bedroom and the fish swimming around the bathroom walls are amusing touches. The bedrooms are compact but each has its own church window. The old schoolroom is now a kitchen/dining room – impressively big and a great place for breakfast. Sarah is ease personified and this is good value.

rooms	3: 1 double, 1 twin, 1 single, sharing 1 bathroom & 1 shower room.
room price	£45. Single £30.
meals	Excellent restaurants & pubs nearby.
closed	Very occasionally.
directions	From Aylesbury, A413 for Buckingham. On reaching Winslow centre, left into Horn St between Bell Hotel & The George. On left.

Sarah Hood
The Congregational Church,
15 Horn Street, Winslow,
Buckinghamshire MK18 3AP

tel   01296 715717
fax   01296 715717

map: 10 entry: 25

CAMBRIDGESHIRE

You are in the middle of an ancient market town with narrow streets and medieval buildings, yet have a beautiful one-acre garden in which to wander, with lawns, shrubbery, orchard and vegetable garden; the Friend-Smiths have retained the original Edwardian garden design. The feel in the bedrooms is traditional English with good quality linen and country antiques and you have lovely views of the garden and cathedral. Sheila serves locally baked bread and home-made marmalade at the long mahogany dining table. The cathedral is just five minutes' walk and Cambridge 15 miles.

rooms	2: 1 double with private bathroom; 1 twin with bathroom.
room price	£50. Single occ. £35–£41.
meals	Breakfast until 9.30am. Dinner 4 minutes' walk.
closed	Christmas & New Year, & for annual holiday.
directions	From Cambridge, A10. Entering Ely, left at lights by Lamb Hotel. Left at next lights, after 200 yds into Egremont St. House last on left. Off-street parking just beyond.

Sheila & Jeremy Friend-Smith
Old Egremont House,
31 Egremont Street, Ely,
Cambridgeshire CB6 1AE

tel   01353 663118
fax   01353 614516

map: 10 entry: 26

CAMBRIDGESHIRE

Breakfasts here are something of a legend: soft cheeses, hams, black puddings, kippers and haddock – the freshest, locally sourced produce is served at 7am if you like. The Ropers bend over backwards to meet guests' needs and many that come to stay are here for the horsey connection: Malcolm's an equine buff and organises racing packages and, of course, the racecourse is close by. Jan, formerly an illustrator, cooks and attends to the décor – old pine, huge cushions, handsome wallpapers and fresh flowers. The Georgian home has a croquet lawn and a conservatory, too.

rooms	3: 1 twin/double, 1 single sharing bathroom; 1 double with shower.
room price	From £60. Single occ. from £30. Occasionally, min. 2 nights' stay.
meals	Breakfast 7-9.15am. Restaurants within walking distance.
closed	Very occasionally.
directions	A142 Newmarket to Ely road, through Fordham & right at Murfitts Lane; at end, right into Carter St; Queensberry 200 yds on left next to Fordham Moor Rd.

Jan & Malcolm Roper
Queensberry,
196 Carter Street, Fordham, Ely,
Cambridgeshire CB7 5JU
tel   01638 720916
fax   01638 720233

map: 11 entry: 27

CAMBRIDGESHIRE

A happy combination of elegance and a bustling family atmosphere in a large 1840 Regency-style home. The former school house hugs the bend of a river on the edge of the quiet, ancient village of Linton and the rooms overlook the large gardens and the river. The conservatory, draped with a mimosa tree, is exceptional and a wonderful spot for summer breakfasts, while in winter one 'repairs' to the dark green dining room. Bedrooms are large, so are the beds, and are stocked with books. This is exceptional value, and so close to Cambridge, too.

rooms	2 doubles, 1 with bath, 1 with bath/shower.
room price	£50-£60. Single occ. £27-£35.
meals	Breakfast 7.30-9.30am. Pub 150 yds.
closed	Very occasionally.
directions	A1307 from Cambridge, left into High St. 1st right after The Crown (on left) into Horn Lane. House on right next to chapel & before ford.

Judith Rossiter
Springfield House,
14-16 Horn Lane, Linton,
Cambridgeshire CB1 6HT
tel   01223 891383
fax   01223 890335

map: 10 entry: 28

CAMBRIDGESHIRE

One cosy yet large and very private bedroom is up its own spiral staircase – a lovely conversion and sure winner of first prize in any Loo With A View competition. In the main house is a fresh blue and white bedroom; those that like their independence will be happy in either room as the Barlows' relaxed 'take-us-as-you-find-us' approach pervades the whole house. There are fruit trees and bees and home-made jam and honey for breakfast and, although this is now an arable farm, sheep still graze the land. Perfectly quiet, and close to Cambridge.

rooms	3 doubles, all with shower room.
room price	£50. Single occ. £28.
meals	Breakfast 7.30-9.30am. Pub/restaurant 3 miles.
closed	Christmas.
directions	Turn off A1198 at Longstowe onto B1046. House on right after 3 miles, before Little Gransden.

Sue Barlow
Model Farm,
Little Gransden,
Cambridgeshire SG19 3EA

tel	01767 677361
fax	01767 677883
e-mail	bandb@modelfarm.org.uk
web	www.modelfarm.org.uk

CHESHIRE

A wonderful farmhouse atmosphere, with friendly hosts. Very quickly you get the feel of Roughlow, planted in its leafy hillside – it is solid, authentic and greatly loved. The cobbled entrance yard is a treasure box of flowering trees and shrubs and from the terrace you can see for 40 miles. Large bedrooms and bathrooms are furnished with artistic flair; the suite is vast. Sally has a good eye and has created a calming, uncluttered space. There's a tennis court and they both collect art. Part of *The Forsyte Saga* was filmed here – the set for Soames's house, Robin Hill, was built in the next field.

rooms	3: 2 doubles, both with bathroom, 1 with sitting room; 1 twin/double with shower room.
room price	£60-£80. Single occ. £40-£50.
meals	Breakfast 8-9am. Good pubs & hotels 1 mile.
closed	Very occasionally.
directions	A51 from Chester. Cross r'bout at Tarvin & A54 to Manchester (not Tarporley). Pass garage. 2nd right & follow signs to Willington. Straight over x-roads & up Chapel Lane. House on right at top.

Sally & Peter Sutcliffe
Roughlow Farm,
Willington, Tarporley,
Cheshire CW6 0PG

tel	01829 751199
fax	01829 751199
e-mail	sutcliffe@roughlow.freeserve.co.uk
web	www.roughlow.freeserve.co.uk

CHESHIRE

Explore the intriguing city of Chester with its Roman history and 900-year-old cathedral before returning the four miles to the farm. You have 250 acres to explore and geese, sheep and, maybe, otters to watch – parts of the farm are cared for under the Countryside Stewardship Scheme. Bedrooms are 'stylish farmhouse' with lovely fabrics – but best of all is the relaxed, family atmosphere created by the Hills. There are touches of luxury, such as huge bath towels and excellent breakfasts, cooked by Clare who was trained by Prue Leith.

rooms	3: 2 doubles, 1 twin, all with bath/shower.
room price	From £50. Single occ. £32.
meals	Pub 1.5 miles.
closed	Very occasionally.
directions	From Chester, A51 east, signed Nantwich. 1.5 miles from city outskirts, right, down Cotton lane, signed Cotton Edmunds. 1.5 miles, on sharp right-hand bend, left. Farm 2nd drive on right.

Clare & Nigel Hill
Cotton Farmhouse,
Cotton Edmunds, Chester,
Cheshire CH3 7PG
tel   01244 336616
fax   01244 336699
e-mail   info@cottonfarm.co.uk
web   www.cottonfarm.co.uk

map: 13 entry: 31

CHESHIRE

David designed some of the furniture, including the vast bed that needs nine pillows. The rooms are sumptuous (TV and video hidden in wooden cabinets) and have great country views – you are on a quiet country lane with the village pub at the end of the drive and Dunham Massey Deer Park five minutes' walk away. David was a professional snooker player. Good value so close to the city (Manchester and its airport are six minutes away), yet so rural. Excellent breakfasts and great hosts, too.
Children over 12 welcome.

rooms	3: 1 double with shower room; 1 double with private bathroom; 1 four-poster with bath/shower.
room price	£58-£70. Single occ. £45-£52.
meals	Breakfast until 9.30am. Pub/restaurant 5 minutes away.
closed	Christmas & New Year.
directions	A556 NE to Manchester, then left on A56 for Lymm. At 1st pub, right down Park Lane. Next to The Swan With Two Nicks.

David & Janice Taylor
Ash Farm Country Guest House,
Park Lane, Little Bollington,
Nr. Altrincham,
Cheshire WA14 4TJ
tel   0161 929 9290
fax   0161 928 5002
e-mail   jan@ashfarm97.fsnet.co.uk
web   www.ashfarm.co.uk

map: 13 entry: 32

Rachel is delightful, warm and friendly. This is Britain at its best with rare trees planted in 1860, flowers everywhere, a pond and a fruitful vegetable garden. The Victorian house is furnished in elegant and traditional style, with garden views from every angle. The proportions of the light-filled drawing room and the big, high-ceilinged dining room feel just right. The bedrooms are inviting, bright and large with attractive fabrics, art, lovely furniture, new mattresses and bedheads. This is a haven for garden buffs, walkers and birdwatchers and there's tennis, too. *Children over 12 welcome.*

rooms	3: 1 double, 1 twin/double, -both with bathroom; 1 twin with shower room.
room price	From £50. Single occ. by arrangement.
meals	Dinner, weekdays only, £20. B.Y.O. Good pub/restaurant 0.5 miles.
closed	Christmas & New Year.
directions	From Chester, A55 west, then A5104 to Broughton. Through Broughton & over A55. 1st left to Kinnerton down Lesters Lane. On right, opposite Mount Farm.

Jonathan & Rachel Major
The Mount,
Higher Kinnerton, Chester,
Cheshire CH4 9BQ

tel	01244 660275
fax	01244 660275
e-mail	major@mountkinnerton.freeserve.co.uk

map: 8 entry: 33

Some hosts 'have it'. They don't have to try – they just stand there, complacently warming their backsides against the fire, knowing that you'll be charmed by their mere presence (while wondering what they have left in the hearth…). This landlady – hirsute but admirably unselfconscious about it – has retired from a long career on Blackpool's seafront. She is less garrulous than many of our hosts but she'll be all ears if you want to burden her with your problems. Be late for your fry-up, however, and even this mild-mannered lady will resort to foot-stamping. The garden is beautifully manicured – she sees to it all herself.

rooms	Stable block: 1 double; Coach House: 1 twin.
room price	£13 – no horse trading.
meals	Cordon Vert – only vegetarians catered for.
closed	Stables doors are often bolted.
directions	From the One-Horse Town, take Cavalry Way. Sharp left at bridlepath, then down unmade drive. Two-legged guests: be careful of potholes; four-legged guests, note super verges for grazing and irresistible windfall apples.

Mr & Mrs Don Key-hotey
Cabullus Castle,
One-Horse Town, Cheshire

tel	01234 567890
e-mail	equusasinus@wildass.com
web	www.dontbeadonkey.com

map: 13 entry: 34

CORNWALL

A ll is immaculate: the vegetable garden, the decoration, the flower arrangements – and run like clockwork by Marion, who loves this special place. The views to the sea are heart-stopping and the ever-changing light casts a spell over the landscape. The dining room is illuminated by fire and candle; the yellow drawing room, with wooden floors and deep sofas, is perfect. Good linen, a regal four-poster and a luxurious half-tester – the bedrooms are exquisite. Swim in the sheltered pool, laze in the pavilion and gaze across the superb garden to the sea – just a three-minute walk away. Irresistible.

rooms	3: 1 four-poster, 1 double, 1 twin/double, all with bath/shower.
room price	£80-£96. Single occ. £50-£58.
meals	Breakfast until 9.30am. Dinner, 3 courses, £26.
closed	Christmas.
directions	From Helston, A3083 south. Just before Lizard, left to Church Cove. Follow signs for about 0.75 miles. House on left behind blue gates.

Peter & Marion Stanley
Landewednack House,
Church Cove, The Lizard,
Cornwall TR12 7PQ

tel 01326 290909
fax 01326 290192
e-mail landewednack.house@virgin.net

map: 1 entry: 35

CORNWALL

T he setting deserves the word 'dramatic'. The little bungalow is perched on the last strip of land before the Atlantic which swirls around the Lizard. Breakfasts, continental and delicious as they are, have to fight for your attention, for your table is set at the big picture window to take in the beauty of the Lizard at England's most southerly point. The bedroom has picture windows and overlooks your private patio – you won't in the least mind waking up. John works in broadcasting and is about to launch a radio station; Jane works locally and both are gentle and easy. It's a five-minute walk to the shoreline.

rooms	1 double with private bath/shower.
room price	£50. Single occ. £25.
meals	Pub & restaurant 0.25 miles.
closed	December-February.
directions	From Helston to The Lizard. 1st right at Lizard Green (head for Smugglers Fish & Chips). Take 1st right & pass wc on left. Road is unmade; on for 400 yds. Double bend. 2nd bungalow on right.

Jane and John Grierson
Carmelin,
Pentreath Lane, The Lizard,
Nr. Helston,
Cornwall TR12 7NY

tel 01326 290677
e-mail pjcarmelin@aol.com
web www.carmelin.ukf.net

map: 1 entry: 36

CORNWALL

CORNWALL

What a stunning position! The house sits in a secluded spot at the top of a wooded valley, just minutes from the coast and the Helford River. The Leiths are attentive and charming hosts who want you to leave feeling refreshed and well looked after. The Georgian rectory, restored with enormous care and style, is both elegant and comfortable with lots of space, light and views. Breakfast, organic from the farm shop, is served in the beautiful turquoise dining room – the magnificent table is a family heirloom. Bedrooms are exceptionally comfortable with lovely colours and great views.

Two – perhaps three – 200-year-old miners' cottages have combined to create a sturdy granite home that sits among other houses in a quiet hamlet. Narrow staircases, low ceilings, stripped pine doors, inglenooks and unpretentious flowery decoration give a typically Cornish feel. There's crisp, ironed cotton in the bedrooms and fresh garden flowers. Moira, a retired midwife, has a passion for gardening. Goff, a potter, joins in, too, and has created a warm, sheltered potager. They are both immensely kind and will bring an early-morning tea tray; bread, jams and marmalades that are all home-made await at the breakfast table.

rooms	2 twin/doubles, both with bath/shower.
room price	From £70. Single occ. by arrangement.
meals	Breakfast 8.15-9.15am. Pub/restaurant 100 yds.
closed	Occasionally.
directions	From Helston, A3083 for the Lizard. Left onto B3293 for St Keverne. Left at Mawgan Cross, past Post Office, & right into tiny slip road. Pass Old Court House pub, house 2nd on right.

rooms	3: 2 doubles, both with bath & shower; 1 twin/double with private bathroom.
room price	£44-£50. Single occ. £22-£25.
meals	Early breakfast for people going to Scillies. Packed lunch from £4.50. Dinner from £12.50. Seafood restaurant, 10 minutes' drive.
closed	Christmas & New Year.
directions	A394 Helston to Penzance, 2nd right after Ashton Post Office for Tresowes Green. After 0.25 miles, sign for house on right.

Susan Leith
The Old Rectory,
Mawgan, Helston,
Cornwall TR12 6AD
tel 01326 221261
fax 01326 221797
e-mail leith@euphony.net
web www.oldrectorymawgan.co.uk

Moira & Goff Cattell
The Gardens,
Tresowes, Ashton, Helston,
Cornwall TR13 9SY
tel 01736 763299
e-mail thegardens@amserve.com

map: 1 entry: 37

map: 1 entry: 38

FOOD
in our Bed & Breakfasts

The vast majority of Special Places will cook
you a breakfast that you'll not forget. You
may have, among other things, home-made
breads and jams, organic milk and yogurt,
eggs and bacon (and sausages) from local
animals, black puddings – even kippers and
kedgeree. Breakfast, however gargantuan and
delicious, is included everywhere; only one
or two houses charge extra for a cooked
breakfast, and we say which they are.

Some of the owners will also do dinner for
you, and we say so in their entry. (Prices are
per person.) You may have to bring your own
wine; do ask. And do, please, turn up on time
for dinner or supper! (Foreign readers should
note that 'supper' is a more modest affair
than dinner.) Some of the meals you
eat will be spectacular.

It's undeniably spoiling – fresh fruit, flowers and bathroom goodies in your room, and a terrace for each pristine bedroom with views to the wild blue yonder and St Michael's Mount. A marvellous position. Come for peace, space and privacy. There are honey-coloured timbers, pretty tea sets, good fabrics and colours. Choose either full English breakfast in the woody kitchen-diner or a continental tray brought to your room. Your hosts are busy people yet will help you discover local walks; a footpath through the field below leads to the village, and Prussia Cove and Cudden Point are walkable, too.

rooms	3 doubles, 2 with bath/shower, 1 with bath.
room price	£60-£74. Single occ. £45-£60.
meals	Breakfast until 9am. Dinner available within walking distance.
closed	Christmas.
directions	From A30 after Crowlas r'bout, A394 to Helston. 0.25 miles after next r'bout, 1st right for Perranuthnoe. Farm drive on left, signed.

Christine & Charles Taylor
Ednovean Farm,
Perranuthnoe, Nr. Penzance,
Cornwall TR20 9LZ

tel	01736 711883
fax	01736 710480
e-mail	info@ednoveanfarm.co.uk
web	www.ednoveanfarm.co.uk

map: 1 entry: 39

Kenneth is a rich mixture of talent and enthusiasm; a baritone and an ex-BBC Singer, he may be in full voice when you arrive. He also cooks divinely and imaginatively (e.g. gunpowder sauce!). He and his delightful mother live on the wildest cliffs, a stroll away from some of Cornwall's loveliest places. It is windswept on a blustery day but exhilerating, traditional and fun, too – a wash basin from an Edwardian train carriage, bedroom views to the Lizard, smart old Victorian beds and a four-poster. It is full of old-fashioned charm, books and personality. *Children over 12 welcome.*

rooms	2: 1 double with wc/shower; 1 twin with private shower.
room price	£60-£70. Single occ. by arrangement.
meals	Supper from £15; dinner from £25. Pubs/restaurants 2-6 miles.
closed	Very occasionally.
directions	A30 to Land's End. 3 miles from Penzance left (at Catchall) onto B3283. Through St Buryan, then left for Lamorna by phone box on green. 2nd right 0.75 miles on (on left-hand bend by woods). Right into drive & on to top.

Kenneth Fraser Annand
Burnewhall Farmhouse,
Nr. St Buryan, Penzance,
Cornwall TR19 6DN

tel	01736 810650
fax	01736 810650
e-mail	burnewhall@btconnect.com

map: 1 entry: 40

CORNWALL

Flowers, fruit and firewood await your arrival in these 200-year-old converted barns where you self-cater. The family in the main house are easy-going and kind and will instantly put you at your ease. Exposed granite, wooden beams, stencilled walls, pieces of local art and a refreshing simplicity set the tone in your holiday home. You have your own patio, but can play in the main garden, too, and there's a barbecue for summer evenings. High beds, comfy sofas, views of wooded hills and distant sea. Good beaches are nearby, yet you feel insulated from the bustle of Penzance.

rooms	2 self-catering cottage suites for 2-4 people.
room price	Cottage £200-£350 p.w. Short breaks available October-March.
meals	Self-catering.
closed	Very occasionally.
directions	Take Penzance bypass for Land's End. Right at r'bout to Heamoor. Through village, right at x-roads for Gulval, 1st left for Bone Valley/New Mill. House on right after 0.5 miles.

Danielle Atkins
Tremearne,
Bone Valley, Penzance,
Cornwall TR20 8UJ
tel   01736 364576
fax   01736 364576
e-mail   danielle@tremearnefarm.co.uk
web   www.tremearnefarm.co.uk

CORNWALL

You'll feel spoilt. A log fire smoulders in the sumptuous sitting room, complimentary afternoon tea is laid out in the huge farmhouse kitchen, and bedrooms are luxurious – the four-poster has pretty *toile de Jouy* wallpaper, a powerful shower and fat pillows. Everywhere there are fascinating artefacts and curios from Gill's travels, designer fabrics and antique pieces. The road ends at Ennys, so the rural bliss is entirely yours. Walk down to the river and along the old towpath, or simply stay here, play tennis, or swim in the heated pool sunk deep into the tropical gardens. *Children over three welcome.*

rooms	5 + 3 cottages: 1 twin with bath; 2 four-posters, both with shower; 2 family suites in barn; 3 luxury self-catering cottages for 2-4.
room price	£60-£85. Single occ. from £50. Self-catering: £250-£450 p.w. 1 bedroom.
meals	Breakfast until 9.15am. Good pub 3 miles.
closed	November-February.
directions	2 miles east of Marazion on B3280, look for sign leading down Trewhella Lane between St Hilary & Relubbus. Keep going to Ennys.

Gill Charlton
Ennys,
St Hilary, Penzance,
Cornwall TR20 9BZ
tel   01736 740262
fax   01736 740055
e-mail   ennys@ennys.co.uk
web   www.ennys.co.uk

A working farm still, the original manor was built in the 1500s and embellished in 1668; it has changed little since. Albertine is rightly proud of this fine house which she has made unpretentiously comfortable, with old pine furniture on wooden floors — wooden panelling and shutters, too. One bedroom has an oak bed specially made for the Leggos and a little granite fireplace. The welcome is of the home-baked-cake variety and there's much to explore: remains of the Cornish mining industry, beaches, St Michael's Mount and the artistic life of St Ives. The pool awaits your return.

For five centuries the house has sat secluded in five acres of this wild and lovely part of Cornwall. The mood is now artistic for the Halls are devoted to the encouragement of the arts in Cornwall. Once the vicarage (the church is next door), the house has polished wooden floors, oriental rugs, faded blue carpet, bird-print curtains and Italian prints. The pretty bedroom and bathroom overlook the Italianate courtyard adorned with hanging flower baskets. The gardens are part of the mood, traditional and beautiful, and your hosts are generous and fun.

rooms	3: 2 doubles, both with bathrooms; 1 twin with private bathroom.
room price	£60. Single occ. £35.
meals	Pub in village 1 mile; restaurant 2 miles.
closed	October-April.
directions	From A30 take Cambourne West. Left to mini-r'bout; right to Conor Downs. Sign on left to Carnhell Green, right at T-junc. between pub and shop; next right Gwinear Lane, past school, first lane on right.

rooms	1 twin/double with bathroom.
room price	£55. Single occ. by arrangement.
meals	Dinner sometimes available. Pub 1.5 miles.
closed	Very occasionally.
directions	From A30 exit Hayle (Pickfords r'bout); 100 yards left at mini-roundabout; 400 yards left for Gwinear; 1.5 miles, top of hill, driveway on right, just before 30mph Gwinear sign.

Mrs Albertine Leggo
Lanyon Manor,
Gwinear Lane, Gwinear, Hayle,
Cornwall TR27 5LA

| tel | 01736 850795 |

Charles & Diana Hall
House at Gwinear,
Gwinear, St Ives,
Cornwall TR27 5JZ

| tel | 01736 850444 |
| fax | 01736 850031 |

CORNWALL

The sea and the peninsula wrap themselves around you – Trevilla House is a great family home in an enviable position, with expansive views over the Fal Estuary. The King Harry ferry gives you easy access to the delights of the Roseland peninsula, too. Your bedroom is comfortable and unfrilly – the high, antique basketwork twin beds have French polished frames – and from here you can take in those views; there is also a small, private sitting room. Breakfast is usually served in the south-facing conservatory overlooking the sea. Perfect *and* Trelissick Gardens are just next door.

rooms	1 twin/family with bathroom & small private sitting room.
room price	£55. Single occ. £30.
meals	Breakfast until 9.30am. Restaurants/pubs 1-2 miles.
closed	Christmas & New Year.
directions	A390 to Truro, left onto A39 to Falmouth. At double r'bout with garage, left off 2nd r'bout (B3289). Pass pub on left. At x-roads, left (B3289). 200 yds on, fork right to Feock. On to T-junc., then left. House 1st on right.

Jinty & Peter Copeland
Trevilla House,
Feock, Truro,
Cornwall TR3 6QG
tel   01872 862369
fax   01872 870088
e-mail   jinty@trevilla.com

map: 1 entry: 45

CORNWALL

What a treat! Catch a tantalising glimpse of the sea from your B&B and wake to the sound of a bubbling stream. Clare's generous and sunny nature is reflected in her lovely home, with its shelves of books, rose-strewn wallpapers and delicious smells of beeswax and baking. She used to run an excellent restaurant and is a superb cook who loves to treat guests to locally-caught bass, brill, mullet, sole. Bedrooms are filled with light: an elegant double/twin and a sweet double with that glimpse of the sea. All this, a garden full of birdsong, a (real) fishing village 500 yards below and the Eden project close by. *Children by arrangement.*

rooms	2: 1 twin/double with bath/shower; 1 double with private bath/shower.
room price	£70-£76. Single occ. by arrangement.
meals	Packed lunch £7.50. Dinner, 2/3 courses, £20/£25.
closed	Occasionally.
directions	From Tregony, A3078 to St Mawes. After 2 miles at Esso garage on left, left to Portloe. Through village until Ship Inn. Right fork after pub car park. Immed. on left between white gate posts up drive under trees.

Clare Holdsworth
Pine Cottage,
Portloe, Truro, Portloe,
Cornwall TR2 5RB
tel   01872 501385
web   www.pinecottage.net

map: 1 entry: 46

A footpath leads from the garden to a big sandy beach – a perfect spot for seaside hols. There's no shortage of spare welly boots for the children either; a great sense of fun echoes around Polsue. Rooms are huge, bedrooms have country eiderdowns, comfy beds and views; there are wooden floors and rugs in the dining room. Annabelle has cooked professionally and her breakfasts are special. Outside: big trees, camellias, a pond, green field views. You are on the spot for the Eden Project, and there are many fine National Trust gardens nearby.

Everything's just right – the setting, the gentle activity of the farm, the windy lanes, and delightful hosts who look after you with huge enthusiasm. What's more, there are freshly decorated rooms, good bathrooms, family antiques and the promise of good food. In the dining room, even with sofas and woodburner, you could turn a cartwheel. An ancient lane leads to Colona Bay: small, secluded and full of rock pools. Blissful. There's an indoor pool and sauna, too, and Heligan and the Eden Project nearby. *Children over 12 welcome. Guided walks by arrangement.*

rooms	3 twin/doubles, all with bath.
room price	£80. Single occ. £50.
meals	Breakfast until 9.30am. Pub 1 mile.
closed	Very occasionally.
directions	A3078 south from Tregony. In Ruan High Lanes, 2nd right (for Philleigh & King Harry Ferry). House 1 mile up on left.

rooms	3: 1 double, 1 twin, both with private bathroom/shower; 1 double with shower room.
room price	£60-£70. Single occ. from £30.
meals	Breakfast 8-9am. Packed lunch from £5. Supper/dinner, £15/£25.
closed	Christmas & New Year.
directions	From St Austell B3273 for Mevagissey. At x-roads on hill, right to Heligan & Mavagissey. Through Gorran, bend left to Portmellon & Mevagissey. After 1.5 miles, right at grass triangle into farm.

Annabelle Sylvester
Polsue Manor,
Ruan High Lanes, Truro,
Cornwall TR2 5LU
tel   01872 501270
fax   01872 501177
web   www.polsuemanor.co.uk

Sally & Tim Kendall
Bodrugan Barton,
Mevagissey,
Cornwall PL26 6PT
tel   01726 842094
fax   01726 844378
e-mail   bodruganbarton@ukonline.co.uk

CORNWALL

Lally and William have transformed a jungle into one of Cornwall's loveliest gardens, whose secret paths lure you into the woodland's dappled delights. Inside the lovely 1730s house shimmering wooden floors are covered with Persian rugs and light pours into every elegant corner. The large guest rooms are gloriously furnished with antiques; breakfast in the large dining room often turns into an early morning house-party, such is Lally's sense of fun and spontaneity. You are in deep and tranquil countryside. The Eden Project and Heligan are nearby. *Children over eight welcome.*

rooms	3: 1 twin/double with bath/shower; 2 twin/doubles, both with private bathroom.
room price	£70-80. Single occ. by arrangement.
meals	Breakfast until 9.30am. Pub/restaurant 1 mile.
closed	Christmas & New Year.
directions	From St Austell, A390 to Grampound. Just beyond clock tower, left into Creed Lane. After 1 mile left at grass triangle opp. church. House behind 2nd white gate on left.

Lally & William Croggon
Creed House,
Creed, Grampound, Truro,
Cornwall TR2 4SL
tel   01872 530372

map: 1 entry: 49

CORNWALL

Your stunning rooms lead onto a pretty private garden with banked lawns – take your breakfast tray and revive yourself gently in the morning sun. The house has been in the family since the 1600s and the young Croggons have renovated this barn extension with such flair and attention to detail: Floris soap, pretty china, squashy sofa, Colefax & Fowler fabrics, seagrass matting, sofa in the huge bedroom, and lovely greys and greens everywhere. Annabel stocks your fridge with chopped exotic fruits, walnut bread, jams and yogurts, to be eaten when you want. Cooked breakfasts are available sometimes, too. A perfect hideaway.

rooms	1 suite with twin/double, breakfast room & bathroom.
room price	£65. Single occ. by arrangement.
meals	Breakfast anytime.
closed	Christmas & New Year; Easter.
directions	From Truro, A390 for St Austell. 6 miles on, through Grampound; on leaving village, at top of hill, right at speed limit sign into Bosillion Lane. House 150 yds on left.

Jonathon & Annabel Croggon
Bosillion,
Bosillion Lane, Grampound, Truro,
Cornwall TR2 4QY
tel   01726 883327

map: 1 entry: 50

Surrounded by a lovely garden open to the public once a year under the National Gardens Scheme, this classical late Regency English country house has the occasional hint of Eastern promise. In the drawing room, where tea is served, a beautiful Chinese cabinet occupies one wall and, in the dining room, is a Malaysian inscribed silk-screen – a thank-you present from Empire days. Upstairs the comfortable bedrooms have antique furniture, views onto the glorious garden and generous baths. The Eden Project and Heligan are nearby. *Children by arrangement.*

Barbara is genuinely keen on doing B&B; their previous house was a glorious listed farmhouse and they have built Oxturn specifically for welcoming guests. The interior is all beiges and creams, fitted furniture, impeccable modernity. Don't expect anything rustic or quaint – you come for Barbara herself (a true Cornishwoman), for the excellent breakfasts, for the views, for the care and attention to detail and comfort. Nothing whacky, eccentric or old here, just B&B of the best kind, in a good position above the village. *Children over 12 welcome.*

rooms	3: 1 four-poster, 1 twin, both with bathroom; 1 double with private bathroom.		rooms	2: 1 double with private bathroom; 1 twin/double with bathroom.
room price	£70-£90. Single occ. £45-£55.		room price	£46-£54. Single occ. by arrangement.
meals	Dinner, 4 courses, £25, B.Y.O.		meals	Breakfast 8-9am. Good village pub, 200 yds.
closed	Christmas & Easter.		closed	December.
directions	A30 for Truro, then left for Grampound Rd. After 3 miles, right onto A390 for Truro. After 200 yds, right where double white lines end. Pass between reflector posts towards house, 200 yds down private lane.		directions	From A30, B3275 south to Ladock. There, turn opposite the Falmouth Arms & follow road uphill for 200 yds. Right 70 yds after 'End 30mph' sign. House on right.

	Alison O'Connor
	Tregoose,
	Grampound, Truro,
	Cornwall TR2 4DB
tel	01726 882460
fax	01872 222427

	Ian & Barbara Holt
	Oxturn House,
	Ladock, Truro,
	Cornwall TR2 4NQ
tel	01726 884348
fax	01726 884248

CORNWALL

CORNWALL

Watch the surfers hug the waves, schools of them, all year. Watch the sun, the sand and, it seems, the world. The vastness of the view astonishes. At high tide you are on an island of granite – but not marooned. The bridge, a breathtaking entry, is the only privately owned suspension bridge in the country – not for those with vertigo. High seas can, spectacularly, wet the house. But all is elegance within: good furniture, deep carpets, family portraits, tradition and luxury with a modern touch. Decking all round for sun bathing, and views to the south, north, east and west. A great escape.

A homely refuge with family furniture and oil paintings and so intimately close to the sea that you might just spot dolphins or a lazy basking shark. You are almost at sea – crashing surf and Atlantic winds in a stunning Daphne du Maurier setting; this is rugged North Cornwall with surfing beaches all around. The cottage, in the family for four generations, was once a 'fish cellar' for processing catches. There's a woodburner in the drawing room and the bedrooms are very simple and unfrilly, but it will be their views that rivet you. An excellent choice for families.

rooms	1 double with private shower room.
room price	£96-£114. Single occ. £48-£57.
meals	Sandwiches & coffee, £5. Excellent pubs/restaurants short walk away.
closed	Very occasionally.
directions	From Treloggen r'bout before Newquay right at Safeways, down hill. Across double r'bout. Left at lights; 1st right Grovesnor Ave. Straight across main road down narrow road, over bridge; 1st left, 1st right down Island Crescent.

rooms	3: 2 twins, both with bathroom. A single can be added to 1 to make a triple.
room price	From £50. Single occ. by arrangement.
meals	Packed lunch from £5. Dinner from £15.
closed	Very occasionally.
directions	From St Merryn, right for Trevose Head. Over sleeping policemen. After toll gate ticket machine right through farm gate. On towards sea; cottage gate at end, on right.

Lady Long
The Island,
Newquay,
Cornwall TR7 1EA
tel   01637 879754
e-mail   helen@towanisland.fsnet.co.uk

Phyllida & Antony Woosnam-Mills
Mother Ivey Cottage,
Trevose Head, Padstow,
Cornwall PL28 8SL
tel   01841 520329
fax   01841 520329
e-mail   woosnammills@compuserve.com

map: 1 entry: 53

map: 1 entry: 54

Tea in the garden or the drawing room when you arrive; the grandeur is so soft and Sarah and her family so natural that you'll immediately feel at home. The Empire sofa, good oils, faded rugs on wooden floors, lovely lamps and an oak chest are just what you might hope for. They, and Sydney the polar bear, all sit beautifully in the 1780s, creeper-clad vicarage. Good period furniture, fresh flowers and quilted bedspreads in the bedrooms; in one a Napoleonic four-poster. The children's room, off the twin, with its miniature beds, is charming.

The Bloors strike the balance between being kind and helpful and unobtrusive. "They are doing a perfect job," said our inspector. The converted barn hunkers down in its own secluded valley and a path leads you through the woods to delightful Epphaven Cove. It's elegantly uncluttered and cool; seagrass contrasts with old oak and the downstairs bedrooms have fresh flowers, quilted bedspreads and doors onto the garden. The shower room – a mixture of rusty reds and Italian marble – is magnificent. Jo's daughter is an aromatherapist – book an appointment. *Children over 12 welcome.*

rooms	3: 1 four-poster, 1 double suite, 1 twin with children's room, all with bathroom.
room price	£40-£60. Single occ. £25-£35.
meals	Breakfast until 10.30am. Good pub food 200 yds up lane.
closed	Christmas Day.
directions	From Wadebridge, B3314 for Rock & Polzeath. After 3.5 miles, left for St Minver. In village, left into cul-de-sac just before Four Ways Inn. House at bottom on left.

rooms	3: 1 double, 2 twins, all sharing 1 bathroom & 1 shower room.
room price	£56. Single occ. by arrangement.
meals	Breakfast 7.30-9.30am. Pub 1.5 miles.
closed	Very occasionally.
directions	A39 to Wadebridge. At r'bout follow signs to Polzeath, then to Porteath Bee Centre. Through Bee Centre shop car park, down farm track; signed on right after 150 yds.

Graham & Sarah Tyson
The Old Vicarage,
St Minver, Nr. Rock,
Cornwall PL27 6QH

tel	01208 862951
fax	01208 863578
e-mail	g.tyson@virgin.net

Jo Bloor
Porteath Barn,
St Minver, Wadebridge,
Cornwall PL27 6RA

tel	01208 863605
fax	01208 863954
e-mail	mbloor@ukonline.co.uk

CORNWALL

CORNWALL

John Betjeman and A.L. Rowse, the historian, both loved 15th-century Bokelly and often wrote about it. The Elizabethan tithe barn, your hosts and the garden are absolutely marvellous, too, and a tennis court and a croquet lawn add to the magic. The house is relaxed and beautiful – unselfconsciously so. There's an exhilarating mix of the exotic (a papier-mâché ship used in a film that Lawrence directed) and the familiar (squishy sofas and traditional carpets). You have your own drawing room with open fire; the Eden Project, coastal paths and surfing beaches are nearby. Special indeed.

Cornish slate and stone, a real candelabra over the generously big breakfast table, pretty rugs, an old leather Chesterfield, bold art, dark wood chests, open fires and a lovely family dog ready to do his bit to help you settle. The lines of the farmhouse are elegant Georgian, the atmosphere relaxed. There's a huge billiard room with polished slate floor or a garden for those who like to pass their leisure time less competitively. White cotton on an antique brass bed, handmade patchwork quilt and views of horses in a paddock. Daphne and Philip have superb taste. Rock and Polzeath are nearby.

rooms	3: 1 double with bathroom; 1 double, 1 twin, both with private bathroom.
room price	From £60. Single occ. by arrangement.
meals	Pub 1 mile.
closed	Occasionally.
directions	On A39, 7 miles south of Camelford at St Kew Highway, right through village on Trelill Rd. (Do not go to St Kew.) 1 mile on, pass white cottage on right, left over cattle grid past white bungalow, house 0.25 miles down drive.

rooms	1 double with private bathroom.
room price	£60. Single occ. £35.
meals	Wonderful pub 0.25 miles.
closed	Christmas & New Year.
directions	From Camelford, follow A39 to Wadebridge. After 10-15 mins, at brow of hill, right, past Esso garage, then immed. left at pub for 0.75 miles. Post, rails & fir trees on left; bear left into house.

	Maggie & Lawrence Gordon Clark Bokelly, St Kew, Bodmin, Cornwall PL30 3DY
tel	01208 850325
e-mail	bokelly@gordonclark.freeserve.co.uk

	Daphne Gough Tregoid Manor Farm, Trequite, St Kew, Bodmin, Cornwall PL30 3EU
tel	01208 841580
e-mail	philip-gough@uknetworks.co.uk

CORNWALL

A granite stair leads to a suite of rooms in the old part of the 14th-century farmhouse: all yours. Sweet cottagey bedrooms with Victorian beds, old pine, beautiful quilts (Heather is an enthusiastic quilter), good white linen; a dining room and a sitting room too, with open fireplace and bread oven. There is also a flowery loggia for summer breakfasts. Your hosts are great spoilers yet unobtrusive, and their adorable black Labradors will be sure to give you a special welcome. Peace and privacy between moor and sea, and only 30 minutes from the Eden Project. *Children by arrangement.*

rooms	2: 1 double with private bathroom; 1 double available to same party, willing to share bathroom.
room price	From £50. Single occ. £30.
meals	Packed lunch from £5. Supper from £12.50. Dinner from £17.50.
closed	Occasionally.
directions	A30 towards Bodmin. 6 miles after Jamaica Inn, right for Blisland/St Breward. Follow signs for St Mabyn, left over bridge. House 2.5 miles on, on right, on bend with trees, before B3266.

Heather & George Hurley
Penwine Farmhouse,
St Mabyn, Nr. Bodmin,
Cornwall PL30 3DB
tel 01208 841783
fax 01208 841783

map: 1 entry: 59

CORNWALL

From January to October you can only come if you have a child under five! This is an unpretentious, jolly haven for families. Your children can collect eggs, climb in the garden, visit the animals or miniature farmyard, watch a video. Nursery teas begin at 5pm (you can have a cream tea in the garden) and Lucy will babysit while you slink off to the local pub – the highest in Cornwall. One bedroom is modern with new pine, the other two more traditional. Celtic crosses in the garden and original panelling hint at the house's 500-year history.

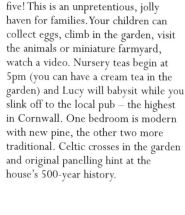

rooms	3 family, all with bath/shower.
room price	From £55. Single occ. by arrangement.
meals	Packed lunch £5. Nursery tea £3.50. Supper £10.50. Dinner £14.50.
closed	Christmas.
directions	From Launceston, A395, then A39 through Camelford. Left onto B3266 to Bodmin. 4 miles on, left (for Wenfordbridge Pottery). Over bridge, past pottery & on brow of hill, left into a lane. House at top.

Lucy Finnemore
Higher Lank Farm,
St Breward, Bodmin,
Cornwall PL30 4NB
tel 01208 850716

map: 1 entry: 60

Rosina modestly refers to her home as offering "simple comfort", but it has so much more. Views of, and walks to, the tidal Camel Estuary, a spot in the garden for sunny summer breakfasts, space to unload sporting gear and gumboots, a sitting room snug with fire in winter: uncomplicated cottage charm. It's 1750s, uncluttered and unfussy, too, with 30 acres of woodland and 40 of grassland. Rosina is a dear and will make sure guests of all ages enjoy their stay. The Camel cycle trail is nearby and you can hire bikes in Padstow or Wadebridge – perfect for a car-free family outing.

One of the most exquisite houses and the setting is magical, too. There are 30 acres with ancient woods, an unrestored water garden, three Celtic crosses and a holy well. In her part-15th-century house Catherine – the loveliest of ladies – has matched fabrics, antique pieces, colours and bed linen with enormous care and flair. One of the bedrooms was part of the old chapel and has ancient stone lintels; all are sunny and have proper bathrooms with lovely old baths. The guest sitting room has a piano, books, beautiful art and fresh flowers. And there's a heated outdoor pool. *Children over 10 welcome.*

rooms	2: 1 double with private bathroom; 1 double sharing bathroom, only let to members of same party.
room price	From £50. Single occ. £25.
meals	Excellent pubs/restaurants 0.5-6 miles.
closed	Very occasionally.
directions	Bypass Wadebridge on A39 for Redruth. Over bridge, pass Esso garage on left; then immed. right to Edmonton. Pass modern houses; then immed. right to Roskear over cattle grid.

rooms	3: 1 twin with bathroom; 2 doubles, both with private bathroom.
room price	£70-£80. Single occ. £35-£40.
meals	Dinner £25. Pub 0.25 miles.
closed	Occasionally.
directions	From A30, turn for Blisland. There, past church on left & pub on right. Take lane at bottom left of village green. 0.25 miles on, drive on left (granite pillars & cattle grid).

Mrs Rosina Messer-Bennetts
Roskear,
St Brock, Wadebridge,
Cornwall PL27 7HU
tel   01208 812805
e-mail   rosinamesserbennetts@ukonline.co.uk

Christopher & Catherine Hartley
Lavethan,
Blisland, Bodmin,
Cornwall PL30 4QG
tel   01208 850487
fax   01208 851387
e-mail   chrishartley@btconnect.com
web   www.lavethan.com

map: 1 entry: 61

map: 1 entry: 62

CORNWALL

M any people never attain their
dream but Charlie, Fee and their
four boys sold up, escaped the rat race
and designed and built a large family
home in a peaceful, rural part of
Cornwall. A 100-year-old millpond
with resident ducks separates the house
from a large, organic fruit, vegetable
and cutting garden, which supplies the
freshest produce to Fee (a creative cook
who once ran her own catering business
in London). The house is flooded with
natural light and full of pleasing colour.
There's a large sitting room with open
fire and a super, comfortable bedroom.

rooms	1 twin with bath.
room price	£50. Single occ. £30.
meals	Dinner £10-£20.
closed	Christmas & New Year.
directions	At end of Bodmin bypass; Innis Downs r'bout A30 exit; immed. 1st right to Lakeview. Straight over x-roads, left 2nd x-roads to Ruthern Bridge; 1st right; 1st left to Withiel. House on left, signed.

Fiona Turner
Trebois,
Withielgoose Mills, Bodmin,
Cornwall PL30 5NN
tel   01208 832901
fax   01208 75699
e-mail fee@trebois.plus.com

map: 1 entry: 63

CORNWALL

M icky and Gelda farm 450 acres at
the head of the beautiful Ruthern
Valley. There are stunning views, grassy
fields, grazing cattle and horses; recline
in the garden hammock, take in the
views, drink in the peace. Gelda has
decorated the house with flair and
there's a generous feel to everything:
swathes of designer fabrics hang in
thick folds at the windows, bathroom
towels are large and soft, sofas are
satisfyingly squishy. Gelda also makes
special efforts to source local produce
and her meals have been much praised;
take breakfast in the garden in summer.
Children by arrangement.

rooms	2 doubles, both with private bathroom.
room price	£70-£80. Special rates available. Single occ. £35-£40.
meals	Dinner £20-£25.
closed	Very occasionally.
directions	From M5, A30 to r'bout south of Bodmin. On A30 for Redruth. 2.2 miles on, right to Withiel. Through Withiel, down hill, over bridge, left at T-junc., for Wadebridge. Drive on right, 0.5 miles on.

Gelda Madden
Higher Tregawne,
Withiel, Bodmin,
Cornwall PL30 5NS
tel   01208 831257
fax   01208 831257
e-mail highertregawne@btinternet.com

map: 1 entry: 64

CORNWALL

There's a treasure round every corner of this fine old manor on the edge of Bodmin Moor. Rich, exotic rugs, cushions and artefacts from around the world, and Louella's sumptuous hand-stencilled fabrics and furniture. Huge beds, coir on the floors and garden flowers in your rooms, and a guest sitting room crammed floor to ceiling with books, many of them Robin's (he's a writer and explorer). A conservatory for breakfast/dinner overlooks elegant lawns, garden, tennis court... and heavenly views. There's even an opera house in a converted barn. Everyone waxes lyrical and you will, too.

Down a wild-flowered drive in a hidden fold, inland from the Fowey river, this is a treasure house, a charming synthesis of style, stone, wood and colour. A Shaker simplicity is sprinkled with pretty touches such as flowers, candles and printed fabrics. There's a settle by the Rayburn and espressos can be brought to you in the garden where goats, chickens and ducks potter happily. Helen is an aromatherapist and reflexologist (do book a treatment); she and Richard are young, enthusiastic and gentle. Bedrooms, reached up a windy stair, are gorgeous. Organic breakfasts, home-made biscuits, fresh fish dinners – wonderful.

rooms	4: 1 double with bath; 2 doubles, 1 twin, sharing 2 bathrooms.
room price	£70. Single occ. £35.
meals	Packed lunch from £5. Dinner, 3 courses, £18.
closed	Christmas & New Year.
directions	6 miles after Jamaica Inn on A30, left signed Cardinham. Through Millpool & straight on, ignoring all further signs to Cardinham. After 2.5 miles, left to Maidenwell 0.75 miles; house right down drive.

rooms	2: 1 double (with extra bed), 1 twin, both with basins, sharing bathroom.
room price	£50-£60. Single occ. £35 from Easter-November.
meals	Dinner with wine, £20-£30. Packed lunch, cream teas and drinks available.
closed	Occasionally.
directions	From Liskeard on A38. At Dobwalls take left fork, A390 for St Austell. After East Taphouse, left onto B3359 for Looe. After 2 miles, right signed Botelet.

Robin & Louella Hanbury-Tenison
Cabilla Manor,
Nr. Mount, Bodmin,
Cornwall PL30 4DW

tel	01208 821224
fax	01208 821267
e-mail	louella@cabilla.co.uk
web	www.cabilla.co.uk

The Tamblyn Family
Botelet,
Herodsfoot, Liskeard,
Cornwall PL14 4RD

tel	01503 220225
fax	01503 220225
e-mail	stay@botelet.co.uk
web	www.botelet.co.uk

map: 1 entry: 65

map: 1 entry: 66

An intriguing 18th-century farmhouse of great character and with outstanding views over unspoiled countryside and the pretty creek side village of Lerryn. A farm with ewes, lambs, chickens, dogs and even otters. It is a very artistic household: Anne sells huge dried hydrangeas and the house is full of their sons' art. The cheerful bedrooms are on the second floor and there is an elegant drawing room for guests. Iain and Anne give a big welcome and serve generous breakfasts on the largest Cornish slate table. Good walks all around and the Eden Project is just 20 minutes away. *Children and pets by arrangement.*

You are at the head of the old smuggling route and an ancient right of way leads you to Polperro's little harbour. The Macartneys have breathed new life into the 14th-century Grade II*-listed hall house and the ancient charm blends perfectly with added comforts. There are three dressing-gowns in descending order of size and you have your own cosy, timbered A-frame sitting room with woodburner, candles, wild flowers; it's stylish, memorably special, and good value. Food is organic and free-range where possible. This is a favourite among guests.

rooms	2: 1 twin, 1 twin/double, 1 with shower, 1 with private bathroom.
room price	£60. Single occ. by arrangement.
meals	Pub 2 minutes.
closed	Christmas & Easter.
directions	From Plymouth, A38 then A390 west. 1 mile before Lostwithiel, 2nd left after Downend garage to Lerryn. Before bridge, left for Couch's Mill, then 1st left into cul-de-sac, up hill for 0.25 miles.

rooms	2: 1 double, 1 single, with shared use of private bathroom & sitting room.
room price	£50-£64. Single from £25-£32.
meals	Dinner, 4 courses, £21.50. B.Y.O.
closed	Very occasionally.
directions	A387 through Looe after approx. 3 miles, B3359 for Pelynt. Less than a mile on, 2nd of 2 turnings on left. After 0.5 miles, left at T-junc., then fork left, signed.

Anne & Iain Mackie
Collon Barton,
Lerryn, Lostwithiel,
Cornwall PL22 0NX
tel 01208 872908
fax 01208 873812

Michael & Ann Macartney
Penellick,
Pelynt, Nr. Looe,
Cornwall PL13 2LX
tel 01503 272372
fax 01503 272372
e-mail penellick@hotmail.com

map: 1 entry: 67

map: 1 entry: 68

Ann is huge fun and a natural entertainer – you'll settle in quickly. This is a wonderfully comfortable house with touches of luxury and matchless views over Plymouth Sound. It is at the top of a steep hill overlooking a charming seaside village of 600 souls. Ann cooks superb meals with wholefood ingredients and local produce and makes her own muesli, bread, yogurt and ice-cream (and can cater for vegans). Bring your own music… there's a 'boudoir grand' to be played as well as a music centre you can use. There's a superb first-floor drawing room with those sea views.

Button and Clive look after you with care and much attention to detail, and their personal touch makes your stay special. Two hundred years ago the Navy used to test canons in the creek at the bottom of the garden but now you hear only wildlife. The 1744 house has been lovingly tended and there are wonderful views from a high brass bed and an antique four-poster. You are brought scones in a sitting room alive with colour and light, and you eat your morning kippers and free-range eggs from a walnut table that cleverly conceals a snooker table. *Minimum stay two nights.*

rooms	3: 1 double with bathroom; 1 twin/double, 1 twin, both with shower room.
room price	From £44. Single occ. by arrangement.
meals	Dinner £16-£25; light supper £10.
closed	Very occasionally.
directions	B3247 for Mount Edgcumbe. Right, before school, for Kingsand. Down hill to right, left fork on bend into Kingsand, 2nd left, then left again. House on left with yellow door. Avoid single track road.

rooms	3: 1 double with private bathroom; 1 four-poster, 1 twin/double, both with shower room.
room price	£75-£100. Single occ. from £52.50.
meals	Breakfast 9-10.30am. Choice of pubs/restaurants 300 yds-4 miles.
closed	Occasionally.
directions	Please contact hosts for directions.

Ann Heasman
Cliff House,
Devonport Hill, Kingsand,
Cornwall PL10 1NJ
tel   01752 823110
fax   01752 822595
e-mail   chkingsand@aol.com
web   www.cliffhse.abel.co.uk

Clive & Button Poole
The Old Rectory,
St John-in-Cornwall, Nr. Torpoint,
Cornwall PL11 3AW
tel   01752 822275
fax   01752 823322
e-mail   clive@oldrectory-stjohn.co.uk
web   www.oldrectory-stjohn.co.uk

ORGANIC B&B
and Alastair Sawday Publishing

Did you know that a group of very fat junk-food addicts in the USA is attempting to sue McDonalds and others for causing their obesity?

It's not as barmy as it sounds, for McDonalds and others have had, in order to ensure continuing growth, to stuff their clients – millions of them - with fattier and fattier food. It's a grim tale, and a salutary one. We forget, at our peril, that our health and our food are inseparable, as we all know. Or do we?

Most of us remain deeply ignorant about food 'issues' – as I have been for most of my life. The organic 'revolution' is misleading, for about about three-quarters of organic food is bought by about ten percent of the buyers. But it's a start, and the growth is profoundly encouraging. Organic farming (and growing) is the single best solution to our agricultural dilemmas, but it takes humility for government to recognise this when so many billions of pounds have been poured into intensive industrial agriculture and the solving of its attendant crises (Foot and Mouth, BSE etc).

Because so many of our B&Bs are in the countryside we are acutely aware of the need for change. Many owners are working hard to support their communities, buying locally and bringing money into their rural economies. We want to support those efforts, hence our determination to introduce an Organic B&B symbol within the next few years – strange but do-able. The Soil Association is working on it now. When it happens, you will be able to sleep between organically-grown-cotton sheets, wash with organic soaps and eat eggs and bacon from 'happy' chickens and pigs. We think that this is a target worth aiming for... and it will all be part of a campaign to generate jobs in the countryside – good jobs.

This is 'Cornwall's Forgotten Corner' and the countryside is gorgeous. The house sits opposite the church, rooted in time and space; massive walls echo their 400 years of history. Farmhouse charm in the kitchen – blue Aga, Welsh dresser, chequered tablecloth – and sheer elegance in the flagstoned sitting room, Farrow & Ball Library Red walls contrasting with heavy calico curtains, off-white sofas and church candles. Bedrooms have crisp cotton and great comfort. Your hosts are easy and fun and there is a games room, too, with bar billiards and table tennis. Excellent value – and wonderful for children.

All of our inspectors have been bowled over by this house. The approach, surrounded on three sides by tidal estuaries, makes your heart leap. The Grade II-listed manor has its own chapel in which a 14th-century fresco still clings to the walls. Its many rooms are filled with thousands of books, pictures and some slightly worn, but massively stylish, fine furniture. Guy is eccentric, funny and passionate about horses – bring your own, or some may be available to competent riders. Rooms, reached via four staircases, are simple and bright with old rugs and scattered books. *Children over 12 welcome.*

rooms	3: 1 double with extra bed, with shower room; 1 double with bath & shower; 1 twin with private bath/shower.
room price	£50. Single occ. £30.
meals	Pub/restaurant 0.5 miles.
closed	Christmas & Boxing Day.
directions	To Sheviock on A374. House opposite church.

rooms	3: 2 doubles, both with bathroom; 1 twin with private bathroom.
room price	£70. Single occ. £40.
meals	Breakfast until 9.30am. Dinner £20. B.Y.O.
closed	Very occasionally.
directions	From Plymouth A38 & cross Tamar Bridge. Through bypass tunnel over r'bout. On top of next hill left to Trematon; through village to Elmgate. Take road to right of white house with letter box, shoulder hard on left.

Carol & Tony Johnson
Sheviock Barton,
Sheviock, Torpoint,
Cornwall PL11 3EH

tel   01503 230793
fax   01503 230793
e-mail   thebarton@sheviock.freeserve.co.uk

Guy Bentinck
Erth Barton,
Saltash,
Cornwall PL12 4QY

tel   01752 842127
fax   01752 842127

map: 2 entry: 71

map: 2 entry: 72

CORNWALL

L ife and art exist in happy communion – Nicky paints with flair and runs courses in life drawing, printmaking and sculpture. This lovely old Georgian farmhouse has breathtaking views over undulating countryside, streams and wooded valleys; set off across fields to discover the Walkers' leat-side trail and don't forget to make a fuss of Polly, the family's Gloucester Old Spot pig, on the way. Delicious breakfasts (in the walled garden in summer), log fires, a good collection of books and two grand pianos. An inspirational place for all. Cottage with good views, too.

rooms	2 + cottage: 1 double with shower; 1 twin with basin & private bathroom next door. Cottage for 6.
room price	£55-£60. Single occ. by arrangement. Cottage £255-£675 per week.
meals	Good pubs & restaurants nearby.
closed	Very occasionally.
directions	A38 through Saltash & on for 3 miles. At Landrake 2nd right for New Barton. After 1 mile, left at white cottage for Tideford. House 150 yds on, on right.

Nicky Walker
Lantallack Farm,
Landrake, Nr. Saltash,
Cornwall PL12 5AE
tel   01752 851281
fax   01752 851281
e-mail   lantallack@ukgateway.net
web   www.lantallack.co.uk

CORNWALL

A n old corn mill with the original water wheel now in the kitchen and with bedroom views down the garden to the salmon/sea trout river. Richard is a keen fly-fisherman and can fix up rods for visitors. Mariebel is a professional portrait painter who taught for many years; she's still happy to teach individuals or groups. Bicton is informal, comfortable and relaxed. Meals are eaten in the huge farmhouse kitchen or in the impressive slate-floored dining/sitting room. The Lynher Valley is unspoilt and enchanting, with lovely walks all round. *Children by arrangement.*

rooms	2: 1 double with shower room; 1 double with private bathroom & wc.
room price	£50-£60. Single occ. by arrangement.
meals	Pubs/restaurants within 7 miles
closed	Very occasionally.
directions	On A388 Callington-Launceston, left at Kelly Bray (opp. garage) to Maders. 400 yds after Maders, left to Golberdon & left at x-roads. After 400 yds, right down unmarked lane. 0.75 miles to Mill by bridge.

Richard & Mariebel Allerton
Bicton Mill,
Bicton, Nr. Liskeard,
Cornwall PL14 5RF
tel   01579 383577
fax   01579 383577

CORNWALL

CORNWALL

The garden has seats positioned to catch the evening sun: perfect for relaxing after a day exploring the gardens and beaches of Cornwall. The peaceful house is named after the hill and you have utter privacy and a private entrance to your fresh, roomy suite: a twin-bedded room and a large, square, high sitting room with double doors giving onto the wooded valley. There's a CD player, music, chocolates and magazines. Jos, a kitchen designer, and Mary-Anne really want you to enjoy your stay; you will. Local produce and free-range eggs are on offer for breakfast.

A Grade II-listed, slate-hung Georgian farmhouse in 30 acres of pastoral loveliness with its own (ancient) Holy Well – can you resist? Your immensely likeable hostess Gillian is full of enthusiasm for her new home where guest rooms have beautiful antique bedspreads and glorious views. (Bask in the morning sun with your head on your pillow.) The vegetable garden is her passion; the freshest produce ends up on the supper table in the Moroccan-look dining room. And you have your own sitting room. The perfect spot on the way to surf, sand and the Eden Project. *Children over five welcome.*

rooms	2: 1 twin with bath/shower, sitting room, & child single next door if needed.
room price	£70. Single occ. £45.
meals	Dinner, 3 courses, £18. B.Y.O.
closed	Christmas.
directions	From Launceston, B3254 towards Liskeard. Through Daw's House & South Petherwin, down steep hill & last left before little bridge. House 1st on left.

rooms	3: 1 double with shower room; 1 double (wc/basin) & 1 twin, sharing separate bathroom with members of same party.
room price	£46-£50. Single occ. £30.
meals	Dinner £15. B.Y.O wine. Pub 1.5 miles.
closed	Christmas.
directions	Heading west, right off A30 onto A395 for Wadebridge. Through Pipers Pool & 3rd left signed Laneast. Left again, through village. House has wooden gates, on left.

Jos & Mary-Anne Otway-Ruthven
Hornacott,
South Petherwin, Launceston,
Cornwall PL15 7LH
tel 01566 782461
fax 01566 782461
e-mail otwayruthven@btinternet.com

Gillian & Anthony ffrench Blake
Laneast Barton,
Laneast, Launceston,
Cornwall PL15 8PN
tel 01566 880104
fax 01566 880103
e-mail affb@totalise.co.uk

The Domesday-listed property of Duke William's half-brother sits in the most glorious garden with manicured lawns and fine outbuildings – the setting is stunning. Inside, there is sober luxury and Muriel runs the house with irreproachable efficiency. If you stay in to eat, you meet fellow guests for drinks before dining in dinner party style; Muriel plans her menus with elaborate care. There are fine paintings, stone-silled windows onto garden views, carefully decorated rooms. Your hosts pride themselves on running an immaculate, peaceful, totally English home.

Built around a cobbled courtyard and tucked into a sheltered hollow, Trevigue, which pre-dates the Norman Conquest, hunkers down against the gustiness of the North Cornish coast. Inside there's little evidence of the original farming activity: all is spick, span and spotless, yet the stone mullions, flagstones and slate are authentic. Breakfasts, using local produce, are generous and there's a restaurant across the courtyard for dinner. Head for Strangles Cove for absolute seclusion; the beach at Crackington Haven – big at low tide – is wonderful for families. *Children over 12 welcome.*

rooms	3 twin/doubles all with bath/shower.
room price	£60–£70. Single occ. £40.
meals	Breakfast 8.30am. Dinner £20.
closed	Christmas Day.
directions	From Wainhouse Corner on A39, follow sign to Crackington Haven. At beach, turn inland for 1 mile, left into Church Park Rd & 1st right into lane.

rooms	3: 2 doubles, both with shower room; 1 twin with bathroom.
room price	£70. Single occ. £40.
meals	Breakfast until 9.30am. Dinner available in farmhouse restaurant.
closed	Very occasionally.
directions	From Crackington Haven follow coastal road keeping sea on right. Up hill & right for Trevigue. Farm 1.5 miles on left on top of cliffs.

Muriel Knight
Manor Farm,
Crackington Haven, Bude,
Cornwall EX23 0JW
tel   01840 230304

Janet Crocker
Trevigue,
Crackington Haven, Bude,
Cornwall EX23 0LQ
tel   01840 230418
fax   01840 230418
e-mail   trevigue@talk21.com

CORNWALL

The road twists and turns, the driveway falls through the spring-fed wooded valley and, suddenly, the secret is yours. The former vicarage – part 16th-century with Georgian and Edwardian additions – is beautiful and within its intriguing garden you are neighbour only to sea, coastal path and fields; nearby are sandy beaches. Lots of light, sea views, seagrass matting, paintings, comfy sofas, pretty fabrics and the feel of a family home. Perfect. Bedrooms are fresh and peaceful, bathrooms charming. What's more, Jane and Anthony share their house without fuss. *Children over five welcome.*

rooms	4: 1 double, 1 twin, both with private bathroom; 1 further twin let to members of same party; 1 small single for child.
room price	£44-£60. Single occ. £32-£40.
meals	Simple supper or dinner, 3 courses, from £12.
closed	Christmas.
directions	Leave A39 at Wainhouse Corner, south of Bude, for St Gennys Church. 2 miles on, fork right by white cottage towards St Gennys Church. Before church, right into lane/drive.

Anthony & Jane Farquhar
St Gennys House,
St Gennys, Bude,
Cornwall EX23 0NW
tel   01840 230384
fax   01840 230537
e-mail ac.farquhar@talk21.com

map: 1 entry: 79

CUMBRIA

The house echoes the enthusiasm and love poured into it by the Duffs. Built in 1753, it has a classic Georgian façade of mellow Eden sandstone. Many original features remain, including an ornate ceiling in the dining room. Seek out the secret door to the billiard room, draw a chair up to the fire, play tennis, or settle on the terrace for a sundowner. Bedrooms and bathrooms are large and freshly painted with far-reaching views over this AONB; there's a super walled garden, too. Shooting, fishing, golf, sailing or riding can be arranged for you. The Duffs are super people. *Children over eight welcome.*

rooms	3: 2 doubles, 1 with shower room, 1 with bath; 1 twin/double with bath.
room price	£70. Single occ. £40.
meals	Supper tray, £20. Dinner, 3 courses, £25. Pub/restaurant, 0.3 miles.
closed	Christmas & New Year.
directions	From M6 junc. 41, follow A6 to High Hesket, right to Armathwaite & follow signs to Newbiggin. There, left at T-junc. 0.5 miles on, right into Cumrew. House straight ahead.

Roddy & Isabel Duff
Cumrew House,
Cumrew, Heads Nook, Carlisle,
Cumbria CA8 9DD
tel   01768 896115
fax   01768 896117
e-mail rabduff@aol.com
web   www.countrysport-lodge.com

map: 18 entry: 80

You look across rooftops towards the towering mass of Skiddaw, the Lake District's third highest mountain. Here is a cottage garden with sweet peas, herbs, vegetables and flowers... all suitably rambling. Roy and Chris have kept most of the original features and there is wood everywhere. Dried flowers, cast-iron tubs, antique linen and patchwork quilts, a collection of christening gowns – all set against a background of wooden floorboards, high bedroom ceilings and a palpable keenness to make it work. Television is delightfully absent, classical music plays. And the Beatys are so friendly.

Everything's well above average... the large and comfortable beds, the linen, the fabrics, the pillows. You feel cossetted. You'll appreciate the sensitivity of the renovations, too – the plasterwork stops here and there to reveal old beam, slate or stone. Peaceful bedrooms are free from clutter and each is named after the mountain that it faces; Swinside brings the 1650s house its own spring water. The breakfast room has separate tables, woodburner, hunting prints and a grandfather clock. Walkers will fall gratefully into the hot spring spa. *Children over six welcome. Self-catering also available.*

rooms	2: 1 double, 1 twin, both with bathroom.
room price	£47-£50. Single occ. £33.50-£35.
meals	Breakfast 8-9am. Inn 300 yds.
closed	December.
directions	From Keswick A591 to Carlisle (approx. 6.5 miles). Right at Bassenthwaite Chapel into village (0.5 miles). Straight on at village green for 170 yds.

rooms	5: 2 doubles, 3 twins/doubles, all with bath/shower.
room price	£80-£88. Single occ. by arrangement.
meals	Breakfast 8.30-9.30am. Packed lunch £6.50. Dinner £22. Tea rooms next door April-October.
closed	Very occasionally.
directions	From M6 junc. 40 west on A66. Past Keswick & on A66 for Cockermouth. Left at Braithmouth onto B5292, Whinlatter Pass. Through forest to Lorton. Left onto B5289 to farm, 1.5 miles on.

Roy & Chris Beaty
Willow Cottage,
Bassenthwaite, Keswick,
Cumbria CA12 4QP
tel   017687 76440
web   www.willowbarncottage.co.uk

5pm.

Hazel Thompson
New House Farm,
Lorton, Cockermouth,
Cumbria CA13 9UU
tel   01900 85404
fax   01900 85421
e-mail   hazel@newhouse-farm.co.uk
web   www.newhouse-farm.co.uk

CUMBRIA

CUMBRIA

Wordsworth's brother-in-law lived here and the great man visited frequently. The views that he enjoyed, over to Barton Fell, are as glorious as ever. The mood is genuine and uncomplicated country hospitality at its best, with communal dining and no ceremony. Much of the atmosphere comes from Mary herself; she is great fun, down-to-earth and friendly, a real farmer's wife. The home-made biscuits in the rooms are a typical gesture. The bedrooms are simple and unfussy, with bathrobes for you, and with those views. There are 300 acres, 850 sheep and a lovely walled garden... all in the National Park.

We can tell you that it is grand, lavish, breathtaking, yet you will arrive unprepared for the luxury and the scale. There is no stinting on *anything*, be it fabric, colour, food or welcome. It is an 1841 Victorian folly with panelled hall, vast drawing room, grand piano, tumbling curtains and rugs galore on polished floors. There are turreted rooms, soaring fairy-tale castle windows and vaulted ceilings. Wendy and Simon spoil you with a happy, family atmosphere, magnificent feasts, huge pillows, handmade chocolates, sherry and massive tubs. Fancy getting married here? You can.

rooms	2 twins/doubles, (each with extra bed) both with shower room. Further bathroom available.
room price	£46. Single occ. £24.
meals	Breakfast until 8.30am. Pub 1 mile & restaurant 3 miles.
closed	1 December-28 February.
directions	From M6 junc. 40, A66 west. At r'bout left on A592. Follow signs to Dalemain house, through car park into courtyard ignoring 'No car' signs. Right for 0.5 miles & right again, at farm building.

rooms	8: 2 twin/doubles, 3 doubles, 3 four-posters, all with bath/shower.
room price	£80-£120. Single occ. £50-£60.
meals	Breakfast from 9am. Dinner (Fri/Sat only) £25; can do for groups, too.
closed	Christmas.
directions	M6 junc. 38, then A685 through Kirkby Stephen. Just before Brough, right signed South Stainmore; house signed on left after 1 mile.

Mrs Mary Milburn
Park House Farm, Dalemain,
Penrith, Cumbria CA11 0HB

tel	01768 486212
fax	01768 486212
e-mail	mail@parkhousedalemain. freeserve.co.uk
web	www.eden-in-cumbria.co.uk/ parkhouse

Simon & Wendy Bennett
Augill Castle,
Brough, Kirkby Stephen,
Cumbria CA17 4DE

tel	017683 41937
e-mail	augill@aol.com
web	www.augillcastle.co.uk

map: 13 entry: 83

map: 13 entry: 84

A Victorian lakeland house, all set about with gables and chimney stacks and light-filtering bay windows, in three supremely peaceful acres on the edge of Grasmere. Rooms are pristine, big and comfortable, with some new pine furniture, matching floral wallpapers and cushions and brass bedside lamps; from two you can see the lake across the wildflower meadow cultivated by the Kirkbrides. There's a pay phone, and a boot-and-drying room, too. Walk from the house, row round the lake or make a pilgrimage to Wordsworth's cottage, a minute's walk. *Children over 10 welcome.*

An ancient cottage so pretty that many artists have painted it. It is just about perfect with tumbling roses, dry stone walls, slate roof and views that lift the spirit; the conservation village of Troutbeck lies below and the bumpy bridleway approach is all part of the charm. The interior of the 1626 shepherd's cottage is simple and cosy with electric heaters, a fire in the sitting room and windows that give on to views up and down the hill. Revel in privacy: you'll not be disturbed. If you don't fancy tumbling out of bed too early, Anne will slip in quietly and leave a continental breakfast tray downstairs for you.

rooms	3: 2 doubles, 1 with bath, 1 with shower; 1 four-poster with bath/shower. Self-catering cottage also available. Ask for price.
room price	£65-£75. Single occ. £47.50.
meals	Breakfast until 8.45am.
closed	November-February.
directions	Enter Grasmere from A591, turn opposite St Oswald's church. After 100 yds, right into Langdale Road. House on left.

rooms	2: 1 double with shower room; 1 twin with private shower room.
room price	£60. Single occ. £30.
meals	Good pub 0.5 miles.
closed	Christmas & New Year.
directions	Turn left when facing Post Office in Troutbeck up Robin Lane. 1st cottage on right, 100 yards from Post Office.

Lyn & John Kirkbride
Ryelands,
Grasmere, Cumbria LA22 9SU

tel	015394 35076
fax	015394 35076
e-mail	kirkbride.ryelands@virgin.net
web	www.ryelandsgrasmere.co.uk

Stephen & Anne Kelly
Dorothy's Cottage,
Robin Lane, Troutbeck,
Cumbria LA23 1PF

tel	01539 432780
e-mail	skelly99@hotmail.com
web	www.robinlane.co.uk

CUMBRIA

CUMBRIA

Philip and Alison's welcoming smiles and great love of Low Jock make this house very special. You're immediately wrapped in the Midwinters' enthusiasm, just as Low Jock Scar itself is folded into the valley; the scar in the name refers to the wall of rock on the far side of the stream. This is a spotless country guest house, and from the conservatory you are lured out to ramble in the flourishing gardens, the pride of your hosts. Listen out for the burbling beck and rest on its banks in the evening to recover from the five-course feast at dinner.

You won't find another B&B like this in the Lakes. Splashes of colour – Barbie pink, lime, lemon, peppermint – give a fresh, exciting feel to the house. Blinds, no frills, modern art, black and white checked hallway and the odd Conran piece set it apart from other B&Bs on Windermere's busy 'Golden Mile'. The dining room in the conservatory is café-style, but fun, and there are lots of places nearby for dinner. The lovely terraced garden at the rear leads to a stream and, beyond that, woodland protected from development. Pat is super and works hard to make you feel welcome.

rooms	5: 1 twin, 2 doubles, 2 with bath, 1 with shower; 1 twin, 1 double, sharing bathroom.
room price	£49-£60. Single occ. from £34.50.
meals	Packed lunch £3.50. Dinner £18.
closed	November-mid-March.
directions	From Kendal, A6 to Penrith. After 5 miles, Plough Inn on left, turn into lane on left after 1 mile.

rooms	5 doubles, all with shower.
room price	£48-£70. Single occ from £34.
meals	Breakfast 8.30-9am. Light evening meals, £10. Many pubs and restaurants very close.
closed	Very occasionally.
directions	A591 to Windermere. Left by Tourist Information & through village. House on right after less than 0.5 miles, opp. modern church.

Alison & Philip Midwinter
Low Jock Scar,
Selside, Kendal,
Cumbria LA8 9LE

tel	01539 823259
fax	01539 823259
e-mail	ljs@avmail.co.uk

Pat Downes
The Coach House,
Lake Road, Windermere,
Cumbria LA23 2EQ

tel	01539 444494
fax	01539 443476
e-mail	info@coachhouse.net1.co.uk
web	www.lakedistrictbandb.com

map: 13 entry: 87

map: 13 entry: 88

Louise and Stephen are bubbly and fun and give a big, generous welcome with not a hint of stuffiness. Bedrooms are sunny and bright with huge comfy beds, fat pillows and super quilted throws, and overlook a wonderful variety of trees – open the windows and let the birdsong in. You'll find it easy to relax by the fire in the winter with a glass of wine, or in the secluded garden in summer. After a splendid breakfast – lots of choice and home-made bread and Aga pancakes too – stroll to lake, fells or village, just five minutes away. *Children by arrangement.*

The Grahams are passionate about conservation, their house and the rich wildlife which populates the 14 acres of private woodland and grounds. The Edwardian Arts & Crafts-style house has been built with great attention to detail: beautifully made oak doors with wooden latches, motifs moulded into plasterwork, local stone fireplaces, green Lakeland slate roof and great round chimneys. Bedrooms, reached via a spiral staircase, are simple and, like the panelled sitting room, allow the architecture to breathe. Distant views of mountains and lakes are stupendous. *Babies & children over six welcome.*

rooms	3: 1 twin/double with shower; 1 family suite (1 double, 1 twin) with bath.
room price	£56–£72. Single occ. from £38. Half price for children.
meals	Breakfast 8.30–9.30am. Pubs/restaurants 5 minutes' walk.
closed	Christmas & New Year.
directions	From Kendal, A591 to Windermere & follow signs to Bowness. There, bear left at bottom of hill & 1st left opp. church. Past garage on left. House 50 yds on, on right.

rooms	3: 1 double with shower room; 1 twin with bathroom; 1 further double for members of same party.
room price	£55. Single occ. £37.50.
meals	Excellent pubs/restaurants locally.
closed	Christmas & New Year.
directions	From M6, junc. 36, A590/A591 to r'bout, then B5284 for Hawkshead (via ferry) for 6 miles. After golf club, right for Heathwaite. Bear right up hill past nursery. Next drive on right – central part.

Louise & Stephen Broughton
Low Fell,
Ferney Green,
Bowness-on-Windermere,
Windermere, Cumbria LA23 3ES
tel   015394 45612
fax   015394 48411
e-mail   lowfell@talk21.com
web   www.low-fell.co.uk

Rhoda M. Graham
Gillthwaite Rigg,
Heathwaite Manor,
Lickbarrow Road, Windermere,
Cumbria LA23 2NQ
tel   015394 46212
fax   015394 46212
e-mail   tony_rhodagraham@hotmail.com

CUMBRIA

A flagstoned hall with panelling, eager dogs to greet you; there's a real heart to this Lakes B&B and Jean, kind and capable, is the icing on the cake. You are just inside the Lake District National Park and the whole place is swimming in views – Brigsteer, the exceptionally pretty village, is a stroll away and the food at its village pub is legendary. Jean puts an arrangement of cottage garden flowers on each breakfast table and the meal itself is a typically generous affair. Bedrooms and the dining room have co-ordinated striped and floral pelmets, drapes and bedspreads, and are restoratively peaceful.

rooms	3: 2 doubles, 1 twin, all with shower room.
room price	£50-£60. Single occ. £30.
meals	Breakfast until 9am. Good pub 0.5 miles.
closed	November-March.
directions	From Windemere, A5074 from Bowness-on-Windemere (signed Lancaster) & left to Brigsteer about 1 mile past Lyth Valley Hotel.

	Jean Macbeth
	Low Plain Farmhouse,
	Brigsteer, Nr. Kendal,
	Cumbria LA8 8AX
tel	015395 68464
fax	015395 68916
e-mail	farmhouse@lowplain.co.uk
web	www.farmhouse

map: 13 entry: 91

DERBYSHIRE

Explore the new 'jungle garden' or the two acres of herbaceous beds, kitchen garden, lovely terraces of stone walls, hidden patios, sculptures and streams. This is garden heaven. Hens, ponies and doves animate the charming old stable yard and, inside the 1783 house, Margaret has created more magic. Her fine eye for detail has brought together perfect colours, fabrics and pieces of furniture to create a house that is inviting throughout. Breakfast is served in the old schoolroom – organic eggs, honey, home-made jams and, of course, garden fruit. Glorious setting… and place. *Children over five welcome.*

rooms	3: 1 double with bath/shower; 1 family, 1 twin sharing bathroom & separate wc.
room price	£46-£55. Single occ. from £30.
meals	Breakfast 8-9am. Pub 1 mile.
closed	23 December-4 January.
directions	M1, junc. 29, A617 to Chesterfield, then B6051 to Millthorpe. Horsleygate Lane 1 mile on, on right.

	Margaret Ford
	Horsleygate Hall,
	Horsleygate Lane, Holmesfield,
	Derbyshire SI8 7WD
tel	0114 289 0333
fax	0114 289 0333

map: 14 entry: 92

DERBYSHIRE

DERBYSHIRE

People come from far for the magic of this beautifully restored farmhouse; such are the bedroom views of moor, valley and heather that guests rarely close the curtains. It is deeply cared for, from the flagstoned hall with ticking grandfather clock to the pretty drawing room with yellow walls and stunning chintz at the windows. Flowers everywhere, oak furniture, fine rugs and ancestral bits and pieces, Chippendale chairs and a Louis XV rosewood bed. The terraced garden is a fine place for star-gazing. Drink – even bathe in – pure spring water; it is delicious. Mary is a delight and the house emanates a nourishing peace.

Views in all directions and farmhouse life at its luxurious best in the heady surroundings of the Peak District. Water from the spring, breakfasts with eggs and fruit from the farm, local sausages, oat cakes and home-made preserves. The farmhouse was built by the family in 1880 and has been deftly and smartly decorated – all rooms are closely carpeted and well lit and have elaborate window treatments. Bedrooms are pristine yet homely and one takes in views of the Peaks. Pam, South African, capable and welcoming, serves home-made cake and tea on arrival.

rooms	2: 1 double, 1 four-poster, both with shower.
room price	From £60. Single occ. from £45.
meals	Breakfast until 9am. Good pubs/restaurants nearby.
closed	Christmas.
directions	From Sheffield A625 into Hathersage. Right into School Lane. After 100 yds, left fork up 'Church Bank'. 50 yds on, right fork, then 0.5 miles. Over cattle grid. Signed.

rooms	3: 1 double with shower room; 1 double with bathroom; 1 twin/double with bath/shower.
room price	£50-£70. Single occ. £35.
meals	Plenty of local pubs & restaurants within 3 miles.
closed	December-February.
directions	From A6 follow Chinley signs. At Chinley Lodge Hotel leave B6062, over bridge, left into Stubbins Lane. After 0.25 miles, left fork onto farm road, over cattle grid & almost 0.5 miles into farmyard.

Mary Bailey
Carrhead Farm,
Hathersage, Hope Valley,
Derbyshire S32 1BR
tel 01433 650383
fax 01433 651441

Pamela & Nick Broadhurst
Cote Bank Farm,
Buxworth, High Peak,
Derbyshire SK23 7NP
tel 01663 750566
fax 01663 750566
e-mail cotebank@btinternet.com.
web www.cotebank.co.uk

map: 14 entry: 93

map: 14 entry: 94

DERBYSHIRE

You are on the precipice of a spectacular limestone gorge – on some days, cloud is at window level. This is a former mill owner's house, a magnificent William IV property with truly panoramic views over the River Wye and to the green hills beyond. Don't be surprised if you see Len in the sky – he is famed for his hang-glider landings in the 30 acres of parkland. Inside, bedrooms are simple, but sympathetic renovation is ongoing; the orangery has just been completed. The Hall buzzes with family life – four generations live here and dynamic Bobby is central to it all.

rooms	3: 2 doubles, 1 twin, all with bath or shower.
room price	£65-£95. Single occ. from £55.
meals	Packed lunch & dinner by arrangement.
closed	Christmas & New Year.
directions	From Ashford-in-the-Water, B6465 to Monsal Head. Left at Monsal Head Hotel, follow valley to Cressbrook Mill, fork left. Left, at lodge building with white fence & 'Private Drive' sign.

Bobby & Len Hull-Bailey
Cressbrook Hall,
Cressbrook, Nr. Buxton,
Derbyshire SK17 8SY
tel   01298 871289
fax   01298 871845
e-mail stay@cressbrookhall.co.uk
web   www.cressbrookhall.co.uk

map: 14 entry: 95

DERBYSHIRE

Elisabeth, immensely kind, is an avid gardener and bird lover and has designed her garden to encourage wildlife; it works. She also bakes bread, buys 'best local' and has generally made this big country house a real pleasure to visit. The double bedroom has walnut furniture, chintz, silk flowers and a superb view; you bathe in a cast-iron bath. The twin shares the fabulous view and its Victorian/Edwardian furniture fits with the period of that part of the house; the rest is 150 years older. Great walking all around and Chatsworth 10 minutes away.

rooms	2: 1 double with private bathroom; 1 twin with private shower room.
room price	£50. Single occ. £40.
meals	Breakfast 8-9am. Pubs and restaurants within walking distance.
closed	Christmas & New Year.
directions	On A6, 1.5 miles from Bakewell, right to Ashford-in-the-Water. Right to Monsal Head & right at Monsal Head Hotel into Little Longstone. Pass Pack Horse pub on left. House almost opposite.

Elisabeth Chadwick
The Hollow,
Little Longstone, Bakewell,
Derbyshire DE45 1NN
tel   01629 640746

map: 14 entry: 96

DERBYSHIRE

DERBYSHIRE

The whole village is listed, and most of it is estate-owned – but Sarah and Ray own the house. Hence the passionate commitment to restoring the best bits to their original splendour, such as flagstoned hall, fireplaces and big old iron bath. There are some beautiful pieces of furniture – an 18-foot dining table and handsome beds – and some striking decorations – Georgian with some earlier Tudor bits. Originally Tudor, it was the Master's House where tenants came to pay their rent. Wonderful countryside, fine walking and a bubbly hostess who buys local produce for your breakfast.

This house hasn't always had such easy-going hosts; in 1821 its owner was involved in the last fatal illegal duel in England. Entering the 16th-century mellow limestone house, one feels the warmth of the beamed sitting room with its Derbyshire stone fireplace and part-flagged floor. The elegant dining room looks out to the walled country garden and you can dine on Marsha's freshly prepared breakfasts, with farm-cured bacon. Large bedrooms look down the conservation village towards the National Trust market hall. Freshly renovated bathrooms have a William Morris theme.

rooms	2 doubles/twins, both with private bathroom.
room price	£54. Single occ. £35.
meals	Packed lunch £3-£5. Good pubs 10 minutes' walk & drive.
closed	Very occasionally.
directions	A6 East of Bakewell; right onto B5006 to Ashbourne. Follow signs to Youlgreave & Alport 1.75 miles. House 1st on right in hamlet.

rooms	3: 1 double with bath/shower; 1 double, 1 twin, both with private bathroom.
room price	£85. Single occ. £60.
meals	Breakfast 7.30-9.30am. Packed lunch £3.75. Pub/restaurant 300 yds.
closed	Christmas & New Year.
directions	3 miles from Matlock on A6 for Bakewell. Left on B5057 signed Winster for 3 miles. House at end of Main Street.

Sarah Copley & Ray Shannon
Rock House,
Alport, Bakewell,
Derbyshire DE45 1LG

tel   01629 636736

John & Marsha Biggin
The Dower House,
Main Street, Winster,
Derbyshire DE4 2DH

tel   01629 650931
fax   01629 650932
e-mail fosterbig@aol.com

You'll be hit by the wow factor. One of the four-poster rooms is *huge*, decadent, lavish – over-the-top, even – but you'll revel in the generosity of it all. Soft white robes, masses of pillows, a chandelier and a vast bathroom with an enticing tub sitting right in the middle. New-laid eggs for breakfast, fresh fruits and home-made breads are the finale to a grand performance. The solid Victorian farmhouse sits in 370 peaceful acres and Kedleston Hall Park with its Robert Adam masterpiece provides a stunning backdrop. The generosity extends to the price, too; this is good value. *Children over eight welcome.*

A beautiful house generously furnished with many fine pieces to admire. There are two sitting rooms with books and antiques, some oriental. The twin has mahogany beds and a Regency chair; the double has rose-patterned, cotton fabrics and a deep cast-iron bath. Sue's competence does not overshadow her sense of humour; she's frank and friendly and guests have written to tell us of their delight at discovering house and owner. The garden is an added treat – rose walkways, a brook and lawns that open onto fields: a tranquil setting for tea. Fruit platter, scrambled eggs and smoked salmon will tempt you from your bed.

rooms	3: 1 double with bath/shower; 1 double with shower room; 1 double with private bathroom.
room price	£65-£80. Single occ. £40-£45.
meals	Good eating places within 20 minutes' drive, closest is 1 mile.
closed	Christmas.
directions	From A52/A38 r'bout west of Derby, A38 north. 1st left for Kedleston Hall. House 1.5 miles past Park on x-roads in Weston Underwood.

rooms	2: 1 twin, 1 double, both with private bathroom. Coach House for 4 people.
room price	£70. Single occ. £45.
meals	Dinner £22.
closed	Christmas & New Year.
directions	From Ashbourne A515 for Lichfield. 3 miles on, right to Snelston. Follow road for 1.25 miles to centre of village. House opp. war memorial. Drive to rear.

Linda & Michael Adams
Park View Farm,
Weston Underwood, Ashbourne,
Derbyshire DE6 4PA

tel 01335 360352
fax 01335 360352
e-mail enquiries@parkviewfarm.co.uk
web www.parkviewfarm.co.uk

Edmund & Sue Jarvis
Oldfield House,
Snelston, Ashbourne,
Derbyshire DE6 2EP

tel 01335 324510
fax 01335 324113
e-mail suejarvis@beeb.net

Lush greenness surrounds the house which is up a tiny country lane with long views over the Dove Valley; there's a fine garden, too. An ancestor of Peter was Lord Mayor of London in 1681, hence the memorabilia; Cynthia is Australian. They are a delightful and genuinely friendly couple. Although elegant, the house is nevertheless a home and guests are treated as friends – no off-limits, although there is a small, book-lined sitting room just for you. The hall sets the tone: white tiles, Indian rugs, woodburning stove and ancestral paintings. The bedrooms are impeccable. *Children over 12 welcome.*

They are the kindest, most gracious hosts. Robert, who has a connection with Beatrix Potter, races vintage cars and Patricia who tends the beautiful garden anticipates your needs. Their splendid Georgian mansion, listed by Pevsner, was 'improved' in 1840 with pillars and again later with a high Victorian conservatory where breakfast, overlooking the beautiful garden, is not to be missed. Shutters, antique furniture and fine country or garden views sit well with the elegant Georgian proportions. The bedrooms are in keeping, with plenty of space, traditional quilts and excellent bathrooms.

rooms	2: 1 double with bathroom; 1 double with private bathroom.
room price	£54–£60. Single occ. £35.
meals	Good pub 2 miles.
closed	Christmas.
directions	From Ashbourne, A515 Lichfield road. After 4 miles, right onto B5033. After 1 mile, 2nd lane on right. 0.5 miles on, on right.

rooms	3: 2 doubles, both with bath/shower; 1 twin with shower room.
room price	£64–£70. Single occ. from £45.
meals	Dinner, 3 courses, £20.
closed	Christmas.
directions	Leave M1 at junc. 23a. At Isley Walton, right to Melbourne. Left in centre of village, then on Ashby road. Right at Melbourne Arms on to Robinsons Hill.

Peter & Cynthia Moore
Rose Cottage,
Snelston, Ashbourne,
Derbyshire DE6 2DL

tel	01335 324230
fax	01335 324651
e-mail	pjmoore@beeb.net

Robert & Patricia Heelis
Shaw House,
Robinsons Hill, Melbourne,
Derbyshire DE73 1DJ

tel	01332 863827
fax	01332 865201
e-mail	robert.heelis@onetel.co.uk

map: 9 entry: 101

map: 9 entry: 102

DERBYSHIRE

A former monastery dating from 1642, this Grade II*-listed rambling family house is set in 18 acres of rolling lakeside gardens and woodland. Rooms are large but cosy, spotless and flower-filled with views over the gardens and surrounding countryside. Bold chintzy fabrics complement the classic English furniture, and bathrooms have Victorian claw-footed baths. Meals are eaten in the linen-fold panelled dining room overlooking the gardens where you may stroll, play croquet or just relax and enjoy the friendly, peaceful atmosphere. Can you resist? Don't even try.

rooms	3: 1 twin with private bathroom; 2 doubles, both with bath.
room price	£56-£64. Single occ. £35-£40.
meals	Packed lunch, from £3-£5. Dinner, from £17.50 or light suppers.
closed	Christmas & New Year.
directions	M42, junc. 11, A444 for Burton-on-Trent for 2 miles, left immediately before Cricketts Inn for Netherseal. Gate is 0.5 miles on right at end of long red brick wall.

Clemency Wilkins
The Old Hall,
Netherseal, Swadlincote,
Ashby de la Zouch,
Derbyshire DE12 8DF
tel   01283 760258
fax   01283 762991
e-mail   clemencywilkins@hotmail.com

map: 9 entry: 103

DEVON

The house is one of the few remaining thatched Devon longhouses in the area and sits at the head of its own valley with wonderful walking and beaches nearby. It is more like a hotel than a private house and you will be pampered. Lots of attention to detail – a fridge for drinks, Molton Brown toiletries in the bathroom, boxed stationery, lavender-scented linens and afternoon tea on arrival. Every window is dressed with swags, tails and tie-backs. Breakfast will be free-range, organic, local and seasonal; bread is baked daily and jam and muesli are home-made. *Children by arrangement.*

rooms	3: 1 twin/double, 1 double, both with shower room; 1 four-poster with bath.
room price	£80-£120. Single occ. £55-£75.
meals	Breakfast 9-11 am. Dinner, £35, minimum 6 people.
closed	Christmas.
directions	In Marlborough, turn opp. Texaco garage into Collaton Rd. Approx. 0.3 miles on, left for Collaton. Keep left at grass island, for Higher Collaton. At end of private lane.

Mark Andrews
The Yeoman's Country House,
Collaton, Salcombe,
Devon TQ7 3DJ
tel   01548 560085
fax   01548 562070
e-mail   yeomanshouse@easicom.com
web   www.yeomanshouse.com

map: 2 entry: 104

DEVON

A cottage and a bakery used to sit side-by-side – 200 years on, the dividing walls have gone. You are less than a mile from the coastal path at Hope Cove (once a smugglers' den) and local materials have been sourced in the renovation – beams from wood from Plymouth docks and panelling in the bedrooms from Dartmouth church. You have breakfast in a small book-filled, geranium-scented conservatory. There are stripped pine doors, a tongue-and-groove panelled bathroom, some lovely oak and pine furniture; bedrooms are cosy and low ceilinged. Paddy and Griselda, who ran a restaurant in Salcombe, are delightful.

rooms	3 doubles, 2 with bath, 1 with shower room.
room price	£46-£50. Single occ. £35-£45.
meals	Pub/restaurant in Hope Cove, 1 mile.
closed	Christmas.
directions	From Kingsbridge on A381, right to Hope Cove. In Galmpton, cottage is 200 yds on left, past village sign.

Paddy & Griselda Daly
Rose Cottage,
Galmpton, Salcombe,
Devon TQ7 3EU
tel 01548 561953
fax 01548 561953
web www.rosecottagesalcombe.co.uk

map: 2 entry: 105

DEVON

The view from Nonsuch is staggering. From the conservatory or the lovely terraced garden you watch the ever-changing scene of boats sailing up and down the estuary. The delights of Kingswear and Dartmouth are linked by a little ferry that will take you and your car across the water in a matter of minutes. But Nonsuch does not rest on its natural laurels; everything about it is captivating. The guests' sitting room has its own balcony, there are great fresh breakfasts, large, extremely comfortable bedrooms, top quality bathrooms, views and more views. *Children over 10 welcome.*

rooms	3 twin/doubles, 1 with bathroom, 1 with private bathroom, 1 with shower.
room price	From £80. Single occ. by arrangement.
meals	Dinner, 3 courses, £21.50, cheese course, £3.50. Not Tuesday or Wednesday.
closed	Very occasionally.
directions	2 miles before Brixham on A3022, take A379. After r'bout, fork left (B3205) downhill, through woods, left up Higher Contour Rd, down Ridley Hill. At hairpin-bend.

Christopher Noble
Nonsuch House,
Church Hill, Kingswear, Dartmouth,
Devon TQ6 0BX
tel 01803 752829
fax 01803 752357
e-mail enquiries@nonsuch-house.co.uk
web www.nonsuch-house.co.uk

map: 2 entry: 106

From a narrow decorative window you see a charming vignette of Devon: a winding country lane edged by fat hedgerows, a hillside dotted with cows. The 18th-century former gamekeeper's cottage is folded into Devon's gentle green softness. Bedrooms are fresh and charming, the drawing and dining rooms formal and immaculate with fine furniture. Tim and Sally – gentle, and new to B&B – serve tea and home-made cake on arrival; they used to run a clematis nursery and the terraced garden is lovely. An excellent pub and the sea are nearby; at night you can see the beam from Start Point lighthouse.

Breakfast, served at a table by the sitting room's French windows, is a hearty affair with own free-range eggs and home-made marmalade and jam. The bright, spotless bedrooms have sofas and super bathrooms, one with a double-sized shower and the other a luxuriously large corner bath. Scented roses and climbers flourish on the local stone walls of this pleasing barn conversion and you cross a primrose-banked stream to an old orchard; Petrina and Kevin, easy-going and friendly, harvest apples for cider which they sell at the local farmer's market.

rooms	3: 1 double, 1 twin/double, both with shower room; 1 double with bathroom.
room price	From £50. Single occ. by arrangement.
meals	Breakfast 8.30-9.30am. Packed lunch £5. Pubs 600-800 yds.
closed	Christmas.
directions	A381 from Totnes to Halwell, then A3122 for Dartmouth. After Dartmouth Golf Club, right at sign to house & Blackawton. 0.3 miles before Blackawton, on right.

rooms	2: 1 double with shower; 1 twin/double with bath.
room price	£52-£64. Single occ. £31-£37.
meals	Excellent pub 2 miles.
closed	Christmas & New Year.
directions	From M5, A38 for Plymouth, A384 for Totnes, A381 for Kingsbridge; through Harbertonford, Halwell & The Mounts. 0.25 miles on, right for Grimpstonleigh. House on left at end of lane.

Tim & Sally Adams
Woodside Cottage,
Blackawton, Nr. Dartmouth,
Devon TQ9 7BL

tel 01803 712375
fax 01803 712761
e-mail info@woodsidedartmouth.co.uk
web www.woodsidedartmouth.co.uk

Petrina & Kevin Frost
Lower Grimpstonleigh,
East Allington, Totnes,
Devon TQ9 7QH

tel 01548 521258
fax 01548 521258
e-mail grimpstonleigh@ukgateway.net
web www.grimpstonleigh.com

map: 2 entry: 107

map: 2 entry: 108

The exterior is newly painted and Jackie is planning more improvements; the interior is as lovely as ever. The Coopers have unleashed their arty, bohemian taste and created a magnificent backdrop of colour for interesting artefacts, huge sofas and wood and slate. They are interesting people, green-leaning farmers who produce their own organic range of soups and sauces. Jackie's breakfasts – platters of fruits and meats *and* the full English – are quite something. Gorgeous bathrooms, large bedrooms and a heated outdoor pool – come for a wonderful, informal time.

Gaze down on the sparkling Dart estuary from the snug warmth of your double bed. A maritime theme plays throughout this 18th-century home with its pebble collections and flotilla of model ships. Fresh, flower-filled bedrooms have tea, coffee and chocolates and your guest sitting/breakfast room is cosy with open fire, comfortable chairs, books, and French windows that open onto the terrace. Gulls call overhead; a ferry takes you to Dartmouth and Totnes. Hugh and Jill are lovely and adore having guests. *Children by arrangement.*

rooms	4: 3 doubles, all with bath/shower; 1 twin with basin & private jacuzzi bath.
room price	£80-£105. Child in same room, £10. Single occ. by arrangement.
meals	Dinner in summer, £18-£25.
closed	Christmas.
directions	A3122 from Totnes for Dartmouth. Left at Forces Tavern, then follow signs to Cornworthy. At Tideford Cross, house opp. with wooden fence. Right, then left into drive over cattle grid.

rooms	2 doubles, 1 with bath & shower, 1 with private bathroom.
room price	£65-£70. Single occ. £40-£50.
meals	Good pubs a short walk.
closed	Christmas.
directions	Coming downhill into Dittisham, sharp right immed. before Red Lion Inn. Along The Level, up narrow hill & house entrance opp. at junc. of Manor St & Rectory Lane.

Jackie Cooper
Higher Tideford,
Tideford Cross, Cornworthy, Totnes,
Devon TQ9 7HL
tel   01803 712387
fax   01803 712388

Hugh & Jill Treseder
The White House,
Manor Street, Dittisham,
Devon TQ6 0EX
tel   01803 722355
fax   01803 722355

DEVON

DEVON

Your generous host has given you the best room in the house. The bedroom opens onto a large terrace high above the spectacular garden: 11 wondrous acres of rhododendron, magnolia, fuchsia, a lily-strewn pond, lawns and paths that dip and rise through areas of wild flowers. Richard is a gifted gardener and the archetypal gardener's modesty and calm have penetrated the house itself. It is uncluttered, serene and comfortable. There's a sheltered corner for breakfasts and you are welcome to find a spot to read or simply sit and absorb the tranquillity.

William of Orange is said to have held his first parliament here. The ancient, rambling, thatched house has blossomed with the attention to detail that you'd expect from two designers. Wallpapers, napkins, *toile de Jouy* – they're all Carole's own design; fresh whites and plain, painted wood are the perfect backdrop for the many pretty touches. Cooked breakfast, along with home-made marmalade, fruits and yogurt, is served on pretty china. Bedrooms are supremely comfortable, one with a cast-iron fireplace and hand-stencilled paper. The garden, with many enchanting corners, is a joy.

rooms	1 twin with bath.
room price	£56. Single occ. £35.
meals	Excellent pub in village.
closed	Very occasionally.
directions	From Totnes to Kingsbridge (A381) for 1 mile. Left, for Ashprington. Into village then left by pub ('Dead End' sign). 0.25 miles on right.

rooms	3: 1 twin/double, 1 double, both with private bathroom; 1 single sometimes available.
room price	From £55. Single occ. £35.
meals	Pubs/restaurants within 2 miles.
closed	Occasionally.
directions	From Totnes, A385 Paignton rd. 2 miles on, look for South Hams Motors on right. Right. House 1st on right. Just past house to parking area on right.

Richard Pitts
Avenue Cottage,
Ashprington, Totnes,
Devon TQ9 7UT
tel   07719 147475
fax

Carole & Harry Grimley
Parliament House,
Longcombe, Totnes, Devon TQ9 6PR
tel   01803 840288
e-mail   parliamenthouse@openworld.com

map: 2 entry: 111

map: 2 entry: 112

DEVON

DEVON

Walk through the pretty garden, past seats strategically placed to soak up the sun, to your own entrance and private terrace right outside your bedroom door. The bedroom is large, with wooden floors, an extremely comfortable brass bed, pieces of Spanish pottery, and biscuits on the tea tray. It's an immaculate yet homely place, just above the rural town of Modbury and only three miles from the sea. The Ewens are friendly and easy company, and their two spaniels will welcome you, too. Generous breakfasts are served in the oak-beamed dining room. *Children over 10 welcome.*

The woodpecker comes at 8.10 every morning; this is a haven for wildlife. Even the cat enters the mood, keen to join you in your room, and there is a goat to take for a walk. The 1860s house was part of the Flete estate – 5,000 acres which run from the South Hams to the sea – and has big, bright bedrooms with velux windows and cheerful colours. Carol and Peter couldn't be nicer and are clearly happy in their chosen spot. Cream tea if you arrive before 5pm, gin and tonic after. *Children over 10 welcome.*

rooms	1 double with shower room.
room price	£45. Single occ. £30.
meals	Good inn 300 yds.
closed	Christmas.
directions	A379 from Plymouth for Modbury. On reaching Church St at top of hill, before Modbury, fork left at Palm Cross, then 1st right by school into Back St. Cottage 3rd on left, past village hall.

rooms	3: 1 double, 1 twin/double, both with bath & shower; 1 double with private shower.
room price	£55. Single occ. £27.50.
meals	Packed lunch £5. Dinner £15.
closed	Very occasionally.
directions	From Modbury, A379 for Plymouth. After 1.5 miles, left to Orcheton. Right after 50 yds. 3rd on right.

	Maureen Ewen
	Orchard Cottage,
	Palm Cross Green, Modbury,
	Devon PL21 0QZ
tel	01548 830633
fax	01548 831127

	Peter Foster & Carol Farrand
	Goutsford,
	Ermington, Nr. Ivybridge,
	Devon PL21 9NY
tel	01548 831299
fax	01752 601728
e-mail	needhams@exchange.uk.com

DEVON

DEVON

Fascinating! The Tamar is magnetic and there's a ruin of an ivy-clad engine house and mine count house from the days when lead and silver were mined here. The lovely Trish makes bread and will procure beef and lamb, or salmon fresh from the river below. Martha the donkey helps Trish win the battle with nature but prefers to have her front feet in the kitchen. Sail in, through the SSSI and AONB: there are moorings and a jetty, even an RYA skipper to give you lessons; or book in for a writing or poetry course. It's characterful, fun, charming. Local branch line connects with Plymouth.

History oozes from every cranny of this Devonshire manor farmhouse which predates the Domesday Book: granite mullioned windows, slate floors and beamed ceilings are all impressive. Ros gives a big welcome – she loves her ancient smallholding with chickens and carthorse. Guest bedrooms have their own entrance and a lovely feel – pretty fabrics and a sofa in the double, apricot walls and crocheted bedspreads in the twin. This is beautiful walking and riding country, and there's stabling and grazing for your horse. If you're looking for utter peace – and privacy – you'll be smitten.

rooms	2: 1 double with bathroom; 1 twin/double with bathroom & extra single/dressing room.
room price	£50-£55. Single occ. £25-£27.50.
meals	Packed lunch £5. Supper £12.50. Dinner £15.
closed	Very occasionally.
directions	Into Bere Alston on B3257, left for Weir Quay. Over x-roads. Follow Hole's Hole sign, then right for Hooe. Fork left for South Hooe Farm. 300 yds on, turn sharply back to your left & down track.

rooms	2: 1 double with private bathroom; 1 twin with private shower room.
room price	From £46. Single occ. from £25.
meals	Breakfast until 9.30am. Packed lunch £5. Dinner £12.50.
closed	Very occasionally.
directions	From Tavistock B3357 for Princetown. At 1st x-roads, right for Whitchurch Down. Next x-roads 'Warren's Cross', left for Samford Spiney. 2nd right at national speed limit sign, past 1 cottage on left. Next house on left.

Trish Dugmore
South Hooe Mine,
Hole's Hole, Bere Alston, Yelverton,
Devon PL20 7BW
tel 01822 840329
e-mail trish@weir-quay.com

Ros Spedding
Samford Manor,
Samford Spiney, Yelverton,
Tavistock,
Devon PL20 6LH
tel 01822 853442
fax 01822 855691
e-mail manor@sampford-spiney.fsnet.co.uk
web www.sampford-spiney.fsnet.co.uk

map: 2 entry: 115

map: 2 entry: 116

DEVON

A n enchanted guest wrote: "If your life is full of stress, there is no better place to recover". Everything is geared to your comfort: enticing four-poster and half-tester beds in cottagey rooms and deep, free-standing baths. It is Joanna and Graham, though, who give that extra something. A lovely Devon couple, they have worked hard to restore the former gardener's *bothy*; Graham made much of the furniture. The guest sitting room has a slate floor, pine Victorian fireplace and leather sofas. There's a thriving organic vegetable garden, ponds, a stream and Nelson, newly retired from the rigours of the Pony Club.

rooms	3: 1 four-poster, 1 double, both with private bathroom; further single available.
room price	From £50. Single occ. from £25.
meals	Dinner, 3 courses, £15.
closed	Very occasionally.
directions	From Tavistock B3357 to Princetown. 0.25 miles on, after Mount House School, left. Drive past lake to house.

Mr & Mrs G. H. Moule
Mount Tavy Cottage,
Tavistock,
Devon PL19 9JL
tel   01822 614253
web   www.mounttavy.freeserve.co.uk

map: 2 entry: 117

DEVON

Y ou come for the glory of the setting and the unpretentiousness of it all, not for huge luxury or sterile scrupulousness. The 17th-century longhouse has a gorgeous cobbled yard (laid by Judy), a bridge across to the island (shades of Monet) and goats. The family produces its own moorland water, all its fruit and vegetables and they even make cheese. The rooms are in simple country style, the attitude very 'green' – hedge-laying, stone wall-mending – and the conversation fascinating. You can wander through two acres of young woodland, too.

rooms	4: 2 twins, 2 singles, all with basins, sharing bathroom.
room price	£25-£50. Under 2s free, under 5s half price in parents' room.
meals	Dinner occasionally available, £12.50; also good pub.
closed	Christmas.
directions	Leave A38 at 2nd Ashburton turning for Princetown. After 2 miles, fork left to Holne. Pass inn & church. After 240 yds, right; after another 150 yds, left to Michelcombe. Over bridge & left. Farm 200 yds on right.

Judy Henderson
Dodbrooke Farm,
Michelcombe, Holne,
Devon TQ13 7SP
tel   01364 631461
e-mail   judy@dodbrooke.freeserve.co.uk
web   www.dodbrookefarm.com

map: 2 entry: 118

DEVON

The exterior's imposing Victorian, the interior youthful and fresh. You'll find Fiona, a former film producer, and her furniture-making husband (he's a potter, too), children, ducks, dogs and chickens; bucolic charm with convenience thrown in. Coir matting, bold colours, a kitchen/dining room which makes breakfast a friendly affair, turquoise floorboards and a bedroom for wheelchair users. Ashburton is a gateway onto Dartmoor, a charming, unspoilt town (so rare!) with good restaurants, proper butcher's and baker's and book, antique and art shops that are perfect for browsing.

rooms	2: 1 double, 1 twin, both with bathroom.
room price	£44-£50. Single occ. £27-£30.
meals	Excellent pubs/restaurants a short walk away.
closed	Very occasionally.
directions	From Exeter, A38 for Plymouth for approx 12 miles. Exit at Ashburton & follow signs to town centre. Pass fire & police station on right and church on left. House on right opp. war memorial.

Fiona Daly
Roborough House,
85 East Street, Ashburton,
Devon TQ13 7AL

tel	01364 654614
e-mail	roborough@btinternet.com
web	www.roboroughhouse.co.uk

map: 2 entry: 119

DEVON

You quickly feel that this elegant, Devon farmhouse (part 14th century) has always been a happy family home. Sarah is capable and jolly and she and husband Michael clearly enjoy guests. The two bedrooms are large – the linen has that lovely, fresh, garden-dried smell – and each has a tray with pretty china, two types of tea, coffee and local spring water. By the bed you'll find a selection of bedtime reading but sleep comes too easily for you to get through much of it. There are hens that give breakfast eggs, a pond and orchard, and excellent food in the pub just up the road.

rooms	2: 1 double with bath/shower; 1 twin with private bathroom.
room price	£48-£52. Single occ. £24-£26.
meals	Packed lunch £3-£4. Dinner £12-£15.
closed	Christmas.
directions	From Newton Abbot, A381 for Totnes. After approx. 2.5 miles, right for Broadhempston. Past village sign, down hill & 2nd left. Pass pub on right & left 170 yds on into courtyard.

Sarah Clapp
Manor Farm,
Broadhempston, Nr. Totnes,
Devon TQ9 6BD

tel	01803 813260
fax	01803 813260
e-mail	clappfamily@members.shines.net

map: 2 entry: 120

DEVON

A rchitect Clough Williams-Ellis (of Portmeirion fame) did more than design an elegant house, he made sure it communed with nature. Light pours in from every window and the most lovely views of the enchanting woodland garden and Devon farmland lift the spirits. The proportions and spaces work and the deep comfort gilds the lily. At every turn, antiques and heirlooms, elegant furniture and welcoming sofas. The Gregsons take huge pride in having created an idyllic retreat and love guests to enjoy the house and the garden; they are charming, excellent hosts. You are welcome to play tennis on the all-weather court.

rooms	3: 1 twin/double with private bath; 1 double with private shower; 1 double/family with private shower.
room price	From £60. Single occ. from £36.
meals	Dinner occasionally available. Good pub 1 mile, excellent one 5 miles.
closed	Very occasionally.
directions	A38 west to Plymouth, A382 turn off, & 3rd turning off r'bout, signed Bickington. There, right at junc. (to Plymouth), right again (to Sigford & Widecombe). Over top of A38. 1st entrance on right.

Madeleine & Michael Gregson
Penpark,
Bickington, Newton Abbot,
Devon TQ12 6LH
tel 01626 821314
fax 01626 821101
e-mail gregson.penpark@ukgateway.net
web www.penpark.co.uk

map: 2 entry: 121

DEVON

T he seductive charm of this hideaway miner's cottage will soothe even the most stressed souls. At the end of a long track you find a lush oasis carved out of woodland. Mary, gently-spoken, loves to see guests unwind; both she and Dick have a finely-judged sense of humour. There's a pretty American patchwork quilt on the brass double bed and a small bathroom off it (this also leads to a twin room). The sound of the river and birdsong fill each room. Local sausages and bacon for breakfast, excellent dinners, a pool and 12 acres to explore; they even have their own water supply. You'll want to return.

rooms	2: 1 double, 1 twin, both with bath/shower.
room price	From £46. Single occ. £23.
meals	Supper £12.50. B.Y.O.
closed	Very occasionally.
directions	From A38, A382 at Drumbridges for Newton Abbot. 4th left at r'bout for Bickington. There, down hill & past garage on left. Right for Haytor. Under bridge, 1st left & down long, bumpy track, past thatched cottage to house.

Mrs Mary Lloyd-Williams
Hooks Cottage,
Bickington, Nr. Ashburton,
Devon TQ12 6JS
tel 01626 821312
e-mail hookscottage@yahoo.com

map: 2 entry: 122

Come to be engrossed in the routines of a wild, engagingly chaotic haven. Ann and William are friendly, kind and extrovert; guests adore them and keep coming back. There is comfort, too: warm curtains, a four-poster with lacy drapes, early morning tea. Gentle giant shire horses live at the shippon end where the cows once stood, and there's medieval magic with Bronze Age foundations. A wonderful place for those who love the rhythm of real country life – and the Two Moors Way footpath is on the doorstep. *Children over 10 by arrangement.*

Restoring Bagtor House has been a labour of love; the family feel a deep attachment to their "friendly, happy" house. The kitchen and the breakfast room, with inglenook fireplace and oak panelling, are tangibly ancient: 14th century. Among this ancient beauty – where John Ford, dramatist, was born in 1586 – there is no stinting on modern comforts; bedrooms, beds and bathrooms are big. You breakfast on home-laid eggs and in this leafy, lush spot in the Dartmoor National Park, you can watch fat sheep graze, wander in the garden or walk to Bagtor, just behind the house.

rooms	2: 1 four-poster, 1 twin, sharing bathroom.
room price	£40-£50. Single occ. £20-£25.
meals	Pubs 2 miles.
closed	Occasionally.
directions	From A38 2nd Ashburton turn for Dartmeet & Princetown. In Poundsgate pass pub on left; 3rd signed turning right for Corndon. Straight over x-roads, 0.5 miles further, farm on left.

rooms	2 doubles (1 with extra single), both with private bathroom.
room price	From £50. Single occ. by arrangement.
meals	Excellent restaurant & real-ale pub 0.5 miles.
closed	Christmas.
directions	From Bovey Tracy, B3387 for Widecombe-in-the-Moor. After 2.5 miles, left for Ilsington. After 0.75 miles, fork right to Bickington. Next right to Bagtor. House on right 0.75 miles on.

Ann & William Williams
Corndonford Farm,
Poundsgate, Newton Abbot,
Devon TQ13 7PP
tel 01364 631595

Nigel & Sue Sawrey-Cookson
Bagtor House,
Ilsington, Dartmoor,
Devon TQ13 9RT
tel 01364 661538
fax 01364 661538
e-mail sawreysue@hotmail.com

map: 2 entry: 123

map: 2 entry: 124

There is a peacefulness about the Dagnalls and Easdon Cottage that immediately strikes you. Come to unwind in the enchanting, beautifully proportioned cottage or, if you want total privacy, book into the warm, peaceful barn (also available for self-catering) which shares the same moor views as the house. Throughout there's a successful mix of pictures, oriental rugs, books, plants, granite walls and some handsome Victorian finds. Liza and Hugh are vegetarian and dedicated users of organic produce, some of which is home-grown. Immediate access to Easdon Down. *Children and pets by arrangement.*

Walks from the house (a 17th-century ex-wool-mill) are reason enough to come here – the owners and the atmosphere are an added bonus. On the edge of one of Dartmoor's prettiest villages, the mill's lawned gardens run down to the Bovey river. There are sparkling wooden floors, walking sticks for hikers, whitewashed walls, wood carvings, stone fireplaces and candles in the dining room. The bedrooms have superb views over woodland and the river, and your delightful, and delightfully modest, hosts provide superb organic and local produce. Peter spins wool, makes honey, plays the sitar.

rooms	2: 1 twin/double with bath. In barn: 1 double with sofa bed & bunk, with private bathroom.
room price	£48. Single occ. £24. Self-catering £175-£280 p.w.
meals	Supper from £10. Pubs/restaurants from 10 minutes' away.
closed	Very occasionally.
directions	A38 from Exeter; A382 for Bovey Tracey. There, left at 2nd r'bout for Manaton. 2 miles beyond Manaton, right at x-roads for M'hampstead. 0.5 miles on, right, signed Easdon. On left up track.

rooms	5: 3 doubles with bath; 1 double with shower; 1 single with private bathroom.
room price	£60-£72. Single occ. £47.
meals	Breakfast 8.30-9am. Dinner £24, not Sun or Mon. Good pub in village.
closed	January & February.
directions	From M5, A30 to Okehampton. Look for Marsh Barton sign onto B3212 to Moretonhampstead. There, take Princetown road, left at newsagent for North Bovey.

	Liza & Hugh Dagnall
	Easdon Cottage,
	Long Lane, Manaton,
	Devon TQ13 9XB
tel	01647 221389
fax	01647 221389
e-mail	easdondown@btopenworld.com

	Peter Hunt & Hazel Phillips
	Black Aller,
	North Bovey, Moretonhampstead,
	Devon TQ13 8QY
tel	01647 440322
fax	01647 441131
e-mail	peter@blackaller.fsbusiness.co.uk
web	www.blackaller.co.uk

map: 2 entry: 125

map: 2 entry: 126

Winding, high-hedged Devon lanes lead to Great Sloncombe – a working Dartmoor farm with milking cows and a pedigree Aberdeen Angus herd. There are few traces of its 13th-century origins – the house is listed – but there are pieces of old oak and granite everywhere, to which the Merchants have added their own antiques and old photographs. Doorways are tiny, bedrooms are country-style cosy – one has a pine four-poster – and all have views to meadows teeming with wildlife. Trudie, who is very involved with carriage driving, cooks dinners of home-grown meat and vegetables.

Such care is taken with everything that you can't fail to feel spoiled; John and Sheila are consummate hosts and clearly love their 15th-century hall house in this delightful conservation village. Dinners here are a real treat, too – maybe free-range chicken breasts cooked in sherry and served on a bed of celeriac with home-grown veg – and you dine by candlelight off crisp white table linen. You have your own sitting room with a vast, granite fireplace and bedrooms are traditional with floral fabrics. A pool in the large, secluded gardens overlooks woodland and moors.

rooms	3: 1 double, 1 twin, 1 four-poster, all with shower room.	rooms	3: 2 twins/doubles, 1 with bath/shower, 1 with shower; 1 double with private bath/shower.
room price	£46-£50. Single occ. by arrangement.	room price	£60. Single occ. £36.
meals	Dinner £14.	meals	Breakfast 7.30-8.45am. Packed lunch available. Dinner, 4/5 courses, £18. B.Y.O wine.
closed	Very occasionally.	closed	Very occasionally.
directions	From Bovey Tracey A382. After Moretonhampstead, look for signs to farm.	directions	From Moretonhampstead via Pound Street to North Bovey (1.5 miles). House is 25 yds off North Bovey's village green, down Lower Hill past village inn on left.

	Trudie Merchant		**John & Sheila Williams**
	Great Sloncombe Farm, Moretonhampstead, Devon TQ13 8QF		The Gate House, North Bovey, Devon TQ13 8RB
tel	01647 440595	tel	01647 440479
fax	01647 440595	fax	01647 440479
e-mail	hmerchant@sloncombe. freeserve.co.uk	e-mail	gatehouseondartmoor@talk21.com
web	www.greatsloncombefarm.co.uk	web	www.gatehouseondartmoor.co.uk

map: 2 entry: 127

map: 2 entry: 128

Only 900 years old and still humming with life; goats, a pony, cats, guinea-fowl, rabbits and foxes share the rambling gardens. Sally-Anne is artistic, fun, slightly zany and dizzy – it's an adventure to stay here. Expect to be wrapped in perfect peace rather than perfect comfort: huge flagstone fireplaces, wobbly floors, interesting modern art, books, pianos, wellies, muddle and charm. Robustly rustic, the house is a historic gem – the BBC twice filmed here for *Down to Earth*. Duck your head to avoid those beams and keep an open mind. Such peace, and hills and fields of waving wheat as far as the eye can see.

A charming, small terraced cottage full of 16th-century nooks and crannies and beams worth ducking. The setting is exquisite – the garden leads into fields of sheep, the Dartmoor Way goes through the town and the Two Moors Way skirts it. Shelagh, a lovely lady, gives guests their own sitting room with a fire – lit on cool nights; breakfasts, served in the cosy dining room, are fresh and free-range. Up the narrow stairs and into the flowery bedrooms – a small double and a tiny twin. A perfect house and hostess – and a perfect village, with its pubs, fine restaurant and delicatessen for picnickers.

rooms	2: 1 twin, 1 double, sharing bathroom.
room price	£50. Single occ. £30.
meals	Restaurants 0.5 miles' walk.
closed	Christmas & New Year.
directions	A30 to Okehampton. After 10 miles left exit into Cheriton Bishop, 2nd left between 2 cottages. Down & up hill. Road turns sharp left. Down lane; signed.

rooms	2: 1 double with private bathroom; 1 twin with shower room.
room price	£40-£50. Single occ. £22-£27.
meals	Good pub 300 yds & excellent restaurant 400 yds.
closed	Christmas.
directions	In Chagford leave church on left & take 1st right beyond Globe Inn. House 150 yds on right.

Carter-Johnson Family
Higher Eggbeer Farm,
Cheriton Bishop, Nr. Exeter,
Devon EX6 6JQ
tel   01647 24427

Shelagh Weeden
Cyprian's Cot,
47 New Street, Chagford,
Devon TQ13 8BB
tel   01647 432256
e-mail   shelagh-weeden@lineone.net

DEVON

Your warm and expansive hosts, he a photographer, she a painter, have created an enchanting and atmospheric home from a thatched longhouse that once belonged to the author Doris Lessing. You'll love this 14th-century, Grade II-listed house in the heart of Dartmoor National Park; each of the beamy, low-ceilinged bedrooms overlooks a cottage garden resplendent with wild flowers. Woodburning stoves, oriental rugs, warm yellow walls, four-poster beds and, outside, a boules pitch, duck pond and the moor with all its wild treasures.

Lavish, spoiling, decadent – Maureen's professionalism and desire to please means that nothing is left to chance and every detail of your stay is carefully thought out. Bedside truffles, fresh fruit, flowers, Cava and soft robes in smart bedrooms. Bathrooms, too, have all that you need and each room has an open fireplace and a private terrace or conservatory. The garden is idyllic, full of secret corners, with fountains colourfully lit at night and paths and steps to guide you through the beauty; a stream runs by and the pool is heated. Breakfasts are served in the (fountained) sunroom. *Minimum stay two nights.*

rooms	2 four-posters, 1 with shower, 1 with bath.
room price	£70. Single occ. £45.
meals	Breakfast 8.30-9.30am. Excellent pubs/restaurants 0.75 miles.
closed	Christmas & New Year.
directions	Exit A30 for Okehampton & Belstone. Follow signs to Belstone. In centre of village right after red telephone box. After 0.75 miles cross cattle grid. House on left.

rooms	3: 2 doubles, 1 twin/double, all with bath/shower.
room price	£130. Single occ. £89. Special deals available.
meals	Breakfast until 9.30am. 3 miles to nearest pubs/restaurants.
closed	Christmas & New Year.
directions	In Chillaton keep pub & Post Office on your left, up hill for Tavistock. After 300 yds, right (Bridlepath sign). Cottage at end of lane.

John & Maureen Pakenham
Tor Down House,
Belstone, Okehampton,
Devon EX20 1QY
tel 01837 840731
fax 01837 840731
e-mail info@tordownhouse.co.uk
web www.tordownhouse.co.uk

Maureen Rowlatt
Tor Cottage,
Chillaton, Nr. Tavistock,
Devon PL16 0JE
tel 01822 860248
fax 01822 860126
e-mail info@torcottage.co.uk
web www.torcottage.co.uk

map: 2 entry: 131

map: 2 entry: 132

DEVON

S onia and Geoffrey are wonderful, natural hosts; they have lived all over the world and are now palpably happy in their converted mill in this corner of Devon. You can walk, ride or sail on or around the Roadford Reservoir which is close by, or put your artistic inhibitions to one side and set off with Sonia, a keen landscape painter, to capture the natural beauty of your surroundings. You'll be folded in human warmth, offered a glass of wine in their large, homely kitchen and be given plenty of ideas for exploring the area. *Children by arrangement.*

rooms	1 twin with bath/shower & sitting room. Bed in studio also available, with shower room.
room price	£50. Studio, when twin is full, £30.
meals	Light supper £10 (not Sundays). Excellent pubs/restaurants within 2 miles.
closed	Christmas & New Year.
directions	From Launceston-Holsworthy road (A388), east for Ashwater. There, 1 mile north, at Thorney Cross, & take 1st drive to left, then right down driveway.

	Geoffrey & Sonia Archer
	Renson Mill,
	Ashwater, Devon EX21 5ER
tel	01409 211665
fax	01409 211665
e-mail	soniaarcher@globalnet.co.uk

DEVON

S tewart & Jennie gave up working in London to take over the estate that has been in the family for 900 years and look after the house (Georgian with Victorian façade) and 150 acres almost single-handedly. You'll find a real country home with history oozing from every stone, painting, piece of furniture and panelling. The large, newly-decorated guest room has brass bedsteads and a big bathroom. The breakfast room is lined with ancient books; the snooker room has a grand piano and an open fire. Walk the old carriage drive to Black Torrington or fish the river running through the estate.

rooms	1 twin with bathroom.
room price	£52. Single occ. £30.50.
meals	Pub 2 miles.
closed	Christmas & New Year.
directions	From Okehampton, A386 for Hatherleigh. There, left onto B3072 for Holsworthy. After 4 miles, through Highampton, then right to Black Torrington. Left at Post Office. Entrance 750 yds on right.

	Stewart & Jennie
	Coham-MacLaren
	Coham Manor,
	Black Torrington, Beaworthy,
	Devon EX21 5HT
tel	01409 231514
fax	01409 231514
e-mail	enquiries@coham.com
web	www.coham.com

You approach the 16th-century traditional Devon farmhouse across open farmland and within minutes of entering you can feel the love that Ann and Richard have for the old place. They are vastly talented and artistic and have worked in harmony to restore it all. Richard made the dresser and uncovered everything of ancient beauty; he's also created a pond that's now home to a family of mallards and two pairs of geese. Ann has laid brick paths, stencilled, stitched and painted, all with a wonderful eye for colour. All this and free-range home eggs for breakfast in the garden room.

The Bradiford Valley is pretty and lush and runs down to glorious beaches. The deceptively big, creaky, comfortable 17th-century home is wrapped in the most lovely garden that stretches up the hill. Old rugs give a warm passage over slate floors, and chintz and pretty wallpapers add to the rural charm. One bathroom, with a huge bath under a long sloping ceiling, has views of a hilltop crowned with trees, the handsome main bedroom has wiggly walls and wicker furniture and there's a drying room downstairs for walking gear. Very easy, unstuffy people. *Children over 12 welcome.*

rooms	2: 1 double with shower; 1 twin with bath & shower.
room price	£50. Single occ. £30.
meals	Breakfast 8-9am. Dinner, 2 courses, £12.50.
closed	20 December-5 January.
directions	From A39, left into Bideford, round quay, passing old bridge on left. Follow signs to Torrington. 1.5 miles on, right for Buckland Brewer. 2.5 miles on, left, also signed. 0.5 miles on, right over cattle grid and down track.

rooms	3: 2 doubles, 1 twin, all with basins, sharing bathroom & separarate shower room.
room price	£36-£44. Single occ. £20-£25.
meals	Breakfast until 9.30am. Good pubs 400 yds-2 miles.
closed	Christmas & New Year.
directions	From Barnstaple, A361 for Braunton. At 2nd set of lights, right for Bradiford. Next T-junc., sharp left, over bridge, up hill for 50 yds, 2nd lane to right. House 1st on left.

Ann & Richard Dorsett
Beara Farmhouse,
Buckland Brewer, Bideford,
Devon EX39 5EH
tel   01237 451666

Jane & Tony Hare
Bradiford Cottage,
Halls Mill Lane, Bradiford,
Barnstaple,
Devon EX31 4DP
tel   01271 345039
fax   01271 345039
e-mail holidays@humesfarm.co.uk
web   www.humesfarm.co.uk

map: 2 entry: 135

map: 2 entry: 136

Bright, fresh colours, antique furniture and charming decorative touches in this Georgian farmhouse. Fresh fruit and flowers in the bedrooms, and a deeply inviting king-size bed in one. Organically reared meats, fresh fish; organic veg, eggs from their own hens and home-made cakes, too. Delicious. Liz and Tony created the stunning formal garden from a green field: a spring-fed pool, a pleached lime walk, pergola, herbaceous beds and ongoing parterre. A bold straight grassy avenue leads to the ponds, much enlarged in 2002. There's an abundance of wildlife; look – and listen – for the tawny owl.

The Weeks have brought a vibrancy to this 300-year-old longhouse with old pine pieces, real candelabras, pretty fabrics and bright colours, yet the old bones of the place – wood, stone floors and beams – are allowed to breathe. The brass double bed is pure farmhouse charm, with Laura Ashley fabrics and papers. Pillows and cushions are stacked high and there are home-made biscuits and an electric blanket. The sparkling bathroom gives onto blossom trees and the garden. Shelley loves cooking and is such easy company.

rooms	2 doubles, both with bath.
room price	£58. Single occ. £29.
meals	Dinner £20.
closed	Occasionally.
directions	From Tiverton, B3137 west. 3 miles on, B3042 to Eggesford. There, right onto A377. 5 miles on, B3226, right. 1 mile on, right for Kings Nympton. Through village; over crossroads; house drive is 0.75 miles on left.

rooms	1 double with bathroom.
room price	£50. Single occ. by arrangement.
meals	Dinner occasionally available.
closed	Occasionally.
directions	From Eggesford, right off A377, for Chawleigh. At very top, bear right through village. 2-3 miles out othe side of village, at Burridge Moor Cross, left for Cheldon. Less than 0.25 mile, on S-bend, drive straight ahead.

Tony & Liz Williams
Lower Hummacott,
Kings Nympton, Umberleigh,
Devon EX37 9TU
tel   01769 581177
fax   01769 581177

Shelley Weeks
Great Burridge Farm,
Chawleigh, Chulmleigh,
Devon EX18 7HY
tel   01363 83818
e-mail   shelleyweeks@smartone.co.uk

map: 2 entry: 137

map: 2 entry: 138

Fun, hugely surprising, very simple and refreshingly different – with brilliant food. Michael has a deserved reputation as an inspired cook and his meals in the kitchen-cum-dining room are great value. The adventure begins as you meander down a lane towards this former 18th-century wheelwright's shop – three miles from a numbered road in any direction; what a reward – bedrooms have polished wooden floors and whitewashed walls, bathrooms are rag-rolled and fluorescent and the stairs painted green. Jellicoe's is fresh, vibrant, Mediterranean. Come for restorative peace... and views.

Lofty ceilings and large windows bring light and space to this traditionalfamily house. The former coaching inn stands at the top of a steep hill (how the horses must have toiled) with exhilarating views of farmland and Exe Valley. Dining and drawing rooms are on a grand scale with some good furniture. One bedroom has a Victorian four-poster; the ground floor double opens onto the gardens. A good place for breaking a journey or for those on business in Tiverton. Barbara is an efficient, kind, no-fuss hostess.
Children over 12 welcome.

rooms	3: 2 doubles, both with shower; 1 twin/family room with bath.
room price	£44. Single occ. £22.
meals	Breakfast 7.30-9.30am. Packed lunch £2.50. Dinner, 3 courses, £12.
closed	Very occasionally.
directions	Leave A396 at Bickleigh, right for Crediton, then immed. right again for Cadeleigh. Through Cadeleigh. Left at 'Post Box Cross', & right for Upham. House 2nd on left.

rooms	3: 1 double with shower room; 1 four-poster with private bath/shower; 1 twin with private bathroom.
room price	From £46. Single occ. £25.
meals	Breakfast 7-9am. Dinner, 4 courses, £15.
closed	Very occasionally.
directions	At junc. 27 (M5), A361 for approx. 4.5 miles. Turn off at Gornway Cross, for Grand Western Canal. At Canal Hill, 1st right into Exeter Hill. House at top on left.

Michael Jellicoe
Jellicoe's, Higher Holn,
Upham, Cheriton Fitzpaine,
Crediton,
Devon EX17 4HN

tel	01363 866165
fax	01363 866165
e-mail	enquiries@jellicoes.co.uk
web	www.jellicoes.co.uk

Barbara Pugsley
Hornhill,
Exeter Hill, Tiverton,
Devon EX16 4PL

tel	01884 253352
fax	01884 253352
e-mail	hornhill@tinyworld.co.uk
web	www.hornhill-farmhouse.co.uk

map: 2 entry: 139

map: 2 entry: 140

HOW TO USE THIS BOOK

sample entry

CORNWALL

Watch the surfers hug the waves, schools of them, all year. Watch the sun, the sand and, it seems, the world. The vastness of the view astonishes. At high tide you are on an island of granite – but not marooned. The bridge, a breathtaking entry, is the only privately owned suspension bridge in the country – not for those with vertigo. High seas can, spectacularly, wet the house. But all is elegance within: good furniture, deep carpets, family portraits, tradition and luxury with a modern touch. Decking all round for sun bathing, and views to the south, north, east and west. A great escape.

rooms	1 double with private shower room.
room price	£96-£114. Single occ. £48-£57.
meals	Sandwiches & coffee, £5. Excellent pubs/restaurants short walk away.
closed	Very occasionally.
directions	From Treloggen r'bout before Newquay right at Safeways, down hill. Across double r'bout. Left at lights; 1st right Grovesnor Ave. Straight across main road down narrow road, over bridge; 1st left, 1st right down Island Crescent.

	Lady Long
	The Island,
	Newquay,
	Cornwall TR7 1EA
tel	01637 879754
e-mail	helen@towanisland.fsnet.co.uk

① ② ③ ④ ⑤ (entry markers)

⑥

⑦ map: 1 entry: 53

explanations

❶ rooms

We do not use the words 'en suite'. If a bathroom is 'en suite' we say **with bath** or **with shower**.

If a room is not 'en suite' we say **with private bathroom** or **with shared bathroom**: the former you will have to yourself, the latter may be shared with other guests or family members; both will have a wc, basin and either a bath or a shower.

❷ room price

The price shown is for B&B for two people sharing a room. A price range incorporates room/seasonal differences. We also give single occupancy rates – the amount payable by one person staying in a room for two.

❸ meals

Prices are per person. All meals must be booked in advance. Ask the owner if you may bring your own wine. Some entries say B.Y.O.

❹ closed

When given in months, this means for the whole of the named months and the time in between.

❺ directions

Use as a guide; the owner can give more details.

❻ symbols

see the last page of the book for fuller explanation:

- 🐸 all children welcome
- ♿ wheelchair facilities for one bedroom/bathroom
- 👣 step-free access to bathroom/bedroom
- 🚭 no smoking anywhere
- 🚬 smoking restrictions exist.
- 🏠 this house has pets
- 🐕 pets can sleep in your bedroom
- 💳 credit cards accepted
- 🌱 vegetarians catered for with advance warning
- 🥕 mostly home-grown/local/organic produce used
- 🍷 licensed premises
- 🐄 working farm
- 🚲 bike
- 🚶 walk

❼ Map page number; entry number.

An Irish attitude to life dominates the house, says Charlotte – that means friends, family and guests mingle naturally. There's plenty of company and activity to enjoy: polo ponies (tuition available), fishing, the garden to explore – or simply enjoy the privacy of your room. Sit and catch the morning sun in the dining room. Bedrooms have handsome, traditional furniture, fat pillows, new mattresses, cotton linen and a tray with whisky decanter, mineral water and biscuits. For breakfast, home-reared organic sausages and bacon, and home-grown melon in season. Your horse can come, too. *Children over 10 welcome.*

rooms	1 twin with bath, sitting room & mini kitchen.
room price	£70. Single occ. from £45.
meals	Breakfast until 9.30am. Picnic lunch £15. Dinner £25.
closed	Christmas & New Year.
directions	From M5, junc. 26 or 27, A38 for Exeter for 6 miles, then left to Culmstock. In Culmstock, over bridge & 1st right into Silver St. Last drive on right.

Roger & Charlotte Horne
Woodhayne Barton,
Culmstock,
Devon EX15 3JG

tel	01884 840708
fax	01884 841479
e-mail	rogercharlotte@hornewoodhayne. demon.co.uk
web	www.hornewoodhayne.demon.co.uk

map: 2 entry: 141

Fay puts masses of thought into looking after her guests. Large panelled bedrooms have lots of little extras – hairdryers, sewing kits, mints, bathrobes, stationery – and floral curtains with matching duvets. The Downs' great love in life is breeding and racing horses and there are 180 acres of organic farm, parkland and views around the 300-year-old house. Breakfast, including home-made marmalade and fresh fruit, is served in the oak-panelled dining room which has a conservatory leading from it... look for the recently revealed inscription dated 1760. Within a short walk is a lovely lake for fishing. *Children over 12 welcome.*

rooms	3: 1 double, 1 twin, both with shower; 1 double with bath. Another bath & shower available.
room price	£44-£50. Single occ. £30.
meals	Great pubs within 2 miles.
closed	Christmas.
directions	M5, junc. 28, head for Cullompton, then left for Broadclyst. Through town & left at 'Sports Centre' sign. Right at T-junc. Cross over m'way bridge. Next left (for Plymtree). House next lane on left.

Fay Down
Upton House,
Cullompton,
Devon EX15 1RA

tel	01884 33097
fax	01884 33097

map: 2 entry: 142

DEVON

DEVON

The round-headed oak door frame in the back bedroom hints at this Grade II-listed farmhouse's 16th-century origins — James will tell you all about its history. Orchards, paddocks and ponds outside; homeliness and comfort within. You'll want for nothing with Sîan (once a nurse) your attentive yet unobtrusive hostess. Bedrooms are whitewashed and simple, with charming old windows and deep sills. The odd beam to be ducked, a soppy black Lab to be fussed over... a delightful place. Only eight miles from Exeter and a dream for walkers, too. *Children by arrangement.*

Lapping, almost, at the riverside garden is the Exe estuary, wide and serene. Birds and boats, the soft hills beyond, a gorgeous Georgian house on the river and kind hosts — silly to wish for more. Yet the garden, too, is beautiful, full of topiary, old apple trees and box hedging; you may breakfast there or in the conservatory. Every corner of the house has been considered. The bedrooms are luxurious, peachy, soft, chintzy and have antique white bedspreads. Topsham is an unspoilt conservation area. A remarkable marriage of nature and human intervention.

rooms	3: 1 double with bathroom; 1 double with private bath; 1 twin with shower room.
room price	£46-£54. Single occ. £28-£32.
meals	Breakfast until 9.30am. Packed lunch £3.
closed	Very occasionally.
directions	From A30, B3180 for Exmouth. 0.75 miles on, right at crossroads for Marsh Green. House 1st on left on entering village.

rooms	2; 1 twin with bath & wc; 1 double, with bath.
room price	£60. Single occ. £35.
meals	Good pubs/restaurants a short walk away.
closed	Christmas & New Year.
directions	M5, junc. 30, follow signs to Exmouth. Right at George & Dragon. After about 1 mile immed. left after level crossing. At mini r'bout, left down The Strand. House last on left by beach.

Mr & Mrs J. B. Wroe
Lower Marsh Farm,
Marsh Green, Exeter,
Devon EX5 2EX

tel	01404 822432
fax	01404 822062
e-mail	lowermarshfarm@eclipse.co.uk

Trevor & Jane Coleman
Beach House,
The Strand, Topsham, Exeter,
Devon EX3 0BB

tel	01392 876456
fax	01392 873159
e-mail	janecoleman45@hotmail.com

Unwind in a home that perfectly matches its owners: friendly, gentle, charming. This old cottage has had many facelifts over the years, hence the delightfully varying ceiling heights. Nurse-turned-reflexologist Joanna wants you to feel at home – play the piano, browse through the family's books (lots of Dickens), try her home-made elderflower cordial. Your creamy coloured bedroom has pine furniture and watercolours by Joanna's father, its garden-to-hillside views are super and there's a Victorian tub in your small bathroom. This is a designated AONB full of wildlife, especially birds. Your sleep will be deep.

Ian, a solicitor, has recently retired to concentrate on looking after his prize-winning Berkshire pigs and guests – he likes both equally! He and Maggie will give you the full Devon B&B experience – home-reared rare-breed pork, bacon and prize-winning sausages, 'ruby' Devon beef and Dorset Down lamb, all with astonishing flavour. 'Combe' means valley and all the farmhouse bedrooms have heart-healing views; there's a private sitting room downstairs and a guest sitting and dining room upstairs. Walk straight from the door onto 70 acres of pasture and ancient woodland carpeted with bluebells in spring and alive with wildlife.

rooms	1 double with basin & private bathroom.
room price	£50. Single occ. £30.
meals	Good pub/restaurant 0.25 miles.
closed	Christmas & New Year.
directions	From M5 junc. 30, A3052 to Sidmouth through Newton Poppleford. 1st left to Harpford.

rooms	4: 1 double with separate bunk room & bathroom; 1 double with bathroom. Ground floor suite: bathroom, bedroom & living room.
room price	£48–£60. Single occ. by arrangement.
meals	Packed lunch £5. Dinner £14.50.
closed	Very occasionally.
directions	From Honiton High St, turn into New St by Lloyds Bank. At mini-r'bout, left, then 1st right. Up hill to golf course & on towards Colyton. 3rd left for Slade. Farm in bottom of valley on right.

Hendrik & Joanna Vollers
Otter House,
Harpford, Nr Sidmouth,
Devon EX10 0NH
tel   01395 568330
e-mail   jovollers@btinternet.com

Maggie Todd
Smallicombe Farm,
Northleigh, Colyton,
Devon EX24 6BU
tel   01404 831310
fax   01404 831431
e-mail   maggie_todd@yahoo.com
web   www.smallicombe.com

map: 2 entry: 145   map: 3 entry: 146

DEVON

Breakfast in the conservatory will seduce you, a drink there before dinner will, too. It is awash with colour, plants and *objets de curiosité*. The garden is outrageously lovely: specimen trees, a fountain and two ponds, mature trees of all kinds, spring carpets of aconites, crocuses, snowdrops and bluebells, huge rhododendrons and camellias. Simon was a pilot, Gill a nurse – the house has lovely paintings, done by Gill when they lived in Japan. It is a splendid place – with large rooms, high corniced ceilings, antiques and fine things – whose freedom you will be given in typically generous spirit.

rooms	1 double with private bathroom.
room price	£70. Single occ. £40.
meals	Packed lunch £5. Dinner £15-£25. Good pubs/restaurants nearby.
closed	Occasionally.
directions	From Tesco/Station r'bout in Axminster, A358 Seaton road up hill. 0.5 miles on, left into Woodbury Lane, after bus stop. House on right 0.5 miles up lane.

	Gill Boston
	Chattan Hall,
	Woodbury Lane, Axminster,
	Devon EX13 5TL
tel	01297 32365
fax	01297 32365
e-mail	boston@chattanhall.co.uk
web	www.chattanhall.co.uk

DEVON

Privacy, stylish comfort and peace in stunning surroundings: after a lot of travelling, these ex-TV producers had a clear vision of what made a perfect place to stay. Each bedroom is self-contained and has a private 'deck' dotted with pots; the woodland views are glorious. No expense has been spared: chrome shower heads are the size of dinner plates, the beds are new and firm, the linen luxurious. They have used local craftsmen and local material in the renovation. Judging by Frank's teatime nut torte, his breakfasts will be excellent. Valley, woodland and bluebell walks start from your terrace.

rooms	3 doubles, all with shower room.
room price	£65. Single occ. £32.50.
meals	Packed lunch from £7.50. Restaurants in Honiton.
closed	Christmas.
directions	Offwell is 3 miles from Honiton & signed off A35 Honiton-Axminster road. In centre of village, at church, down hill. Farm 0.5 miles on.

	Frank & Carol Hayes
	West Colwell Farm,
	Offwell, Honiton,
	Devon EX14 9SL
tel	01404 831130
fax	01404 831769
e-mail	stay@westcolwell.co.uk
web	www.westcolwell.co.uk

A self-contained hideaway for nature lovers – with terrific views. At last Katrina has the opportunity to do B&B, and has converted the stone and slate 'garden shed' into a comfortable two-bed cottage – with sitting room – for guests. Eat the best bacon and eggs for breakfast – all locally produced – on your private patio with those glorious views. Perfect as a couple's hideaway or for families: Katrina has three children of her own and offers babysitting and high tea. The Axe Valley is a designated AONB and the walks are all you'd expect them to be.

You come for the gardens and for the food: organic and local, traditional and delicious. Up to 12 can eat at separate tables. Outside, nine acres with an orchard of damson and cherry trees; then ghinkos, meta sequoia, magnolia, jacaranda and Chinese shrubs. There are even ponds and a bamboo valley, and sheep, ponies, geese and free-range hens. The house is mainly Georgian but parts date back to 1332 and the views are wonderful. Cottage suites have stripped pine, Laura Ashley-style linen and curtains and oak kitchens.

rooms	2: 1 double, 1 twin sharing bathroom.
room price	£50. Single occ. £25. Under 12s half price.
meals	Packed lunch £3. Children's tea £3. Good pubs 1-2 miles.
closed	Very occasionally.
directions	A358 from Chard to Axminster. Through Tytherleigh & 1st right to Alston. Through village & bear left towards Holy City. House down 4th drive on left.

rooms	3: 1 twin/double with bath; 2 cottage suites.
room price	£56-£60. Single occ. £31.50-£35 in high season.
meals	Breakfast until 8.45am. Dinner, with aperitif, £21.
closed	Mid-November-Christmas Eve; 3 January-14 February.
directions	From Chard, A30 Honiton for 0.25 miles. At top of hill fork left. After 3 miles, right after animal sanctuary. Follow signs for Furley. At T-junc., left to Ford, then bear right. House on left.

Katrina Felgate
Beaconhill Cottage,
Chardstock, Axminster,
Devon EX13 7LB

tel	01460 220065
fax	01460 220065
e-mail	katrina_felgate@btinternet.com
web	www.beaconhillcottage.co.uk

Robert & Pat Spencer
Goodmans House,
Furley, Membury,
Devon EX13 7TU

tel	01404 881690
fax	01404 881690
e-mail	enquiries@goodmanshouse.co.uk
web	www.goodmanshouse.co.uk

map: 3 entry: 149

map: 3 entry: 150

DORSET

On a clear day ask for breakfast on the balcony: you'll be wowed by stupendous views across Lyme Bay and beyond. Years of travel and naval lifestyle lie behind the Normans' meticulous and old-fashioned hospitality; they have settled happily in this large 1920s house. Bedrooms under the eaves are thoroughly comfortable; all have chairs, a writing desk and flowers from the garden. Two of the rooms are large and have wonderful coastal views and the third is cottagey; one of the bathrooms is small. *Children over eight welcome.*

rooms	3: 1 double, 2 twins, all with bathroom.
room price	£44-£58. Single occ. £33-£40.
meals	Breakfast 8.15-9am. Supper tray (1st night only) £9.50. Pub/restaurant 400 yds.
closed	Mid-November-early March.
directions	On A3052 to Lyme, house 1st left after 'Welcome to Lyme' sign on right. Up Sidmouth Rd, past Morgan's Grave & Somers Rd. 1st drive on right, opp. junc. sign.

Tony & Vicky Norman
The Red House,
Sidmouth Road, Lyme Regis,
Dorset DT7 3ES

tel	01297 442055
fax	01297 442055
e-mail	red.house@virgin.net

map: 3 entry: 151

DORSET

In the parlour, deep sofas, a woodburner and piles of magazines urge you to rest. This is a thatched dream in 80 acres of bio-dynamic/ organic farmland on which the Bells, specialist food suppliers, graze Aberdeen Angus cattle, Portland sheep and Tamworth pigs (they supply Nigella Lawson and other top chefs). Large guest rooms have comfy armchairs and views of the Jurassic coastline and Golden Cap – the south coast's highest point, so-called because the sun illuminates its peak as it rises over the sea. The farm's fields overlook Lyme Bay and walks and wild flowers are all around. *Children, pets and horses by arrangement.*

rooms	3: 2 doubles, 1 single, all sharing bath/shower.
room price	From £100.
meals	Hampers & packed lunch from £15. Dinner, 3 courses, from £25. Excellent local restaurants.
closed	Occasionally.
directions	Directions given at time of booking.

Denise & Ian Bell
Shedbush Farm,
Muddy Ford Lane,
Stanton St Gabriel, Lyme Regis,
Dorset DT6 6DR

tel	01297 489304
fax	01297 489531
e-mail	heritageprime@aol.com
web	www.heritageprime.co.uk

map: 3 entry: 152

The Royal Commission included this house in its inventory on Historical Monuments in England. Dorset, with its softly folding hills and leafy lanes, is the perfect backdrop for the listed, 17th-century house, and there's stacks of atmosphere – original beams, flagstones, window seats, numerous family treasures, books and pictures. The bedrooms have been generously furnished with fine pieces as has the guests' sitting room. There is a lovely garden, with an orchard leading to a stream, and the sea is one mile away. Mrs Tennant is a quiet, thoughtful hostess. *Children over 10 welcome.*

What views! Catch them from the bedrooms and the sweeping gardens. This handsome house stands in a glorious position up and away from the summer crowds and joins National Trust land; the Jurassic Coast – a World Heritage Site – lies below and you are in an AONB. Jane and Adrian, good company and well-travelled, have created a hugely comfortable home and B&B. Antique furniture and books in the main rooms; bedrooms with colour-washed walls and pretty fabrics. You are a five-minute walk from Seatown beach and the Anchor Inn.

rooms	2: 1 double with private bathroom; 1 twin sharing bathroom, let only to members of same party.
room price	£60-£70. Single occ. by arrangement.
meals	Many pubs & restaurants 0.75 miles.
closed	Christmas & New Year.
directions	From Bridport, A35 into Chideock. Right at church. 0.75 miles up 'No Through Road' to T-junc. Turn right, house 7th on right (thatched with 2 porches). Drive to end of house, through gate to car park.

rooms	3: 2 doubles sharing bathroom; 1 twin/double (+ single bed) with shower room.
room price	From £55. Single occ. £32.50.
meals	Breakfast 8-9am. Packed lunch £5. Dinner £15.
closed	Christmas & New Year.
directions	Into Chideock on A35, take Bridport & Honiton rd. Left at sign to Seatown, then right fork. At top of hill take access road on right hand side. Signed on right.

	Mrs M. Tennant
	Champ's Land,
	Brighthay Lane, North Chideock,
	Bridport,
	Dorset DT6 6JZ
tel	01297 489314

	Jane & Adrian Tamone
	Seahill House,
	Seahill Lane, Seatown, Chideock,
	Dorset DT6 6JT
tel	01297 489801
fax	01297 489526
e-mail	jane@seahill.co.uk
web	www.seahill.co.uk

map: 3 entry: 153

map: 3 entry: 154

Sydney and Jayne share a gift for unwinding stressed souls – and producing memorable food and wine. Ten acres of orchard, valley and wooded hills, wrapped in peace and quiet and, inside, 17th-century stone walls, low-beamed ceilings and a warm French flair. Bedrooms have antique French beds, bold colours and crisp linen; in the sitting room are books, a log fire and soft, deep chairs. Jayne makes compotes from the orchard fruit; taste them at breakfast with cured ham, pains au chocolat and American pancakes. Cliff walks, beaches and fields to explore – a perfect place.

The house is set in a maze of paths that run through ancient wildflower meadows and medieval woodland; the views from the ramparts of Eggardon's hill fort are superb. From up there you can gaze down on the soft stone farmhouse and sleepy flower-decked lanes. The former shooting lodge has enormous flagstones, stripped floors, chunky studded doors and exposed beams. The tranquillity of the bedrooms complements Rosie's vibrant paintings. Explore the secret valleys and bumpety hills of West Dorset or the spectacular World Heritage coast. Enchanting seclusion.

rooms	4: 3 doubles, 1 twin, all with bath.
room price	£65-£80. Single occ. (weekdays only), £50.
meals	Breakfast 8.45-9.30am. Dinner, 3 courses, £18.50. Potage supper for late arrivals £15.50.
closed	October, Christmas & New Year.
directions	From Dorchester A35 for Bridport. After 13 miles 2nd road signed left to Shipton Gorge & Burton Bradstock. 1st left up long drive.

rooms	2: 1 double/family with bath/shower; 1 twin with bathroom.
room price	From £48. Single occ. £30.
meals	Breakfast 7-10am. Award-winning pubs, 3 miles.
closed	Occasionally.
directions	On A37, then A356 from D'chester, left at 1st sign for Toller Porcorum. Through village & up hill for 1 mile. At x-roads, right for Powerstock, under bridge. Track 0.5 miles on left, opp. white post by lane. At end, on left.

Sydney & Jayne Davies
Innsacre Farmhouse,
Shipton Gorge, Nr. Bridport,
Dorset DT6 4LJ
tel   01308 456137
e-mail   innsacre.farmhouse@btinternet.com

Rosie & Roger Britton
Gray's Farmhouse,
Toller Porcorum, Dorchester,
Dorset DT2 0EJ
tel   01308 485574
e-mail   rosieroger@farmhousebnb.co.uk
web   www.farmhousebnb.co.uk

DORSET

Breakfast with newspapers in the large, beamed kitchen or in the walled courtyard in summer. The well-travelled Jackie and David make light of the practicalities of looking after guests; they and their 200-year-old cottage have huge quantities of character and charm. One immaculate twin bedroom has fresh blue and white checks and access to the garden; another, attractive chintz. The sitting room has pretty pink sofas, an inglenook fireplace and window seats. The River Frome – a chalk stream favoured by local fishermen – is within 150 yards of the grounds. Convenient for the A35, yet peaceful.

rooms	3: 1 twin with (downstairs) shower room; 1 twin with private bathroom. 1 single also available.
room price	£50. Single occ. £35.
meals	Pub/restaurant 1.25 miles.
closed	Easter & Christmas.
directions	From r'bout at top of Dorchester, west on B3150 for 100 yds. Right onto Poundbury Rd (before museum). 1 mile on, over another road, then 2nd concrete track on right beyond Whitfield Farmhouse sign. Cottage set back from road.

Jackie & David Charles
Whitfield Farm Cottage,
Poundbury Road, Nr. Dorchester,
Dorset DT2 9SL

tel	01305 260233
fax	01305 260233
e-mail	dc.whitfield@clara.net
web	www.dc.whitfield.clara.net

map: 3 entry: 157

DORSET

An impossibly pretty English cottage – 400 years old with a stream to cross and a pretty flowery garden – in a lovely village with fields and hills all around. Nicky, independent, enthusiastic and knowledgeable about walks and visits in Hardy Country, will leave you to your own devices once you are properly advised. Inside, a stone-flagged hall and bedrooms with lathe and plaster ceilings, and chalk/limestone walls that feel unmistakably cottagey. They're characterful and you'll feel comfortable. Home-made jam and free-range eggs for breakfast. *Children over eight welcome.*

rooms	3: 2 doubles (1 with room for extra bed), 1 twin, all with basins, sharing 2 bathrooms.
room price	£44. Single occ. £27.
meals	Breakfast until 9.30am. Good food available locally.
closed	Very occasionally.
directions	From Dorchester, A37 north. After 5 miles, in Grimstone, right under r'way bridge to Sydling St Nicholas. Lamperts is 1st thatched cottage on right, in village.

Nicky Willis
Lamperts Cottage,
Sydling St Nicholas, Dorchester,
Dorset DT2 9NU

tel	01300 341659
fax	01300 341699
e-mail	nickywillis@tesco.net

map: 3 entry: 158

DORSET

DORSET

The oldest house in the village (1622) in the beautiful Piddle valley; wild deer frolic on the hillside, ducks splash in the village stream. Robin and Liz are the friendliest of hosts and keen to do a good job of caring for you; they have renovated their home and stable block with enormous care. One bedroom is in the house, simple and charming with low-beamed ceilings and white walls; the rooms in the old stables are more modern, and equally comfortable. Breakfast is served round a gleaming mahogany table in a flagstoned, rugged dining room. The Cerne Abbas Giant, cut into the chalk hillside, beckons.

Solid, Elizabethan grandeur in this magnificent 1590s Grade I-listed manor. Something to delight at every turn: huge, impressive carved antique beds, enormous staircases, beautiful rugs on stone and wooden floors, fabrics which perfectly suit the period, fine views to the lake. Pevsner described the Manor as being "refined to a point of perfection". The splendours are varied and the grounds live up to the house. Andrew and Mulu will pamper you in great style; Mulu can even give you a massage/beauty treatment in the salon. *Children over 12 by arrangement.*

rooms	5: House: 1 twin with bath. Stables: 3 twin/doubles, 2 with bath/shower, 1 with shower room; 1 twin with bath/shower.
room price	£50. Single occ. £32.50.
meals	Breakfast until 9.30am. Packed lunch from £3. Pubs/restaurants short walk away.
closed	Christmas & New Year.
directions	From Dorchester, A35 for Bere Regis for 1 mile. B3143 left to Piddlehinton. Through village. On left 100 yds after Thimble pub.

rooms	3: 1 four-poster, 1 twin, both with bathroom; 1 double, with shower room &/or with private bathroom.
room price	£90-£110. Single occ. £60-£70.
meals	Dinner, 4 courses, £25.
closed	Mid-December-end-February.
directions	At r'bout on A35, 1 mile NE of Dorchester, follow sign to Kingston Maurward gardens & animal park. In grounds, follow signs to house.

Robin & Liz Adeney
Whites Dairy House,
Piddlehinton, Dorchester,
Dorset DT2 7TD
tel   01300 348386
e-mail   robin.adeney@care4free.net
web   www.whitesdairyhouse.co.uk

Andrew & Mulu Thomson
The Old Manor,
Kingston Maurward, Dorchester,
Dorset DT2 8PX
tel   01305 261110
fax   01305 263734
e-mail   thomson@kingston-maurward.co.uk
web   www.kingston-maurward.co.uk

DORSET

Smart, spruce, country-style décor – windy corridors, sloping floors and the odd wonky wall. It's a listed farmhouse of two halves – the front is 100 years younger than the back. Rooms are generous, particularly the cream suite, which has a very pretty bathroom, dressing room and views of garden and paddock; all have mineral water, good towels and mattresses. Lisa and Tim are utterly at ease with guests and serve delicious, locally sourced breakfasts. The place hums with birdsong and the garden is lovely. You are only five minutes from Dorchester and, yes, there are Thomas Hardy connections – he used to visit the church next door.

rooms	3: 1 double with bath; 1 double with extra single & private bath; 1 double with private bath.
room price	£50-£60. Single occ. £32.
meals	Breakfast 8-9.30am. Packed lunch £3.50. Dinner £15.
closed	Occasionally.
directions	From Dorchester bypass A354 to Weymouth. 1st left to Winterbourne Herrington; at T-junc. right, on for 1 mile; look out for golf course, next left to house.

Lisa Bowden
Higher Came Farmhouse,
Higher Came, Dorchester,
Dorset DT2 8AP
tel   01305 268908
fax   01305 268908
e-mail   highercame@eurolink.ltd.net
web   www.highercame.co.uk

map: 3 entry: 161

DORSET

Thomas Hardy and his brother were so taken by the neighbouring 12th-century church that they helped restore it; Hardy's home, Max Gate, is nearby. This 300-year-old thatched cottage hugs the church boundary and has been diligently restored. Sink into comfortable mattresses on king-size beds – bedrooms are simple, serene and softly lit. The village is genuinely quaint and there's a local pub that does excellent food a short stroll away. Good breakfasts with local, free-range eggs, honey, home-made yogurt and preserves. Renée also offers reflexology.

rooms	2: 1 twin/double, 1 double, both with bath/shower.
room price	£50-£60. Single occ. by arrangement.
meals	Breakfast until 9.30am. Good pub 500 yds.
closed	Christmas & New Year.
directions	A352 Wareham road from Dorchester bypass. Left at sign to West Knighton, or on to Broadmayne & left for West Knighton at x-roads. On for 0.5 miles; cottage just after church.

Peter & Renée East
Church Cottage,
West Knighton, Dorchester,
Dorset DT2 8PF
tel   01305 852243
e-mail   info@church-cottage.com
web   www.church-cottage.com

map: 3 entry: 162

The mood is of restrained luxury and uncluttered, often beautiful, good taste. Bedrooms are cream with mahogany furniture, sloping ceilings, beams, a radio and armchairs. There's a large drawing room and good paintings are all around. The Hipwells are easy; the house, and the garden, are a refuge. Views are soft and lush yet you are in the main square of this attractive town; the house was rebuilt in 1762 after a great fire, on the foundations of a 13th-century goldsmith's house. *Children over 10 welcome.*

Halfway between Corfe Castle and Kingston, and minutes from the coastal path, the 'Isle of Purbeck' is a glorious area. Here is an 18th-century wisteria-strewn house – two cottages that have grown together – which demands that you unwind and enjoy yourself. Bedrooms are comforting, full of pictures, old pieces and country prints; the double most homely with Victorian button armchair and mahogany dressing table. The small twin is perfect for children. Breakfast – from Bron's Aga – is at tables overlooking courtyard and garden. If you spot wild deer munching on the roses, tell Bron.

rooms	3 twin/doubles, all with private bathroom.
room price	£50-£55. Single occ. £30-£35.
meals	Dinner £12, available in winter. Good restaurants 50 yds.
closed	Christmas & New Year.
directions	From A35, A351 to Wareham. Follow signs to town centre. In North St, over lights into South St. 1st left into St John's Hill; house on far right-hand corner of the square.

rooms	2: 1 double with private bath/shower; 1 twin with shower room.
room price	£50. Single occ. £32.50.
meals	Breakfast 8-9.30am. Good inns 0.5 miles.
closed	Christmas & New Year.
directions	A351 from Wareham to Corfe Castle. At end of village fork right on B3069 for Kingston. Left in 0.5 miles down track (signed).

Anthea & Michael Hipwell
Gold Court House,
St John's Hill, Wareham,
Dorset BH20 4LZ
tel   01929 553320
fax   01929 553320

Mrs H. B. Burt
Lower Lynch House,
Kingston Hill, Corfe Castle,
Dorset BH20 5LG
tel   01929 480089

map: 3 entry: 163

map: 3 entry: 164

The views of Poole Harbour and yachts are enough; the sumptuousness of the bedrooms and bathrooms is the icing on the cake. Choose from a harbour-facing suite with its own balcony or a double garden room. Sherry, every bathroom treat, robes, sweets, fruit… "More luxury than many a five-star hotel," says our inspector: Renate wants your stay to be memorable. Breakfasts are served on Spode china, outside, maybe, among the birds, the flowers and the sea breeze. There's always fresh fruit, maybe Parma ham, smoked salmon or kedgeree. Truly spoiling.

A large house kept in pristine condition by Sara and John – the huge and enchanting garden comes in for the same careful treatment, too. Furnishings are sedate, and some newer pieces are well mixed with family antiques. The twin, with patterned carpet, has a good collection of books and the double has views from both windows. Sara pays attention to detail: new toothbrush for the forgetful, linen table napkins, a choice of teas. Every view is onto green Hardy Country… or the lovely garden. Bring your racquets – there's a tennis court.

rooms	2 twins/doubles, both with bath & shower.
room price	£58-£70. Single occ. by arrangement.
meals	Pub 400 yds, restaurants 1 mile.
closed	Very occasionally.
directions	From A350 Upton x-roads take Blandford Road south for Poole. After 1.5 miles, right at Red Lion pub into Lake Road. Under narrow bridge towards water's edge, then left down Brank Sea Ave; on left.

rooms	3: 1 double, 1 twin, 1 single sharing 2 bathrooms. Possible use of private bathroom.
room price	From £46. Single £23.
meals	Breakfast 7.30-9.30am. Pub/restaurant 400 yds.
closed	Very occasionally.
directions	From Wimborne B3078 to Cranborne. Right to Holt. After 2 miles Thornhill on right, 200 yds beyond Old Inn.

Renate & John Wadham
53 Branksea Avenue,
Poole,
Dorset BH15 4DP

tel 01202 673419
fax 01202 667260
e-mail johnrenate@lineone.net

John & Sara Turnbull
Thornhill,
Holt, Wimborne,
Dorset BH21 7DJ

tel 01202 889434
e-mail scturnbull@lineone.net

DORSET

Below is the River Stour which winds through the valley and under the medieval, nine-arched bridge; above is an Iron Age hillfort; between is Crawford House. Soft and pretty, the house has floor-length windows in the sitting and dining rooms that allow sun to stream through in the most uplifting way. Bedroom colours are neutral and calm, offsetting floral curtains. One room has charming four-poster twin beds with chintzy drapes. Downstairs, there are lovely oils on the walls and Andrea brings you breakfast in the pale green dining room. Ferry ports are 25 minutes away.

rooms	3: 1 twin/double with bathroom; 2 twins sharing bathroom.
room price	£50. Single occ. £25.
meals	Pub in village, 0.5 miles.
closed	Mid-October–mid-April.
directions	1st gateway immed. on left after crossroads (B3075) on A350 going north after entering Spetisbury.

Andrea Lea
Crawford House,
Spetisbury, Blandford,
Dorset DT11 9DP
tel   01258 857338
fax   01258 858152

map: 3 entry: 167

DORSET

An encapsulation of much that is charming about Dorset – a soft, delightful, thatched cottage in an enviable rural setting. Sandy and Paul have poured love into this Grade II-listed farmhouse and garden, the latter bursting with lupins, poppies, foxgloves, clematis, delphiniums… Sandy is very welcoming; Paul, brought up in South America, is full of stories and fluent in Spanish, Portuguese and French. Excellent bedrooms with good prints, pretty bedheads and lovely pieces of furniture. The garden room with exposed flintstone walls has its own door to the garden. Very special indeed. *Children over 10 welcome.*

rooms	3: 2 doubles, 1 ground-floor twin, all with shower room.
room price	£50. Single occ. £30.
meals	Packed lunch from £5.
closed	Christmas & New Year.
directions	Leave Blandford for SW, cross river Stour. Hard right after Bryanston school, for W. Stickland (4.5 miles). There, down North St, right signed W'bourne Houghton. House 150 yds on left with 5-bar gate.

Sandy & Paul Crofton-Atkins
Stickland Farmhouse,
Winterborne Stickland,
Blandford Forum,
Dorset DT11 0NT
tel   01258 880119
fax   01258 880119
e-mail   sticklandfarmhouse@
sticklanddorset.fsnet.co.uk

map: 3 entry: 168

DORSET

DORSET

Breakfast by the log fire in the elegant dining room in winter; you'll enjoy a memorable feast of free-range eggs, home-made jams and marmalades. There is a walled half-acre garden and herbaceous border (Tia's passion). All rooms are beautifully decorated – lovely prints, many lamps – and have stunning views. After a day out or a good walk, sit beside the fire with a pile of their books in the large drawing room. On a quiet road, this is a fabulous old house, comfortable and easy, and Holly the Labrador is as welcoming as her owners.

A magical place. Complete peace: the garden runs down to the River Stour and has uninterrupted views over the water meadows. The millhouse, 16th-century and Grade I-listed, is as warm and interesting as the owners. The inside is no surprise: an original moulded plaster ceiling, a half-tester bed in one room, a real four-poster in another, rich decoration and large table in the dining room. There is no sitting room for guests, but the rooms are big and who cares when the house is so magnificent? *Children over 12 welcome.*

rooms	3: 1 double with bath/shower; 1 twin/double with shower; 1 single with private bathroom.
room price	£45-£54.
meals	Breakfast until 9am. Supper tray, £8 on first night. Pub 600 yds.
closed	Christmas.
directions	From Dorchester, B3143 into Buckland Newton over x-roads; On right opp. village cricket pitch.

rooms	3: 1 double, with bath; 1 double, 1 four-poster sharing bathroom.
room price	£45-£60. Single occ. from £30.
meals	Breakfast 7-9am. Pub/restaurant 5 minutes' walk away.
closed	Very occasionally.
directions	On A357 between Sturminster Newton & Blandford. Look for well-marked turning on north side between S. Newton & Fiddleford.

Tia Bunkall
Holyleas House,
Buckland Newton, Dorchester,
Dorset DT2 7DP
tel	01300 345214
fax	01305 264488
e-mail	tiabunkall@holyleas.fsnet.co.uk
web	www.holyleashouse.co.uk

Mr & Mrs A. & J. Ingleton
Fiddleford Mill,
Fiddleford, Sturminster Newton,
Dorset DT10 2BX
| tel | 01258 472786 |

map: 3 entry: 169

map: 3 entry: 170

Across the road the water meadows descend to the river that winds round Sturminster Newton. Australian Margie is fun and easy-going and the house is reassuringly homely, with some attractive, convivial clutter. There's a huge fireplace in the hall and a smaller one in the snug sitting room with its matted carpet and jolly rugs. Bedrooms are big, spotless and attractive with plain Wilton carpets; one of the bathrooms has pretty handmade tiles. Breakfasts, served from the vast and friendly kitchen, are feasts of local sausage, home-made marmalade and fruit salad. A wonderful house.

Deep in the Wessex countryside, where Ancient Britons sleep, lies Stourton Caundle and, standing off the road, Golden Hill Cottage. Look out of your bedroom window at the flowers and the fields, descend to platters of local bacon and sausages and more of home-made jams and Dorset honey, then step outside and immerse yourself in the past – to Sherborne, Kingston Lacy, Badbury Rings. Unwind in the elegant sitting room – all yours – at the end of the day. When hunger strikes you are spoilt for choice: the Modern Britons who run the pubs are wide awake and know how to cook.
Babes in arms welcome.

rooms	4: 1 double with bathroom; 1 double with private bathroom; 1 twin, 2 singles sharing bathroom & wc.
room price	£50. Singles from £27.50.
meals	Packed lunch, from £3. Good pub within walking distance.
closed	Christmas.
directions	On A357 Sherborne to Blandford road. House 0.25 miles west of Sturminster Newton bridge, on south side of road.

rooms	1 twin with shower.
room price	£48. Single occ. £24.
meals	Good pubs/restaurants within 3 miles.
closed	Very occasionally.
directions	From Sherborne, A352 to Dorchester; after 1 mile, left onto A3030; on to far end of Bishops Caundle, left to Stourton Caundle; after sharp left into village street, house 200 yards on right.

Charles & Margie Fraser
Newton House,
Sturminster Newton,
Dorset DT10 2DQ
tel   01258 472783
fax   01258 473235
e-mail   carolinepass@lineone.net

Anna Oliver
Golden Hill Cottage,
Stourton Caundle,
Sturminster Newton,
Dorset DT10 2JW
tel   01963 362109
fax   01963 364205
e-mail   andrew@oliver.net
web   www.goldenhillcottage.co.uk

The Benjamins worked in the States and have imported the country's high standard of B&B. Bedrooms are more 'grand luxe' than cottagey and the beds are big and of the finest quality; the four-poster has steps up to it. Lovely *toile de Jouy* curtains throughout and a feeling of opulence. State-of-the-art bathroom fittings, power showers (of course) and fluffy towels. The garden was professionally designed and there is much of interest – they have space for wedding party marquees, too, so just ask. Sylvia's other passion is antiques – you can buy some of her finds if you wish – and they run bridge, art and pampering weekends.

An attractive and quiet Victorian townhouse with a country feel. The view from the rear belies the fact that the centre of Sherborne with its abbey, shops restaurants, tea rooms and weekly market stalls is just minutes from the house. The gentle country feel pervades the interior of the house, too: the colour scheme is predominantly soft green and there are pretty chintz fabrics in the bedrooms and drawing room. Bathrooms are new, modern, white and fresh with excellent fittings. *Children over 12 welcome.*

rooms	6: 4 doubles, 2 twins, all with bathroom. Studio: double, campbeds, cot, kitchenette & shower.
room price	£72–£90. Single occ. £39–£49. Studio £75–£85 for 2; extra beds £15 each.
meals	Restaurants within walking distance.
closed	Very occasionally.
directions	From Sherborne follow signs to A3030, then to Alweston, 2 miles. Past Post Office on right, parking sign on left, next left into Munden Lane. House behind Oxford Bakery.

rooms	2: 1 twin/double with bath; 1 double with private bath.
room price	From £65. Single occ. by arrangement.
meals	Several pubs and restaurants within walking distance.
closed	December & January.
directions	From A30, left into North Rd, left at first x-roads into Newlands, then sharp right at Castletown x-roads into Long St. House on left 150 yards from x-roads.

Sylvia & Joe Benjamin
Munden House,
Alweston, Sherborne,
Dorset DT9 5HU

tel	01963 23150
fax	01963 23153
e-mail	sylvia@mundenhouse.demon.co.uk
web	www.mundenhouse.demon.co.uk

Mrs Pamela Rae
Tudor Lodge,
Long Street, Sherbourne,
Dorset DT9 3ED

tel	01935 813970

This rambling, rose-clad Georgian farmhouse is English to the core. Rooms are stylishly cluttered with lovely old pieces, paintings and prints – books, delightful objects and flowers at every turn. Bedrooms under the eaves are deliciously cosy – and chic, with matching curtains and bedheads in creamy chintz. Breakfast is served in the farmhouse kitchen amid copper pans and colourful plates picked up on Richard & Jenny's travels – and under the vine-strewn loggia in summer. The garden overflows with honeysuckle and roses: a Dorsetshire dream.
Children over 12 welcome.

Altogether a surprising house – the austere Gothic exterior doesn't prepare you for the exuberance of the interior. It's a pleasant surprise – striking mixtures of fabrics and furniture that blend east and west. Anthony, from Hong Kong, is an excellent chef – at weekends, when he cooks, you really must eat in. Much of his food is Mediterranean with an oriental influence: Thai crabmeat cake with stir-fried veg, wild sea bass with shitake mushrooms. The Chinese bedroom is wonderfully showy with black and gold lacquer half-tester bed and furniture. Splendid views, too.
Children over five welcome.

rooms	2: 1 double, 1 twin (only let to same party), with private bathroom.
room price	£55. Single occ. £32.50.
meals	Breakfast until 9.30am. Packed lunch £3. Dinner £15–£20.
closed	Christmas.
directions	From Wincanton, A357 for Templecombe. Take 2nd signed turning to Stowell on right opp. entrance to Horsington House. Down hill past church. 0.5 miles on. House on left after phone box.

rooms	6: 3 doubles, 3 family, all with bath/shower.
room price	£58–£100. Single occ. £42–£59.
meals	Breakfast until 9.30am. Dinner £20–£26, Fri & Sat only. Pub/restaurant 200 yds.
closed	January.
directions	From Sherborne A30 to Milborne Port. House 2nd on right on entering village.

Richard & Jenny Gold
Windrush Farm,
Stowell, Sherborne,
Dorset DT9 4PD
tel   01963 370799
e-mail   jennygold2@hotmail.com

Mr Anthony Ma & Jorgen Kunath
The Old Vicarage,
Milborne Port, Sherborne,
Dorset DT9 5AT
tel   01963 251117
fax   01963 251515
e-mail   theoldvicarage@milborneport.
freeserve.co.uk
web   www.milborneport.freeserve.co.uk

map: 3 entry: 175

map: 3 entry: 176

DORSET

DORSET

Lucy and Tim are tangibly happy in this converted forge; it was built in the 1700s and the wheelwright and carriage-builder from the local estate used to work here. Tim is a classic car restorer and has rebuilt a 1934 Lagonda; Lucy rides long-distance on her Arab horse. The attic bedrooms are snug, with Lucy's quilts, country antiques and sparkling bathrooms. Breakfasts include organic sausages and bacon and eggs from the Kerridges' free-ranging chickens and ducks. The Downs beckon keen walkers; warm corners invite readers. A lovely setting.

It's a short stroll into the centre of town, yet so quiet, thanks to the magnificent one-acre walled garden, open to the public once a year. With delicate, decorative details, the house is a Regency gem and there are many of them in this historic town. Have tea in the garden on arrival and, in the morning, take full English breakfast there with black pudding, kippers, home-made jams, eggs every way... There's an elegant drawing room for you and one bedroom has views of the church and Melbury Hill and a vast and luxurious bathroom. A delight.

rooms	3: 1 double/family with shower room; 1 double, 1 single (let to same party) sharing bathroom. 2 self-catering cottages for 2 & 3.
room price	£45-£57.50. Single occ. £40.
meals	Breakfast 8-9.30am. Pub/restaurant 4 miles.
closed	Very occasionally.
directions	From Shaftesbury, A350 to Compton Abbas. 1st on left before Compton Abbas sign. Left; entrance on left through 5-bar gate.

rooms	2 twins, both with bathroom.
room price	£60. Single occ. £45.
meals	Breakfast until 9.30am. Good restaurants locally.
closed	Christmas Day.
directions	From Shaftesbury, B3091 for Sturminster Newton. After 0.25 miles down St John's Hill, house 1st on right, parking next to garage.

Tim & Lucy Kerridge
The Old Forge, Fanners Yard,
Compton Abbas, Shaftesbury,
Dorset SP7 0NQ

tel	01747 811881
fax	01747 811881
e-mail	theoldforge@hotmail.com

Diana Pow
Cliff House,
Breach Lane, Shaftesbury,
Dorset SP7 8LF

tel	01747 852548
fax	01747 852548
e-mail	dianaepow@aol.com
web	www.cliff-house.co.uk

DORSET

A new house that will soften with age and Ella has great plans for the garden, including a breakfast terrace (in her former Special Place she had a vineyard that produced wonderful wine). In the dining room there's a large collection of books, and dining chairs sporting Ella's tapestry work, designed to match the curtains. Thoughtful extras in the comfortable bedroom – spring water and fresh flowers – and an antique mahogany chair and towel rail. This is a quiet spot in an AONB; there's a pub and a church in the charming village. *Children over 10 welcome.*

DURHAM

For lovers of horses this is irresistible – there are over 40 of them, the Booths are mad about them and you can learn to ride – or to do so more elegantly. Once a hunting lodge, Ivesley is at the end of an avenue of beech trees planted in the 1350s to commemorate the end of the Black Death. Half the house is new, discreetly so; the floorboards that creak are in the old part. The big bedrooms are very much 'country house', with antiques, and the grandeur of the dining room and drawing room belies their recent birth. Only 15 minutes from the centre of Durham. *Children over eight welcome.*

rooms	1 twin with private bathroom.
room price	£50. Single occ. from £35.
meals	Breakfast until 9.30am. Several pubs within 3 miles.
closed	Very occasionally.
directions	From Shaftesbury, A30 east. Through Ludwell, then left at bottom of hill signed The Donheads. At T-junc. follow sign to Donhead. Pass Foresters Inn on right, fork left after 150 yds. House on right after 300 yds.

rooms	3 doubles/twins, all with bath or shower.
room price	£62. Single occ. from £49.
meals	Breakfast until 9am. Dinner £22.
closed	Christmas Day.
directions	A1, then A68 to Tow Law. Right onto B6301, signed Lanchester. After 3.7 miles, right at sign. Drive is 0.7 miles up hill on left.

Ella Humphreys
Oakdale House,
Donhead St Andrew, Shaftesbury,
Dorset SP7 9EG

tel   01747 828767
e-mail   oakdale@eurolink.ltd.net

Roger & Pauline Booth
Ivesley Equestrian Centre,
Waterhouses,
Durham DH7 9HB

tel   0191 3734324
fax   0191 3734757
e-mail   ivesley@msn.com

DURHAM

DURHAM

Such privacy: your bedroom is sybaritically comfortable, and your own sitting room has a deep sofa and cosy armchairs. Coves House is a rare jewel: a Grade II*-listed, early 17th-century farmhouse with later additions, one of only 20 similar listed buildings in the county. The kitchen has the original bread oven, and Marguerite produces mouthwatering meals served in the dining room before an open fire. Hiddledy-piggledy charm combines with huge comfort; you are off the beaten track in magical scenery yet only 12 miles from Durham. A place you won't forget.

A walker's paradise, with pure air, deer, and woodpeckers. The Georgian shooting lodge is in an open glade with views of the moors – you drive for two miles through the forest to get to 5,000 acres of woodland, moors, becks, rivers and ancient trees. The Art Nouveau furniture and fittings are a refreshing change from traditional furnishings and there are some dramatic touches, such as the shocking pink bathroom. Big downstairs rooms, small bedrooms, open fires and books. Helene is an exceptional cook and has lived here all her life. *Children over eight welcome.*

rooms	1 twin with sitting room & bathroom in own wing.
room price	£70. Single occ. £45.
meals	Dinner, 4 courses, £25.
closed	Occasionally.
directions	West on A689, approx. 1 mile west of Wolsingham, left at Kingfisher Country Park sign. Over bridge, sharp left over disused r'way line. 0.5 miles up track, fork right through ford. House 200 yds further.

rooms	3: 2 doubles, both with bath/shower; 1 twin with shower room.
room price	£53-£65. Single occ. £36.50-£42.50.
meals	Packed lunch £4. Dinner £22.50.
closed	20 December-3 January.
directions	A68 from Darlington, left to Hamsterley. On for 2 miles (ignore forest signs) into village, then right, signed The Grove, then left. Right (signed), after 3 miles, over stone bridge, house opposite.

Anthony & Marguerite Todd
Coves House Farm,
Wolsingham, Weardale,
Durham DL13 3BG
tel 01388 527375
fax 01388 526157

Helene Close
Grove House,
Hamsterley Forest,
Bishop Auckland,
Durham DL13 3NL
tel 01388 488203
fax 01388 488174
e-mail xov47@dial.pipex.com
web www.grovehouse.ws

map: 14 entry: 181

map: 14 entry: 182

DURHAM

DURHAM

The renovation of the 1825 Regency villa was an enormous job and Sarah-Jane has tackled it with her evident good humour and energy. It's a fine country home – close to so many of the delights of Barnard Castle – and seems to have come alive since being nurtured back to its former glory. The sitting room is huge, with comfy sofas and a fire that's lit on chilly evenings. Bedrooms are freshly and simply decorated and have good views. Mature gardens envelop the house and merge with a buttercup field. Explore the rose garden and parkland and delight in finding the many rare plants in the woods.

This Georgian townhouse stands impressively horizontal on The Bank in 'Barney'. There you can meet Digby, Eva, Ian and George – in that order. Digby's an Old English sheepdog and George is the resident ghost whose manners are unfailingly polite. Eva and Ian merely run the place. Ian cooks the breakfasts; Eva arranges them artistically because that's her thing. They love their guests, provide beautiful rooms, and what more could you ask? After the meal stagger forth to see the rest of Barney on the Tees: the castle, the antique shops and restaurant next door where Cromwell really stayed.
Children over 12 welcome.

rooms	3: 1 double with shower; 2 twins, 1 with bath, 1 with private bathroom.
room price	£55-£65. Single occ. from £37.50.
meals	Breakfast until 9.30am. Dinner, 3 courses, £22.50.
closed	Christmas & New Year.
directions	From A1, at Scotch Corner, A66 for B. Castle. 7 miles on, approaching 1st section of dual c'way, 1st right for B. Castle to lights. Right over bridge. At T-junc. left for B. Castle Town. Pass school & museum, through gates on left.

rooms	2: 1 twin with private bathroom; 1 double with bath/shower.
room price	£50. Single occ. £35.
meals	Good pubs/restaurants nearby.
closed	Occasionally.
directions	At A1 Scotch Corner, A66 west for 7 miles. Then 1st dual carriageway; right for Barnard Castle. At lights right over bridge, left at T-junc. to Butter Market. Left down bank, house on left.

Sarah-Jane Ormston
Spring Lodge,
Newgate, Barnard Castle,
Durham DL12 8NW

tel	01833 638110
fax	01833 630389
e-mail	ormston@telinco.co.uk

Ian & Eva Reid
Number 34,
The Bank, Barnard Castle,
Durham DL12 8PN

tel	01833 631304
fax	01833 631304

DURHAM

We loved this place – the cobbled courtyard that evokes memories of its days as a coaching inn (Dickens stayed here), the River Greta that runs through the estate, the lovely garden and potager, the fine breakfasts (kipper and smoked haddock). Above all, Peter and Mary, your kind, unstuffy and dog-adoring hosts. Every creature comfort has been attended to in the cosy, Beatrix-Potterish bedrooms: crisp linen, soft lights, embroidered pillows and, in the bathrooms, big soft towels and heated rails. A perfect, rural stepping-stone to Scotland – or to the south.

ESSEX

The house is minutes from wild walking; the island of Mersea is secluded, surprising; the sea murmurs across the saltings where the Brent geese wheel and the great Constable skies stretch. The house began in 1343 – nearly as old as the exquisite church. The Georgians added their bit, but the venerable beams and uneven old construction shine through. It is a sunny, comfortable, beautiful house. There is a snug, book-filled sitting room, a terracotta-floored conservatory and much wood and soft colours. It is a privilege to stay here, with such agreeable hosts.

rooms	2 doubles/twins, 1 with bath/shower, 1 with private bathroom.
room price	£70. Single occ. £45.
meals	Packed lunch £5. Dinner, 3 courses, £20.
closed	Very occasionally.
directions	A1(M) to Scotch Corner. A66 west until Greta Bridge turn-off. House on left just before bridge.

rooms	2: 1 double, 1 twin, both with private bathroom.
room price	£56-£70. Single occ. £30.
meals	Restaurant 1 mile away, pub within walking distance.
closed	Very occasionally.
directions	From Colchester B1025, over causeway, then bear left. After 3 miles, pass Dog & Pheasant pub. Take 2nd right into Bromans Lane. House 1st on left.

Peter & Mary Gilbertson
The Coach House,
Greta Bridge, Barnard Castle,
Durham DL12 9SD
tel   01833 627201
e-mail   info@coachhousegreta.co.uk
web   www.coachhousegreta.co.uk

Ruth Dence
Bromans Farm,
East Mersea,
Essex CO5 8UE
tel   01206 383235
fax   01206 383235

ESSEX

ESSEX

As fascinating as the area it lives in, the Grade II*-listed 'Old Hall' House has two mainly 14th-century cross wings, and a 'new' 15th-century wing where you breakfast in front of a log fire. A forest fell, surely, to provide the beams. The interior is as beguiling as the house itself, with wonderfully strong colours, and bedrooms are cosy and welcoming, with undulating floors and 'museum corners' enshrining original features. The road goes close by but there is the enchanting garden and good insulation. Beams, sofas, handsome furniture, books, a sense of history – and immensely likeable hosts.

An Elizabethan jewel in a superb rural setting. Exposed timber ceilings, open fireplaces, nooks and crannies: this 'farmhouse' trumpets its history at every turn. The two-acre garden has old-fashioned roses and a pond that attracts many birds. The Wordsworths (yes, they are related to the poet) are engaging and solicitous people, who delight in their guests. Anne, an excellent cook, serves home-grown organic vegetables with dinner and the hens and bantams provide organic eggs for breakfast served in the Aga-warm kitchen. The perfect retreat from London and so close to Stansted airport, Cambridge and Duxford.

rooms	3: 1 double/family room with bathroom; 1 twin with private bathroom; 1 single with private shower room & wc.
room price	£45-£60. Single £27.50-£35.
meals	Good pubs 100 yds.
closed	Very occasionally.
directions	On A1124, 2.5 miles west of A12 junction. House is on left beyond Cooper's Arms & opposite Queens Head. Parking in courtyard.

rooms	2: 1 double with bath/shower; 1 twin with private bathroom.
room price	£80. Single occ. £50.
meals	Supper/dinner £18-£25. B.Y.O.
closed	Very occasionally.
directions	From S. Walden B1053 (George St) to Radwinter. Right at church & 1st left after 1 mile (at grass triangle on sharp right-hand bend). Signed.

	Patricia & Richard Mitchell
	Old House,
	Fordstreet, Aldham, Colchester,
	Essex CO6 3PH
tel	01206 240456
fax	01206 240456

	Antony & Anne Wordsworth
	Little Brockholds Farm,
	Radwinter, Saffron Walden,
	Essex CB10 2TF
tel	01799 599458
fax	01799 599458
e-mail	as@brockholds99.freeserve.co.uk
web	www.brockholds.co.uk

map: 11 entry: 187

map: 10 entry: 188

ESSEX

Floors slant and the old elm creaks – this timber-framed, 13th-century, Grade II*-listed Essex hall house is tangibly ancient. You have your own drawing room with stunning silk curtains and can be a cherished only guest, or things can be moved around to accommodate a larger group. Strong (Designer's Guild) colours in the twin bedroom and fresh blues and white in the large double. Stansted airport is 20 minutes away, Chelmsford 12, yet this is very rural: the tennis court is hard by open fields and there are ponds, an island and tame ducks.

GLOUCESTERSHIRE

The magnificent, softly undulating countryside has inspired musicians, writers and poets; you'll see why. Sit on the terrace – which is candlelit in the evenings – and take in the views; Michael and Jo will bring you a glass of award-winning wine produced at the neighbouring vineyard. They are genuine, kind, fun and you will relax immediately. Michael loves old cars – the Puma racing car was made right here – and they often tour in France. The house is a converted grain barn and the pretty and immaculate bedroom has a soaring A-frame ceiling. You will be very comfortable.

rooms	2: 1 double, 1 twin, sharing private bathroom.
room price	£60-£74. Single occ. £30-£37.
meals	Breakfast 6-10am. Dinner, £22.50.
closed	Occasionally.
directions	From Stansted, A120 east, then right onto A130. After Ford End, right at r'bout to Gt. Waltham. There, right at Beehive Pub into Barrack Lane. 1.3 miles on, right down track in between cottages. Left through gate before barn.

rooms	2: 1 twin with private bathroom. In cottage, 1 twin with bath (& wheelchair access), occasionally available on B&B basis.
room price	£60-£70. Single occ. £30-£35.
meals	Dinner from £18. Pub/restaurant 1 mile.
closed	Very occasionally.
directions	From Gloucester A40 to Ross-on-Wye, right onto B4215 for Newent. After approx. 7 miles, right (for Dymock). After '3 Choirs Vineyard', next right (before M50). House 1 mile down lane, 3rd on right.

Mrs Roslyn Renwick
Fitzjohns Farmhouse,
Mashbury Road, Great Waltham,
Chelmsford,
Essex CM3 1EJ
tel   01245 360204
fax   01245 361724
e-mail   rosrenwick@aol.com

Stop press!
No longer doing B&B

map: 11 entry: 189

map: 9 entry: 190

GLOUCESTERSHIRE

Petrina is a natural and imaginative cook – a eulogy from a French chef in the visitors' book endorses this – and both she and James thrive on the bustle and conversation of guests; you'll feel immediately at ease. Very early risers can help themselves to tea and coffee. There's plenty of space for everyone – bedrooms are large and airy, the beds emperor-size, no less. Large gardens and sweeping views of May Hill and the Malverns and an attractive and elegant house to which the Pughs bring a real sense of fun.

rooms	3: 2 twins/doubles, with bath/shower; 1 double with private shower room.
room price	£60. Single occ. £30.
meals	Dinner £17.50; gourmet dinner £22.50.
closed	Very occasionally.
directions	A40 from Gloucester for Ross-on-Wye, then B4215 (for Newent/Highnam). Whitehall Lane 2 miles on left. House approx. 0.75 miles down lane, on right, behind laurel hedge.

James & Petrina Pugh
Whitelands,
Whitehall Lane, Rudford,
Gloucestershire GL2 8ED

tel	01452 790406
fax	01452 790676
e-mail	pughwhitelands@hotmail.com

GLOUCESTERSHIRE

Come in spring and the nightingale's song is the only sound that could disturb your slumber; but this is a year-round, soothing retreat, a hunting lodge with views over the rolling Cotswold Hills. You enter an enchanted wood surrounded by a RSPB sanctuary and a pine arboretum planted by Thomas Gambier Parry in 1844. Carol and David are friendly, unobtrusive and knowledgeable about organic gardening, as reflected in the 13-acre grounds. The bedrooms with new beds and bathrooms have the most wonderful garden views.

rooms	2 doubles/twins, 1 with bathroom, 1 with shower room.
room price	£50-£60. Single occ. £30-£35.
meals	Dinner £17.50. Pub/restaurant 4 miles.
closed	Very occasionally.
directions	From Gloucester A40/A48 r'bout follow A40 (Ross) for 0.7 miles. At brow of hill right up drive of black & white cottage; follow track for 0.75 miles into woods. House at top through iron gates. Drive round house to front door.

David & Carol Wilkin
The Pinetum Lodge,
Churcham,
Gloucestershire GL2 8AD

tel	01452 750554
fax	01452 750402
e-mail	c.wilkin@amserve.net

Boards creak and you duck – it is a farmhouse of the best kind: simple, small-roomed, stone-flagged, beamed and delightful. The walls are white, the furniture is good and there are pictures everywhere. In spite of great age (16th century) there are lots of windows and good light. They farm 400 acres organically (cows and sheep) and your horse can come, too. Your welcome will be as generous as your farmhouse breakfast. The views across the Severn estuary to the Cotswolds are stupendous and there is, simply, no noise – unless the guinea fowl are in good voice.

A perfect English scene… a late 18th-century house tucked down a lane off the country's longest village green. It's a wonderful house and Carol wants you to treat it as home. When we visited, the Aga was being nurtured back to optimum health, there was a jigsaw puzzle that invited a challenge, dogs and cats happily co-existed; the visitors' book was inscribed: "We'll be back" (and return they do). There are lovely gardens, hens for breakfast eggs and orchards, and Carol has decorated big bedrooms in muted yellows and rich velvety plums. *Children over 10 welcome.*

rooms	2: 1 double, 1 twin, with shared or private shower room.
room price	£40-£50. Single occ. £25.
meals	Breakfast 7-10.30am. Packed lunch £5. Pub 2 miles.
closed	Occasionally.
directions	2 miles south of Newnham on A48, opp. turn for Bullo Pill, there is large 'pull-in' with phone box on right. Turn here. Follow farm track to end.

rooms	2: 1 twin/double, 1 twin, both with bath/shower.
room price	£53. Single occ. £26.50.
meals	Pubs in village. Excellent restaurant 5 miles.
closed	Christmas & New Year.
directions	A38 for Bristol, west onto B4071. 1st left & drive length of village green. 300 yds after end, right into Whittles Lane. House last on right. 3 miles from junc. 13 on M5.

Penny & David Hill
Grove Farm,
Bullo Pill, Newnham,
Gloucestershire GL14 1DZ

tel   01594 516304
fax   01594 516304
e-mail   davidandpennyhill@btopenworld.com

Carol & William Alexander
The Old School House, Whittles
Lane, Frampton-on-Severn,
Gloucestershire GL2 7EB

tel   01452 740457
fax   01452 741721
e-mail   bedandbreakfast@f-o-s.
freeserve.co.uk
web   www.the-oldschoolhouse.co.uk

GLOUCESTERSHIRE

Deep authenticity in this magnificent, Grade-I listed house in a fascinating village. The family has lived here since the 11th century – and Mrs Clifford, in her eighties, soldiers nobly on with extra help. There are exquisite examples of carved wood and the hall has an impressive Doric frieze. One bedroom has a Flemish tapestry and a four-poster bed with hand-embroidered curtains; the other, lovely views, antiques and panelling. Dutch ornamental canal, lake, old-master views… gorgeous! And a Strawberry Hill Gothic orangery for self-catering.

rooms	2: 1 four-poster with dressing room with a single bed & private bathroom; 1 twin with bathroom.
room price	£90-£100.
meals	Breakfast 8.30-10am. Restaurants & pubs close by.
closed	Very occasionally.
directions	From M5 junc. 13 west, then B4071. Left through village green, then just look to left! Entrance between 2 trees 200 yds on left.

Mrs Henriette Clifford
Frampton Court,
Frampton-on-Severn,
Gloucestershire GL2 7EX
tel   01452 740267
fax   01452 740698
e-mail   clifford.fce@farming.co.uk

GLOUCESTERSHIRE

Country roads swoop through soft countryside and into honey-coloured villages full of tempting shops and inns; neighbouring Nailsworth has stacks of good restaurants. At the Mill your surroundings are bucolic and the large lake at the side of the house is at windowsill level, giving you a strange feeling of being underwater! The lake, the mill race and Judy – genuinely friendly – make this place special. You have your own wing and entrance with sitting room. Bedrooms are fresh and simple. Bring the family and climb the hills.

rooms	2: 1 twin/double (extra single if needed), 1 twin both with shower room.
room price	£50-£56. Single occ. £32-£35.
meals	Several pubs close by.
closed	Christmas.
directions	From Stroud, A46 for Bath. After 2 miles right to North Woodchester then 2nd left, down hill, sharp right up short drive.

Mrs Judy Sutch
Southfield Mill,
Southfield Road, Woodchester,
Stroud,
Gloucestershire GL5 5PA
tel   01453 872896
fax   01452 872896
e-mail   judysutch@hotmail.com

GLOUCESTERSHIRE

GLOUCESTERSHIRE

A treat: utterly delightful people with wide-ranging interests (ex-British Council and college lecturing; arts, travel, gardening…) in a manor-type house full of beautiful furniture. The house was born of the Arts & Crafts movement and remains fascinating: wood panels painted green, a log-fired drawing-room for guests, quarry tiles on windowsills, handsome old furniture, comfortable proportions… elegant but human. The garden's massive clipped hedges and great lawn are impressive, as is the whole place. Refined but nevertheless easy.

Boyts is a handsome 16th-century stone farmhouse in two acres of superb, Italianate-style gardens. A magnolia climbs around wooden mullioned windows and there's more magic behind the oak front door: stone flags, huge fireplaces, Georgian panelling, polished wooden stairs. Stewed fruits from the garden for breakfast, served in a dining room whose walls are hung with interesting pictures. Bedrooms are lovely, and one comes with an original Thirties' bathroom. John and Sally are keen gardeners and it shows: wonderful ornamental ponds, orchards, ha-ha's, paddocks, a canal and plants for sale. Perfect peace, farmland views, gentle people.

rooms	3: 1 double, 2 twins, 1 with private bath/shower, 2 with shared bathroom.
room price	£68. Single occ. £44.
meals	Breakfast until 9.15am. Dinner £17.50. B.Y.O.
closed	December – January.
directions	B4060 from Stinchcombe to Wotton-under-Edge. 0.25 miles up long hill, house at top on left; gateway marked.

rooms	2: 1 double, 1 twin, both with bathroom.
room price	From £70. Single occ. from £35 – £40.
meals	Pub with restaurant 3 minutes' walk.
closed	21 December-2 January.
directions	From M5 junc. 16, A38 for Gloucester. Tytherington turn after 6 miles. From north, leave M5 at exit 14 & south on A38 for Bristol. Tytherington turn after 3 miles.

	Hugh & Crystal St John Mildmay
	Drakestone House,
	Stinchcombe, Dursley,
	Gloucestershire GL11 6AS
tel	01453 542140
fax	01453 542140

	John & Sally Eyre
	Boyts Farm,
	Tytherington, Wotton-under-Edge,
	Gloucestershire GL12 8UG
tel	01454 412220
fax	01454 412220
e-mail	jve@boyts.fsnet.co.uk

map: 9 entry: 197

map: 9 entry: 198

The Kings have farmed here for 75 years and 40 of those have been shared with B&B guests; Sonja really knows her stuff and the whole family is involved in the arable and dairy enterprise. The famous Westonbirt Arboretum – breathtaking whatever the season – is a stroll away across the field; the Kings' fine cedar tree sadly succumbed to the elements but its grand trunk is being planked to make a summer house. Bedheads have drapes that give the impression of a half-tester – and throughout the house are two generations' worth of fine needlework. An honest, good-value place without pretentions.

A glorious, sunny house in a park-like setting with large trees – the sense of space, peace and seclusion is memorable. There are family photographs, lovely furniture, interesting pictures, a grand piano and a musical atmosphere; bedrooms are pale and restful with books and pretty tea trays. Breakfasts of butcher's sausages, home-made bread and marmalade are taken in the formal dining room with views into the garden. There are walks all around this conservation area – Shipton Moyne is an award-winning village with its own famous pub, Westonbirt is next door and picnics for the Beaufort Polo Club can be arranged.

rooms	3: 1 double, 1 twin, both with shower room; 1 twin with shower room & separate wc.
room price	From £50. Single occ. £30.
meals	Pub 200 yds.
closed	Very occasionally.
directions	A433 from Tetbury for 5 miles. On entering Knockdown, farm on right before crossroads.

rooms	2 doubles, both with bath.
room price	£80. Single occ. by arrangement.
meals	Dinner, 2 courses, £25.
closed	24th December–1st January.
directions	From Tetbury, A433 for Bath. 1st left to Shipton Moyne. After 1 mile 1st right to Westonbirt. House 0.8 miles on left.

Sonja King
Avenue Farm,
Knockdown, Tetbury,
Gloucestershire GL8 8QY
tel   01454 238207
fax   01454 238033
e-mail   sonjames@breathemail.net

Susie & Antony Brassey
Hillcourt,
Shipton Moyne, Tetbury,
Gloucestershire GL8 8QB
tel   01666 880280

THE LITTLE EARTH BOOK

The Little Earth Book

Only dead fish float with the current;
live fish swim against it.

Did you know we
publish this remarkable
little book? It has sold
over 30,000 copies in
the last two years.

- It makes complex issues understandable. Many
  of us have browsed the 'environmental' or
  'economics' shelves in bookshops, have pulled
  down a book or two and then put them back. They
  are simply too academic. Or they demand too much
  commitment to reading time.

- It makes them quick to read about. It takes about
  under five minutes to get through each chapter –
  polish off the book in a series of sessions in the bath.

- It brings them all together so you may see the links.
  Thus, what on earth does Third World Debt have to
  do with Microbes and Cod? Lots – the book tells you.

- It inspires you. Some readers shift their views; others
  take up cudgels.

- It gives you the knowledge you need to act. There is
  stacks of pithy information/quotes/facts.

- It lightens it all up a bit! We try not to be too
  furrowed-browed about it all.

This third edition is, given the imminent Johannesburg
summit and the awful events of September 11th, of
huge importance.

Mike and Carolyn are inspiring – they've opened a fully organic restaurant above which sits an absolutely charming B&B. "We do it for spirit, not money," says Carolyn and it's a place with heart that we are delighted to include. Your bedroom may share a bathroom but each room is delightful – huge, like a studio, with oak floors or seagrass matting and lovely art on the walls. They've used local craftsmen to make the beds, light fittings, fire baskets, tables and crockery and you have your own entrance opposite the Herb Wheel.

Three cottages were knocked together to create this perfect little house, now listed and dripping with wisteria. Beams are exposed, walls are pale and hung with prints, floors are close-carpeted (pinky beige), curtains are floral, the sitting room is formally cosy, heavily beamed and classically English. You eat breakfast – probably organic and always local – in the conservatory overlooking the walled garden. The village is delightful, well-filled with good places to eat and drink. Many guests return time and again.

rooms	3: 2 doubles sharing bathroom; 1 twin with bathroom.
room price	£60. Single occ. £35.
meals	Fully organic restaurant.
closed	Last 2 weeks of January.
directions	M5, junc. 13, A419 to Stroud, then A46 south to Nailsworth. Right at r'bout & immed. left; restaurant & house are opp. Britannia Pub.

rooms	3: 1 double/family with shower room; 2 doubles, sharing bathroom.
room price	From £50. Single occ. £30.
meals	Good pub 100 yards.
closed	Very occasionally.
directions	From Cirencester A419 for Stroud. After 7 miles right to Bisley. Left at village shop. House 50 yds on right.

Carolyn & Mike Findlay
Heaven's Above at The Mad Hatters,
3 Cossack Square, Nailsworth,
Gloucestershire GL6 0DB
tel   01453 832615
fax   01453 832615
e-mail   mafindlay@waitrose.com

Brenda & Mike Hammond
Nation House,
George Street, Bisley,
Gloucestershire GL6 7BB
tel   01452 770197
e-mail   scott@earswick.fsworld.co.uk

A very special place: good taste, good value, warmth, peace, undaunting luxuriousness and homeliness – and a complete lack of pretension. Bridget, too, is delightful. The house has been here in the appropriately named hamlet of Calmsden ('place of calm') for 500 years and little seems to have changed. There's a lovely drawing room, wonky floors, beams that go the wrong way, ceilings that need ducking and lovely views. The double bedroom is gloriously sunny and light and you unwind among fat pillows and magazines. The smell of home-baked bread will lure you to the wood-panelled dining room. *Children by arrangement.*

rooms	3: 1 twin with bath/shower; 1 double with shower; 1 twin with private bathroom.
room price	£60-£70. Single occ. £35-£40.
meals	Excellent pub 1.5 miles away.
closed	December-February.
directions	From Cirencester A429 north. After 5 miles, 2nd left for Calmsden, just before Hare & Hounds pub. On for 1.5 miles. 3rd house on right.

Bridget Baxter
The Old House,
Calmsden, Nr. Cirencester,
Gloucestershire GL7 5ET
tel   01285 831240
fax   01285 831240
e-mail   baxter@calmsden.freeserve.co.uk

map: 9 entry: 203

English to the core – and to the bottom of its lovely garden where there many delightful places to sit. Steep honey-coloured gables, mullioned windows and weathered stone tiles enclose this lovely 17th-century house on a quiet village lane. Caroline is a calmly competent hostess with a talent for understated interior décor. You may sit in the very large dining room to read and the two ample, airy bedrooms are furnished with antiques and have either a *chaise longue* or easy chairs. Caroline can organise hire bikes to be delivered to the door.

rooms	2: 1 double, 1 twin, both with bath/shower.
room price	From £66. Single occ. £43.
meals	Excellent pub within easy walking distance.
closed	December – January.
directions	South through village from A417. Right after Masons Arms. House 200 yds on left.

Roger & Caroline Carne
The Old Rectory,
Meysey Hampton, Nr. Cirencester,
Gloucestershire GL7 5JX
tel   01285 851200
fax   01285 850452
e-mail   caroline.carne@lineone.net

map: 9 entry: 204

You feel the energy of a new start in old surroundings: here is a home created from a barn that just 10 years ago was derelict. The décor is fresh – so are the flowers – and the furniture and books old; all is bright and the conservatory looks over the garden that the Barrys have created. The charming owners are happy and proud to have you in their home. Beds are incredibly comfortable with excellent sheets and pillows; there are fine furniture and lovely paintings. This is unspoilt Cotswolds and this delightful house sits in splendid, peaceful isolation.

Chickens strut on the lawn – and what a manicured lawn for a working farm! Your charming hosts built the honey-stone house 20 years ago and have kept it immaculately. Light pours into perfectly proportioned rooms through windows hung with velvet and chintz; china sits in alcoves on both sides of the fireplace. Bedrooms, with lovely views, feel just right. After your expertly cooked breakfast – with eggs from those happy hens – you'll be ready for a swim or a game of tennis. Jeanie and James can organise fishing locally, and watersports, cycling and golf, too.

rooms	3: 1 double with bathroom; 1 double, 1 twin, sharing bath/shower.
room price	£64-£70. Single occ. by arrangement.
meals	Breakfast 8-9am. Excellent pubs & restaurants 0.3 miles.
closed	Christmas, New Year & Easter.
directions	From Cirencester A417 for Lechlade. At Meysey Hampton crossroads left to Sun Hill. After 1 mile left at cottage. House is 400 yds down drive.

rooms	2: 1 twin with bathroom; 1 twin/double with private bathroom.
room price	£60. Single occ. £40.
meals	Pubs/restaurants 1-4 miles.
closed	Christmas & New Year.
directions	A417 Cirencester-Fairford road. Pass Meysey Hampton sign & entrance on right opp. sign for Waitenhill & Cherry Tree House. Approx 1 mile from Meysey Hampton or 0.5 miles Fairford.

Richard & Jill Barry
Hampton Fields,
Meysey Hampton, Cirencester,
Gloucestershire GL7 5JL
tel   01285 850070
fax   01285 850993
e-mail   richard@hampflds.fsnet.co.uk

Jeanie Keyser
Lady Lamb Farm,
Meysey Hampton, Cirencester,
Gloucestershire GL7 5LH
tel   01285 712206
fax   01285 712206
e-mail   jekeyser1@aol.com

GLOUCESTERSHIRE

GLOUCESTERSHIRE

Look over the garden wall as you breakfast on home-made jams and home-laid eggs and enjoy those wonderful, long views. The garden, too, is worth a look – it has featured in magazines and James and Karin are passionate about it. The 16th- and 17th-century manor house has a flagstoned hall, huge fireplaces, sit-in inglenooks and Cotswold stone mullioned windows. One of the bedrooms has a secret door that leads to a surprising fuchsia-pink bathroom. The other, though smaller, has wonderful garden views. An easy-going and lovely house with owners to match.

Masses of charm and style here – this 1789 Cotswold farmhouse is clearly much loved: it lured Angela and Michael away from the city. Outbuildings, courtyards and cartsheds in the same warm stone, and a pool. Your hosts are friendly and fun and terrific cooks: Angela's *Cordon Bleu* trained. Breakfasts and dinners are served in the lovely, low-ceilinged dining room where oil paintings offset the beams and flagged floors. Country bedrooms have generous curtains in Colefax florals and *toile de Jouy*. There are robes in the bathrooms and walking and riding country all around. Ask if you may swim.

rooms	2: 1 double with bath/shower; 1 twin/double with bathroom.
room price	£70. Single occ. £50.
meals	Breakfast usually 8-9.30am. Pub/restaurants 5-15 mins' drive.
closed	Christmas.
directions	From Cirencester, A429 for Stow. Right at Apple Pie House Hotel, for Clapton. In village, pass triangular green on left & house straight ahead on left on corner.

rooms	3: 2 doubles (1 with extra single), 1 twin, all with bathroom.
room price	£70-£80. Single occ. £35-£45.
meals	Breakfast until 9.30am. Packed lunch £7. Dinner £25. Excellent pub within walking distance.
closed	Christmas.
directions	In middle of village, past Plough Inn on left; look for gates on right.

Karin & James Bolton
Clapton Manor,
Clapton-on-the-Hill,
Nr. Bourton-on-the-Water,
Gloucestershire GL54 2LG
tel 01451 810202
fax 01451 821804
e-mail bandb@claptonmanor.co.uk

Angela Storey
Grove Farm House,
Cold Aston, Cheltenham,
Gloucestershire GL54 3BJ
tel 01451 821801
fax 01451 821108
e-mail angela@cotswoldbedandbreakfast.com
web www.cotswoldbedandbreakfast.com

GLOUCESTERSHIRE

Cardinal Wolsey allegedly owned Rectory Farmhouse, then Henry VIII took it from him and gave it to Christ Church College, Oxford. Since then it has had only two private owners, such is its immense charm. Passing a development of converted farm buildings to get to the warm Cotswold stones of this place makes the discovery doubly exciting. Sybil, an interior decorator, has created something cool, beautiful and immaculate. Bed linen is white, walls cream; the huge enamel bath has a stunning pink exterior. Sybil used to own a restaurant; breakfast, next to the Aga, is a cosy affair.

rooms	3: 1 double with bath/shower; 1 double with bathroom; 1 suite with sitting room & shower room.
room price	From £68. Single occ. £45.
meals	Pub/restaurant 1 mile.
closed	Christmas & New Year.
directions	B4068 from Stow to Lower Swell, left just before Golden Ball Inn. Far end of gravel drive on right.

Sybil Gisby
Rectory Farmhouse,
Lower Swell, Stow-on-the-Wold,
Gloucestershire GL54 1LH

tel	01451 832351
e-mail	rectory.farmhouse@cw-warwick.co.uk

GLOUCESTERSHIRE

Astonishing! It feels palpably old – Elizabethan even – with superb mullioned windows, gables and great expanses of stoned, slated and thatched roofs with those unexpected corners which make old buildings so fascinating. Yet unbelievably, it was started in 1951. Cecil, a retired builder, and his family have thrown their home open to guests with generosity and bonhomie. There's an outdoor swimming pool flanked by an all-weather tennis court, croquet, a snooker/billiard room, a folly, a prize-winning garden and an arboretum with almost 300 species of trees. Immaculate and sumptuous, but also fun and special.

rooms	3: 2 doubles, both with bathroom; 1 double with private bathroom.
room price	£80. Single occ. £60.
meals	Good inn opposite. Restaurant/pub 100 yds.
closed	Very occasionally.
directions	Approach from Stow on A424 for 2 miles. Opposite Coach & Horses, right by postbox down single track lane. Entrance 100 yds on left.

C. J. Williams
Windy Ridge,
Longborough, Moreton-in-Marsh,
Gloucestershire GL56 0QY

tel	01451 832328/830465
fax	01451 831489
e-mail	cjw@windy-ridge.co.uk
web	www.windy-ridge.co.uk

The part-Tudor, part-Georgian house is named after the little river flowing through its back garden; Sudeley Castle is next door – just pass through the kissing gate into the glorious grounds. David (an organic grain merchant) and Felicity are gentle-mannered and easy and treat you to breakfasts with home-made and organic produce. One bedroom has a very comfortable, ornately carved four-poster; the twin, under the eaves, its own sun terrace. In the drawing room: oils on walls, antiques, an honesty bar and open fire. Winchcombe is such a satisfying little town, with useful shops, buzzing inns and a real sense of community.

Ample space for everyone to feel at ease – and you do so in luxury and style. You are on the site of an extinct medieval village that is mentioned in the Domesday book: until 1610 this was the village church. The hall and ground floor are stone-flagged, with rugs for colour, and there are delightful touches of exotica everywhere. One bedroom is massive. The gardens, set in 37 acres, are simply beautiful, with a trout lake, tennis court, pool and wonderful views. John and Camilla are wickedly funny and easy-going. Our inspector didn't want to come home. *Children over seven welcome.*

rooms	3: 1 double with shower room; 1 twin with private shower room; 1 four-poster with bath/shower.
room price	£60-£80. Single occ. £45-£60.
meals	Breakfast 8-9.30am. Excellent pubs/restaurants 2-5 minutes.
closed	Christmas and possibly Easter.
directions	Winchcombe is on A4632 between Cheltenham and Broadway. Turn into Castle St by White Hart in centre of village. House on left at bottom of steep hill.

rooms	3: 2 doubles, both with bath; 1 single with private bathroom.
room price	£48-£85.
meals	Supper £24. Excellent pub and restaurant nearby.
closed	Christmas.
directions	4 miles north of Moreton-in-Marsh on A429, left to Aston Magna. At 1st building, immed. right. House 0.75 miles on right, up drive.

Felicity & David King
Isbourne Manor House,
Castle Street, Winchcombe,
Cheltenham,
Gloucestershire GL54 5JA

tel	01242 602281
fax	01242 602281
e-mail	felicity@isbourne-manor.co.uk
web	www.isbourne-manor.co.uk

John & Camilla Playfair
Neighbrook Manor,
Nr. Aston Magna,
Moreton-in-Marsh,
Gloucestershire GL56 9QP

tel	01386 593232
fax	01386 593500
e-mail	info@neighbrookmanor.com
web	www.neighbrookmanor.com

map: 9 entry: 211

map: 9 entry: 212

GLOUCESTERSHIRE

Everything you could want from a glorious, truly English country home. The magnificent Georgian manor sits in 15 acres. The two-acre lake is alive with wildfowl and there's a little boat to paddle off in. You really should come with friends and make a house party of it; there are luxurious self-catering cottages in the old coaching yard. You can play tennis or croquet, swim, ride and clay pigeon shoot on the Bredon Hills. You can even get married here. Antique furniture, sumptuous beds and drapes and the super Herford family. Perfection. *Minimum stay two nights at weekends.*

rooms	5: 3 four-posters, 1 twin/double, 1 twin, all with bathroom. Self-catering cottages & Coach House sleep 2-11.
room price	£95-£120. Single occ. up to £75.
meals	Breakfast served in bed at no extra cost! Dinner: manor, from £35; cottages, £20. Pubs/restaurants 3 minutes' walk.
closed	Christmas. Self-catering never.
directions	From Cheltenham, A435 north, then B4079. About 1 mile after A438 x-roads, right to Kemerton. Leave road at War Memorial. House behind church.

Bill & Diana Herford
Upper Court,
Kemerton, Tewkesbury,
Gloucestershire GL20 7HY

tel	01386 725351
fax	01386 725472
e-mail	diana@uppercourt.co.uk
web	www.uppercourt.co.uk

map: 9 entry: 213

HAMPSHIRE

Neither theatrical flair nor tradition have been allowed to dominate the interior of the 17th-century home — each has amiably reined in the other. Real attention to detail in the bedrooms: thick robes, beautiful linen, bath oils, sherry. The ground-floor bedroom opens onto the terrace and has a huge walk-in shower. Cushions are piled high on the sofas in the sitting room where you'll find an honesty drinks tray. The conservatory looks onto a weeping willow and a magnolia, and the sea is a short sprint away. A perfect lovers' hideaway — you'll feel thoroughly spoiled. *Babes in arms and children over 10 welcome.*

rooms	3: 1 four-poster, 1 double, both with bath/shower; 1 twin/family room with private bathroom.
room price	£50-£90. Single occ. £50. Children £15.
meals	Breakfast until 9.30am. Restaurants 2 minutes' walk.
closed	Very occasionally.
directions	From Lymington, B3058 for Milford-on-Sea. House on left, just past village green.

Gary Payne & Simon Box
The Bay Trees,
8 High Street, Milford-on-Sea,
Hampshire SO41 0QD

| tel | 01590 642186 |
| fax | 01590 645461 |

map: 4 entry: 214

Wallow in comfort in an atmosphere of restrained elegance. Bedrooms feel fresh and you'll appreciate Josephine's attention to detail: fresh flowers, good reading lamps, radio, mineral water. This is a townhouse – on the road but quiet, especially at night. Lymington's myriad charms – cafés, restaurants and shops – are a stroll away. Narrow and deep, the Edwardian house has many lovely pieces of furniture, a dark red dining room, lots of books and some good oils. Bedrooms are furnished traditionally with tallboys, dressing tables and displays of good china. *Children over eight welcome.*

An excellent spot for anyone who enjoys walking, cycling, riding, wildlife, good country pubs and a sense of space – Sue's smallholding is on the edge of the New Forest. There's plenty of room for wet clothes and muddy boots, and cattle graze within 10 feet of the window. You may hear the call of a nightjar in June; Dartford warblers nest nearby. Sue keeps a few sheep, free-range poultry, a horse and two cats. Guests have their own little sitting room, warm, simple bedrooms, a friendly atmosphere and good home cooking. Uncomplicated country B&B.

rooms	2: 1 twin, 1 double, both with private bathroom.
room price	£50. Single occ. £35.
meals	Breakfast 7.30-9.30am. Good pubs/restaurants 200 yds.
closed	Christmas.
directions	From Brockenhurst A337 to Lymington. Pass hospital to lights on corner of Southampton Rd & Avenue Rd. Left into Avenue Rd. 20 yds on, a short driveway, 1st right, leads to back of house.

rooms	2: 1 double with bath/shower; 1 twin/double with bath.
room price	From £50. Single occ. from £30.
meals	Breakfast 7-9am. Packed lunch £6. Dinner from £13.
closed	Christmas & New Year.
directions	On A338, 1 mile south of Fordingbridge, left at small x-roads for Hyde & Hungerford. Up hill & right at school on corner for Ogdens. Left at next x-roads for Ogdens North. House on right at bottom of hill.

Josephine & David Jeffcock
West Lodge,
40 Southampton Road, Lymington,
Hampshire SO41 9GG
tel   01590 672237
fax   01590 673592
e-mail   jeffcock@amserve.net

Sue Browne
Sandy Corner,
Ogdens North, Fordingbridge,
Hampshire SP6 2QD
tel   01425 657295

map: 4 entry: 215

map: 4 entry: 216

Seagrass matting, Moroccan rugs, antiques and a woodburning stove all contribute to the easy atmosphere in this terrifically light and sunny 200-year-old barn. Lindy, who speaks French and lets out her French holiday home in the Lot, organises garden tours. You can relax on the terrace overlooking her pretty well-tended English garden with cornfields beyond, admire the waterfowl on the pond or saunter to the pub past the thatched cottages of this chocolate-box village. Golf, fishing and antique shops nearby. *Children over 10 welcome.*

A new house for Anthea, but the same enthusiastic welcome as in her previous Special Place. She adores her new home – it dates from the 13th century when Richard de Ranville sailed here from Normandy and settled his family. Now Grade II*-listed, it has herringbone brickwork – fascinating. There are five acres of garden and paddock, lovely prints, lots of books and large beds in big rooms that overlook a courtyard of old barns. The dining room – in the palest grey – has two large decorative carved wall lights. Anthea is a dynamo doing B&B for the fun of it.

rooms	3: 1 double with shower room; 1 twin with private bathroom; 1 studio double across courtyard with shower room & own front door.
room price	£50-£60. Single occ. from £35.
meals	Excellent pub in village.
closed	Christmas & New Year.
directions	From Salisbury, A354 for Blandford, through Coombe Bissett. After 1.5 miles, left on bend to Rockbourne. Through village, 200 yds after 30mph zone, house signed on left. After 50 yds, gravel drive on right.

rooms	3 twin/doubles, all with bath/shower; 1 of these can be a family room.
room price	£50-£60. Single occ. £35-£40.
meals	Pub/restaurant 1 mile.
closed	Christmas & New Year.
directions	Exit M27 at junc. 2, A3090 for Romsey. Climb hill, then look for 'Gardener's Lane' on left. Drive 100 yds further on, on south side of dual carriageway, house marked by a flagpole. Crossing marked with 2 white posts.

Lindy & Tony Ball
Marsh Barn,
Rockbourne, Fordingbridge,
Hampshire SP6 3NF

tel	01725 518768
fax	01725 518380

Bill & Anthea Hughes
Ranvilles Farm House,
Romsey,
Hampshire SO51 6AA

tel	02380 814481
fax	02380 814481
e-mail	antheahughes39@hotmail.com
web	www.ranvilles.com

map: 4 entry: 217

map: 4 entry: 218

Lovely people and a charming house, Georgian in look – rather like an old rectory. It sits in its own 15-acre grounds, yet is just minutes from Winchester and is elegantly decorated, full of antiques and ancestral portraits. The bedrooms have chintz, mahogany furniture and beautiful views. Sue modestly calls herself an "amateur artist" – some of her watercolours decorate the bedrooms. An inspiration to the energetic or the divinely inspired, the house is on the Pilgrim's Way so the walking is ready-made. *Children over 10 welcome.*

Complete privacy in a B&B is rare. Here you have it, and just 12 minutes' walk from the centre of town, cathedral and water meadows. Relax in your own half of a Victorian townhouse beautifully furnished and decorated, and immensely welcoming. Fizzy serves sumptuous breakfasts and fresh flowers abound – guests have been delighted. You are also left with an 'honesty box' so you may help yourselves to drinks. The rooms are small and cosy with lovely big, antique mirrors, bedspreads and furniture; there is a log fire in the sitting room and a small garden, too. *Children over seven welcome.*

rooms	2: 1 twin with bathroom; 1 twin with private bathroom.
room price	£55-£65. Single occ. £35-£40.
meals	Pub/restaurant 250 yds.
closed	Christmas & New Year.
directions	From M3, junc. 9, A272 to W'chester. At next r'bout, straight over. Left at small r'bout for Morestead, then immed. left. 1 mile after M'stead, right to O'bury. Through village, left to Whadden Lane. 200 yds down lane on left.

rooms	2: 1 twin, 1 double, both with shower & bath.
room price	£55-£60. Single occ. £50-£54.
meals	Dinner available nearby.
closed	Christmas.
directions	Leave M3 at junc. 9 & take A272 Winchester exit, then signs for Winchester Park & Ride. Under m'way, straight on at r'bout signed St Cross. Left at T-junc. St Faith's Rd about 100 yds ahead.

Sue & Tim Torrington
Great Hunts Place,
Owslebury, Nr. Winchester,
Hampshire SO21 1JL

tel	01962 777234
fax	01962 777242
e-mail	tt@byngs.freeserve.co.uk
web	www.byngs.freeserve.co.uk

Guy & Fizzy Warren
Brymer House,
29/30 St Faith's Road, St Cross,
Winchester,
Hampshire SO23 9QD

tel	01962 867428
fax	01962 868624
e-mail	brymerhouse@aol.com

Charles Dickens is said to have escaped the helter-skelter of London for the peace of the Test Valley to write at Yew Tree House. The warm red brick was there 200 years before him; the famous, conical-roofed dovecote at the end of the herbaceous border (to which you may have the key) 300 years before that. Here is understated elegance and deep tranquillity: a yellow-ochre bedroom with Descamps bed linen to match, cashmere/silk curtains designed by Philip and Janet's son, a profusion of flowers – the garden is gorgeous. The yew was the symbol of peace and plenty in medieval times; it is a fitting name.

Four generations of Hanbury-Batemans have lived here and much beautiful furniture remains from each. Wooden and stone floors reflect the light that floods in; upstairs, all is carpeted. Intriguing curios, statues and vases that Elisabeth, who is Austrian and an interior designer, brings together: faded elegance meets Edwardian opulence. Comfortable bedrooms have good bedside lamps and generous curtains and a traditional country-house feel. Super, mature gardens – you can play tennis or croquet – and, further afield, plenty of opportunities for fishing and walking. *Babes in arms and children over 12 welcome.*

rooms	2: 1 double with private bathroom; 1 twin, with shower room.
room price	£52. Single occ. £31.
meals	Good pubs in village; restaurants 5 miles.
closed	Very occasionally.
directions	From A30 travelling west of Stockbridge for 1.5 miles, left at minor x-roads. After 2 miles left at T-junc. House on left at next junction opposite Greyhound pub.

rooms	2: 1 twin with bath; 1 twin with basin & private bathroom.
room price	£70. Single occ. £45.
meals	Breakfast 7.30-10.30am. Nearest pub 1 mile, restaurant 5 miles.
closed	Very occasionally.
directions	From Andover, on A303, past petrol station, turn for Longparish. From B3048, 1st right for Forton, then 1st left onto private road.

Philip & Janet Mutton
Yew Tree House,
Broughton, Stockbridge,
Hampshire SO20 8AA
tel   01794 301227

Bill & Elisabeth Hanbury-Bateman
Forton House,
Long Parish, Andover,
Hampshire SP11 6NN
tel   01264 720236
fax   01264 720885
e-mail   bandbbest@aol.com

Super hosts and one of the greatest gardens in the book... seven tended acres sit within 100 acres of woodland. There are Japanese and dahlia gardens, azaleas and camellias, fine specimen trees, a formal terrace and exotica, all managed with flair and imagination. You breakfast in the chinoiserie dining room – the allegorical tableau is charming – and bedrooms are furnished in traditional style and have gorgeous garden views. The tennis court is hidden in the garden among some of the largest Wellingtonia in the country. The perfect English country house. *Children over 12 welcome.*

A lovely, beamy, roomy 16th-century farmhouse on a site with a medieval history. Harriet is planning a sculpture garden to add to the magic of the beautiful, two-acre landscaped gardens – already there is a lake, an upstairs conservatory, a heated covered pool, outdoor chess and a croquet lawn. Splendid breakfasts in the spectacular A-frame dining room, and the bedrooms are large, comfortable and even dramatic; one has a four-poster and a grand marble bathroom. Harriet and Julian are flexible and kind and will tell you about lovely walks in this designated AONB. *Children over eight welcome.*

rooms	2 twins, 1 with bathroom, 1 with private bathroom.
room price	From £60. Single occ. from £40.
meals	Dinner, with wine, £20.
closed	Christmas Day.
directions	South on A3 to lights at Hindhead. Straight across & after 400 yds, right onto B3002. Continue for 3 miles. Entrance (signed) on right in a wood.

rooms	3: 1 double, 1 four-poster, both with bath/shower; 1 twin, with bath.
room price	£60-£72. Single occ. by arrangement.
meals	Breakfast 8-9am. Good pubs within 10 minutes' drive.
closed	Christmas & New Year.
directions	From A272 at Rogate, turn for Harting & Nyewood. Cross humpback bridge; drive signed to right after 300 yds.

Jeremy & Philippa Whitaker
Land of Nod,
Headley, Bordon,
Hampshire GU35 8SJ
tel   01428 713609
fax   01428 717698

Harriet & Julian Francis
Mizzards Farm,
Rogate, Petersfield,
Hampshire GU31 5HS
tel   01730 821656
fax   01730 821655
e-mail julian.francis@hemscott.net

Pink fir-apple potatoes and orchard fruit often end up on the dinner table: food is taken seriously here (they've won awards) and dinner is a four-course banquet. Panache in the décor, too: luxurious drapes and medieval-style high-backed chairs in the dining room, leather sofas and oak floorboards in the sitting room. Bedrooms are fresh and bright; bathrooms are seductive (there's a *chaise longue* in one), candlelit and rather magical. The old farmhouse is perfectly quiet at night and Steve and Jill are warm and well-travelled. You'll feel at home. *Children over 10 welcome.*

A medieval, cruck-framed, house whose timbers – and there are lots – are probably 1,000 years old. Little of the structure has ever been altered. It is an absolute delight: stone floors, warm yellow paint, paned windows, fireplaces everywhere, wooden stairs, a piano and comfortable chairs. The countryside is 'pure', too, with 1,500 acres of National Trust land open to all just five miles away. The bedrooms are small – this was a yeoman's house – but no matter. One is dark blue with white bedcovers and a fireplace in the bathroom. Anita is easy-going and good company. Mind your head.

rooms	3: 1 double with private bathroom; 1 twin with shower room; 1 double with self-catering option (kitchen & shower).
room price	£70. Single occ. £45. Self-catering £60 (min. 3 nights).
meals	Dinner £25.
closed	Very occasionally.
directions	A4110 north to Wigmore. At 'Welcome' sign straight for 150 yds, then right. Drive 1st on left.

rooms	4: 1 twin, with bath; 1 double, 2 singles, sharing bathroom, for family group.
room price	£60. Singles £27.
meals	Dinner £20.
closed	Very occasionally.
directions	From Leominster, A49 for Ludlow. In Ashton, left & house on right behind postbox after 1 mile.

Steve Dawson & Jill Fieldhouse
Pear Tree Farm,
Wigmore,
Herefordshire HR6 9UR
tel   01568 770140
fax   01568 770141
e-mail   steveandjill@peartreefarmco.
          freeserve.co.uk
web   www.peartreefarmco.freeserve.co.uk

Mrs Anita Syers-Gibson
Bunns Croft,
Morton Eye, Leominster,
Herefordshire HR6 0DP
tel   01568 615836
fax   01568 610620

A wonderful place that, after Herculean labours, has been brought back to life by James and Henrietta. It is set in parkland, high above the River Lugg, with views to the Black Mountains. There are comforting features such as a cast-iron bath in an attractive, modern bathroom, huge (and many) windows releasing light into rooms filled with some grand old furniture and interesting prints. It is snug, cosy, grand and without pretence – country house living at its most appealing. They cook a great breakfast, too. *Children over five welcome.*

If you enjoy the luxuries of space and tranquillity, this immaculate house, full of old paintings and fine furniture, will make your heart sing. There are 11 fireplaces in the part-17th-, part-19th-century house, and bedrooms are large and airy, with perfect white linen and carpets soft underfoot; the double is fit for a king. Bathrooms are lavish. In the grounds, handsome lawns, mature trees and two kitchen gardens: Guy not only makes bread but also grows fruit and vegetables. Share them with your kind and considerate hosts at the grand dining table: Amanda loves to entertain. *Children over 12 welcome.*

rooms	3: 2 doubles, 1 twin, all with bathroom.
room price	£50-£60. Single occ. £35-£40.
meals	Dinner, 3 courses, £20.
closed	Christmas & Easter.
directions	From Leominster B4361 north. 0.5 miles on, left for Eyton. 1.5 miles on, left for Kingsland. House 0.5 miles on right.

rooms	2: 1 twin with bath; 1 double with bath/shower.
room price	£70. Single occ. £45.
meals	Packed lunch from £5. Dinner, 3 courses, £25 (with wine and pre-dinner drink).
closed	Occasionally.
directions	From Tenbury Wells to Leysters, on A4112, left at crossroads in village. Ignore sign to Leysters church. House on left, with wooden gate (after postbox in wall).

James & Henrietta Varley
Eyton Old Hall,
Eyton, Leominster,
Herefordshire HR6 0AQ
tel 01568 612551
fax 01568 616100
e-mail varleyeoh@hotmail.com
web www.eytonoldhall.fsnet.co.uk

Guy & Amanda Griffiths
The Old Vicarage,
Leysters, Leominster,
Herefordshire HR6 0HS
tel 01568 750208
fax 01568 750208
e-mail guy.griffiths@virgin.net
web www.oldvicar.co.uk

map: 8 entry: 227

map: 8 entry: 228

HEREFORDSHIRE

HEREFORDSHIRE

A fascinating place and with a butterfly house, too – Leslie is a keen lepidopterist. The 17th-century farmhouse, cider house, dairy, granary and 14-acre private nature reserve are perched at the top of a small valley; the views are tremendous. Excellent food: the Wiles use as many organic ingredients as possible, serve only organic wine, smoke their own fish and meat and make their own bread. One suite is across the courtyard, the other three in the granary annexe; they are all timber-framed and compact and have their own sitting rooms. You can be very private. *Children over eight welcome.*

What a treat to stay in a 17th-century farmhouse set high on a sheep-strewn hill – the views reach to the Cotswolds on a fine day. This is an attractive, listed house on a working farm with tennis court, croquet lawn, stables and extensive garden. More character than luxury lies within: big old fireplaces and beams, comfortable sofas and wonky floors that squeak. Bertie is a dab hand at breakfast, using home-produced free-range eggs; Caroline cooks a delicious dinner. Bedrooms are engagingly timeworn, with good carpets, fine old family furniture and views. Utterly peaceful – and fun.

rooms	4 suites, all with private bath/shower & sitting room.
room price	£67. Single occ. £43.50.
meals	Breakfast until 9.30am. Dinner £16.50–£24.50.
closed	Very occasionally.
directions	From Leominster, A49 north but turning right onto A4122, signed Leysters. Lower Bache then signed after village of Kimbolton. Look out for white butterfly sign.

rooms	2: 1 twin with private bathroom; further twin/double let to members of same party.
room price	£50. Single occ. £30.
meals	Dinner £18.
closed	Occasionally.
directions	From Bromyard Post Office, exactly 3 miles on B4203 for Great Witley. Pass Saltmarsh Castle on left. Next drive with double wooden gates, 60 yds on right.

Rose & Leslie Wiles
Lower Bache House,
Kimbolton, Nr. Leominster,
Herefordshire HR6 0ER
tel 01568 750304
e-mail leslie.wiles@care4free.net

Bertie & Caroline Cotterell
Upper Norton,
Tedstone Wafre, Bromyard,
Herefordshire HR7 4PN
tel 01885 483141
fax 01885 488710
e-mail bertie@woodenconcepts.plus.com

map: 8 entry: 229

map: 9 entry: 230

HEREFORDSHIRE

HEREFORDSHIRE

Breakfast beside the great log fire in the Tudor dining room on chilly mornings, or under the spreading chestnut tree on warm days. The house and your hosts are entirely natural and easy to be with and you will be most comfortable. The rambling old manor with gardens and croquet lawn sits just beside the lovely 12th-century church. Rooms are big, family-style, with books, flowers and garden views; bedrooms are without a whiff of anything designery. Relax after dinner in the cosy little oak-panelled sitting room. Two excellent pubs within walking distance, too.

Just walk into that barn and look up. Wow! The roof is breathtaking, a copse of beams and timbers. Few conversions are as successful as this one, but Judy is an artist, a painter, and impossibly resourceful – so, no surprise. It is fresh, new, bright and clean; comfortable, too, and as they have moved from Prior's Court (in previous editions of our book) they will bring cohorts of loyal fans – so come soon. It is a generous place and they will ferry you to the pub in the evening. Lovely people.

rooms	3: 2 doubles, 1 with bath, 1 with private bath; 1 twin with bathroom.
room price	£50. Single occ. £30.
meals	Breakfast until 9am. Packed lunch on request. Dinner £18.50. Excellent pubs under a mile.
closed	Very occasionally.
directions	From A417 south, left to Ullingswick at x-roads. Through village, left then right at signs to Ullingswick church. Drive on right before church lychgate.

rooms	2: 1 double with bath/shower; 1 twin/double with private bath & shower.
room price	£55. Single occ. £35.
meals	Dinner, 3 courses, £18.50. Pub 1 mile.
closed	Very occasionally.
directions	At Burley Gate r'bout on A417, A465 for Bromyard. At Stoke Lacy church, on right, right then 2nd right to entrance.

Christopher & Susan Dalton
Upper Court,
Ullingswick,
Herefordshire HR1 3JQ
tel   01432 820295
fax   01432 820174
e-mail   dalton.family@virgin.net

Roger & Judy Young
Dovecote Barn,
Stoke Lacy,
Herefordshire HR7 4HJ
tel   01432 820968
fax   01432 820969
e-mail   dovecotebarn@mail.com

HEREFORDSHIRE

An honest, authentic farmhouse with livestock, an assortment of farm buildings and a deep sense of rural peace. Elizabeth, a busy farmer's wife, manages it all efficiently with husband Peter – they were lambing when we were there. This is a traditional livestock and hop farm which still dries its own hops; in September you can watch their oast house at work. You will eat home-produced meat, preserves and vegetables – Elizabeth is a fine cook. The buildings, about 500 years old, ramble and enfold both gardens and guests. Bedrooms are timber-framed with bright fabrics.

rooms	3: 1 twin with shower room; 1 twin, 1 double, both with bathroom.
room price	£40-£50. Single occ. £28.
meals	Dinner, 3 courses, £14.
closed	Very occasionally.
directions	From Hereford, east on A438. A417 into Stretton Grandison. 1st right past village sign, through Holmend Park. Bear left past phone box. House on left.

Elizabeth & Peter Godsall
Moor Court Farm,
Stretton Grandison, Nr. Ledbury,
Herefordshire HR8 2TP
tel   01531 670408
fax   01531 670408

HEREFORDSHIRE

Forests must have fallen to build this house; the 1612 barn behind the Georgian façade is a soaring tangle of timbers, a paean to carpentry. The hall, open to the roof, is beautiful, with Chippendale panels in the staircase; oak beams and timber crucks are on bold display. Guests have a sitting room; breakfast is served in the beamed dining room. The bedrooms are comfortable; in some Judi provides towelling robes for the quick flit to the antique bath. A delightfully unexpected house with a charming hostess, and there is a lovely walled garden, too… all this in the centre of Ledbury.

rooms	3: 1 double with shower room; 1 double, 1 twin, both with basin, sharing bathroom.
room price	£58-£65. Single occ. from £48.
meals	Good selection of pubs/restaurants, 50 yards.
closed	Christmas & New Year.
directions	From Ledbury bypass, A449 for Worcester/town centre. House on left just past Somerfield but before central town crossroads.

Judi Holland
The Barn House,
New Street, Ledbury,
Herefordshire HR8 2DX
tel   01531 632825
e-mail   barnhouseledbury@lineone.net
web   www.thebarnhouse.net

You sleep in the ancient heart of the house, among 12th-century timbers and 18th-century additions. Grove House is wonderfully warm and cosseting – the dark wood gleams and large, luxurious rooms glow in firelight. In the elegant guests' drawing room there are books by the fire and plump armchairs and sofas to sink into and, in the bedrooms, window-seats, ornately carved canopied beds and Jacobean panelling. Michael is an excellent cook and dinner is a special occasion, so do eat in. You can play tennis, swim in the neighbour's pool or walk the Malvern Hills. Perfect.

The front is Georgian, the back Victorian. Inside, thick, thick walls and stone flags speak of a more ancient history. Valerie and Carol are clearly content in their uncontrived home and their grandchildren are regular visitors; your children may share toys in the house and garden. The pretty, traditional bedrooms have marvellous views of the richly wooded countryside and you also have your own large piece of the two-and-a-half-acre garden and use of the tennis court. There's a small library and music appreciation is high on the agenda.

rooms	3: 1 twin/double, 2 four-posters, all with bath/shower.
room price	£73. Single occ. £51.50.
meals	Dinner £24.
closed	Christmas & New Year.
directions	Leave M50 at junc. 2, for Ledbury. 1st left to Bromsberrow Heath. Right by Post Office & up hill. House on right.

rooms	3: 2 doubles sharing bathroom; 1 twin with private bathroom.
room price	£49. Under 5s £5; 5s-12s, £15. Single occ. from £24.50.
meals	Restaurants a short drive.
closed	Very occasionally.
directions	From Ross-on-Wye east on A40 for Gloucester. Right to Hope Mansell. Take 3rd lane on left opp. gallery. After 1 mile, house on left between lane signed 'village hall' & church.

Michael & Ellen Ross
The Grove House,
Bromsberrow Heath, Ledbury,
Herefordshire HR8 1PE
tel   01531 650584
e-mail   rossgrovehouse@amserve.net

**Mrs Carol Ouvry &
Mrs Valerie Godson**
The Old Rectory,
Hope Mansell, Ross-on-Wye,
Herefordshire HR9 5TL
tel   01989 750382
fax   01989 750382
e-mail   rectory@mansell.wyenet.co.uk

HEREFORDSHIRE

HEREFORDSHIRE

A setting that reminds you of much that is special about this corner of Britain: the Monnow Valley, the Brecon Beacons, the Black Mountains – an ever-changing scene of lush tranquillity. The house is small, late Victorian and filled with warmth and charm; you eat Aga-cooked breakfasts and dinners at a long plank table and Caroline is an accomplished cook. The Knights Templar, then the Knights of St John, once owned Garway Church; it is a Norman gem. Somehow, the tranquillity and assurance of the church have communicated themselves to this house. *Children over eight welcome.*

Jamie is a salmon-smoker so breakfast may well be even better than you hoped. Eggs are free-range, sausages are local, china is of fine bone, and beds are huge with sheets of Egyptian cotton: comfort at every turn. It is a handsome house slap in the middle of town, a few paces from the town hall and, of course, the cathedral, traditionally furnished and full of kind touches such as a tea tray with organic shortbread and proper coffee. There is no sitting room, but there's so much right on your doorstep that you won't mind.

rooms	2: 1 twin, 1 four-poster, both with basin, sharing bathroom. Separate shower & wcs.
room price	£40-£50. Single occ. £25-£35.
meals	Dinner from £17.50.
closed	Very occasionally.
directions	From Hereford A49 for Ross. After 5 miles A466 for Monmouth. After 7 miles B4521 for Abergavenny. At Broad Oak right for Garway. 1st right past school to Garway Hill. House 150 yds on right.

rooms	2 doubles, both with bath/shower.
room price	From £60. Single occ. £45.
meals	Packed lunch from £5. Pub/restaurant, 5 minutes' walk.
closed	Very occasionally.
directions	In centre of Hereford, beside town hall in St Owen Street, on right-hand side. Detailed instructions given at time of booking.

	Caroline Ailesbury
	The Old Rectory,
	Garway,
	Herefordshire HR2 8RH
tel	01600 750363
fax	01600 750364
e-mail	garwayoldrectory@yahoo.co.uk

	Jamie & Elizabeth Forbes
	Montgomery House,
	12 St Owen Street, Hereford,
	Herefordshire HR1 2PL
tel	01432 351454
fax	01432 344463
e-mail	lizforbes@lineone.net
web	www.montgomeryhousehereford.com

map: 8 entry: 237

map: 8 entry: 238

HEREFORDSHIRE

An ecclesiastic entrance hall sweeps you into this imposing, red-brick former Victorian vicarage; it was built for a wealthy friend of the diarist Francis Kilvert. Your attentive hostess Jill has redecorated the light and well-proportioned rooms with period furniture, good fabrics and attractive, plain colours: we liked the large double with French bed and roll-top bath. There's a sitting room for guests to relax in and plans for the garden are well under way. Come for peace and elegance in a rural setting. Marvellous Wye Valley views, too.

rooms	2: 1 double with bath & shower; 1 twin with private bathroom.
room price	From £50. Single occ. by arrangement.
meals	Breakfast until 9.30am. Dinner £16. Packed lunch from £3.50. Pub 5 miles.
closed	Christmas.
directions	A438 from Hereford, then A480 to Stretton Sugwas. After 10 miles from Hereford, left to Norton Wood & church. House 1st on right.

Jill & Julian Gallimore
The Old Vicarage,
Norton Canon, Hereford,
Herefordshire HR4 7BQ
tel   01544 318146
e-mail galli@gallimore.me.uk

HEREFORDSHIRE

So, you've decided to escape to some peace and quiet in the Welsh mountains, with the only man-made noise a passing tractor. The good life is here, presided over by intelligent, humorous and unfussy people who have got their priorities right. The feel is homely, the furniture antique, the atmosphere natural. Up the picture-lined staircase to good bedrooms and a deep sleep. Local sausages and bacon for breakfast and a lovely garden to explore; the variety and colour of the springtime flowers is astonishing.

rooms	2: 1 double with private bathroom; 1 twin sharing bathroom.
room price	£50. Single occ. £25.
meals	Dinner £15.
closed	Very occasionally.
directions	A480 from Hereford, after 10 miles right onto B4230 for Weobley. After 1.75 miles turn right; house is 2nd on left over cattle grid.

Dawn & Michael MacLeod
Garnstone House,
Weobley,
Herefordshire HR4 8QP
tel   01544 318943
fax   01544 318197

History comes alive in this gracious 16th-century manor house, visited by Wordsworth and King Charles II (who danced on the landing...); it is in a charming black and white village and surrounded by beautiful gardens and real countryside. The wrought-iron gates were admired by Pevsner and date from 1720. There are period furnishings throughout and you sleep in high brass beds with linen sheets; bathrooms are large and comfortable. Relax in front of the huge fire in the flagstoned hall or sit by the pool in summer.

Super hosts – a concert singer and a wine merchant – in whose company you can't fail to unwind. You have all the advantages of being in a small town with a rural atmosphere thrown in; on one side, the church, on the other, a large garden which disappears into rolling hills. The dining room is magnificent, with full-height Georgian windows and shutters, oak burr sideboard and ornate bookcase. The décor is charming with bare boards and paintwork effects and there are cotton sheets, flowers, lovely china, a roll-top cast-iron bath. For breakfast, home-made marmalades and jams.

rooms	2: 1 twin with bath & shower; 1 double with private bath & shower.
room price	From £50. Single occ. £30.
meals	Dinner from £15. Good pubs/restaurants 3 miles.
closed	Very occasionally.
directions	From Leominster, A44 & follow signs for Brecon. After 6 miles, left into Dilwyn. Round 3 sharp bends. House set back on right behind stone gate piers & railings.

rooms	2: 1 double, 1 twin, both with basin, sharing bathroom.
room price	From £50. Single occ. £30.
meals	Breakfast until 9.30am. Pubs/restaurants 400 yds.
closed	Christmas & New Year.
directions	Coming into Kington, follow signs for town centre. Through middle of town & up long steady hill to St Mary's church. On left opposite.

Tom & Jane Hawksley
The Great House,
Dilwyn, Hereford,
Herefordshire HR4 8HX
tel   01544 318007

Andrew & Lis Darwin
Church House,
Church Road, Kington,
Herefordshire HR5 3AG
tel   01544 230534
fax   01544 231100
e-mail   darwin@kc3.co.uk
web   www.churchhousekington.co.uk

map: 8 entry: 241

map: 8 entry: 242

The house's views alone might earn it a place in this book. But there's so much more… a beautifully furnished interior, an interesting four-acre garden with perfumed rose walk, and Stephanie and John, who work unobtrusively to make your stay relaxing and enjoyable. They are natural hosts, good fun, and have combined vibrant colours with elegance. The rooms are gracious with fine family paintings and furniture; from the sofa in your exceptionally comfortable bedroom gaze across the Wye Valley to the Malvern Hills and west to the Black Mountains – glorious. Stephanie's cooking is worth a detour.

rooms	2: 1 twin with bath, 1 double with private bathroom.
room price	From £56. Single occ. £28.
meals	Breakfast 8-9am. Packed lunch from £3.50. Dinner from £16.
closed	Christmas.
directions	From A438 Hereford/Brecon road, for Kington on A4111 through Eardisley village. 2 miles up hill on left, behind a long line of conifers.

Stephanie & John Grant
Bollingham House,
Eardisley, Herefordshire HR5 3LE
tel   01544 327326
fax   01544 327880
e-mail bollhouse@bigfoot.com

map: 8 entry: 243

Breathtaking in its ancient dignity, most of the house was built in 1500, and its undulating floors, great oak beams and two-foot thick walls are awe-inspiring. There are splashes of colour and candles everywhere and the timber-framed bedrooms are exceptional. The four-poster room has an Indian-style bathroom with ornate carved wood and a huge roll-top bath; the suite has a four-poster bed and a sitting area with two sofas. There's a guest sitting room, too. Jackie spoils you with sherry and wine or chocolates for special occasions. In summer the garden is filled with the scent of herbs and flowers.

rooms	3: 1 double, 1 four-poster, 1 suite with four-poster, all with bathroom.
room price	£56-£74. Single occ. from £42.
meals	Pubs 2 minutes' walk away.
closed	Christmas.
directions	From Hereford, A438 into village. House on left with a green sign & iron gates.

Jackie Kingdon
Winforton Court,
Winforton, Herefordshire HR3 6EA
tel   01544 328498
fax   01544 328498
e-mail winfortoncourt@talk21.com

map: 8 entry: 244

HEREFORDSHIRE

HEREFORDSHIRE

The picture belies the inviting warmth inside – the sitting room is snug with a woodburner and sofas and the kitchen is very much the gravitational centre of the home. Grace is chatty and informal and very settled in her unpretentious, modernised mill house. Rooms are small, with exposed beams and slate window sills, and only the old mill itself interrupts the views of the surrounding greenness. You drift off to sleep to the sound of the Arrow River burbling nearby – a real tonic for frazzled city-dwellers. *Children over four welcome.*

Floorboards squeak and creak in this lovely 17th-century grain barn, renovated by the Tong family with weatherboarding and stone tiling. It has a vast open threshing bay which frames the Welsh border woods and hills – an old-time idyll of rural England. The cattle byres house the conservatory; the bedrooms have simple modern furniture and share a shower room (a quick trot downstairs for those in the family room). Ann makes her own bread and preserves which she serves to guests. Superb views, honest value and rustic simplicity.

rooms	3: 1 double with shower; 1 double, 1 twin, sharing bathroom & wc.
room price	£36-£44. Single occ. £18-£22.
meals	Dinner from £12.
closed	Christmas.
directions	A438 from Hereford. After Winforton & Whitney-on-Wye & after toll bridge on left, sharp right for Brilley. Left fork to Huntington, over x-roads & next right to Huntington. Next right into 'No through' road, then 1st right.

rooms	2: 1 family (double & single), 1 twin, sharing shower & wc.
room price	£44. Single occ. £22. Under 12s, £16.
meals	Breakfast about 8.30am. Packed lunch from £3. Dinner £16. B.Y.O.
closed	Very occasionally.
directions	From Hay, B4350 to Clifford. Pass castle & right to Bredwardine. 3rd left at top of hill, for Priory Wood. Pass between chapel & small fenced playing field. Barn is ahead on right.

Grace Watson
Hall's Mill House,
Huntington, Kington,
Herefordshire HR5 3QA
tel   01497 831409

Ann Tong
Castleton Barn,
Priory Wood, Clifford,
Nr. Hay-on-Wye,
Herefordshire HR3 5HF
tel   01497 831690
fax   01497 831296

map: 8 entry: 245

map: 8 entry: 246

HEREFORDSHIRE

Gleaming oak floors and staircases are a proud feature of this 17th-century Grade II-listed cottage. Bedrooms are large and beds comfortably firm. The welcome from Linda is friendly but reserved, with guests free to come and go as they please; she and Ed tend to keep to their own part of the house. A postbox by the front door is all that remains of the cottage's past. Tired walkers can recover here after a stint in the Welsh Borders; bookworms can seek out the second-hand bookshops of Hay-on-Wye. Whichever activity you choose, you'll be captivated by the beauty of the area. Superb vegetarian breakfasts are served.

rooms	3: 1 double/family, 1 twin/double, 1 double, all with shower room.
room price	£56. Single occ. £28.
meals	Breakfast from 8.30am. Good pub 2 miles. Pubs/restaurants in Hay-on-Wye.
closed	Very occasionally.
directions	From Hay-on-Wye take Brecon road. After 0.5 miles, left, signed to Llanigon. On for 1.5 miles & left before school. Old Post Office is white building on right opp. church.

Linda Webb
The Old Post Office,
Llanigon, Hay-on-Wye,
Herefordshire HR3 5QA

tel	01497 820008
web	www.oldpost-office.co.uk

HERTFORDSHIRE

Lutyens built this wonderful 1901 house, set down a long drive in six acres of beautiful gardens and fields, for his mother-in-law, Lady Lytton. Each elevation of the house is different. Architectural peculiarities – such as internal, octagonal windows – abound and Samantha has applied her considerable artistic skills to the interior; the downstairs rooms, particularly, are elegant and formal. Unusual colour schemes offset magnificent antiques, tapestries and chinoiserie. The family are happy to share their home, can converse in a clutch of languages and will book tables and taxis if required.

rooms	3: 1 double with shower; 1 family suite (1 double/1 twin) with bath; 1 double with private shower sometimes available.
room price	£70. Single occ. £45. Family suite £70 for 2, £15 per extra person.
meals	Breakfast from 7.15am. Pub 15 minutes' drive.
closed	20 December-3 January.
directions	Into Knebworth on B197, turn into Station Rd which becomes Park Lane. 300 yds after crossing m'way bridge, left into public footpath. After 300 yds, bear left through lodge gates. House at end.

Samantha Pollock-Hill
Homewood,
Knebworth,
Hertfordshire SG3 6PP

tel	01438 812105
fax	01438 812572
e-mail	sami@pollock-hill.fsnet.co.uk
web	www.homewood-bb.co.uk

HERTFORDSHIRE

O ld-fashioned roses, pelargoniums, a willow tunnel and 40 (thriving) varieties of clematis – a horticultural haven amid open fields. Sue, relaxed and friendly, will point you towards rare wildflower sites in this remote spot. Her green fingers have been at work in the pretty conservatory too, where you eat breakfast – local sausages and home-made muffins – surrounded by greenery and memorable views. Bedrooms are cottagey: we liked the double with its white and brass bed. The peachy guest sitting room is elegant and has doors that open onto the garden. *Children over 12 welcome.*

rooms	3: 1 double with shower room; 1 twin, 1 single, both with private bathroom.
room price	From £65. Single occ. from £35.
meals	Pub 0.5 miles.
closed	Christmas & New Year.
directions	South on A413 from Wendover. Pass Jet station, left to Kings Ash. 2 miles on, left at x-roads to Old Swan pub. Pass pub. 0.5 miles on, ignore sharp right, but go sharp left onto bridlepath. 2nd gate along.

Mike & Sue Jepson
Field Cottage,
St Leonards, Nr. Tring,
Hertfordshire HP23 6NS
tel 01494 837602
fax 01494 837137
e-mail michael.jepson@lineone.net

map: 10 entry: 249

HERTFORDSHIRE

T he whole place is peppered with antiques and has an undeniable charm, but you don't have to tiptoe for fear of spoiling a contrived tidiness – Julia is easy-going and natural. Bedrooms are beamy and snug; the en suite room is under the thatch with garden views, the other two look onto an avenue of horse chestnuts that were planted on the village green to commemorate the jubilee of George V. There's a duck pond and an excellent village pub. Hard to believe that this 15th-century cottage is only five minutes' drive from Stansted; no noise here, though – the flight path is in the opposite direction.

rooms	3: 2 doubles, 1 twin, all with bath.
room price	From £55. Single occ. from £35.
meals	Packed lunch £3-£5.
closed	Very occasionally.
directions	From Stansted Mountfitchet B1051 for approx. 3 miles, through Elseham. Left for Henham. Right at war memorial. Wood End Green on right with avenue of large trees. Cottage on far right corner.

George & Julia Griffiths
Pleasant Cottage,
Wood End Green, Henham,
Bishops Stortford,
Hertfordshire CM22 6AZ
tel 01279 850792
fax 01279 850792
e-mail george@pleasantcott.fsnet.co.uk

map: 10 entry: 250

You sleep on a French rosewood bed, and there's a huge cast-iron bath *in* your room – ideal for wallowing in by candlelight with a glass of wine. There's a head-clearing simplicity to this unique 'first-floor' Saxon house with living space on top and the windowless ground floor reserved for defence purposes or storage. Limewashed walls, wooden floors and exposed A-frame beams in both bedrooms – and there's a secluded garden. The cottage with huge sofa and Shaker-style dining furniture is equally stunning. *Children over 12 welcome.*

The Harrisons bought this stunning Jacobean pile for its matchless gardens: 15 acres of pathed wilderness, exotic and subtropical flowers. A stroll is an adventure; you come across an old swimming pool with cascading plants, a bench on a lofty vantage point, a crystal clear stream banked with bamboo, a smooth lawn, a walled garden, a sunken rose garden and a grass tennis court. In a quiet village in lovely downland this massive house has inviting rooms and acres of space. Come to the Isle of Wight if only to see the garden.

rooms	2 + cottage: 1 double with bath; 1 double with bath/shower. Self-catering cottage sleeps 4+.
room price	£60-£80. Single occ. by arrangement. Cottage £300-£620 p.w.
meals	Good pub 1.5 mile.
closed	Never.
directions	0.5 miles south of Chale Green on B3399; after village, left at Gotten Lane; house at end of lane.

rooms	6: 3 doubles, 3 twins, all with bath/shower, in two separate wings.
room price	£50-£65. Single occ. £34-£45.
meals	Breakfast 8-9.15am. Light meals sometimes available. Pub 3 minutes' walk through gardens.
closed	Christmas.
directions	From Newport, drive into Shorwell, down a steep hill, under a rustic bridge & right opp. thatched cottage. Signed.

Caroline Smith
Gotten Manor,
Gotten Lane, Chale,
Isle of Wight PO38 2HQ
tel   01983 551368
fax   0870 1369453
e-mail   b&b@gottenmanor.co.uk
web   www.gottenmanor.co.uk

John & Christine Harrison
North Court,
Shorwell,
Isle of Wight PO30 3JG
tel   01983 740415
fax   01983 740409
e-mail   christinenorthcourt@msn.com
web   www.wightfarmholidays.co.uk/
          northcourt

map: 4 entry: 251

map: 4 entry: 252

This beautiful, porticoed, brick house has a gorgeous drawing room, fabulous antiques and family portraits. There's a secret garden within the grounds and an arbour and a pond. The large front bedroom is tremendous, more like a suite, with good furniture, fine views and an open fire in winter – a rare treat. Bathrooms have towelling robes, shower caps, etc. John is unflappable and a touch mischievous; Gillian welcomes you into their home with well-judged humour and easy charm – you'll like them. *Children over 12 welcome.*

The six acres of gardens with pond, obelisk and orchards are immaculate, the views in this AONB are magnificent and Susan and Markham genuinely enjoy meeting new people. This is a large, traditional country house – strong colours contrast well with dark, antique furniture and Liberty prints; the hall is hung with Chinese silk carpet and Thai and Indian pictures. The music room has an organ that Markham plays, occasionally giving concerts for charity – guests are welcome to attend. There is a luxurious indoor pool.

rooms	3: 1 double with bathroom; 2 doubles, both with private bathroom.
room price	From £70. Single occ. £40.
meals	Breakfast until noon. Dinner £25.
closed	Christmas & New Year.
directions	From Dover, M2 to Medway Services. Into station, on past pumps. Ignore exit signs. Left at T-junc., 1st left & on for 2 miles. Left at next T-junc. House 3rd on left.

rooms	3: 1 double, 1 twin, 1 four-poster, all with shower room.
room price	£64-£70. Single occ. £38-£41.
meals	Breakfast until 9.15am. Dinner, 2 courses, £17.
closed	Christmas.
directions	From A2 at Faversham, Brogdale road to Eastling. 1.5 miles past Carpenters Arms, right (by postbox). House 0.5 miles on right.

Gillian & John Yerburgh
Hartlip Place,
Place Lane, Nr. Sittingbourne,
Kent ME9 7TR

tel	01795 842583
fax	01795 842763
e-mail	jyerburgh@aol.com

Susan & Markham Chesterfield
Frith Farm House,
Otterden, Faversham,
Kent ME13 0DD

tel	01795 890701
fax	01795 890009
e-mail	enquiries@frithfarmhouse.co.uk
web	www.frithfarmhouse.co.uk

A charming, compact, Regency house built by a Sandwich brewer of ginger beer. Katie has decorated, sponged and stencilled to perfection; the rooms are gorgeous, spotless, dotted with much-loved antiques, fresh with flowers. Bathrooms are warm and well-equipped; one big, cast-iron bath has great taps that fill it in seconds. There are rare and spectacular oriental plane trees on either side of the main gate and stunning hedges and lawns. The area hums with history and Katie and Neil – who runs an Audio Book Library from the converted stables – are enchanting. *Children over eight welcome.*

The welcome is big and genuine, the feel is family and the value terrific. You are encouraged to relax into the space: a sitting room with two inglenooks, a lovely big garden, and another sitting room in your own wing. Chris, an umpire, runs a hockey and cricket shop and the two grown-up boys play county level/national sport. Jac cheerfully deals with everyone's needs – she'll drive you into Canterbury, babysit and prepare suppers; Chris cooks a great breakfast. Bedrooms are spotless and fresh with floral borders; bathrooms are modern and sparkling.

rooms	2 doubles/twins, both with bath/shower.
room price	£80. Single occ. £55.
meals	Dinner £26. Light suppers on request.
closed	Christmas & New Year.
directions	From Canterbury A257 for Sandwich. On approach to Ash, stay on A257 (do not enter village), then 3rd left at sign to Weddington. House 200 yds down on left.

rooms	3: 1 double, 1 twin/double, both with shower; 1 double with adjoining twin (only let to same group) with bath.
room price	From £40. Single occ. by arrangement. Children £5-£15.
meals	Lunch £5. Dinner £10.
closed	Very occasionally.
directions	From M20 exit 11, B2068 for Canterbury. After crossing A2, house, with postbox in wall, is 100 yds on right. (Head for county cricket ground & phone if lost.)

	Katie & Neil Gunn
	Great Weddington,
	Ash, Nr. Canterbury,
	Kent CT3 2AR
tel	01304 813407
fax	01304 812531
e-mail	traveltale@aol.com
web	www.greatweddington.co.uk

	Chris & Jac Bray
	Sylvan Cottage,
	Nackington Road, Canterbury,
	Kent CT4 7AY
tel	01227 765307
fax	01227 478411
e-mail	jac@sylvan5.fsnet.co.uk

map: 6 entry: 255

map: 6 entry: 256

Rolling hills and woodland, long views over luscious Kent, and a lovely garden that Alison has created entirely herself. This is a modern bungalow, a rare phenomenon in this book, a Scandia house built from a Swedish kit. It is brilliant for wheelchair users and altogether easy and comfortable to be in, with floral-covered sofas and chairs and plain reproduction furniture. Alison is sweet, very much a 'coper' who used to live here with her disabled father. The house is so close to Dover that it is worth staying here for the night before embarking on the ferry fray.

Peter and Mary make a happy team and their conversation is informed and easy. Anthony Eden stayed here during the Second World War to be close to the Channel defences; today you may stay for Chunnel convenience. Downstairs are many beams, large leather Chesterfield sofas, a polished dining table, wooden floors. And there's much magic outside: a wisteria-smothered façade, a croquet lawn, a tennis court and sheep happy to keep the field clipped. Food is excellent. And the bedrooms? One has a Delft-tiled fireplace, one is half-timbered, and the single has a wonderful pink marble sink.

rooms	2: 1 double with bath/shower; 1 twin with private bath/shower.
room price	£70. Single occ. £35.
meals	Dinner occasionally available. Pubs within walking distance.
closed	Christmas.
directions	From A2 Canterbury-Dover, Barham & Kingston sign. Right at bottom of hill by bus shelter, into The Street, Kingston to top of hill and right fork. 1st left on sharp right bend. 100 yds left into farm keeping right of barn.

rooms	3: 1 double, 1 single, both with bath/shower; 1 twin, with private bath/shower.
room price	£54-£60. Single £30.
meals	Dinner £20. Good pubs & restaurants 1 mile.
closed	Christmas.
directions	A2 Canterbury to Dover road; take Barham exit. Through Barham to Elham. After Elham sign 1st right signed Park Gate 0.75 miles. Over brow of hill; house on left.

Alison Crawley
Hornbeams,
Jesses Hill, Kingston, Canterbury,
Kent CT4 6JD
tel 01227 830119
fax 01227 830119

Peter & Mary Morgan
Park Gate,
Elham, Nr. Canterbury,
Kent CT4 6NE
tel 01303 840304
fax 01227 450498

map: 6 entry: 257

map: 6 entry: 258

The Lathams are well-travelled, friendly and active, yet firmly attached to their home and its surrounding 200 acres. The house has an interesting mix of styles: Tudor, Georgian and modern co-exist in harmony. High ceilings and a conservatory with terracotta-tiled floor, brimming with greenery, conjure up images of the decadent Twenties. You'll find good furniture, yet the house is homely; bedrooms are comfortable with traditional bathrooms. Guests have their own log-fired drawing room with wonderful views of all that countryside. Only 10 minutes from the Chunnel. *Children over 10 welcome.*

Not only are you in the depths of the country but you are wonderfully private too: your ground-floor bedroom is reached via a corner of the garden that is all your own. Through the garden to the breakfast room, a cosy place, with old pine table and dresser, flowers and greenery, for bacon and eggs – or three-course dinner. (If you don't feel like emerging Sarah is happy to bring you breakfast in your room.) This is a good stopover point for the Channel – and you're just 15 minutes from Canterbury Cathedral. *Babies welcome.*

rooms	3: 2 twins, both with bath/shower; 1 double, let only to members of same party willing to share a bathroom.
room price	From £55. Single occ. £32.50.
meals	Breakfast until 9.30am. Dinner £20-£25.
closed	Christmas & New Year.
directions	From M20 junc. 11, B2068 north. After 4.6 miles, left opp. Jet garage. House at bottom of hill on left, after 1.7 miles. Left into drive.

rooms	1 double with bath/shower.
room price	£60. Single occ. £30.
meals	Breakfast until 9.30am. Packed lunch £5. Dinner, 3 courses, £20.
closed	Very occasionally.
directions	From A2, 2nd exit to Canterbury. Follow ring road & B2068 for Hythe. Over A2, on for 2 miles, through Lower Hardres, past Granville pub. Right for Petham & Waltham. 1.5 miles after Waltham, right into Hassell St. 4th on left.

Richard & Virginia Latham
Stowting Hill House,
Stowting, Nr. Ashford,
Kent TN25 6BE
tel   01303 862881
fax   01303 863433
e-mail   vjlatham@hotmail.com

Sarah Rainbird
Woodmans,
Hassell Street, Hastingleigh,
Nr. Ashford,
Kent TN25 5JE
tel   01233 750250

map: 6 entry: 259

map: 6 entry: 260

Lord (Bob) Boothby once occupied the timber-framed Wealden house; the snug double above the study was his bedroom. So robust is the building that it survived intact when it slid 50 feet down the escarpment in a dramatic subsidence in 1726. A striking entrance leads straight to the huge sitting room, with massive fireplace and panelled oak staircase. Everywhere 18th- and 19th-century paintings gaze down – some are for sale. Bedrooms are suitably simple and all have 40-gallon iron bathtubs and panoramic views. On a fine day you can see France; the Shuttle terminal and Dover are only minutes away: perfect for wine runs.

You are right on Romney Marsh which begs to be explored. A pretty home: roses and climbers decorate the pink and blue brickwork, and gabled windows look onto rolling fields. Inside is homely: books, paintings, photos, two little dogs… in the garden are sunloungers to while away the afternoon on. The double bedroom has pink and white *fleur-de-lys* wallpaper while the secluded stable twin is very popular with guests: it's private with its own terrace and garden furniture. Adele is lovely – warm and down-to-earth. *Children over 10 welcome.*

rooms	3: 2 doubles, both with bath/shower; 1 with adjoining twin for children.
room price	£60. Single occ. £35.
meals	Breakfast until 9.30am. 10 minutes' drive to nearest restaurants.
closed	Christmas & New Year.
directions	From M20 at junc. 11, A20 south, then B2068 (Stone St), to Lympne. Approx. 0.25 miles on is County Members pub, & school sign on right. Left opp. convex mirror. House at end of lane.

rooms	3: 1 twin in stable with sitting room & bathroom; 1 double, 1 twin, both with private bathroom.
room price	£50-£70. Single occ. from £30.
meals	Excellent pub 1.5 miles.
closed	Very occasionally.
directions	M20, exit 10 for Brenzett. A2070 for approx. 6 miles. Right for Hamstreet, & immed. left. In Hamstreet, right onto B2067, left for Warehorne church. Through Warehorne to level crossing. House 1 mile on, on right.

Peter & Matty Gaston
The French House,
Lympne, Nr. Hythe,
Kent CT21 4PA

tel	01303 265974
fax	01303 262545
e-mail	gastons@frenchouse.freeserve.co.uk
web	www.frenchhouse.freeserve.co.uk

Adele Sherston
Terry House,
Warehorne, Ashford,
Kent TN26 2LS

tel	01233 732443
fax	01233 732443
e-mail	jsherston@ukonline.co.uk

Views from the doorstep are tremendous – you won't want to move. There's not a road or railway line within sight of this working farm which has been in the family since 900. Without, it is handsome and imposing; within, comfort and elegance go hand-in-hand: large dining and drawing rooms, high ceilings and beautiful mahogany furniture. Rosemary, kindness itself, looks after guests well – they always comment on the peace and quiet. Bedrooms – huge, light, never fussy – have very large bathrooms... and those views! *Children over 12 welcome.*

Traditional country with a dash of city style: inglenooks, bright colours, dark wood, wrought-iron candelabras. Little Hodgeham, 500 years old, is revelling in the love and care given by the Bradburys. Mouthwatering meals come from a state-of-the-art kitchen – Mark usually cooks and does wonders with green back bacon, Bethersden sausages and hash browns; dinners are superb too, and are taken in the green and gold dining room. Mark and Anne are discreet hosts and are happy to let you revel in privacy, and use their pool. *Self-catering suite in barn, ideal for families.*

rooms	3: 1 twin with bathroom; 1 twin, 1 double, both with private bathroom.
room price	£55-£64. Single occ. by arrangement.
meals	Breakfast until 9am; until 9.30am Sunday. Dinner from £12.50.
closed	December-January.
directions	At lights in centre of Hawkhurst, A268 for Rye. 1.5 miles after lights, at Four Throws, immed. right into Conghurst Lane. Driveway signed after 1.25 miles on left.

rooms	4: 1 four-poster, 1 twin/double, both with bath. Barn: 1 double, 1 twin, shower, sitting room & kitchen.
room price	£70-£75. Single occ. £45-£50. Barn, £100 per night, £250-£400 p.w.
meals	Dinner, 3 courses, £22; weekday supper £12.50.
closed	Christmas & New Year.
directions	From Tenterden, A28 for Ashford. At Bull pub in Bethersden, turn off for Smarden. Beamed yellow house on right after 2 miles.

Rosemary Piper
Conghurst Farm,
Hawkhurst,
Kent TN18 4RW
tel 01580 753331
fax 01580 754579
e-mail rosa@conghurst.co.uk

Mark & Anne Bradbury
Little Hodgeham,
Smarden Road, Bethersden,
Kent TN26 3HE
tel 01233 850323
fax 01233 850006
e-mail little.hodgeham@virgin.net
web www.littlehodgeham.co.uk

KENT

David lives gardening, and the High Weald of Kent is the Garden of England. So ask him about his ever-evolving work of art: his newly-walled vegetable garden, his orchard, lily pond, terraces and herbaceous border. Airy bedrooms are filled with pine and wicker, stripped or painted. Is it the main purpose of these to provide sleep, or a view that makes your heart stop to the bottom of the garden and the hop fields beyond? Fresh flowers erupt from vases, printed ones from the walls. There's a mini-library of very good garden books so you can mug up before visiting Sissinghurst or Kent's other lovely gardens.

rooms	2: 1 double with private bathroom; 1 twin with shower room.
room price	£55.
meals	Breakfast until 9am. Good pubs within walking distance.
closed	October-March.
directions	From A21 onto A262 for 2 miles. Before Goudhurst right onto Bluecoat Lane, signed Kilndown. At crossroads, right into Ranters Lane; house on right.

David & Margaret Sargent
Mount House,
Ranters Lane, Goudhurst,
Kent TN17 1HN
tel 01580 211230
fax 01580 212373
e-mail davidmargaretsargent@compuserve.com

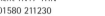

map: 6 entry: 265

KENT

Annie goes the extra mile for guests – breakfasts, especially, are a treat and the extras are home-made compotes and jams, locally-baked croissants and brioches. It's friendly, fun and informal and the Parkers have a good sense of humour and hospitality. The bedrooms in this Edwardian house are in the low, more modern wing with easy garden access; both are light and bright and there are treats on the tea tray. The drawing room where you have breakfast was once the house library. It's a splendid room, huge, with ribbon-and-wreath cornicing and a panelled ceiling. *Children over five welcome.*

rooms	2: 1 double with private bathroom; 1 twin with shower room.
room price	£55. Single occ. £40.
meals	Good pubs within 2-mile radius.
closed	Christmas & New Year.
directions	A262 to Goudhurst. There, B2079 to Marden. House is 2 miles from village, on left.

Annie Parker
West Winchet,
Winchet Hill, Goudhurst, Cranbrook,
Kent TN17 1JX
tel 01580 212024
fax 01580 212250
e-mail jeremyparker@jpa-ltd.co.uk

map: 6 entry: 266

KENT

The Wettons are genuinely smiley and easy, their house "just gorgeous inside and out". The small manor house in the beautiful conservation village of Hunton was built in the 1600s by a wealthy wool merchant as a place for storage and display. It's a delightfully artistic, beamed home whose ancient character and architectural details have survived intact. Bedrooms are charming and lack nothing. Grand piano and open fire in the drawing room (just for you), a conservatory for breakfast and a country garden to explore. The resident alpacas do most of the 'mowing'. Enchanting.

rooms	3: 2 twins, 1 with bath, 1 with bath/shower; 1 double with shower.
room price	£56-£66. Single occ. £28-£33.
meals	Restaurants 2-5 miles.
closed	Christmas & New Year.
directions	A229 Maidstone/Hastings. At lights at Linton x-roads, turn for Coxheath & through village. 1st left down Hunton Hill. Pass church, park & school, then right into Grove Lane.

Gavin & Anne Wetton
The Woolhouse,
Grove Lane, Hunton,
Kent ME15 0SE
tel   01622 820778
fax   01622 820645

KENT

Carolyn is experienced and easy-going with guests; you will settle in quickly. Her Grade II-listed, 16th-century, beamy house was begun in 1545. A small flock of sheep and two horses graze the 20 acres; dogs, cats and chickens (own eggs for breakfast) roam freely. Both the Carrells' children were raised and married from here and happy family vibes remain. The bedheads in the twin were made from old Horsmonden church pews; all rooms are light and airy with pastel colours, floral curtains and green views. Guests can use the drawing room and there's a terrace for tea. *Children over 10 welcome.*

rooms	3: 1 twin with private bathroom; 2 singles, both with basins, sharing bathroom & wc.
room price	£50-£56. Singles £25-£27.
meals	2 pubs in village, 1 mile.
closed	November-March.
directions	4 miles south of Tunbridge Wells on A267. 1 mile south of Frant, on left. Sign on fence at bottom of drive.

Mrs Carolyn Carrell
Rowden House Farm,
Frant, Tunbridge Wells,
Kent TN3 9HS
tel   01892 750259

Immerse yourself in fascinating history, ancient beauty and stunning architecture. The house twists, turns, rises and falls; its old stone and wood captivates. There's an easy atmosphere created by a family in a home that they love. It is part-Edwardian, part-Tudor and the Streatfields have been in Chiddingstone for centuries. Some furniture is well-worn and faded but everything feels authentic. Bedrooms are huge, with views over the gardens, grazing sheep and hills. There's a stable bedroom, too, but we recommend staying in the main house. *Minimum stay two nights at weekends.*

Nicholas is known to the family as Marco Pierre Morris. An enthusiastic cook, he loves to prepare breakfasts of home-made breads, jams, yogurt, eggs and, maybe, hash browns or kippers; on arrival, you may try his home-made cakes and drop scones. Guests have their own beamed sitting room in the old Bake House and bedrooms are simple, but fresh. The house dates from about 1750 and, curiously, manages to be in two places at once – the parish boundary runs straight through the middle with one half in Leigh, the other in Chiddingstone.

rooms	4: Main house: 1 twin, 1 double, sharing bathroom; 1 double with private bathroom. Annexe: 1 double with bath.
room price	£55-£60. Single occ. £30-£40.
meals	Breakfast 7-9am. Light supper & dinner £12.50-£20.
closed	Christmas & New Year.
directions	From A21, Hildenborough exit. Follow signs to Penshurst Place, then to vineyard. Pass it. Right at T-junc. for Edenbridge. Through village, bear left, for Edenbridge. House 0.5 miles on left.

rooms	3: 2 twins, 1 with shower, 1 with bath; 1 twin with private bathroom.
room price	£45-£50. Single occ. £35.
meals	Breakfast 7-9.30am. Excellent pub 5 minutes' walk.
closed	Very occasionally.
directions	B2027 0.5 miles north of Chiddingstone Causeway. Equidistant between Tonbridge, Sevenoaks & Edenbridge.

Mr & Mrs Mervyn Streatfield
Hoath House,
Chiddingstone Hoath,
Nr. Edenbridge,
Kent TN8 7DB
tel 01342 850362
fax 01342 841066
e-mail jstreatfeild@hoath-house.freeserve.co.uk

Nicholas & Ginny Morris
Charcott Farmhouse,
Charcott, Leigh, Tonbridge,
Kent TN11 8LG
tel 01892 870024
fax 01892 870158
e-mail nicholasmorris@charcott.freeserve.co.uk

map: 5 entry: 269

map: 5 entry: 270

KENT

Sue is a gifted garden designer and bursting with ideas for making her three acres even more special. This year she is, intriguingly, creating a planet garden, and is also restoring an old shepherd's hut to use as a summer house. All around the clothes line she has planted oregano and thyme so that the bed linen picks up the sweet scent in the breeze. All the rooms feel light, airy and comfortable; bedrooms and bathrooms are excellent. Play tennis or croquet, or walk into historic Westerham. The feel is bucolic and Sue spoils you.

rooms	3: 1 twin, 1 double, both with basin, sharing bathroom; 1 double with private bathroom.
room price	£50. Single occ. £40.
meals	Breakfast 7-9am or by arrangement. Excellent places for dinner nearby.
closed	Christmas week.
directions	M25 junc. 6, follow signs to Westerham (A25). After town sign & 30mph sign, 1st left into Farley Lane. After approx. 200 yds, left at top, then left again.

Sue & Alastair Marr
Worples Field,
Farley Common, Westerham,
Kent TN16 1UB

tel	01959 562869
e-mail	marr@worplesfield.com
web	www.worplesfield.com

LANCASHIRE

The stream meanders and the wild deer roam – the Ribble Valley, an AONB, feels like a time-locked land. The Queen is a frequent visitor to the local royal estate and she knows well the charm of the area. The Smiths are easy and comfortable to be with; here, in the former 18th-century tithe barn, where old church rafters support the guest sitting room, you settle among plump sofas, antiques, and some lace and flounces. You have the whole of the top floor and your own entrance. Breakfast is a feast – the jams and the muesli are home-made – and the garden is a peaceful retreat, full of interesting plants and wildlife.

rooms	3: 1 double with bath/shower; 1 double with private bath; 1 twin/double with shower.
room price	From £50. Single occ. £30.
meals	Lots of good restaurants within 10-minute drive.
closed	Christmas & New Year.
directions	M6 junc. 31, A59 to Skipton, left to Clitheroe. Through Clitheroe & Waddington, on for 0.5 miles, left along Cross Lane. 0.75 miles on, past Colthurst Hall, house on left.

Jean & Gordon Smith
Peter Barn Country House,
Cross Lane/Rabbit Lane,
Waddington, Clitheroe,
Lancashire BB7 3JH

tel	01200 428585
e-mail	jean@peterbarn.fsnet.co.uk

LEICESTERSHIRE | LEICESTERSHIRE

Passing traffic is less frequent than passing horses. The lasting impression of this 17th-century cottage is of an uplifting lightness and brightness; the house is filled with laughter and the Cowdells are terrific hosts. There's a fine collection of paintings and furniture, double oak doors lead from the dining room to the guest sitting room, and there are fresh flowers everywhere. Bedrooms are restful and fresh – one has three-way views – and the garden was designed by Bunny Guinness from *Gardeners' Question Time*. A good base if travelling from East Midlands airport. *Children over 12 welcome.*

Each room has panelling and an open fireplace, enough reason for wanting to sleep here. The panelling is painted in the plain, gentle colours that suit beautiful and traditional rooms; they're generous and faultless. It is a fine and grand house, done to the standards expected of the National Trust. High and ornate plaster ceilings, two handsome main staircases, floor-to-ceiling drapes and your own sitting room. There is even a lake – one mile long, no less – for you to row on and acres and acres of grounds divided into several gardens, some walled.
A wonderful place to do your own thing.

rooms	3: 2 twins/doubles, 1 with bathroom & extra single bed, 1 with shower room; 1 ground-floor family with bath & shower.
room price	From £45. Single occ. £27.50.
meals	Packed lunch £3. Pub 100 yds.
closed	Occasionally.
directions	From A46 Newark-Leicester, onto B676, for Melton. At staggered x-roads, straight for Grimston. 1 mile on, right to Grimston. There, up hill, past church. House on left, just after right-hand bend at top.

rooms	3: 1 double, 1 twin, both with bath/shower; 1 twin with private bathroom.
room price	£80. Single occ. £40.
meals	Good pub 2 miles.
closed	Christmas, New Year and some weekends.
directions	From A1 at Grantham A607 to Waltham on the Wolds. Sign to Eastwell by Royal Horseshoe pub; 1st left to Goadby Marwood. 50 yds past phone box right down Towns Lane; gates 100 yds on left.

Mr & Mrs R. L. Cowdell
The Gorse House,
Main Street, Grimston,
Melton Mowbray,
Leicestershire LE14 3BZ
tel 01664 813537
fax 01664 813537
e-mail cowdell@gorsehouse.co.uk
web www.gorsehouse.co.uk

Mrs Vicky Westropp
Goadby Hall,
Goadby Marwood,
Melton Mowbray,
Leicestershire LE14 4LN
tel 01664 464202
fax 01664 464092
e-mail h.westropp@compuserve.com

map: 10 entry: 273 | map: 10 entry: 274

LINCOLNSHIRE

LINCOLNSHIRE

The farmhouse is 200 years old and John Wycliffe, who translated the Bible into English, was rector at the village church in the 14th century. Christine is one of the most welcoming and helpful people we have met; she also bakes a delicious cake. Bill, newly-retired from farming, is friendly, too. You have your own sitting room with open fire and a dining room with garden views. The bedrooms are light, airy and peaceful; one is as plain and simple as the other is floral. Guests keep coming back. *Children over five welcome.*

Wide open Lincolnshire farmland on the edge of the Wolds – you'll love your bedroom views. This immaculately kept farm has been in the family for five generations and an award-winning farm trail helps you explore – or maybe you just want to watch the sunset by the trout lake (or sink into squashy leather sofas after supper in front of the fire). Sarah is young, energetic and welcoming and brings you delicious home-made cake on arrival. Bedrooms have dark wooden beds; bathrooms are spick and span. Donkeys graze in the paddock in the winter and your horse is welcome, too.

rooms	2: 1 double with private bathroom; 1 twin with shower room.
room price	£45. Single occ. by arrangement.
meals	Breakfast 7.30-9.30am. Good pubs 2-4 miles.
closed	Christmas & New Year.
directions	From Lincoln, A15 north. 2nd left after Scampton RAF station signed Fillingham. 1st right onto B1398. 2nd left to Fillingham. 1st house at bottom of hill on right.

rooms	2 doubles, both with bathroom.
room price	£47. Single occ. £30.
meals	Packed lunch £5. Supper from £10. Dinner, 3 courses, £15. B.Y.O. No meals at harvest time.
closed	Christmas & New Year.
directions	Turn off A157 in East Barkwith at war memorial, into Torrington Lane. House 0.75 miles on right after sharp right-hand bend.

Christine & Bill Ramsay
Church Farm,
Fillingham, Gainsborough,
Lincolnshire DN21 5BS
tel   01427 668279
fax   01427 668025
e-mail fillinghambandb@lineone.net

Sarah & Jonathan Stamp
The Grange,
Torrington Lane, East Barkwith,
Lincolnshire LN8 5RY
tel   01673 858670
e-mail jonathanstamp@farmersweekly.net

map: 15 entry: 275

map: 15 entry: 276

LINCOLNSHIRE

LINCOLNSHIRE

One guest's summing up reads: "Absolutely perfect – hostess, house, garden and marmalade." Ann loves having people to stay and makes you feel utterly at home. You have the run of downstairs: neat and traditionally smart, with elegant family antiques, parquet and chintz, flowers and space. Dreamy views of the gardens and small lake, and divine dinners, too: game casserole, ginger and meringue bombe... Perfect stillness at the base of the Lincolnshire Wolds and a lovely one-mile walk along the line of the old railway that starts from the door. Special indeed. *Children over 12 welcome.*

A warm, calm Sawday idyll: we promise you'll be enchanted. There's tea on arrival and, maybe, some Lincolnshire plum bread, and you can chat in the kitchen lined with good, original artwork. The Collards have carried out sympathetic restoration of original tiles and shutters, claw-footed baths and wooden doors. Frances is a furniture historian and museum curator; both are cultured, unassuming hosts, keen on excellent, organic food. There's immediate access to miles of walks packed with architectural and historical interest. You are in the Wolds and the landscape will surprise you. *Children over seven welcome.*

rooms	2: 1 twin with shower; 1 double with bath.
room price	£50. Single occ. by arrangement.
meals	Dinner £15. B.Y.O wine. Pub 0.75 miles.
closed	Christmas.
directions	From Wragby A157 for Louth. After approx. 2 miles, at triple road sign, right. Red postbox at drive entrance, past graveyard.

rooms	3: 1 double with bath & shower; 1 twin/double with private bath & shower; 1 extra single occasionally available.
room price	£50. Single occ. £25.
meals	Pub in village; restaurant 2 miles.
closed	Christmas & New Year.
directions	From Spilsby A16 north for 1 mile. In Partney bear left at church for Grimsby (A16). Drive 60 yds on left, down grassy track.

Ann Hobbins
The Manor House,
West Barkwith,
Lincolnshire LN8 5LF
tel   01673 858253
fax   01673 858253

Frances & Anthony Collard
The Grange,
Partney, Spilsby,
Lincolnshire PE23 4PQ
tel   01790 753151
fax   01790 753151
e-mail   antonline@onetel.net.uk

Just nine miles from Boston 'Stump' – Britain's largest parish church. Michael, ex-MP, ex-Navy, was active in the quest to illuminate the church's glories at night; you can now see it from miles around. The Brothertons are smashing people, massively interesting and easy and they both enjoy cooking and tending their huge fruit and vegetable garden. The impressive Queen Anne vicarage was built in 1707 with local handmade bricks which have mellowed gloriously. The typical square Lincolnshire hall has stone flags leading to a red-pine-panelled staircase. The double room is large, light and charming; the twin is simpler.

rooms	2: 1 double, 1 twin, both with private bathroom.
room price	£45-£55. Single occ. £32.50-£37.50.
meals	Packed lunch £4.50. Dinner, with drinks, £24.50.
closed	Christmas & Boxing Day.
directions	Wrangle is 9 miles north of Boston on A52. In village follow signs to Angel Inn. House opppsite. church by War Memorial.

Michael & Julia Brotherton
The Old Vicarage,
Wrangle, Boston,
Lincolnshire PE22 9EP
tel   01205 870688
fax   01205 871857
e-mail   jb141@aol.com

It's hard to believe this single-storey house was built in the '60s – its interior has more character than that of many period homes. Bridget is an interior decorator and her talent is everywhere. There's a conservatory feel to the light-filled, stone-floored dining room with French windows onto the garden – so pretty in summer. Checked curtains, matching, padded headboards and a gilt-trimmed Edwardian copy of a Louis XIV chair in the bedroom; a full-height mirror in the bathroom with deep, cast-iron bath. Looking after guests comes easily to Bridget and she does so without fuss.

rooms	1 twin with private bathroom across the hall.
room price	£39.50.
meals	Dinner from £14. Excellent pubs/restaurants nearby.
closed	Christmas & New Year.
directions	A607 Grantham to Lincoln road. On reaching Carlton Scroop 1st left for Hough Lane. Last house on left.

Mrs Bridget Hankinson
Churchfield House,
Carlton Scroop, Grantham,
Lincolnshire NG32 3BA
tel   01400 250387
fax   01400 250241

Deep comfort is yours at Pipwell, with an extra big welcome from Lesley who has looked after guests for years. The sitting room invites you in with tea and home-made cakes and, on wintery days, a blazing log fire. Pipwell is lovingly decorated in rich blues and greens, each room with its own character; an attractive country house scene of old pine tables, fresh and dried flowers and the smell of those cakes. The peace, the marshes, the solitude: in summer you can cycle for miles – and the bikes are free. In April the surrounding fields are a sea of yellow daffodils.

Drift off to sleep on a cloud of rose scent: Ozric makes the only genuine English rose oil and water, distilled here in an outbuilding. Outside your bedroom: three and a half acres of roses – magical. The house is full of intriguing features such as two boat-shaped windows that open onto the garden and a vast studio/sitting room built in the 1900s by Gardner of the R.A., filled with paintings and African carvings. There are some fearsome fish on the Portuguese tiles around the claw-footed bath, but Ozric and Chantal are extremely friendly and warm.

rooms	3: 1 double with bath/shower; 1 twin with shower; 1 double with private shower.
room price	From £46. Single occ. £35.
meals	Breakfast 7-9am. Packed lunch £4. Pub 1 mile, restaurant 1.5 miles.
closed	Christmas & New Year.
directions	Turn off A17, 1.5 miles north-east of Holbeach, into Washway Rd. Past phone box, pub & garage; house on left.

rooms	3: 1 double with bathroom; 1 twin, 1 double, both with private shower room.
room price	From £60. Single occ. £35.
meals	Pub/restaurant 1 mile.
closed	Christmas & New Year.
directions	From Bourne, A15 north for Sleaford, 1st hamlet on left signed to Cawthorpe. House last on right before road becomes a track.

Lesley & John Honnor
Pipwell Manor,
Washway Road, Saracen's Head,
Holbeach,
Lincolnshire PE12 8AL
tel   01406 423119
fax   01406 423119
e-mail   honnor@pipwellmanor.
           freeserve.co.uk

Ozric & Chantal Armstrong
Cawthorpe Hall,
Bourne,
Lincolnshire PE10 0AB
tel   01778 423830
fax   01778 426620
e-mail   bandb@rosewater.co.uk
web   www.rosewater.co.uk

LINCOLNSHIRE

An old, stone, listed farmhouse deep in Lincolnshire countryside with freshly decorated bedrooms (one in blues and whites, one in sunny yellows) that look onto paddock and fields. Anne, who twinkles with good humour, is a fine Aga cook, so you'll enjoy the local bacon, home-grown eggs and home-made preserves. Chris is great fun too, and his love of the countryside is infectious. Walk the mile to Barnack to visit a nature reserve bursting with orchids and rare Pasque flowers, or explore the fascinating BBC *Gardeners' World* gardens nearby. You can walk to shops and pub: the village is at the door.

rooms	2: 1 double, with half-size bath/shower; 1 twin with private bathroom.
room price	£50-£60. Single occ. £35-£40.
meals	Pubs 1 mile.
closed	Christmas & New Year.
directions	Leave A1 at Wansford, travelling towards Peterborough on A47 for 0.75 miles. Left to Southorpe; through village, house 100 yds after phone box on right.

Anne Harrison-Smith
Midstone House,
Southorpe, Stamford,
Lincolnshire PE9 3BX

tel	01780 740136
fax	01780 749294
e-mail	ahsmidstonehouse@amserve.net

map: 10 entry: 283

LONDON

The luxury of a good hotel – excellent beds, gorgeous bathrooms, even air conditioning – yet here you have the personal touch we so like. You eat breakfast in the big, colourful, kitchen, complete with Aga, wooden floor and table, and take Carole's advice on what's on in London. Bright, comfortable bedrooms have sisal flooring, brass beds, crisp linen, bathrobes and contemporary décor. The open space and delightful shops and restaurants of Primrose Hill are nearby.

rooms	2: 1 double with private bath/shower; 1 twin with bath/shower room.
room price	£100. Single occ. £80.
meals	Breakfast 8-9am Mon-Fri, 8.30-9.30am Sat/Sun. Many pubs & restaurants nearby.
closed	Rarely.
directions	5 minutes' walk from Chalk Farm tube: cross Adelaide Road, right for 20 steps, left into Bridge Approach, cross bridge, right. Free parking weekends, ticket parking nearby.

Andrew & Carole Ingram
30 King Henry's Road,
Primrose Hill,
London NW3 3RP

tel	020 7483 2871
fax	020 7209 9739
e-mail	mail@caroleingram.com
web	www.30kinghenrysroad.co.uk

map: 5 entry: 284

LONDON

A modern walled and tranquil home made of African teak and glass. The open plan living area is a fabulous use of space decorated with ethnic ornaments from far flung holidays and opening to a courtyard garden. Halogen lighting and a pyramid of glass on the roof brightens still further. Climb the wooden staircase to find very special bedrooms, both in Japanese style: low platform beds, modern chairs; the double has two walls of glass. A famous market and lots of good places to eat nearby. Rodger and Sue are a delight and Peckham the parrot completes the picture. *Children by arrangement.*

rooms	2: 1 double, 1 single, sharing bathroom (let only to same party).
room price	£90. Singles from £45.
meals	Extensive continental breakfast 7.30–10am.
closed	Very occasionally.
directions	From Camden Town tube, take Camden Rd towards Holloway. Pass Camden Rd BR station & 4th right into Murray St. House on corner of Murray Street & Camden Mews. Free parking at weekends; meters during week.

Sue & Rodger Davis
66 Camden Square,
London NW1 9XD
tel   020 7485 4622
fax   020 7485 4622
e-mail rodgerdavis@btinternet.com

map: 5 entry: 285

LONDON

In the heart of vibrant Camden Town, well set back in a quiet, wide, tree-lined street, moments from Regent's Park, this is a superb central London base. The large and stunning kitchen was designed by Peter (an architect and lighting specialist) and every room in the modernist house has had the best brought out of it – small rooms are cleverly laid out and there's a really super large double. All is distinctive and understated with cool colours and fresh flowers. The Bells run this established B&B with a cool professionalism. *Near to Camden Lock and market.*

rooms	3: 1 small double, with shower; 1 twin with bunks, 1 twin/double sharing bathroom.
room price	£90–£100. Single occ. £45–£60.
meals	Breakfast 7–10am. Pubs/restaurants nearby.
closed	Very occasionally.
directions	From Camden Town tube (Northern Line), up Parkway. Albert St 2nd on left. House on left. Parking free Sunday; otherwise meters.

Joanna & Peter Bell
78 Albert Street,
London NW1 7NR
tel   020 7387 6813
fax   020 7387 1704

map: 5 entry: 286

There's a dramatic vibrancy to Valerie's home, which is just off Upper Street with its many restaurants, and right by the Almeida and Sadler's Wells. She has many artists and actors to stay and has a theatre background herself. The Victorian house is stuffed with oriental, French and Italian pieces, and the basement bedroom filled with light and character. Walls, doors and much of the furniture are ragged, sponged and stencilled in the colourful style of the Bloomsbury set; the theatrical mood continues in the conservatory, crammed with tropical plants, ferns, seashells and candles. An inspiring place to stay.

Wonderful rooms in an 1860s Kensington Victorian townhouse. The newly decorated bedrooms are in one of the lightest basements that we've ever seen and you have your own key and entrance. The rest of the house is still the family home. There's an easy formality: mahogany table and dresser, antique chairs and floral fabrics, and breakfast is served in the dining room overlooking the charming, secluded garden. Nanette really enjoys people. *Near to Kensington Gardens, Holland Park, High Street Kensington. Children over 12 welcome.*

rooms	1 double with private shower room.
room price	£85. Single occ. £65-£70.
meals	Breakfast 8-9am; extensive continental only.
closed	Rarely.
directions	From Highbury & Islington tube, right out of station. Down Upper Street, past Town Hall. Left immed. before Shell garage. Free overnight & weekend parking (Sat 6.30pm on); otherwise meters & car parks.

rooms	3: 2 twins, both with bath/shower; 1 double with shower room.
room price	£85-£95. Single occ. £70.
meals	Cooked breakfast 8.30-9am (Mon-Fri), 9-9.30am (Sat-Sun).
closed	Very occasionally.
directions	Left out of Earl's Court tube, over Cromwell Rd, left into Pembroke Rd. Warwick Gardens 3rd on right. Parking £6 per day next door. Public transport: High St Kensington/Earl's Court tube (8 mins' walk).

Valerie Rossmore
26 Florence Street,
Islington,
London N1 2FW
tel   020 7359 5293

Nanette Stylianou
47 Warwick Gardens,
London W14 8PL
tel   020 7603 7614
fax   020 7602 5473
e-mail   nanette@stylianou.fsnet.co.uk

SPECIAL PLACES – WHAT'S OUR SECRET?

Our first book was about French Bed and Breakfast, an easy one because France has such a deep appeal to the British. Sleeping in an old château is a seductive prospect when faced with a modern roadside hotel or an unreliable old village inn. But for centuries the French have had a reputation for aloofness, stemming partly from their custom of receiving strangers in the local café rather than at home. But the chambres d'hôtes system has persuaded thousands of them to open up – and they are enjoying it hugely.

So we found those with the greatest character and warmth, and put them into a book. It worked. We quickly established a reputation, for honesty and dependability. Readers came to rely on us. They also liked our lightness of touch, evidenced in the spoofs. We also avoided the tired cliché of estate agents and many guide-writers.

Our next book, on Britain, was up against a plethora of books on the subject. But it worked - again, we suspect, because we were, somehow, refreshing. Look at most B&B and hotel books and you will find a blandness of style and an absence of discrimination. The ugly will be mixed with the beautiful, the dull with the exhilarating, and pomposity will be confused with elegance. Lastly, the presence of 'stuff' – power showers, lush carpets, 'courtesy trays' and televisions – will be mistaken for charm and character.

My own preference is for simplicity, beauty and personality. I am a bit puritanical, perhaps, and my work as an environmentalist has made me resent wastage and excess. Hence our focus on good people, architecture, honest food and good value. And we try not to take ourselves too seriously. We seem to have tapped into a longing for **'real'** experience, rather than the nonsense peddled by those who trumpet the 'cool', 'exclusive' and 'prestigious'.

Holland Park is one of London's most sought-after addresses and Sunny's gorgeous family home is right opposite the park. The whole top floor is generally given over to guests. Both rooms are in gentle yellows and greens, with pale green carpets, soft, white duvets, pelmeted windows, big porcelain table lights, fresh flowers and treetop views. The bathroom is marble-tiled and sky-lit, with a deep cast-iron bath; great comfort is guaranteed. Near to Kensington Gardens, and the Number 9 or Number 10 bus will drop you off at the Albert Hall, Knightsbridge or Piccadilly. *Children over 10 welcome.*

rooms	2: 1 double, 1 single, sharing bathroom.
room price	£80-£90. Single room from £45.
meals	Lots of places to eat nearby.
closed	Occasionally.
directions	Public transport: nearest tube Holland Park, 7 minutes' walk, or High St Kensington. Best buses, 9 & 10 to Knightsbridge. Off-street parking sometimes available.

Sunny Murray
101 Abbotsbury Road,
London W14 8EP

tel	020 7602 0179
fax	020 7602 1036
e-mail	sunny@101abb.freeserve.co.uk

All the personality, charm and individual attention of a private house – right in the heart of London, too. But also a huge canopied four-poster bed, private telephone, fax and laundry facilities, a great bathroom and use of the sitting room. Continental breakfast with newspaper is equally inspired. Everything is prepared by Jenny the housekeeper; this means the orange is freshly squeezed and the jams are home-made. You will not find better comfort in central London at these prices. *Near to Westminster Abbey, Tate Gallery, Buckingham Palace. Good shopping in nearby Knightsbridge and Sloane Square.*

rooms	1 four-poster with bathroom.
room price	£110-£120. Single occ. £100.
meals	Breakfast 8-9am; continental included; full English £8. Many excellent local restaurants nearby.
closed	Christmas.
directions	1 min from Pimlico tube (Rampayne St exit), or 5 mins from Victoria Station. Best bus, 24 to Trafalgar Sq. Parking: NCP or 2-hour meters.

Mrs Helen Douglas
Number Ninety-Six,
96 Tachbrook Street,
London SW1V 2NB

tel	020 7932 0969
fax	020 7821 5454
e-mail	helen@numberninety-six.co.uk
web	www.numberninety-six.co.uk

LONDON

A family home, just a step from the King's Road. Breakfast is continental — London-style — but Jane will cook eggs and bacon if you wish. It is served in the stunning kitchen conservatory which overlooks a beautiful garden; everyone remarks on the peace and the greenery. Jane, who lectured at St Martin's School of Art, gives you top-floor bedrooms that are simple, sunny and cheerful and have interesting books and unique views of Sir Christopher Wren's magnificent Royal Hospital.

rooms	2: 1 twin, 1 family room (single & double futon), sharing bathroom (bath & shower).
room price	£80-£90. Single occ. £55.
meals	Continental breakfast only. Dinner £20. B.Y.O.
closed	Very occasionally.
directions	Parallel with King's Road between Smith Street & Royal Avenue. Off-street parking available.

Jane Barran
17 St Leonard's Terrace,
London SW3 4QG

tel	020 7730 2801
fax	020 7730 2801

LONDON

Just around the corner from the New King's Road, Amanda's home has indisputable comfort and her attention to detail and happy way of doing things make the place special. Harrods' jams and pancakes for breakfast, either in the kitchen or the garden; candles everywhere; and Huggy the dog, an erstwhile star of the silver screen, who turned down the movies and the promise of a chauffeured limousine for the quiet life in Fulham. The downstairs bedroom is lovely: big and bright, warm and airy and excellent for longer stays; the Italian-tiled bathroom next door just the ticket. *Children over 12 welcome.*

rooms	3: 1 twin/double with bathroom; 1 twin/double, 1 single, both with private bathroom.
room price	£80. Single occ. £55.
meals	Extensive continental breakfast. Good restaurants nearby.
closed	Rarely.
directions	3 mins from Parsons Green tube (District Line, Wimbledon branch). Straight over green, keeping White Horse on left; Bradbourne St is over King's Rd, ahead. House on left. Parking free 5pm-9am & all Sunday; otherwise Pay & Display.

Mrs Amanda Turner
3 Bradbourne Street,
Fulham,
London SW6 3TF

tel	020 7736 7284
e-mail	info@luxuryinlondon.clara.co.uk
web	www.luxuryinlondon.co.uk

LONDON

Caroline mixes the sophistication of the city with the human warmth of the countryside and her lovely big kitchen is clearly the engine-room of the house. It leads through to a light breakfast room on seagrass matting, with doors onto a pretty brick garden with its chairs and table – hope for fine days. The house is long and thin – Fulham style – and reaches up to the guest room in the eaves, which needs no more explanation than the picture below. A really warm place to stay in a very accessible part of the metropolis. *Near to King's Road antique shops.*

rooms	1 twin/double with shower & private bathroom.
room price	£80-£90. Single occ. £70.
meals	Continental breakfast only, 8.30-9.30am (Mon-Fri), 8.30-10am (Sat-Sun).
closed	Very occasionally.
directions	Public transport: 4 minutes' walk to Parsons Green tube. Parking: £9 per day in street.

Caroline Docker
8 Parthenia Road,
Fulham,
London SW6 4BD
tel   020 7384 1165
fax   020 7371 8819
e-mail   caldock@btinternet.com

map: 5 entry: 293

LONDON

Rachel is generous and thinks nothing of it; her house glows warm gold as you enter, courtesy of Osborne & Little on the walls, and excellent lighting – you immediately know you've chosen well. Upstairs, an exceptionally pretty double with pink checks and garden views, fresh flowers and a sparkling bathroom. The hub of the house is back downstairs in the kitchen, where you can sit on the sofa, or open the French windows and enjoy the serenity of a small London garden. The street runs down to the Fulham Road and far too many irresistible shops and restaurants. *Children over 10 welcome.*

rooms	2: 1 double with bath/shower; 1 single with private bath.
room price	£75-£80. Single occ. from £50. Single £45.
meals	Continental breakfast until 9.30am. Choice of pubs/restaurants within walking distance.
closed	Very occasionally.
directions	2 minutes from Parsons Green tube (District Line, Wimbledon branch). Bus 14 to Knightsbridge. Parking in street all day.

Rachel Wilson
29 Winchendon Road,
London SW6 5DH
tel   020 7731 3901
e-mail   rachel.k.wilson@talk21.com

map: 5 entry: 294

Come here for peace and undemanding luxury; this 1890 Victorian cottage with delightful courtyard garden is a perfect antidote to the rigours of city life. You breakfast in the dining room: the full English works (unusual for London); across the hall in the sitting room with gilt-framed mirrors, wooden blinds and plump-cushioned sofa is a piano you are welcome to play. Upstairs, very comfy bedrooms with pretty linen, books, even guides. The next-door bathroom is fabulous with porthole windows and a radio to entertain you as you soak. *Convenient for Chelsea Flower Show, Battersea Park and the South Bank.*

Barnes is London's loveliest village: ducks still live on the village pond opposite a pub where cricketers meet to quench a collective thirst, there's the Thames, towpaths, lovely shops and a wild common. Helen's immaculate home has boundless style: plantation shutters in the large sitting room, a shiny wooden floor in the big, bright kitchen. Bedrooms have big beds, Australian damask cotton sheets, all the spoiling extras. The top room has skylights (stargaze from bed) and a crisp elegance; the grander double, an Edwardian *bergère* sofa and a purple claw-foot bath in a divine en suite. *Children over 12 welcome.*

rooms	2: 1 double with private bathroom; 1 double for guests in same party, sharing bathroom.
room price	£70-£80. Single occ. £60.
meals	Breakfast until 9am Mon-Fri; flexible Sat & Sun. Good restaurants 200 yds.
closed	Occasionally.
directions	Please call for directions. Nearby r'way stations (6 mins Waterloo or 3 mins Victoria) or 137 bus (Sloane Square 10 mins). Parking £4 per day, 9.30-5.30pm Mon-Fri; otherwise free.

rooms	2: 1 double, with bath; 1 double with private bathroom.
room price	From £70. Single occ. £45.
meals	Breakfast until 9.30am. Pubs/restaurants 500 yds.
closed	Christmas & New Year.
directions	From Great West Rd, Hammersmith Bridge to Barnes. At lights by Browns Restaurant, right along Lonsdale Rd for just over 1 mile. Left into Gerard Rd & 1st left into Charlotte Rd. House 1st on left. Free parking.

	Barbara Graham
	20 St Philip Street,
	Battersea,
	London SW8 3SL
tel	020 7498 9967
fax	020 7498 9967
e-mail	barbaragraham@telco4u.net

	Helen Smith
	1 Charlotte Road,
	Barnes,
	London SW13 9QJ
tel	020 8741 5504
fax	020 8741 5504

A smart 1880s family home in a leafy conservation area. There's a snug library with club fenders round the fire, a stylish dining room flanked by *trompe l'oeil* pillars and an elegant sitting room with antique furniture which opens to a secluded garden. Big bedrooms have comfy mahogany furniture, pretty fabrics, tartan blankets. Best of all is the huge room at the top: it has two sofas – with masses of space all around – and twin beds hidden up in the eaves, so it's perfect for families. Viveka does excellent continental breakfasts – go Swedish and have jam on your cheese.

Privacy is the key element here – you have exclusive use of your own Coach House (only one party at a time), separated from your hosts' home by a stylish terracotta-potted courtyard. Breakfast in your sunny kitchen, or let the gracious Meena treat you to an all-organic full English (she's a whizz at porridge, too). The big but cosy main attic bedroom has *toile de Jouy* bedcovers, cream curtains, rugs on dark polished floors; the brick-walled ground-floor twin is pleasant, light and airy. An exceptionally quiet south London B&B. *Minimum stay three nights; two nights in January & February. Children by arrangement.*

rooms	3: 1 double with bathroom, 1 family suite (double & twin) with private shower room.
room price	Doubles £60. Single occ. £45. Family suite by arrangement.
meals	Continental breakfast 8-9am. Restaurants and pubs 5-10 minutes' walk.
closed	Occasionally.
directions	Ring on arrival at Tooting Bec tube (Northern line) & you'll be collected. Free off-road parking.

rooms	2: 1 twin with private shower; 1 family with bathroom.
room price	£75-£165.
meals	Dinner, all organic, £35. Pub/restaurant 200 yds.
closed	Very occasionally.
directions	From r'bout on south side of Wandsworth Bridge, head south down Trinity Rd on A214. At 3rd set of traffic lights, 1.7 miles on, left into Upper Tooting Park. 4th left into Marius Rd, then 3rd left.

Viveka & Chris Collingwood
34 Ambleside Ave,
London SW16 1QP
tel 020 8769 2742
fax 020 8677 3023
e-mail info@bednbrek.com
web www.bednbrek.com

Meena & Harley Nott
The Coach House,
2 Tunley Road,
London SW17 7QJ
tel 020 8772 1939
fax 0870 133 4957
e-mail coachhouse@chslondon.com
web www.coachhouse.chslondon.com

map: 5 entry: 297

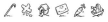

map: 5 entry: 298

It's a handsome house in a conservation area that manages to be both elegant and cosy. The cream-coloured bedroom has comfy furniture, fine fabrics and original features; the en suite bathroom is light and airy. The restful dining room overlooks a secluded terrace and garden and there are newspapers at breakfast. On a quiet, tree-lined street, here is a relaxing city base with friendly owners. Maximum comfort and good value for London. *Minimum stay two nights.*

rooms	1 double with bath.
room price	£60. Single occ. £45.
meals	Breakfast 8-9.30am (10am Sat & Sun). Dinner, 3 courses, £25. Good restaurants nearby.
closed	Occasionally.
directions	From Tooting Bec tube, along Balham High Roadd towards Balham. 3rd road on right. 7 minutes' walk from tube. Free parking weekends, otherwise meters or daily rate of £2.50.

	Mary & David Hodges
	108 Streathbourne Road,
	London SW17 8QY
tel	020 8767 6931
fax	020 8672 8839
e-mail	mary.hodges@virgin.net
web	www.streathbourneroad.com

Not a hard house to find – just knock at the door of the wildest pad on the street. Beatrice is an artist and her 1860s home is an extension of both work and self – funky, easy-going and welcoming. There are big, light-swamped rooms, polished wood floors and groovy colours – 21st-century B&B. The hub is the big kitchen with its farmhouse table for generous continental breakfasts and a glass wall that gives onto the garden. Beatrice's other half, James, is a Kiwi garden designer – one of London's best; wander at will and find old dock timbers, a sari-shaded Mexican hammock, tall, willowy grasses and a water garden.

rooms	1 twin with shower.
room price	£70-£80. Single occ. £45.
meals	5 minutes' walk for dinner.
closed	Very occasionally.
directions	From Brockley station, cross Brockley Road & up Cranfield Road; cross at church & cont. along road. until Breakspears Road. Free parking. Trains: Brockley to London Bridge. Buses: 171 & 36 to centre.

	Beatrice Fraser
	57 Breakspears Road,
	London SE4 1XR
tel	020 8469 3162
e-mail	bunzl@btinternet.com

LONDON

The downstairs room is worthy of an expensive hotel: the crispest linen, bamboo blinds, Chinese screens and a marble bathroom. Anne is originally from Borneo; Tim was 'our man in East Malaysia' some 35 years ago. They have travelled widely, are full of life, and now live on the side of a hill above a carpet of London lights. Hats on the hat stand, old maps on the walls, everything sparkles. Two more bedrooms upstairs, one in country house style, the other in contemporary yellow. Anne will do you a steaming hot oriental cooked breakfast or the 'full English'. It's a short walk downhill to buses, tubes and trains.

rooms	3: 1 double, 1 twin/double, both with bath/shower; 1 twin with private bathroom.
room price	£75-£85; single occ. from £37.50.
meals	Dinner £26. B.Y.O.
closed	Occasionally.
directions	From Elephant & Castle r'bout, A2 (New Kent/Old Kent/New Cross Rd) to junc. with Queens Road. Right for Queens Road. 1st left into Erlanger Road, left into Sherwin Rd. Right into Pepys Rd up hill. House opp. Telegraph Hill Park.

Mrs A. Marten
113 Pepys Road,
London SE14 5SE
tel	020 7639 1060
fax	020 7639 8780
e-mail	annemarten@pepysroad.com
web	www.pepysroad.com

map: 5 entry: 301

NORFOLK

Mrs Garnier has become a legend among B&B-ers – she has done it for so long and looks after her stupendous Grade II*-listed house single-handedly. She tells colourful stories of the house and her family's long local history: from 1349 until the Dissolution of the Monasteries, it was a college of priests; later, it was saved from ruin and brought back to life. It has a stunning panelled dining room, big bedrooms (the sky-blue one is particularly pretty) and great views. Incredible value for such a special house. *Children over seven welcome.*

rooms	3: 1 double with private bath; 1 twin, 1 twin/double, both with bath. Also extra shower & wc.
room price	From £50. Single occ. £25.
meals	Afternoon tea included. Pub, 1 mile.
closed	Very occasionally.
directions	From Thetford A1075 north for Watton. After 9 miles, left to Thompson. After 0.5 miles 2nd left at red postbox on corner. Left again, house at dead end.

Mrs Garnier
College Farm,
Thompson, Thetford,
Norfolk IP24 1QG
tel	01953 483318
fax	01953 483318
e-mail	collegefarm@amserve.net

map: 11 entry: 302

So many interesting objects it takes time to absorb the splendour; in the drawing room, gorgeous prints and paintings, unusual furniture, decorative lamps... Caroline has a fine eye for detail. The guest room has a Regency-style canopied king-size bed and decoration to suit the era of the house (1850). The large garden is just as fascinating, with rooms and a very large, jungly pond that slinks between the trees. You can eat in the courtyard or the conservatory; Caroline prepares lovely dinners using much local produce. *Children over nine welcome.*

A house on a hill – unusual for East Anglia; the lawns fall away and views stretch out over farmland. Richard and Patricia are utterly charming and so easy to talk to; their respective passions are fishing and gardening – the garden is superb. There are fresh flowers, family photographs, agricultural prints and a feeling of light and space. The guest sitting room is generously furnished and Patricia will light a fire for you. The double, predominantly green bedroom is the biggest; all have thick carpets and a quiet Victorian elegance. *Rooms let to same party willing to share bathroom.*

rooms	2: 1 double, 1 single, both with private bathroom.
room price	£50. Single £25.
meals	Packed lunch £5. Lunch £10. Dinner £15.
closed	Christmas & New Year.
directions	A11 Attleborough-Wymondham. Take Spooner Row sign. Over x-roads by Three Boars pub. At T-junc. left to Wymondham. 1 mile on, look for rusty barrel on left. Turn into farm track.

rooms	2: 1 twin/double, 1 double sharing bath. Extra wc & basin available.
room price	From £50. Single occ. £30.
meals	Pub/restaurant 1 mile.
closed	Very occasionally.
directions	A143 Diss/Yarmouth for 9 miles. At r'bout left for Harleston, then immed. left to Starston. Over x-roads, into village, over bridge, immed. right. After 0.5 miles, drive on left by white railings.

Caroline Musker
Sallowfield Cottage,
Wattlefield, Wymondham,
Norfolk NR18 9PA
tel   01953 605086
e-mail   caroline.musker@tesco.net

Mrs Patricia Lombe Taylor
Conifer Hill,
Low Road, Starston, Harleston,
Norfolk IP20 9NT
tel   01379 852393
fax   01379 852393

A truly grand, imposing house run with what feels like appropriate, irreproachable efficiency. The moat was used by Flemish flax weavers to wash their flax before hanging it in the magnificent barn to dry. The house is Grade II*-listed, red-brick and mellow and on a grand scale: soaring ceilings, handsome fireplaces, huge sash windows, cast-iron baths, parquet floors, good, large, beds. It's full of light, and chandeliers, balustrades and frescos add grandeur. You have your own sitting room but do explore the garden with its pretty archways, a scented rose walk, an impressive mix of trees and a tennis court.

Old, and beautiful, a large tapestry hangs in the stairwell and foot-square stone slabs make up the ground floor. The rugs are old, too, from Persia and the East. This is the sort of house we love to include: we value the well-worn dignity, furniture and style of such unassuming good taste. The mature garden is a place for badminton, croquet or relaxing with a book in the gazebo. Meanwhile, musical guests are welcome to play the grand piano. Home-grown eggs for breakfast; the double and one twin can become a self-contained flat with sitting room and kitchen. Marvellous value.

rooms	3: 2 doubles, both with private bathroom; 1 twin with bathroom.
room price	£80. Single occ. £50.
meals	Dinner £27.50.
closed	Occasionally.
directions	A143 Yarmouth/Beccles road. In Toft Monks take Post Office Rd (opposite Toft Lion pub) for 0.4 miles to T-junc. Right down Aldeby Rd for 0.1 mile, fork right. House on right, 0.2 miles on.

rooms	3: 1 double with bathroom; 2 twins, both with private bathroom.
room price	£50. Single occ. by arrangement.
meals	Breakfast until 9.30am. Supper £15. B.Y.O.
closed	Occasionally.
directions	10-15 minute drive from Norwich. Bramerton is signed from A146 (Norwich-Lowestoft rd). House opp. church, with white 5-bar gate.

Richard & Teena Freeland
The Elms,
Toft Monks, Beccles,
Norfolk NR34 0EJ
tel   01502 677380
fax   01502 677362
e-mail   richardfreeland@btconnect.com
web   www.freelandenterprises.co.uk

Elizabeth Perowne
The White House,
Bramerton, Norwich,
Norfolk NR14 7DW
tel   01508 538673
e-mail   e.perowne@amserve.net

map: 11 entry: 305

map: 11 entry: 306

NORFOLK

NORFOLK

The best of both worlds: a lovely family buzz in the neighbouring Manor Farmhouse where you take breakfast, and privacy in the converted barn where you stay. You can come and go as you please and curl up with a book in front of the fire if it's raining… perfect. The thatched, late 16th-century barn has three bedrooms – two lofty – and everything is fresh, new and luxurious; one has views to Happisburgh's red and white striped lighthouse. There's a vaulted sitting room, a courtyard garden and a billiard table in the flint stable. Your hosts are charming. *Children over seven welcome.*

Conservation farmland all around, and acres of wild heathland busy with woodpeckers and owls just a stride from your door. Life in this 17th-century farmhouse revolves around the great kitchen and the draw of the Aga is irresistible on Fiona's bread-baking days. Good, traditional bedrooms, cosy with rugs and *objets* from diplomatic postings abroad, have views onto farmyard and gardens. All is space and light and, when the teenage children are at home, family chatter and laughter too. Breakfasts are a feast with Norfolk kippers, home-grown eggs, sausages and real marmalade. There's tennis, too.

rooms	3: 2 doubles, both with bath & shower; 1 twin/double with bath.
room price	From £44. Single occ. by arrangement.
meals	Dinner, 3 courses, from £12.50.
closed	Christmas & New Year (available then as a holiday let).
directions	From Norwich, A1151/A149 almost to Stalham. Left, for Walcott. At T-junc. left again. 1 mile on, right for H'burgh. Next T-junc., right. Next T-junc. left. Past houses & fields. Road bends right, look for house sign by fence.

rooms	2: 1 double with bath; 1 double with private bathroom.
room price	£50. Single occ. £30.
meals	Packed lunch £5. Dinner available. Good pubs 2 miles.
closed	Occasionally.
directions	A1151 from Norwich for Stalham. Just before Stalham, left to Happisburgh. Left at T-junc. On for 3 miles then 2nd left after East Rushton church, signed Foxhill by-way. Right at cross roads. House 1 mile on right.

David & Rosie Eldridge
Manor Farmhouse,
Happisburgh,
Norfolk NR12 0SA
tel 01692 651262
fax 01692 650220
web www.northnorfolk.co.uk/manorbarn

Mrs Fiona Black
The Old Rectory,
Ridlington,
Norfolk NR28 9NZ
tel 01692 650247
fax 0870 1335719
e-mail blacks7@email.com

map: 11 entry: 307

map: 11 entry: 308

Elegance and prettiness in equal measure. Light, airy rooms with long Georgian windows have been dressed in beautiful fabrics – checks, *toile de Jouy* and elegant ochre stripes. Each of the bedrooms is most attractive, and one opens onto a sweet little sleeping area for children with toys and books. Bibby, a *Cordon Bleu* cook, uses local produce and vegetables from the lovely garden. Worstead, the birthplace of the worsted cloth, is a charming village and only a stroll away; come at the end of July and you can join in the fun of the village festival. There's also a large, heated pool.

A gorgeous place! Sarah has opened up the Georgian Old Laundry beside Heydon Hall, one of Norfolk's finest Grade I-listed Elizabethan houses. The white walls, scrubbed tables and stone flags are still in place, but immense luxury has been added. For breakfast you have your own sunny dining/sitting room with cream furniture and mellow stone floors. Bedrooms have pretty fabrics at the windows and on the headboards; one has a bathroom with a fireplace and a free-standing bath. You have a private courtyard and there's a swimming pool that you can use if you ask.

rooms	2: 1 double/family, with bathroom; 1 twin with basin & private shower.
room price	£46-£50. Single occ. £33-£35.
meals	Packed lunch available. Dinner, 2 courses £12.50, 3 courses £16.
closed	Christmas & New Year
directions	From Norwich, B1150 (N. Walsham road). At Westwick, right for Worstead. Under railway bridge. On entering village, left at Manor House, on to school on left. House on right opposite. pond.

rooms	2 twins/doubles, 1 with bathroom, 1 with private bathroom.
room price	£60. Single occ. in high season, £40.
meals	Dinner, 3 courses, £16, by arrangement. Good pub 0.5 miles. Restaurant 5 miles.
closed	Self-catering only at Christmas.
directions	From Norwich, B1149 for 10 miles. 2nd left after bridge, for Heydon. After 1.5 miles, right into village, straight into park, over cattle grid, past Hall to left & follow signs.

Michael & Bibby Horwood
Holly Grove,
Worstead, North Walsham,
Norfolk NR28 9RQ

tel	01692 535546
e-mail	michaelhorwood@freenetname.co.uk
web	www.broadland.com/hollygrove

Sarah Bulwer-Long
The Old Laundry,
Heydon Hall, Heydon,
Norfolk NR11 6RE

| tel | 01263 587343 |
| fax | 01263 587805 |

map: 11 entry: 309

map: 11 entry: 310

Play croquet, find a cosy spot to read, doze – we applaud Clare's ease and willingness to share her home. The house has a contemporary barn feel and, with clever use of space, light and aspect, Clare has created varied sitting areas in the open-plan ground floor. In one bedroom there is coir matting and a double brass bedstead and striking vine-patterned fabric; the twin is equally stylish and large. Wood everywhere and lovely stone, a formal garden, ponds, a summer house and two self-catering barns. Two National Trust houses are nearby and, by the coast, thousands of acres of sky, sea and sand.

Arrive on a summer afternoon and the Norfolk longhouse will be bathed in sunlight. The welcome from the Heals will be equally warm. The large bedrooms in this handsome and cosy house face west, ensuring views of sunsets in the vast Norfolk skies, and the old furniture, rugs and pictures give a feeling of unpretentious ease. The Grade II-listed house is all that remains of Burgh Parva after the village was deserted in the Great Plague of 1668. The breakfast eggs are fresh from the hens in the garden, the vegetables are home-grown and there is plenty of game in season.

rooms	3: 1 double with shower room; 1 double, 1 twin, both with bath/shower.
room price	£70–£80. Single occ from £35.
meals	Dinner, 2 courses, £12.50; 3 courses, £19.50.
closed	Occasionally.
directions	From Norwich, A140. On entering Roughton, left into Back Lane. After 0.75 miles, pass one cottage on left. Grove Farm is 30 yds on right.

rooms	2: 1 double with bath/shower; 1 twin with private bathroom.
room price	From £50. Single occ. from £30.
meals	Breakfast until 9.30am. Dinner £20.
closed	Very occasionally.
directions	Fakenham A149 for Cromer. At Thursford B1354 for Aylsham. Just before Melton, speed bumps, left immed. before bus shelter; 1st house on right after farmyard.

Clare Wilson
Grove Farm,
Back Lane, Roughton,
Norfolk NR11 8QR

tel   01263 761594
fax   01263 761605
e-mail   grovefarm@homestay.co.uk
web   www.grove-farm.co.uk

Judy Heal
Burgh Parva Hall,
Melton Constable,
Norfolk NR24 2PU

tel   01263 862569
fax   01263 862569
e-mail   judy.heal@btinternet.com

map: 11 entry: 311

map: 11 entry: 312

NORFOLK

NORFOLK

Everything is of hotel-like perfection – breakfast, coffee, beds, furnishings – yet the level of care is personal (a perfect combination for many). The river laps at the walls of the 18th-century windmill and a magnificent sitting room overlooks the marshes; some bedrooms take in the endless seascape and one has a walk-around balcony. Jeremy took over the Mill in 1998 – a guest who fell in love with the place. He upped sticks from his Battersea restaurant and now does wonders with local ingredients: caught-that-day fish or the delicious seamarsh samphire. Don't forget the binoculars.

A fairy-tale house – you almost expect Hansel and Gretel to come skipping out from the woods. Mary has brought deep luxury to this historic former gamekeeper's flint lodge. There are two private guest suites with their own entrance, sitting room, double room and bathroom. Luxury, too: king-size brass beds, excellent mattresses and high spec bathrooms. Mary, an art historian, is solicitous and wants you to feel cossetted; you will. Charcoal used to be burnt in the woodland and the surrounding countryside is enchanting: under the huge Norfolk skies are bird-watching reserves, sandy beaches and salt marshes.

rooms	7: 3 twin/doubles, 4 doubles, all with bathroom.
room price	£74-£112. Single occ. rate by arrangement.
meals	Breakfast 8.30-9am. Dinner £17.50.
closed	Very occasionally.
directions	From Holt take Cley Road, through only street in Cley. Mill signed on left. Over bridge to car park.

rooms	2 double suites, with private sitting room, both with bath/shower.
room price	£85-£100. Single occ. £90.
meals	Excellent pubs and restaurants within 3 miles.
closed	Christmas.
directions	Off A148 onto B1156 for Blakeney. At x-roads, straight over (pass sign to Saxlingham). Approx. 0.5 miles on, house on right with gravel drive & lamp post.

Jeremy Bolam
Cley Mill,
Cley-next-the-Sea, Holt,
Norfolk NR25 7RP
tel 01263 740209
fax 01263 740209

Mary Alexander
The Map House,
Smokers Hole, Saxlingham, Holt,
Norfolk NR25 7JU
tel 01263 741304
e-mail enquiries@maphouse.net
web www.maphouse.net

map: 11 entry: 313

map: 11 entry: 314

NORFOLK

NORFOLK

Norfolk at its best – huge skies, and views that go on forever from this fine Georgian vicarage. An elegant staircase springs from the flagstoned inner hall lit by the glass pyramid high above. Two lovely bedrooms – one facing west captures terrific sunsets – have good furniture, books, china and pictures. The dining room is sunlit, too, and Rosie produces local fare: Cley kippers, mussels, crab, home-produced eggs and preserves and game in season. Just five miles from the coast – swim, sail, walk, cycle, visit the seals...
Use of grass tennis court by arrangement. French spoken.

You can have a real fire in one of the bedrooms – Mary will light it if you ask. She runs a bustling, welcoming household with good humour; "clean, but not always tidy", which is fine by us. There's a natural, family feel – a homely kitchen with old, cream Aga, jade woodwork and bright china – and a bold design sense, too; much that is wooden has been painted and everything draped in brightly coloured coverings. Upstairs, faded carpets, fresh flowers, good sheets, a lovely bathroom and A-frame ceilings. In the sitting room: deep sofas, a log-burner, wooden floor and beams.

rooms	2: 1 double with private bathroom; 1 twin/double with bathroom.
room price	From £50. Please ask about single occ. and children's rate.
meals	Dinner, 3 courses, £18. B.Y.O.
closed	Christmas & New Year.
directions	From Fakenham to Cromer for 6 miles. Left at Crawfish pub into Hindringham, down hill & left, before church, into Blacksmith's Lane. Follow lane, bear right, house on left at top of hill, flinted entrances.

rooms	2: 1 double with bathroom; 1 double with private shower. Cot & fold-up bed available.
room price	£50-£60. Single occ. £27.50-£32.50.
meals	Pub 3 minutes' walk.
closed	Christmas.
directions	From Burnham Market, follow signs to Fakenham for 2 miles; next village is North Creake. Over bridge, sharp left, 0.25 miles on right.

Rosie & Robin Waters
The Old Vicarage,
Blacksmith's Lane, Hindringham,
Norfolk NR21 0QA

tel	01328 878223
e-mail	watersrobin@hotmail.com

Mary & Jeremy Brettingham
Glebe Farmhouse,
Wells Road, North Creake,
Fakenham,
Norfolk NR21 9LG

tel	01328 730133
fax	01328 730444
e-mail	info@eastnortheast.co.uk

map: 11 entry: 315

map: 11 entry: 316

The luxury of a hotel combined with the friendliness of a B&B: it's is a gem. Tucked into a hollow, enfolded by gardens, the 18th-century barn has been decorated in huge style; Allan, a trained chef, welcomes you with tea and scones fresh from the Aga. Floor-to-ceiling windows in the lofty suite with mezzanine bedroom, solid, white-painted stone walls, rugs, books, magazines, even a grand piano. Breakfasts are special – home-made breads and preserves, fresh stewed fruits, local kippers, eggs from next door – and dinner is served at a mahogany table. Alan spoils you from start to finish; he'll even do your laundry.

rooms	3: 1 suite with bath; 1 twin & 1 single, both with private bath/shower. Also 2-bed self-catering cottage.
room price	£70–£80; single occ. £35–£40.
meals	Breakfast 7.30-9.30am. Packed lunch £7.50. Dinner £20.
closed	Occasionally.
directions	From A1067 south of Fakenham towards Stibbard. There right into Wood Norton Rd, then left split (not to Guist); Tylers Barn signed 2nd on left after split.

Allan Urquhart
Tylers Barn,
Wood Norton Road, Stibbard,
Fakenham,
Norfolk NR21 0EX
tel   01328 829260   01263 740228
fax   01328 829260
e-mail allanurquhart@freenet.co.uk

The garden was alive with spring bulbs when we visited and a squadron of white ducks joined in the welcome; they give lovely breakfast eggs, says Jo, but they do trample the tulips! This 17th-century rectory is a big, easy-going family home with a large, jolly drawing/dining room, a double bedroom with a canopied brass bedstead and a croquet lawn. Your children are more than welcome and the grown-up family is fun. Jo is an enthusiastic local and architectural historian; she and Giles are keen sailors. Swim, sail or seal-watch on the nearby coast. *All-weather tennis court available by arrangement.*

rooms	2: 1 double with bathroom; 1 twin with private bath, shower & wc.
room price	£52. Single occ. £37.50.
meals	Dinner £15. B.Y.O.
closed	Christmas & New Year.
directions	From Fakenham A1067 for Norwich. At Guist clock tower, left; second of 2 turnings to Wood Norton. House on right after 100 yds, through overgrown entrance, over 2 cattle grids.

Jo & Giles Winter
The Old Rectory,
Wood Norton,
Norfolk NR20 5AZ
tel   01362 683785

Elizabeth is capable and funny – a winning combination. Recently she got the local church bells ringing again after years of silence (tractor grease did the trick). This is a mainly arable farm with hens, geese and chicks in spring, yet the house is unusually elegant. You have your own sitting room and bedrooms have high ceilings and pretty details – hand-painted tiles above the basins, padded headboards, lovely prints… Organic farm eggs for breakfast and Elizabeth's excellent lemon cake for tea; city-dwellers will feel that they have escaped from it all. *Children over 12 welcome.*

A conservation-award-winning farm tucked away in the heart of rural Norfolk; you are next door to a tiny 13th-century church and within lovely gardens (the coast is only 20 minutes away). The two guest rooms, with large sitting room and small kitchen, are in the converted stables – which are beautiful. Antiques, lovely rugs, cushions and artefacts add to the luxury. Breakfast is delicious, with home eggs, bacon and sausages and is served in the dining room of the main house. Libby and Robin have created something special. Kennel and stable available. *Children over 10 welcome.*

rooms	3: 1 double, 1 twin, sharing bathroom; 1 twin with bathroom.
room price	£42–£50. Single occ. in season, £26–£30.
meals	Breakfast 8–9.30am. Dinner in winter £15.
closed	Christmas & New Year.
directions	From Fakenham B1146 for East Dereham. After 2 miles, left to Gt. Ryburgh. In village, 2nd left up Highfield Lane opp. pink cottage & on for 0.5 miles; house on right.

rooms	2: 1 double, 1 twin in stable annexe, both with bathroom.
room price	£56–£70. Single occ. £35–£45.
meals	Breakfast until 9.30am or by arrangement. Pub 1.5 miles.
closed	Very occasionally.
directions	A1065 Swaffham & Fakenham road. 6 miles on, through Weasenham. After 1 mile, right for Wellingham. There, house on left, next to church.

	Elizabeth Savory
	Highfield Farm,
	Great Ryburgh, Fakenham,
	Norfolk NR21 7AL
tel	01328 829249
fax	01328 829422

	Elisabeth Ellis
	Manor House Farm,
	Wellingham, Nr. Fakenham,
	Kings Lynn,
	Norfolk PE32 2TH
tel	01328 838227
fax	01328 838348
e-mail	l.ellis@farming.co.uk

map: 11 entry: 319   map: 11 entry: 320

For the whole of the 19th century this was Litcham's doctor's house and today, over 200 years after it was built, the red-brick Hall remains at the centre of the community, with church fêtes held in the three-acre garden. This is a thoroughly English home with elegant proportions. The hall, drawing room and dining room are gracious and beautifully furnished. There are good reading lights and books by the beds and the big-windowed guest rooms look onto the lovely garden. John and Hermione are friendly and most helpful. *Children and dogs by arrangement; use of pool similarly.*

Extraordinarily kind and generous hosts – a guest wrote to tell us so – and they really enjoy having people in their 200-year-old converted barn/smithy. There are bees and free-range hens, and vegetables and fruit are home-grown organic; Jane is an imaginative cook. There are farmland views and a wildflower garden and fresh juice before breakfast – in the large friendly kitchen where candles are suspended above the table and dried flowers from the beams. One bedroom is carpeted and the other is more rustic with seagrass matting. The coast and Walsingham are close by and there's plenty of inspiration for artists.

rooms	2 twins, both with private bathroom. Sitting room available. Extra room available occasionally.
room price	£50-£65. Single occ. by arrangement.
meals	Dinner £20.
closed	Christmas.
directions	From Swaffham, A1065; right to Litcham after 5 miles. House on left on entering village. Georgian red brick with stone balls on gatepost.

rooms	2: 1 twin/double with private bathroom; 1 twin/double with private shower room.
room price	£45. Single occ. from £22.50.
meals	Dinner, 3 courses, £15. B.Y.O wine.
closed	Christmas.
directions	A148 from Fakenham for Kings Lynn, then left for Dunton. Straight through Dunton. Keep on main country lane. Barn on left before phone box.

John & Hermione Birkbeck
Litcham Hall,
Litcham, Nr. Kings Lynn,
Norfolk PE32 2QQ
tel   01328 701389
fax   01328 701164
e-mail   j.birkbeck@amserve.com

Michael & Jane Davidson-Houston
Manor Farm Barn,
Tatterford, Nr. Fakenham,
Norfolk NR21 7AZ
tel   01485 528393

map: 11 entry: 321

map: 11 entry: 322

A bustling, easy-going, lived-in farmhouse with comfortable touches of elegance such as grand piano and gilt cornicing. Two of the bedrooms are huge and high-ceilinged, with chairs from which to admire the view through the long windows. Bedrooms are neither designery nor lavish, but homely and generous with towels, bathrobes and other extras, such as a fridge and sofa. There are plenty of dogs and horses (stabling available) and delightful farming hosts – walls bear the proofs of their successes at point-to-points and shows. *Children over 12 by arrangement.*

A perfectly shaped 18th-century house – its setting is utterly rural and the large grounds deserve exploration. You can play tennis, swim in the heated outdoor pool, shelter under an arbour or cross the bridged pond to an enchanting island. This is a very traditional house with displays of china, an oak, oval dining table that seats 12 and antique furniture; bedrooms are coolly elegant and there are good views all around. This is a place of peace – close to Sandringham, good sailing, walking, golf courses and beaches.

rooms	3: 1 double with shower room, 1 double with bath/shower; 1 twin with private bathroom & wc.
room price	£40-£56. Single occ. £25-£35.
meals	Pub/restaurant 800 yds.
closed	Very occasionally.
directions	From Kings Lynn, A148 for Cromer. 3 miles after Hillington, 2nd of 2 turnings right to Harpley (no signpost) opp. Houghton Hall sign. 200 yds on, over x-roads & house 400 yds on left.

rooms	1 twin/double with bath.
room price	£70-£75. Single occ. £50.
meals	Dinner, 2-3 courses, £21.50-£25.
closed	Christmas.
directions	From Kings Lynn A47 for Swaffham. 4 miles on, left at Middleton, by church & left again into Hill Rd. Right into drive (opp. Paul Drive).

Amanda Case
Lower Farm,
Harpley, Nr. Kings Lynn,
Norfolk PE31 6TU
tel   01485 520240
fax   01485 520240

Mrs C. Knight
The Old Hall,
Middleton, Kings Lynn,
Norfolk PE32 1RW
tel   01553 840490
fax   01553 840708
e-mail   emidas@talk21.com

The 1970s exterior belies the comfort and elegance within. Tessa's family once owned a house near this site and much of the antique furniture lives on here; her ancestors include a lover of Elizabeth, Empress of Austria, hence the imperial memorabilia on display. Tessa and her ex-Army husband, David, have lived all over the world and the warm domesticity of the house reflects their desire to 'come home to roost'. You are given a charming welcome and a delicious breakfast with eggs from the chickens and other fowl that wander the garden.

rooms	2 twins, both with basin, sharing bathroom.
room price	£60. Single occ. £40.
meals	Breakfast 7-10am. Packed lunch £5. Dinner £25. Good pubs locally.
closed	Occasionally.
directions	From A14, A508 south for Northampton, 1st right to Haselbech. At sharp r-h bend, left past church to Cottesbrooke, 0.25 miles. Left between 2 red cottages & then 1st right between fields. Tarmac drive to house.

Tessa Le Sueur
Haselbech House,
Haselbech Hill, Northampton,
Northamptonshire NN6 9LL
tel   01604 686266
fax   01604 686544
e-mail lesueur@haselbech.freeserve.co.uk

map: 10 entry: 325

Part of the Althorp estate, this former 1840s farmhouse is a family home at the end of a grand avenue of lime trees; in the garden you'll see traces of medieval ridge-and-furrow farming methods. Valerie and Ian, who collect and sell blue and white Staffordshire pottery, are great company; they are also very knowledgeable and enthusiastic about the area and pull off the trick of giving you both comfort and privacy. Their daughter runs a livery – the riding is superb and your horse is welcome, too. The large simple bedrooms have sofas, armchairs and great views.

rooms	3: 1 double, with bath, plus 1 extra twin, let only to members of same party; 1 twin with private bath.
room price	£50-£60. Single occ. from £30.
meals	Dinner £15. B.Y.O wine.
closed	Very occasionally.
directions	From N'hampton, A45 for Daventry. After approx 1.5 miles, 3rd exit at r'bout (for Althorp). After 1 mile, 1st exit at r'bout (for Nobottle). House just beyond Nobottle on left, on brow of hill.

Valerie Cocks
Nobottle Grange,
Nobottle, Northampton,
Northamptonshire NN7 4HJ
tel   01604 759494
fax   01604 590799
e-mail nobottlegrange@hotmail.com

map: 10 entry: 326

A beautiful 300-year-old stone thatched cottage, with converted barn, stables, conservatory and garden. Inside, something special at every turn: a Bechstein piano in the cottage sitting room, a Jacobean trunk in the single room, Gothic headboards in the twin, a beautiful bureau in the bathroom. And then there's Liz – a charming and gracious hostess; guests have said that "staying here is like staying with a good friend". *Cordon Bleu* dinners and the lovely conservation village of Staverton complete the idyll. *Children over eight and babes in arms welcome.*

Eileen and Clive fell in love with the place when they first saw the valley from the top of the hill 11 years ago. They are the friendliest hosts and have created splendid comfort; one of the large bedrooms has a huge shower, said by one American to be "the best in England". Built as a coach house in the 1850s, it adjoins the site of a former priory founded in 1175. The garden is gorgeous – watch the ducks or fish on the small lake. Unspoilt open countryside and the Jurassic Way beckon walkers; there may be apricot cake on your return…

rooms	4: 2 doubles, 1 twin, all with bath/shower; 1 single with bathroom.
room price	£77. Single occ. £48.50.
meals	Dinner, 3 courses, £25.50.
closed	Christmas & New Year.
directions	From Daventry, A425 to Leamington Spa. 100 yds past Staverton Park Conference Centre, right into village, then 1st right. Keep left, & at 'Give Way' sign, sharp left. House immed. on right.

rooms	2: 1 double with private bathroom; 1 twin with shower room.
room price	£70. Single occ. £45.
meals	Pub 1 mile, restaurants within 5 miles.
closed	Very occasionally.
directions	At Staverton on A425 Daventry to Leamington Spa; take road to Catesby opp. Countryman pub for 2 miles. 200 yds after sharp bend right to Lower Catesby. House to left of clock at foot of hill.

	Mrs Elizabeth Jarrett
	Colledges House,
	Oakham Lane, Staverton, Daventry,
	Northamptonshire NN11 6JQ
tel	01327 702737
fax	01327 300851
e-mail	lizjarrett@colledgeshouse.fsnet.co.uk

	Clive & Eileen Gardiner Wood
	The Old Coach House,
	Lower Catesby, Daventry,
	Northamptonshire NN11 6LF
tel	01327 310390
fax	01327 312220
e-mail	coachhouse@lowercatesby.co.uk
web	www.lowercatesby.co.uk

NORTHAMPTONSHIRE

In this wonderful corner of England you're immersed in a restorative peace. The church and the ironstone, listed vicarage have sat side by side since the 18th century. Birdsong and the sound of tennis being played on the grass court add to the Englishness of it all; you will effortlessly sink into the country-house pace. The cream twin and the pale green double are extremely comfortable. Lots of choice for breakfast and your favourite newspaper can be waiting on the table. *Children by arrangement.*

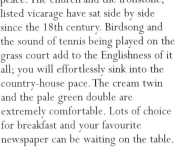

rooms	2: 1 double with shower room; 1 twin with private bathroom.
room price	From £60. Single occ. £35.
meals	Packed lunch £3-£5. Dinner £12-£15.
closed	Christmas.
directions	From M40 junc. 11, dual c'way for N'thampton. 0.75 miles on, left at r'bout for N'thampton, & left again 2 miles on. Follow signs for Canons Ashby to Moreton Pinkney. There, fork right across green on track. Beside church.

Colonel & Mrs T. J. S. Eastwood
The Old Vicarage,
Moreton Pinkney, Daventry,
Northamptonshire NN11 3SQ

tel	01295 760057
fax	01295 760057
e-mail	tim@tandjeastwood.fsnet.co.uk
web	www.tandjeastwood.fsnet.co.uk

NORTHUMBERLAND

The topiary is magnificent! And the old dovecote fascinates foreigners. This is a solid, Victorian house set in expansive, breathtaking Northumbrian scenery – a magnet for walkers and nature lovers. Your gentle, hospitable hostess welcomes families now that her children have fled the nest, though their Beatrix Potter books and little knick-knacks remain. Lots of photographs, too, mostly of the family on horseback. Twin bedrooms are straightforward but large and perfectly adequate. All have wonderful views.

rooms	3 twins (2 with basin) sharing 2 bathrooms.
room price	£50. Single occ. from £30.
meals	Breakfast from 7am. Dinner from £20.
closed	Occasionally.
directions	From A68, south of Tyne at r'bout, east for Stocksfield. Take B6309 right signed Hindley. 1st left, then biggest house at end.

Mrs J. Aldridge
Old Ridley Hall,
Stocksfield,
Northumberland NE43 7RU

tel	01661 842816
e-mail	oldridleyhall@talk21.com

NORTHUMBERLAND

NORTHUMBERLAND

Lynne has made many improvements to this 18th-century gentleman's residence and there are more delights promised. Bedrooms all have original Georgian shutters; some have waxed floors with rugs. Guests love the comfy beds. Substantial breakfasts are served in the lovely dining room with its antique oak dresser and other good pieces. All rooms have exceptional views of the Northumberland countryside which beckons the walker, the naturalist, the stressed city soul. A pretty garden, a newly-built stable block, an outdoor arena set in five acres and a big family welcome.

The Clydes have striven for perfection: every picture, ornament, piece of china, fabric and colour has been chosen to perfectly complement each artfully designed room. Bedrooms have bold William Morris wallpapers, excellent beds and windows that are elaborately dressed. Your hosts are generous, too – with their breakfasts, enticing tea trays, fluffy robes, toiletries displayed among shells and glassware and bowls of fruit… They ran a restaurant for 22 years, are down-to-earth and keen walkers. *Children by arrangement.*

rooms	3: 2 doubles, both with shower, 1 family room with bathroom.
room price	£55. Single occ. £35.
meals	Restaurants within a short drive.
closed	December & January.
directions	A69 signed Ovington, on left if travelling to Hexham. Through Ovington. House signed on left, after sharp corner.

rooms	2: 1 double with bathroom; 1 twin with shower room.
room price	£70-£75. Single occ. £45-£47.50.
meals	Packed lunch £4. Dinner £24.
closed	Very occasionally.
directions	From Haydon Bridge, left onto B6319. After 300 yds cross railway. 1st right (B6319). After 2 miles farmhouse on left.

	Lynne Moffitt
	Ovington House,
	Ovington, Prudhoe,
	Northumberland NE42 6DH
tel	01661 832442
fax	01661 832442
e-mail	lynne.moffitt@btopenworld.com

	Angela Clyde
	Allerwash Farmhouse,
	Newborough, Nr. Hexham,
	Northumberland NE47 5AB
tel	01434 674574
fax	01434 674574
web	www.allerwash.ntb.org.uk

Readers have written to tell us how happy they have been here. Just three miles from Hadrian's Wall the house is at the end of a long drive – over the burn and an old stone bridge, surrounded by ancient woodland and birdsong. It is well lived-in, elegant and comfortable; the large bedrooms are pretty and thoughtfully furnished with antiques and lovely prints. There is a walled garden and breakfast can be taken on the terrace. Katie grew up in this lovely house and can tell you all about the area. *Children over seven and babes in arms welcome.*

Guests stay in recently converted farm buildings round a courtyard and each suite is named after the wood used within: Stephen makes and restores antique furniture and there's an example of his artistry at every turn. You have use of a sitting room and a beautiful library within the courtyard, while meals are taken in the oak-beamed main house (once the home of Capability Brown's family). Celia is a friendly, attentive hostess who loves cooking, and many ingredients are home-grown; Stephen tops up your drinks from the bar. There's a small but varied wine list, too. A super place.

rooms	3: 1 double, 1 twin, both with bathroom; 1 twin with private bathroom.
room price	£70. Single occ. £45.
meals	Breakfast 7.30-9am. Three good eating pubs locally.
closed	October-February.
directions	7 miles north of Corbridge on A68. Left on A6079 & after 1 mile, right through Lodge gates with arch. House 0.5 miles down drive.

rooms	3: 1 four-poster, 1 double, 1 twin, all with bath/shower.
room price	£58-£70. Single occ. £40.
meals	Dinner, 4 courses, £20. Good pub 6 miles.
closed	November-February.
directions	From Newcastle A696 (for Jedburgh). 5 miles north of Belsay, right onto B6342. House on left after 300 yds.

Simon & Katie Stewart
The Hermitage,
Swinburne, Nr. Hexham,
Northumberland NE48 4DG
tel 01434 681248
fax 01434 681110
e-mail katie.stewart@themeet.co.uk

Celia & Stephen Robinson-Gay
Shieldhall,
Wallington, Morpeth,
Northumberland NE61 4AQ
tel 01830 540387
fax 01830 540490
e-mail robinson.gay@btinternet.com
web www.shieldhallguesthouse.co.uk

map: 19 entry: 333

map: 19 entry: 334

Enid seems to thrive on hard work and company, and that combination makes a perfect B&B hostess – you couldn't hope to meet a nicer woman. You could choose any of her five large homely bedrooms and stay there for a week – awash with comfort, old paintings, silk fabrics, masses to eat and drink and views to the horizon – without wanting or having to leave. But if you stray downstairs past the log fire and the groaning table (dinner is good value) there are 600 acres of farmland around you and a few million more of the Cheviots beyond that. There's much to explore.

Farmhouse B&B at its traditional best: pine furniture, flowery curtains, big duvets, plain walls. It is cosy and friendly, your hosts are kind and the countryside will be a wild surprise if you don't yet know it. Be there at the right time and see fields full of gambolling lambs; revel in the way the salmon and trout on the River Coquet fight for a place on your hook. The National Park is all around you, as are more castles and fortifications than in any other county. Breakfasts are good with fresh fruit, yogurts and local produce.

rooms	5: 4 doubles, 1 twin, all with bath/shower.
room price	£50. Single occ. £35.
meals	Breakfast 7.30-9.30am. Dinner, 3 courses, £14.
closed	Christmas.
directions	Leave A1 for A697 for Coldstream & Longhorsley; 2 miles past Longhorsley, left at Todburn sign; 1 mile to x-roads, then right; on 1 mile over white bridge; 1st right, right again, over cattle grid.

rooms	3: 2 doubles, both with bath/shower; 1 twin with shower.
room price	£50. Single occ. £30.
meals	Good pubs/restaurants 2-6 miles.
closed	Christmas & New Year.
directions	Left in Rothbury along Bridge St; take 1st immed. right over bridge, follow B&B & County Council signs for Great Tosson, approx 2 miles.

	Henry & Enid Nelless
	Thistleyhaugh,
	Longhorsley, Morpeth,
	Northumberland NE65 8RG
tel	01665 570629
fax	01665 570629
web	www.thistleyhaugh.co.uk

	Ann Foggin
	Tosson Tower Farm,
	Great Tosson, Rothbury, Morpeth,
	Northumberland NE65 7NW
tel	01669 620228
fax	01669 620228
e-mail	ann@tossontowerfarm.com
web	www.tossontowerfarm.com

Sophisticated, gracious living in an immaculately elegant Georgian villa perched on a rocky promontory – the sea views are magnificent. The Athertons are avid antique collectors, charming and friendly, amusing and energetic perfectionists. Breakfasts are feasts of fresh fruit, organic yogurt, croissants, scones and fruit compotes; weekend breakfasts are 'full English' with locally-smoked Craster kippers or smoked salmon. Superb bedrooms have beautiful curtains, huge French mahogany beds and luxurious linen and towels. There is a sumptuous drawing room with a grand piano, and a well-stocked library. Perfect.

Dorothy takes pride in creating an easy, sociable atmosphere – three couples who met here one weekend returned for a reunion. This is a pretty spot and the Jacksons know every inch of the countryside and coastline that surrounds their 1715 home. They farm 400 acres of mixed arable land that sweeps down to the coast yet still find time to greet and get to know their guests. The bedrooms are large, bright and well-furnished; there is a conservatory at the back (where you can have tea on arrival), an airy guests' sitting room and splendid views to the sea.

rooms	3: 2 doubles, both with bathroom; 1 double with private shower room.
room price	£90. Single occ. £70.
meals	Breakfast 8-9am. Pub/restaurant 5 miles.
closed	Christmas & New Year.
directions	A1068 Warkworth/Alnmouth. On entering High Buston, Hall is 1st building on right.

rooms	3: 2 doubles, 1 twin, all with shower room. Bathroom also available.
room price	£54. Single occ. £27-£37.
meals	Packed lunches from £3.50. Dinner £14.50.
closed	Christmas & New Year.
directions	From Alnwick, A1068 to Alnmouth. At Hipsburn r'bout follow signs to station & cross bridge. 1st lane to left, approx. 0.5 miles down drive.

Ian & Therese Atherton
High Buston Hall,
High Buston, Alnmouth,
Northumberland NE66 3QH
tel   01665 830606
fax   01665 830707
e-mail   highbuston@aol.com
web   www.members.aol.com/highbuston

Brian & Dorothy Jackson
Bilton Barns,
Alnmouth, Alnwick,
Northumberland NE66 2TB
tel   01665 830427
fax   01665 830063
e-mail   dorothy@biltonbarns.co.uk
web   www.biltonbarns.co.uk

map: 19 entry: 337

map: 19 entry: 338

NORTHUMBERLAND

NORTHUMBERLAND

Sylvia is a doyenne of farmhouse B&B, with 25 years' experience under her belt. She recently received an MBE for her 'Household and Farming Museum' and is justly proud of her gong. She has a wonderful sense of community and Charlie, even if he's been up since dawn with his sheep, will come and have a chat as you have breakfast. Large bedrooms, long views, handmade quilts, family furniture, generous breakfasts. True farmhouse B&B. *Children over 10 welcome.*

A totally surprising one-storey house, full of beautiful things. It is an Aladdin's cave, larger than you could imagine. The garden/breakfast room is the hub of the house and has a country cottage feel to it; here you'll eat locally-smoked kippers, award-winning 'Bamburgh Bangers' and home-cured bacon from the village butcher. There's a sun-trapping courtyard full of colourful pots for summer breakfasts. Guests have a cheerful sitting/dining room and bedrooms have fresh flowers and very good books. Mary is welcoming, amusing and has stacks of local knowledge.

rooms	3: 2 doubles, both with shower room; 1 twin with private bathroom.
room price	£60. Single occ. £40.
meals	Breakfast 7.30-9am. 4miles Restaurants.
closed	Christmas & New Year.
directions	6 miles north of Alnwick on A1, left when you hit dual carriageway, for North Charlton. House 300 yds up on left through trees.

rooms	2: 1 double, 1 twin, sharing private bathroom.
room price	£50-£55. Single occ. £32.50-£35.
meals	Dinner £18.50.
closed	Christmas & occasionally in winter.
directions	From Newcastle A1 north, then right for Bamburgh on B1341. To village, pass 30mph sign & hotel, then 1st right. 400 yds on right.

Charles & Sylvia Armstrong
North Charlton Farm,
Chathill, Alnwick,
Northumberland NE67 5HP
tel   01665 579443
fax   01665 579407
e-mail   ncharlton1@agriplus.net
web   www.northcharlton.com

Mary Dixon
Broome,
22 Ingram Road, Bamburgh,
Northumberland NE69 7BT
tel   01668 214287
e-mail   mdixon4394@aol.com

map: 19 entry: 339

map: 19 entry: 340

NORTHUMBERLAND

NORTHUMBERLAND

Few houses can match the majesty of this Northumberland landscape – Pallinsburn challenges it. The architecture spans several centuries; the heart of the house is Jacobean and there are interior columns and ornate plasterwork. The bedrooms are on the expected grand scale and are generously furnished with antiques, chairs, *chaise longue*. From the window seats you can gaze at the Cheviot Hills. The finest linen and fresh flowers complete the luxury. A fire can be lit for you in the panelled dining room and Mrs Westwood, the housekeeper, will expertly settle you in. *Children over five welcome.*

A south-facing Georgian farmhouse overlooking the Tweed with Holy Island in the distance and not a whisper of noise. You know that Berwick is two miles away and Edinburgh and Newcastle only 45 minutes by train, but you can't feel it. There's broad appeal here for sightseers, birdwatchers, anglers, golfers, deerstalkers and country lovers. The luxury is irresistible: bedding as soft as the landscape; food and wine flawless. Susan is a trained cook, Richard a retired wine-shipper. Anything else you'd like to know before you sit down for dinner? *Children over 12 welcome.*

rooms	2 four-posters, both with bath.
room price	£80-£96. Single occ. £55-£63.
meals	Dinner occasionally available. Pubs/restaurants 1-10 miles.
closed	Occasionally.
directions	North from Newcastle on A1. Left on A697 north of Morpeth turn. On for 5 miles south of Coldstream. Pass Bluebell Inn on left. Drive on right 0.5 miles on. Lodge at gate.

rooms	2: 1 double with shower/bath; 1 twin/double with shower room.
room price	£64-£68. Single occ. from £42.
meals	Breakfast until 9am. Packed lunch £6. Dinner, 3 courses, £19; 4 courses, £22.
closed	Christmas.
directions	Travelling north on A1 level with Berwick, cross bridge over River Tweed; after 1.5 miles take 2nd left signed Low Cocklaw. House on left after 0.5 miles.

Mr & Mrs Lyell
Pallinsburn,
Coldstream, Berwick-upon-Tweed,
Northumberland TD12 4SG
tel   01890 820202

Richard & Susan Persse
High Letham Farmhouse,
by Berwick-upon-Tweed,
Northumberland TD15 1UX
tel   01289 306585
fax   01289 304194

map: 19 entry: 341

map: 19 entry: 342

Jillie's grandmother studied at the Slade and her paintings line the walls; glass and china ornaments adorn every surface. The wisteria-clad Victorian vicarage next to the 12th-century church was falling down when the Steeles bought it; now it is an elegant and traditional country home. Long windows are generously draped and pelmeted, there are tall-backed dining chairs, silver and crystal and lovely oils. Bedrooms are large and the baths have claw feet. You can play tennis or croquet while Jillie prepares a traditional supper using fresh vegetables from the kitchen garden. *Children over 12 welcome.*

When owners love their home and enjoy sharing it with guests you can't fail to have a good time. Colin and Erica are such people and have nurtured the well-proportioned house, built in 1917, into its present happy state. Numerous rooms lead off a big, open hall filled with flowers; guests have two sitting rooms with deep sofas and log fires; and there's lots to do: golf (six holes), snooker, darts, croquet, tennis, swimming... if the weather's dreary, there are more games to play by the fire. Bedrooms have ample lounging-around space and fireplaces; bathrooms are big and one has black and cream Edwardian tiles.

rooms	3: 1 double, 1 twin, each with bath & shower, 1 small double with shower.
room price	£70–£77. Single occ. £45–£47.50.
meals	Dinner £20.
closed	Occasionally.
directions	From A1, A46 to Lincoln & left onto A1133 for Gainsborough. Drive through Langford, 1 mile on, & left for Holme. House 100 yds on, on right, by church.

rooms	3: 2 doubles, 1 with private bathroom, 1 with shower; 1 twin with bathroom.
room price	£56. Single occ. £33.
meals	Breakfast 7–10am. Dinner, for 4 people or more, £22; light supper from £12. Good pub 3 miles.
closed	Christmas.
directions	From A617 Newark to Mansfield, 0.25 miles west of Kirklington; right at 2 small white bollards, just before turn to Eakring.

	Jerry & Jillie Steele
	The Old Vicarage,
	Langford, Newark,
	Nottinghamshire NG23 7RT
tel	01636 705031
fax	01636 708728
e-mail	jillie.steele@virgin.net

	Erica McGarrigle
	Archway House,
	Kirklington, Newark,
	Nottinghamshire NG22 8NX
tel	01636 812070
fax	01636 812200
e-mail	mcgarrigle@archway-house.co.uk

A village house close to Southwell's minster – "the most rural cathedral in England". Hilary has lived here for 38 years and can recommend good places to eat, all within walking distance, and much to see and do. The four bedrooms are cottagey and the dining room is two connecting rooms, with separate tables, that lead to a conservatory. The feel is more guest house than private home B&B. Hilary is a one-off, a special host: she's chatty and fun and never happier than when the house is full of guests. Breakfasts are generous.

From the front bedrooms and the majestic drawing and dining rooms you look beyond the lawns and cherished roses to a glorious view: it feels as if the Vale of Belvoir is at your feet. The house has been in the family for generations – it doesn't bustle with life and warmth and the bedrooms are a little dated but the gilt-framed portraits, the grandfather clock and the formal rooms vividly recall a grander age. Use of the swimming pool and tennis court can be arranged. The hill behind is the highest between here and the Urals in Russia. *Horse B&B by arrangement.*

rooms	4: 1 twin, 1 double, both with bath/shower; 1 double with shower; 1 twin with private bathroom.
room price	From £68. Single occ. from £40.
meals	Plenty of pubs & restaurants within walking distance.
closed	Very occasionally.
directions	From Nottingham, A612 to Southwell. Right into Westgate & pass Minster. 100 yds on, fork right at library & almost immed. right down alley beside Old Forge.

rooms	4: 2 doubles, 1 twin, all with private bathroom; 1 twin with shower.
room price	£45-£50. Single occ. £25-£30.
meals	Good pubs nearby.
closed	Christmas.
directions	On A606 between Nottingham (12 miles) & Melton Mowbray (7 miles). Coming north drive to top of hill, then sharp right into Colonel's Lane. Signed.

Hilary Marston
The Old Forge,
Burgage Lane, Southwell,
Nottinghamshire NG25 0ER
tel   01636 812809
fax   01636 816302

Hilary Dowson
Sulney Fields,
Colonel's Lane, Upper Broughton,
Melton Mowbray,
Nottinghamshire LE14 3BD
tel   01664 822204
fax   01664 823976
e-mail   hillyc@talk21.com

map: 10 entry: 345

map: 10 entry: 346

The architecture and the grounds are immediately captivating and the late Georgian interior is impressive in scale, with the light, height and space you expect from this period. The hall is galleried and the staircase, elegantly delicate, sweeps you regally up to the bedrooms. All rooms are large – bathroom suites hark back to the '70s – and all except one look onto the garden and far beyond. Guests have a large drawing room, woodland to explore, tennis and croquet to play; French windows open onto the grounds. Brian and Wendy are super hosts. *Children over 12 welcome.*

A baby grand that beckons those who can play and fires lit on cold evenings. It's all utterly soothing and easy and reinforces the wonders of English country life. Persian rugs in the sitting room and ethnic touches here and there reflect Sue's passion for real travel. More rugs in pretty bedrooms that are unmistakably 'country' and light; low ceilings and uneven floors reveal their 18th-century origins. There are eight acres of grounds with all-round views and gorgeous walks through Beech Woods strewn with bluebells in May. *No bookings after noon on day of stay, please.*

rooms	5: 2 doubles, 2 twins, 1 single, all with bathroom.
room price	£65. Single occ. £45–£55.
meals	Breakfast 7.30–9.45am. Pub 0.5 miles.
closed	Occasionally and Christmas.
directions	From Henley, A4155 for Reading. After 2.5 miles, College on left & pub on right. Before pub turn into Plough Lane. House 1 mile on left.

rooms	2 twins/doubles, both with bath/shower.
room price	£58. Single occ. £40.
meals	Breakfast 8–9am. Good choice of pubs/restaurants 0.5 miles.
closed	September–April.
directions	From Henley NW on Peppard road for 3 miles, then right for Shepherds Green. House on right after 0.3 miles. Phone to advise time of arrival.

Brian & Wendy Talfourd-Cook
Holmwood,
Shiplake Row,
Binfield Heath, Henley,
Oxfordshire RG9 4DP

tel   0118 947 8747
fax   0118 947 8637

Sue Fulford-Dobson
Shepherds,
Shepherds Green, Rotherfield Greys
Henley-on-Thames,
Oxfordshire RG9 4QL

tel   01491 628413
fax   01491 628413

OXFORDSHIRE

Horse-loving Joanna will teach you to ride, by arrangement, and even offers B&B to itinerant horses and their riders. Her husband, who is passionate about roses, may be able to organise rough shooting for field sports enthusiasts, complete with gun dog. Simple comfort in peaceful surroundings is the watchword at this extended, semi-detached old worker's cottage; clean, functional, no-frills, lemon-yellow rooms are in a separate garden flat overlooking a courtyard. If roses, wine, shooting, hunting and stud farms are your thing, you could do no better. Probably not for *Guardian* readers.

They are as laid back as they are efficient... the perfect owners for a ravishing house. The décor is oak floors, white walls, wood, antiques, fine prints; there's a minimalist feel, with the odd dash of exotica from much long-haul travel. The drawing room has a vast, magnificent fireplace for winter. Anthea and Stephen are fun – clocks are their main business and the drawing room has a large, projected clock on the wall. Everywhere there is head-clearing simplicity that allows the original features the space to impress.

rooms	2 twins in garden flat, both with private bathroom & garden access.
room price	From £45. Single occ. from £25.
meals	Short drive to restaurants.
closed	Very occasionally.
directions	Junc. 8/9 M4 to Henley. A4130 to Oxford. Crowmarsh Gifford r'bout, left onto Wallingford bypass. Right at next r'bout, over river, left at 1st of double r'bouts to Moulsford. 1 mile on, right into Caps Lane. Cottage 1st on left.

rooms	3: 1 double with bathroom; 1 double with private bathroom; 1 twin/double, with shower room.
room price	£80.
meals	Pub/restaurant 0.5 miles.
closed	Christmas & New Year.
directions	From M40, A329 for Wallingford. In Stadhampton take lane immed. after mini-r'bout, left across village green. House straight ahead.

Mrs Joanna Alexander
The Well Cottage,
Caps Lane, Cholsey,
Oxfordshire OX10 9HQ
tel 01491 651959
fax 01491 651675
e-mail joanna@thewellcottage.com
web www.thewellcottage.com

Anthea & Stephen Savage
The Manor,
Stadhampton,
Oxfordshire OX44 7UL
tel 01865 891999
fax 01865 891640
e-mail action@timebeam.com

map: 4 entry: 349

map: 9 entry: 350

OXFORDSHIRE

OXFORDSHIRE

This beautiful farmhouse was once owned by St John's College, Oxford – the date stone above the entrance reads 1629, but parts of the house are even older. There's the happy buzz of family life here; it's relaxed and informal and you settle in easily, welcomed by Mary Anne with tea and home-made shortbread and by the equally friendly Robert. Bedrooms are light and airy with small stone-arched and mullioned windows; there are Tudor fireplaces, timbered and exposed walls. The huge, twin bedroom has ornate plasterwork and views over the garden and church; the green and peach double is cosier, again with views.

Ten acres in which to dream – this 18th-century stone house sits behind a Norman church in a perfect Cotswold hamlet. "England at its most idyllic," said our inspector. The beautifully renovated farmhouse combines character and elegance: a comfortable sitting room, sweet bedrooms (one with its own sitting room) and flowers from a garden that is Clare's delight. She and Robin are friendly, vibrant, easy with children – there are children's arts and crafts workshops in the holidays and ponies in the yard which children can ride. The surrounding fields provide glorious views. *Self-catering possible.*

rooms	2: 1 double, 1 twin, both with shower room.
room price	£52-£54. Single occ. £36-£38.
meals	Breakfast until 9am. Good pub 2 minutes' walk.
closed	Mid-December-mid-January.
directions	From Oxford, A420 for Swindon for 8 miles & right at r'bout, for Witney (A415). Over 2 bridges, immed. right by pub car park. Right at T-junc.; drive on right, past church.

rooms	3: 1 double, 1 twin, both with private bathroom; 1 twin/double with bathroom & sitting room.
room price	£58-£80. Single occ. £44-£55.
meals	Dinner from £20. Good pubs and restaurants in town.
closed	Very occasionally.
directions	From Burford, A40 for Cheltenham. 1st left, for Westwell. 2 miles to T-junc., then right, through village. Right to Aldsworth then 1st right onto drive. On to end.

Mary Anne & Robert Florey
Rectory Farm,
Northmoor, Nr. Witney,
Oxfordshire OX29 5SX
tel 01865 300207
fax 01865 300559
e-mail pj.florey@farmline.com

Clare & Robin Dunipace
The Glebe House,
Westwell, Burford,
Oxfordshire OX18 4JT
tel 01993 822171
fax 01993 824125
e-mail clare.dunipace@amserve.net
web www.oxford-cotswolds-holidays.com

map: 9 entry: 351

map: 9 entry: 352

Our inspector calls it "a Sawday idyll". Bridget is gracious and elegant, the house and setting intoxicating. This is country elegance with few concessions to modernity: rugs and furniture fit beautifully, the kitchen is stone-flagged and wood-boarded. The Garden House is a wonderful B&B or self-catering hideaway – hunker down with books, play the piano, stroll out into the garden; you have your own bedroom, kitchen, sitting room and log fire. The River Windrush trickles through the garden, the church and the ruins of Minster Lovell Hall sit beside it.

A charming Cotswold stone house – originally the village inn – with a 14th-century core; there's a special elegance and atmosphere. Breakfasts are served in the wooden-framed conservatory with spectacular views – on a clear day you can see for over 30 miles. The light and airy bedroom that looks out onto the village green has extremely comfortable beds with a delightful bathroom. The professionally landscaped, newly planted one-acre garden has a series of rooms and lovely views and contains many unusual plants and trees. A delightful, homely and welcoming house in a beautiful setting.

rooms	1 double in Garden House with bath/shower.
room price	£75. Single occ. £47.50.
meals	Good pubs within walking distance.
closed	Very occasionally.
directions	From Burford, A40 for Oxford. At next r'bout, left for Minster Lovell, across bridge. Through village, house on right before church, in cul-de-sac marked 'Unsuitable for motor vehicles'. Through green gates on right.

rooms	1 twin with bathroom.
room price	£70. Single occ. £45.
meals	Breakfast until 9.30am.
closed	Christmas.
directions	From Witney, 4 miles for Charlbury on B4022, then left to Leafield. There, pass church & fork left by flagpole & school sign. 100 yds on, house on left, with lawn in front. Turn into gravel drive.

Ms Bridget Geddes
The Old Vicarage,
Minster Lovell,
Oxfordshire OX29 0RR
tel   01993 775630
fax   01993 772534
e-mail   ageddes@lix.compulink.co.uk

Mrs Tania Llewellyn
Old George House,
Leafield,
Oxfordshire OX29 9NP
tel   01993 878632
fax   01993 878700

map: 9 entry: 353

map: 9 entry: 354

Helen and John radiate pleasure and humour; join them at the oak table by the rough-hewn fireplace and the ancient dresser. Blenheim is a short walk down the lane and this soft old stone house is perfect for any delusions of grandeur: good prints and paintings, venerable furniture, gentle fabrics – nothing cluttered or overdone. Shallow, curvy, 18th-century stairs lead past grandfather's bronze bust to the splendid double room; the tiny twin beyond the fine green shower room has its own challenging spiral staircase to the cobbled courtyard. A delight of a garden and a quiet village complete the picture.

All the nooks, crannies and beams you would expect in such an ancient thatched cottage in a Cotswold village, but much more besides: music, fun and laughter, not to mention a wealth of inside information about gardens to visit. Judith is a keen gardener who writes books on the subject; her passion for plants is palpable in her own wonderful cottage garden. Her style and intelligence are reflected in the lived-in, elegant house. Charming, bright pastel bedrooms, thoroughly relaxed atmosphere – and fresh everything…

rooms	2: 1 double, 1 twin, sharing shower room.
room price	From £48. Single occ. from £35.
meals	2 pubs within walking distance.
closed	Christmas.
directions	A44 north from Oxford's ring road. At r'bout, 1 mile before Woodstock, left onto A4095 into Bladon. Take last left in village. House on 2nd bend in road, with iron railings.

rooms	2: 1 double, 1 twin, both with bath.
room price	£70. Single occ. £45.
meals	Dinner, 4 courses, £25. Excellent restaurant, 150 yards.
closed	Christmas & New Year.
directions	Sibford Gower is 0.5 miles south off B4035 which runs between Banbury & Chipping Campden. House on main street, same side as church & school.

Helen Stevenson
Manor Farmhouse,
Manor Road, Bladon, Nr. Woodstock,
Oxfordshire OX20 1RU

tel 01993 812168
fax 01993 812168
e-mail helstevenson@hotmail.com
web www.oxlink.co.uk/woodstock/manor-farmhouse/

Judith Hitching
Gower's Close,
Sibford Gower, Nr. Banbury,
Oxfordshire OX15 5RW

tel 01295 780348
e-mail j.hitching@virgin.net.co.uk

map: 9 entry: 355

map: 9 entry: 356

There's a marvellous glow to this lovingly restored house. A rare, original and fine example of a large 1650s Yeoman farmhouse, it has more than its fair share of oak beams, stone-mullioned windows, big fireplaces and bread ovens. What's more, there are fine antiques, paintings and, in the attic, a games room with a full-size billiard table. Beamed bedrooms are large, light and airy, with views to the valley or to the church; this is an exceptionally pretty village with a proper green. The Hainsworths' two lovely dogs are "weird-haired" pointers, apparently!

Parish records suggest that on the site of the 1760 house there was once a monastic farm where teachers at Oxford would come for enlightenment and inspiration; today you reap the same benefits, and in considerable comfort. Stephen and Sara happily share their books, piano, tennis court, gardens, lake and local knowledge. Sara is an interior designer; cushions, curtains and sofas are made from beautiful fabrics and the colours throughout are excellent. The beds are memorably comfortable, with goose down pillows and duvets. Breakfast is an easy-going affair and there's a guest drawing room with fire.

rooms	2: 1 double, 1 twin, both with bathroom.
room price	From £75. Single occ. £50.
meals	Excellent pub & restaurant in village.
closed	Very occasionally.
directions	From A422, 7 miles north-west of Banbury, left down hill through Alkerton, then up hill. 1st left by church. House on right.

rooms	3: 1 twin/double with shower room; 1 twin/double with bathroom; 1 twin/double with bath/shower.
room price	£64. Single occ. £40.
meals	Dinner £20. Excellent pubs 600 yds.
closed	Very occasionally.
directions	In Kings Sutton follow signs to Charlton but, before leaving Kings Sutton, take last right turn down lane, off Astrop rd, opp. a tree with a seat around it. At end of lane.

	Keith & Maggie Hainsworth
	Mill House,
	Shenington, Banbury,
	Oxfordshire OX15 6NH
tel	01295 670642

	Sara & Stephen Allday
	College Farmhouse,
	Kings Sutton, Banbury,
	Oxfordshire OX17 3PS
tel	01295 811473
fax	01295 812505
e-mail	seallday@aol.com

OXFORDSHIRE

Our inspector really loved this place. The Grove-Whites are super and they run their B&B as a real team. The house is charming: low ceilings, exposed beams and stone fireplaces and the bedrooms, perched above their own staircases like crows' nests, are decorated with rich, floral fabrics. All rooms are unusual and full of character, old and luxurious; the family's history and travels are evident all over. They have two delightful dogs – Ulysses and Goliath – and it's all so easy that you may not want to leave. There's a barn room, too, with its own entrance.

RUTLAND

The stable yard is hung with roses and the delightful garden overlooks the croquet lawn and Rutland Water – England's largest lake – around which you may sail, fish, cycle or ride. Rutland is a 'mini-Cotswolds' of stone villages, gentle hills, market towns and good pubs; historic houses and castles, bird sanctuaries and Georgian Stamford are nearby. Inside the house are high ceilings, stone archways, antique furniture and beds spread with fine linen. Do eat here – Cecilie is a charming hostess and a brilliant cook.

rooms	3: 1 double, 1 twin/double, both with bath/shower; 1 twin/double with private bathroom.
room price	£68. Single occ. £44.
meals	Breakfast 8-9am. Dinner £24. Supper £16.
closed	Christmas.
directions	From M40, junc. 10, A43 for Northampton. After 5 miles, left to Charlton. There, left & house on left, 100 yds past Rose & Crown.

rooms	3: 1 twin, 1 double, both with private bathroom; 1 single, with shared bathroom.
room price	£70. Single occ. £35-£45.
meals	Dinner £20.
closed	Occasionally.
directions	From A1 Stamford bypass A606 for Oakham for 3 miles. Fork left for Edith Weston. Past village sign take 1st right, Church Lane. Past church right again down hill. House on right on left bend.

	Col & Mrs Grove-White
	Home Farmhouse,
	Charlton, Nr. Banbury,
	Oxfordshire OX17 3DR
tel	01295 811683
fax	01295 811683
e-mail	grovewhite@lineone.net
web	www.homefarmhouse.co.uk

	Cecilie Ingoldby
	Old Hall Coach House,
	Edith Weston, Oakham,
	Rutland LE15 8HQ
tel	01780 721504
e-mail	cecilieingoldby@aol.com

Anyone seeking a second childhood should pay this former pub a visit. All kinds of toys and games add to the attractive clutter and illustrations from children's books adorn the walls. The real joy is Susan herself: generous with her time, spirit and hospitality, she will quickly engage you in lively conversation; her laughter is echoed by Polly the parrot. Other natural sounds are provided by the trickle of the stream which meanders through the enchanting garden where you can picnic by the river.

An atmosphere of life, warmth, elegance and good taste pervades and guests return time after time. Pam – theatrical, laughing, genuine – is just lovely. The house is ancient, magpie-gabled and the church and pound are 800 years old. Beams criss-cross the rooms and vertical framing has been exposed to great effect. There's a grand piano in the drawing room and, on the rambling first floor, bedrooms are pretty and double-glazed. Pam's breakfasts are as generous as her spirit. *Children over 11 welcome.*

rooms	2: 1 double, 1 single, both with private bathroom.
room price	£40. Single £20.
meals	Packed lunch £5. Dinner, 3 courses, from £10. Excellent restaurant 0.5 miles.
closed	Occasionally.
directions	From Oswestry, A483 from A5 for Welshpool. 1st left to Maesbury; 3rd right at x-roads with school on corner; 1st house on right.

rooms	3: 1 twin, 1 double, both with shower; 1 family (1 double, 2 singles) with bath/shower.
room price	£48-£52. Single occ. from £30.
meals	Breakfast 7.30-9.30am. Packed lunch available. Good pub within walking distance.
closed	Very occasionally.
directions	From Shrewsbury, A5 north. Through Nesscliffe & after 2 miles, left to Knockin. Through Knockin, past Bradford Arms. House 150 yds on left.

Mrs Sue Barr
Pinfold Cottage,
Newbridge, Maesbury,
Oswestry, Shropshire SY10 8AY
tel   01691 661192
fax   01691 670563
e-mail   suebarr100@hotmail.com

Pam Morrissey
Top Farmhouse,
Knockin, Nr. Oswestry,
Shropshire SY10 8HN
tel   01691 682582
fax   01691 682070
e-mail   p.a.m@knockin.freeserve.co.uk
web   www.topfarmknockin.co.uk

map: 8 entry: 361

map: 8 entry: 362

A Georgian farmhouse, square except for its sandstone portico, set in five acres of paddock and garden; the half-timbered barn looks 200 years older than the house. Animals surround you and reflect the family's interests: three dogs, a cat, two horses, a clutch of hens and a ferret; game birds grace the walls and elephants graze on the mantelpiece. One bathroom has a marble-topped washstand and a lovely roll-top bath. Clare is determined to give guests the sort of treatment she loves to receive herself, and succeeds. You can even bring your horse.
Children over 12 welcome.

David's family has farmed here for four generations – he tends a 250-acre arable and stock farm. The Breidden Hills and views of the Severn dominate the setting and the simple garden, sensibly, does not try to compete with the scenery. There are three bedrooms in this 1740s border farmhouse: one with Sanderson curtains and borders and a half-tester bed with rope-twist columns, a twin with Victorian wrought-iron bedsteads, and a double with brass bed. Try venison sausages from a local deer herd with your farm eggs for breakfast. A smashing place – simple and excellent value.

rooms	2: 1 double, 1 twin, sharing bathroom.
room price	£50. Single occ. £30.
meals	Packed lunch available. Excellent pubs nearby.
closed	Christmas & New Year.
directions	A528 (north out of Shrewsbury), becomes B5476 at Harmer Hill signed Wem. After 1.25 miles left at x-roads for Myddle. Large red-brick house 150 yds on right on crown of bend.

rooms	3: 1 double, 1 twin, both with shower room; 1 double with bathroom.
room price	From £45.
meals	Packed lunch £3.50. Pub 3 minutes' walk.
closed	Very occasionally.
directions	From Shrewsbury A458 Welshpool rd. After Ford, right onto B4393. At Crew Green, left for Criggion. House 1st on left after Admiral Rodney pub.

Clare Sawers
Alderton House,
Harmer Hill, Shrewsbury,
Shropshire SY4 3EL
tel   01939 220324
fax   01939 220324
e-mail   the4sawers@countryside-inter.net

Liz Dawson
Brimford House,
Criggion, Nr. Shrewsbury,
Shropshire SY5 9AU
tel   01938 570235
fax   01938 570235
e-mail   info@brimford.co.uk
web   www.brimford.co.uk

You might expect chintz and a touch of gloom but the interior of this 16th-century cottage holds some surprises. Glorious contemporary colours – bongo jazz, mellow heather, Inca gold, salsa – that light up the house; clean, simple lines that owe much to Ikea; and a stainless steel gate dividing the stairs between guests and family that is a piece of art in itself. Bedrooms are small but neat, colourful, and with some fine furniture, both antique and pine. Two rooms face the road; this is not a country retreat. You may hear the family upstairs, too – but a house full of life is fun, and Christine is a delight.

A heavenly Grade II-listed Georgian house in manicured gardens and a 20-minute stroll from Abbey and town. Joan is a terrific cook – 1998 Aga Cook of the Year, no less – who radiates courtesy and charm; Charles cheerfully assumes the role of 'mine host'. Theirs is an atmospheric home, rich with antiques, polished mahogany and eye-catching wallpapers and fabrics. Home-made biscuits and flowers in every room; we loved the large, sunny double with Victorian painted brass half-tester and *chaise longue*. Summer breakfasts are taken in the conservatory – as is afternoon tea.

rooms	4: 2 twin/doubles; 1 twin, 1 double, all with shower room.
room price	£46-£50. Single occ. £33.
meals	Walking distance from pubs, wine bars & restaurants.
closed	Christmas.
directions	From the A5 bypass, A458 into town. Over 2 r'bouts for Shrewsbury; through lights; house immed. on left, next to Post Office.

rooms	3: 1 double with bath/shower; 1 double with private bathroom; 1 twin with shower room.
room price	£59-£65. Single occ. from £44.50.
meals	Dinner from £25.
closed	Occasionally.
directions	A5/A49 junc. (south of bypass) follow signs to centre. Over 1st mini r'bout, 2nd exit at next, past hotel. 2nd left into Upper Rd. 150 yds on at house on bend, left & immed. right into Church Lane. Drive at bottom on left.

Christine Yates-Roberts
164 Abbey Foregate,
Shrewsbury,
Shropshire SY2 6AL
tel   01743 367750
fax   01743 367750
e-mail chris@164bedandbreakfast.co.uk
web   www.164bedandbreakfast.co.uk

Joan Hathaway
Meole Brace Hall,
Shrewsbury,
Shropshire SY3 9HF
tel   01743 235566
fax   01743 236886
e-mail enquiries@meolebracehall.co.uk
web   www.meolebracehall.co.uk

map: 8 entry: 365

map: 8 entry: 366

SHROPSHIRE

SHROPSHIRE

A large, handsome, solid Georgian farmhouse which has a lovely courtyard with period outbuildings – a classic of its type. In the fine drawing room there are exposed beams and an enormous mirror above the fireplace; the dining room is smart and has deep red walls that have been stencilled with pretty flowers (by a guest). The odd sign here and there suggests this is a very small hotel but amiable George rescues the day; he is super-helpful. Rooms are English to the core: florals and chintz, soft carpets and four-posters. There are extras such as cafetières and fluffy bathrobes. In-house chef Gareth creates "food adventures".

Jean is an immensely kind hostess and has turned her simple Methodist chapel into a warm, homely, walker's retreat: pine furniture, patterned rugs, old wooden floors. The dining/sitting room, with its choir gallery, is open right to the roof – the effect is impressive. There is a small twin with views and an even smaller (and cosier) single with extra pull-out bed. Tea and cakes by the woodburning stove: just what you need after a day's trek on the Devil's Chair Ridge. This is a walker's paradise and Jean will transport luggage to your next stop. Simple, small, good value.

rooms	5: 4 doubles, 1 family/twin, all with bath/shower.
room price	£70–£100. Single occ. by arrangement.
meals	Packed lunch £5. Dinner £25. Gourmet, 5-course, dinner, £35.
closed	Very occasionally.
directions	4 miles south of Shrewsbury on A458. In Cross Houses, left after petrol station, signed Atcham. Down lane & right to Brompton; follow to farm.

rooms	2: 1 twin, 1 single, sharing shower, wc & basin.
room price	£44. Single occ. £24.
meals	Packed lunch available. Pub within walking distance.
closed	Occasionally.
directions	From Shrewsbury A488 for Bishop's Castle. Left on edge of Plox Green for Stiperstones. There, left before pub up Perkinsbeach Dingle. Chapel on right.

George Roberts
Upper Brompton Farm,
Cross Houses, Shrewsbury,
Shropshire SY5 6LE
tel 01743 761629
fax 01743 761679
e-mail upper-brompton.farm@dial.pipex.com
web www.upperbromptonfarm.com

Jean Lees
The Old Chapel,
Perkinsbeach Dingle,
Stiperstones, Shrewsbury,
Shropshire SY5 0PE
tel 01743 791449
e-mail jean@a-lees.freeserve.co.uk

map: 8 entry: 367

map: 8 entry: 368

A lovely calm sense of the continuity of history and family life emanates from this large, comfortable Victorian home. Jackie and Jim are delightful hosts and great fun. Bedrooms welcome you with flowers, bathrobes, books, duckdown pillows… and stupendous views of the Stretton Hills (even from bed). Tuck into a generous breakfast in the dining room – elegant with family portraits and Bechstein grand piano that you are most welcome to play. Explore the garden with its lupins, sweet peas, delphiniums and 50 types of rose that bloom in wild profusion. *Children over 12 welcome.*

Magnificent gardens, a terrific setting and memorable walks all around. Jinlye sits, sheltered, at 1,400 feet surrounded by hills, rare birds, wild ponies and windswept ridges. The skies are infinite and Stretton Hills spring water trickles into the garden. Shining wooden floors stretch through the reading lounge and the dining room; the 14-seater Victorian breakfast table is impressive and breakfasts here are fun. There is much attention to detail from this mother and daughter team and the scent of flowers fills the house in summer. Pristine bedrooms have big and comfortable beds. *Children over 12 welcome.*

rooms	2: 1 double with private bath; 1 twin/double with bath.
room price	£50-£60. Single occ. £35-£40.
meals	Packed lunch from £2.50. Good pubs and restaurants nearby.
closed	Christmas & New Year.
directions	From Shrewsbury, south on A49. 0.5 miles before Leebotwood, right to Smethcott. Follow signs uphill & drive on left just before Smethcott.

rooms	8: 3 doubles, 2 twin/doubles, 2 twins, all with bath/shower; 1 double with private bath. Self-catering also available.
room price	£54-£80. Single occ. £42-£57.
meals	Breakfast 8-9am. Packed lunch available. Excellent pubs and restaurants nearby.
closed	Very occasionally.
directions	From Shrewsbury, A49 to Church Stretton, past Little Chef & right for All Stretton. Right immed. past phone box & up hill to Jinlye.

Jackie & Jim Scarratt
Lawley House,
Smethcott, Church Stretton,
Shropshire SY6 6NX

tel   01694 751236
fax   01694 751396
e-mail   lawleyhouse@easicom.com
web   www.lawleyhouse.co.uk

Mrs Janet Tory
Jinlye,
Castle Hill, All Stretton,
Church Stretton,
Shropshire SY6 6JP

tel   01694 723243
fax   01694 723243
e-mail   info@jinlye.co.uk
web   www.jinlye.co.uk

map: 8 entry: 369

map: 8 entry: 370

From the double room, with hand-printed wallpaper and oak chests, you look to Acton Burnell hill — England's first parliament was held here. The yellow room has lovely views of a lake, the garden and the Welsh hills; sunsets can be spectacular. Wooden doors, floors, carved settle and chests sit well with elegant furniture, lovely prints and photographs. A two-acre garden hugs the house, with a pool for summer and a croquet lawn. Parts of the house were built in 1660; the site is mentioned in the Domesday book. Very special.

A whole mile off the beaten track — such a rural spot. Privacy is yours in the converted dairy (and, new this year, the rustic barn; both have own front doors) across a flower-filled yard. Bedrooms have plump beds, sofa, armchairs, good lighting and peaceful views of fields that roll towards the setting sun. Feel free to wander in the garden with its border hedges and manicured lawns: Fiona, who is charming, easy-going and fun, likes to see the fruits of her labours appreciated. Breakfasts are served in the book-lined dining room of the main house and there's home honey for your bread. A restorative place.

rooms	3: 1 double, 1 twin/double, both with bathroom; 1 family (twin/double, 2 singles) with shower room.
room price	£55–£65. Single occ. £32.50.
meals	Dinner from £15.
closed	Christmas & New Year.
directions	From A5 & Shrewsbury, onto A458 for Bridgnorth. Approx. 200 yds on, right to Acton Burnell. Entering A. Burnell, left to Kenley. 0.5 miles on, left to Acton Pigot. 1st on left.

rooms	2 twins, both with bath.
room price	£50. Single occ. by arrangement.
meals	Pub 1.25 miles, restaurant 4 miles.
closed	Very occasionally.
directions	From Bridgnorth, A458 to Shrewsbury. 0.5 miles after Morville, right onto a stone road & follow signs to farm.

Mrs Hildegard Owen
Acton Pigot,
Acton Burnell, Shrewsbury,
Shropshire SY5 7PH

tel	01694 731209
fax	01694 731399
e-mail	acton@farmline.com
web	www.actonpigot.co.uk

Mrs Fiona Thompson
Hannigans Farm,
Morville, Bridgnorth,
Shropshire WV16 4RN

tel	01746 714332
fax	01746 714332
e-mail	hannigansfarm@btinternet.com

map: 8 entry: 371   map: 9 entry: 372

Where ancient Shropshire rolls down from Brown Clee to Ludlow, cross the ford (arguably the longest in England) in this tiny stone village and there is Carpenters. The renovation, a mix of high spec modern fittings and antique furniture, is a triumph of character, colour and immaculate taste. Norman is a Michelin *Bib Gourmand* chef and was a director of three excellent London restaurants: you really must eat in. The bedrooms are superbly decorated and filled with light, colour and a peaceful atmosphere. The newly transformed gardens are a mix of formal and natural and a brook runs through. Special indeed.

rooms	2: 1 double, with bath/shower; 1 double, with shower room.
room price	£65. Single occ. from £40.
meals	Dinner £25. Good pubs & restaurants 5-7 miles.
closed	Very occasionally.
directions	From A49 at Ludlow, A4117 for Kidderminster. After 0.75 miles fork left onto B4364 for Bridgnorth. After 2.5 miles left to Stoke St Milbrough & Clee St Margaret. There, left through ford, house 2nd on right.

Norman Swallow
Carpenters,
Clee St Margaret, Ludlow,
Shropshire SY7 9DT
tel   01584 823624
fax   01584 823432

A tiny lane leads you to Cleeton Court, a part 14th-century renovated farmhouse. With views over sheep meadows and heathland, you feel immersed in countryside. Ros greets you with fresh coffee and home-made cake – she is genuinely enthusiastic about B&B and allows you to settle into your own pace. You have a private entrance and use of the drawing room – prettily striped in yellow and cream, with comfortable sofas and log fire. Bedrooms are full of character with beams, a four-poster with chintzy drapes and good pieces of furniture. An easy place to relax. *Children over five welcome.*

rooms	2: 1 twin, 1 four-poster, both with bathroom.
room price	£50-£70. Single occ. £35.
meals	Excellent restaurants & pubs 4 miles.
closed	Christmas & New Year.
directions	From Ludlow, A4117 for Kidderminster for 1 mile. Left on B4364, for Cleobury North. On for 5 miles. In Wheathill, right for Cleeton St Mary & on for 1.5 miles. House on left.

Rosamond Woodward
Cleeton Court,
Cleeton St Mary, Ludlow,
Shropshire DY14 0QZ
tel   01584 823379
fax   01584 823379
e-mail   jk.straughan@talk21.com
web   www.cleetoncourt.co.uk

Very much the sense of being invited into someone's home, albeit it a grand one. The stupendous site and size of this early Georgian house reflect the status of the ancestor who built it in 1740. The present-day Salweys are farmers – Mrs Salwey is also a significant gardener – and they know about food so will happily help you decide where to eat in Ludlow (which has Michelin-starred restaurants). The large softly furnished bedrooms have antique chairs and modern bedding; one has a Louis XV bed, another chinoiserie. The Salweys are interesting people and the estate even has a Georgian bath house near the trout lake.

Good-sized bedrooms with fine furniture, luxurious beds, excellent linen, bathrobes and bathroom treats – there is no stinting on generosity. Standing in lush gardens that slope down to a millstream and across meadows to the River Teme, this is a gracious Georgian house with lovely views. It has a millstream and a weir, a motte and bailey castle site, a heronry, a point-to-point course and a ha-ha. Yvonne's reputation for imaginative cooking using local produce is a great attraction for walkers returning from a day in the glorious Welsh Borders. There's an interesting wine list, too. *Children by arrangement.*

rooms	3: 1 double, 1 twin, both with bath; 1 double with private bathroom.
room price	£90. Single occ. £50.
meals	Excellent choice in Ludlow, 1.5 miles.
closed	November–March.
directions	From Ludlow, over River Teme by traffic lights, 2nd right for Presteigne & Richard's Castle on B4361. After about 100 yds, drive is 1st right.

rooms	3: 1 double with shower room; 2 twins/doubles, both with private bathroom.
room price	£56-£70. Single occ. £38-£45.
meals	Dinner £20.
closed	Very occasionally.
directions	From Ludlow, A49 to Shrewsbury. At Bromfield, A4113. Right in Walford for Buckton, on to 2nd farm on left. Large sign on building.

	Humphrey & Hermione Salwey
	The Lodge,
	Ludlow,
	Shropshire SY8 4DU
tel	01584 872103
fax	01584 876126

	Hayden & Yvonne Lloyd
	Upper Buckton,
	Leintwardine,
	Craven Arms, Ludlow,
	Shropshire SY7 0JU
tel	01547 540634
fax	01547 540634

map: 8 entry: 375

map: 8 entry: 376

HOW TO USE THIS BOOK

sample entry

CORNWALL

Watch the surfers hug the waves, schools of them, all year. Watch the sun, the sand and, it seems, the world. The vastness of the view astonishes. At high tide you are on an island of granite – but not marooned. The bridge, a breathtaking entry, is the only privately owned suspension bridge in the country – not for those with vertigo. High seas can, spectacularly, wet the house. But all is elegance within: good furniture, deep carpets, family portraits, tradition and luxury with a modern touch. Decking all round for sun bathing, and views to the south, north, east and west. A great escape.

rooms	1 double with private shower room.
room price	£96-£114. Single occ. £48-£57.
meals	Sandwiches & coffee, £5. Excellent pubs/restaurants short walk away.
closed	Very occasionally.
directions	From Treloggen r'bout before Newquay right at Safeways, down hill. Across double r'bout. Left at lights; 1st right Grovesnor Ave. Straight across main road down narrow road, over bridge; 1st left, 1st right down Island Crescent.

Lady Long
The Island,
Newquay,
Cornwall TR7 1EA
tel   01637 879754
e-mail   helen@towanisland.fsnet.co.uk

6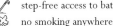
7 map: 1 entry: 53

explanations

1 rooms
We do not use the words 'en suite'. If a bathroom is 'en suite' we say **with bath** or **with shower**.

If a room is not 'en suite' we say **with private bathroom** or **with shared bathroom**: the former you will have to yourself, the latter may be shared with other guests or family members; both will have a wc, basin and either a bath or a shower.

2 room price
The price shown is for B&B for two people sharing a room. A price range incorporates room/seasonal differences. We also give single occupancy rates – the amount payable by one person staying in a room for two.

3 meals
Prices are per person. All meals must be booked in advance. Ask the owner if you may bring your own wine. Some entries say B.Y.O.

4 closed
When given in months, this means for the whole of the named months and the time in between.

5 directions
Use as a guide; the owner can give more details.

6 symbols
see the last page of the book for fuller explanation:

 all children welcome

 wheelchair facilities for one bedroom/bathroom

 step-free access to bathroom/bedroom

 no smoking anywhere

 smoking restrictions exist.

 this house has pets

 pets can sleep in your bedroom

 credit cards accepted

 vegetarians catered for with advance warning

 mostly home-grown/local/organic produce used

 licensed premises

 working farm

 bike

 walk

7 Map page number; entry number.

Enthusiastic collectors of country artefacts, the Whitfields have filled this Grade II-listed, 16th-century farmhouse with the most eye-catching things. Not every kitchen range has an American cowboy's saddle hanging over it; this one echoes Susan's Texan roots. Floors and doors of oak contrast with brightly coloured walls, and there's a calm, happy atmosphere. Much enthusiasm for the village and surrounding countryside, and Susan will give you full English and American breakfasts, using local produce; dinners are special, too. Come to walk or cycle or ride — you can even bring your horse.

In a land of fat sheep and ancient hill forts, this 17th-century mill ended Gill and Andrew's search for a refuge from the city. With seclusion and natural beauty, and an absence of fussiness in the house, this feels like a retreat — just what your hosts (a designer and an illustrator) want. Rooms are comfortable, freshly-decorated and spotless: the double has a Victorian brass bed and newly restored original roll-top bath. The stone and oak extension blends beautifully and has become a large twin room. The River Unk flows through the mill's three acres of meadowland and gardens. *Children over eight welcome.*

rooms	3: 1 double, 1 double bunk with bath; 1 double, 1 single bed with private bath.
room price	£46-£48. Single occ. by arrangement.
meals	Dinner £15-£17.50. Packed lunch £3.50. Good pubs/restaurants nearby.
closed	December.
directions	A49 from Ludlow & onto B4368 at Craven Arms, for Clun. In High St on left 0.5 miles from Clun sign.

rooms	3: 2 doubles, 1 with bathroom, 1 with private bathroom; 1 twin with bath/shower.
room price	£54-£70. Single occ. £37-£50.
meals	Breakfast until 9.30am. Dinner £21.
closed	November-February.
directions	From Clun A488 for Bishops Castle. 1st left, for Bicton. There, 2nd left for Mainstone. 1st right after Llananhedric Farm; house by river at bottom of hill.

	Anthony & Susan Whitfield
	Clun Farm House,
	High Street, Clun,
	Shropshire SY7 8JB
tel	01588 640432
fax	01588 640432

	Gill Della Casa & Andrew Farmer
	The Birches Mill, Clun,
	Nr. Craven Arms,
	Shropshire SY7 8NL
tel	01588 640409
fax	01588 640409
e-mail	gill@birchesmill.fsnet.co.uk
web	www.virtual-shropshire.co.uk/ birchesmill

map: 8 entry: 377

map: 8 entry: 378

Tucked into the folds of Exmoor on the River Quarme lies everybody's fantasy house. The walls inside the white-fronted mill curve and twist, and in the breakfast room the mill machinery is still intact. In the bedrooms, pine floors, Porlock quilts, hand-painted furniture and attention to detail; in the grounds, lambs, ponies and a special Welsh collie; along the bridle path a pub. And all around is still, beyond the gentle splash of water. Sally is unflappable and a *Cordon Bleu* cook, so why not stay by the log fire and let the evening meal come to you? *Children over eight welcome.*

The views from this characterful, old, tree-protected house are of farmland and heath: Edgcott is a haven on the edge of rambling heathland. You'll find few nods to anything 'designery' – two bedrooms are smallish and furniture tends towards basic, but this doesn't detract from the place and its quirkiness. The price is fair, too. Mrs Lamble is a gentle hostess and enjoys cooking using her own garden vegetables. She's also an Exmoor enthusiast and her knowledge of the area is invaluable; rides, walks, village visits galore will be suggested. You may also play the family piano.

rooms	3: 1 double with private bathroom; 1 double with private shower room; 1 twin with shared bathroom.
room price	£50. Single occ. £25.
meals	Packed lunch £5. Dinner available. Good pub 1 mile.
closed	Very occasionally.
directions	Follow A358 from Taunton to Minehead/Raleighs Cross/Wheddon Cross. Straight over x-roads; straight on Exford road, 2 miles. Turn into Luckwell Bridge; house down bridleway on left.

rooms	3: 1 double, 1 twin, both with private bathroom; 1 twin/double with bath/shower.
room price	£44-£50. Single occ. £25.
meals	Dinner, 4 courses, £15. B.Y.O. Excellent pubs in village.
closed	Very occasionally.
directions	From Taunton A358, then left on B3224 to Exford. There, take road to Porlock. 0.25 miles from village.

Sally Pearce
West Mill,
Luckwell Bridge,
Wheddon Cross,
Somerset TA24 7EH
tel   01643 841896
e-mail   sally.pearce1@btinternet.com

Gillian Lamble
Edgcott House,
Exford,
Somerset TA24 7QG
tel   01643 831495
fax   01643 831495
e-mail   enquiries@edgcotthouse.co.uk
web   www.edgcotthouse.co.uk

map: 2 entry: 379

map: 2 entry: 380

The picture-book, 12th-century priory leans against its church, has a rustic gate, a walled garden, a tumble of flowers. Both house and hostess are elegant, unpretentious and friendly; the old oak tables, flagstones, panelled doors, books and higgledy-piggledy corridors are English through and through. But a perfect English house in a sweet Somerset village needs a touch of pepper and cosmopolitan Jane adds her own special flair with artistic touches here and there. One of our favourites. There's a roomy self-catering cottage with colour-washed walls and a log fire, too.

A little lane tumbles down to the centre of Dunster – the fascinating village is just two minutes' walk away – yet up here you have wide open views of fields, sheep and sea. Janet, helpful and kind, loves people to explore by bike or foot and can help with luggage and transport; Exmoor footpaths start behind the house. The 1860s house retains its Victorian features and bedrooms are quiet and simple – the double has a view to Blue Anchor Bay, the castle and church. Stripped pine, cream curtains, fresh flowers – it's homely. Garden fruit for breakfast and home-laid eggs, too. *Children and pets by arrangement.*

rooms	3: 1 double with private shower; 1 twin, 1 four-poster, both with bath.
room price	£60-£70. Single occ. by arrangement. Cottage from £175 per week.
meals	Good restaurants and pubs nearby.
closed	Christmas.
directions	From A39 into Dunster, right at blue sign 'unsuitable for goods vehicles'. House adjoined to church.

rooms	3: 1 double with bath/shower; 2 twins/doubles, both with shower room.
room price	£40-£50. Single occ. £25.
meals	Packed lunch from £3.50. Excellent restaurants nearby.
closed	Christmas.
directions	From Williton, A39 for Minehead for 8 miles. Left to Dunster. There, right fork into 'The Ball'. At T-junc. at end of road, right. House 75 yds on right.

Jane Forshaw
The Old Priory,
Dunster,
Somerset TA24 6RY
tel   01643 821540

Mrs Janet Lamacraft
Higher Orchard,
30 St George's Street, Dunster,
Somerset TA24 6RS
tel   01643 821915
e-mail   lamacraft@higherorchard.fsnet.co.uk
web   www.higherorchard.fsnet.co.uk

The Vincents have made the house 'smile' again – handsome and Georgian, it overlooks Watchet harbour and marina. Both bedrooms are pleasing – the double has duck-egg blue walls and pretty floral curtains and looks down onto a Mediterranean courtyard; the twin, with blue chintz valances and matching curtains, has a sea view. Expect home-made cakes and biscuits and generous breakfasts; Susan holds cookery demonstrations. Relax in the garden within sight and sound of sea and steam railway and with palm trees, ponds, burgeoning borders and a revolving summerhouse. *Children and dogs, by arrangement.*

An unusual-looking house… so no surprise to discover that it was the romantic fantasy of a love-struck local man, George Carew, who built it for his mistress in 1830. The interior is as striking as the Italianate terracotta, triple-gabled exterior. 'Heritage' colours are much in evidence and have been matched with lovely pieces of furniture, polished wood floors and rugs. There's a drawing room for you and the bedrooms are well-proportioned with garden views through leaded windows. Breakfast is a feast of fresh fruit, local sausages and bacon, cheerfully served in front of the log fire in winter.

rooms	2: 1 double with private bathroom; 1 twin with shower room.
room price	From £50. Single occ. from £25.
meals	Breakfast 7.30-10am. Pub/restaurants a short walk away.
closed	Christmas.
directions	From railway station & footbridge in Watchet, up South Road (for Doniford). After 50 yds, left into Beverly Drive. House 50 yds on left.

rooms	3: 2 doubles sharing bathroom & wc; further twin with basins, let only to same party.
room price	£50. Single occ. £35.
meals	Dinner £20. Excellent pubs nearby.
closed	Christmas & New Year.
directions	A358 from Taunton for Minehead, for 9.5 miles (passing Flaxpool garage on left). Next right at brow of hill for Crowcombe & past church. House (with 5-bar gate) 500 yds past pub on right.

Susan & Roger Vincent
Wyndham House,
4 Sea View Terrace, Watchet,
Somerset TA23 0DF
tel   01984 631881
fax   01984 631881
e-mail   rhv@dialstart.net

Rosie Macdonald
Hooks House,
Crowcombe, Taunton,
Somerset TA4 4AE
tel   01984 618691
fax   01984 618357
e-mail   lukemacdd@hookhouse. fsbusiness.co.uk

map: 2 entry: 383

map: 2 entry: 384

Arestrained, elegant style sets off the natural beauty of the 300-year-old farmhouse: handsome furniture and soft colours sit easily with stone flags, beams and wooden panelling. It's a beautiful house, with its own spring, and is meticulously kept by friendly Pamela who also makes all her own jams, marmalade and bread. Bedrooms and bathrooms are a generous size and very attractive. You are 1,000 feet up on the Quantocks where the views are long and the scenery stunning; the Smiths' 20 acres of fields and woodland are alive with songbirds. *Children over 10 welcome.*

The Ritchies devote a huge amount of energy to their B&B and have done a fine job of renovating this exquisite 17th-century farmhouse in Somerset's lovely Quantock Hills. There's a homely feel with splashes of style where they matter – well-framed prints, good fabrics, comfortable sofas – and they've done everything to make you comfortable. Rooms are very pretty, fresh and large and look over the cobbled courtyard or open fields; many look both ways. Breakfast will include home-baked bread and home-made jams. Charles and Jane prepare meals using fresh local ingredients, so do eat in.

rooms	3: 2 doubles, 1 twin, all with bath/shower.
room price	£46-£50. Single occ. £30.
meals	Breakfast until 9.30am. Pubs 0.5 miles.
closed	Very occasionally.
directions	From Taunton, A358 north for Williton. Approx. 7 miles on, right for West Bagborough. Through village, up hill for 0.5 miles. Farm on left.

rooms	3: 1 double with shower room; 1 double with private shower room; 1 twin with private bathroom.
room price	£50-£55. Single occ. £30-£32.50.
meals	Breakfast 8-9am. Dinner £22.50.
closed	Very occasionally.
directions	From M5 junc. 25. A358 for Minehead. Leave A358 at West Bagborough turning. Through village for 1.5 miles. Farmhouse 3rd on left past pub.

Mrs Pamela Smith
Tilbury Farm,
Cothelstone, Taunton,
Somerset TA4 3DY
tel 01823 432391

Charles & Jane Ritchie
Bashfords Farmhouse,
West Bagborough, Taunton,
Somerset TA4 3EF
tel 01823 432015
fax 0870 1671587
e-mail info@bashfordsfarmhouse.co.uk
web www.bashfordsfarmhouse.co.uk

SOMERSET

SOMERSET

The Quantocks are a treat and from here you have at least 38 square miles of great walking. Wildlife bounds, flits and creeps through the garden, woods and heathland: wild deer, hill ponies, badgers and over 50 species of birds. Laze on the terrace or by the ornamental pond in the rambling garden and soak in the views to the Mendips and Glastonbury Tor. You have your own self-contained wing with sitting room, old and antique furniture, china and flowers. Breakfast *al fresco*, have supper by candlelight or eat at the local pub – the Taylor-Youngs will drive you to and fro.

You eat beside an open fire – vegetables from the walled garden, fruit from the orchard, home-baked bread and jams, eggs from the hens. This is an organic smallholding and your enthusiastic hosts have added an easy comfort to their 17th-century rectory farmhouse. Quarry tiled floors, log fires, books and a piano in the cosy sitting room, and American folk art and Susan's pastels add charm. Bedrooms are big with fresh flowers and great views (even from the Victorian bath in the en suite). The natural beauty of the Quantock Hills surrounds you and walks start from the front door.

rooms	1 twin/double with bathroom.
room price	£53-£57. Single occ. £26.50-£28.50.
meals	Packed lunch £4. Supper from £8.
closed	Very occasionally.
directions	From B'water, A39 through Cannington. Main road forks right, straight on & over x-roads to Over Stowey. Left signed Ramscombe Forestry Trail. Keep to tarmac by turning right up hill. Cottage in front; left through gates.

rooms	3: 1 double with shower & extra sofa bed; 1 twin/double with bath & extra pull-out bed; 1 double with shared bathroom.
room price	£42-£50. Single occ. £28.
meals	Dinner, 3 courses, £18. Light supper £7.
closed	Christmas.
directions	From Bridgwater, A39 for Minehead. 7 miles on, left at Cottage Inn for Over Stowey. Village 1.8 miles on. House on right after church.

Michael & Penny Taylor-Young
Friarn Cottage,
Over Stowey, Bridgwater,
Somerset TA5 1HW
tel 01278 732870
fax 01278 732870

Susan Lilienthal
Parsonage Farm,
Over Stowey, Bridgwater,
Somerset TA5 1HA
tel 01278 733237
fax 01278 733511
e-mail suki@parsonfarm.co.uk
web www.parsonfarm.co.uk

map: 3 entry: 387

map: 3 entry: 388

Massive stone walls, heavy timbers, flagged floors and lack of fussiness give this Grade I-listed 15th-century farmhouse a real solidity and atmosphere. Explore the West Bedroom with timbered walls, a ceiling open to the beamed roof and a four-poster bed, and don't miss the oak-panelled Gallery Bedroom with recently uncovered secret stairway. Feel baronial while seated for breakfast beside the Great Hall's massive fireplace at the 16-foot oak table. There's a new stable room, too — although less architecturally stunning, it's perfect for wheelchair users. And Ann is kind and smiley.

A former farmhouse begun in the 17th century, with the main rooms in a late Victorian extension. Diamond-patterned tiles and stained glass in the entrance hall, stripped wooden floors and open fireplaces create a turn-of-the-century atmosphere designed to welcome rather than impress. The bedrooms are large, with easy chairs and beds that can be adapted into singles or doubles. Breakfasts involve local eggs and sausages and even cappuccinos — a rare treat. Carol is a keen cook and gives monthly gourmet dinners which you can enjoy in a candlelit setting.

rooms	4: 3 doubles, 1 family, all with bath/shower.
room price	£48-£56. Single occ. £32-£35.
meals	Breakfast until 9.30am. Pub 500 yds.
closed	Very occasionally.
directions	From Bridgwater, A39 west around Cannington. After 2nd r'bout, follow signs to Minehead. 1st left after Yeo Valley creamery. Farm 1st house on right.

rooms	3: 1 double, 1 twin/family, 1 twin, all with bath/shower.
room price	£60. Single occ. £40.
meals	Breakfast 7-9.30am. Dinner, 3 courses, £18.
closed	Very occasionally.
directions	A39 for Minehead. After B'water cont. 1 mile, pass garage, down hill & at double bend right for Wembdon. Immed. left for Perry Green. After 0.75 miles follow 'No Through Road'; 2nd on left.

Ann Dyer
Blackmore Farm,
Cannington, Bridgwater,
Somerset TA5 2NE

tel	01278 653442
fax	01278 653427
e-mail	dyerfarm@aol.com
web	www.dyerfarm.co.uk

Richard & Carol Wright
Model Farm,
Perry Green,
Wembdon, Bridgwater,
Somerset TA5 2BA

tel	01278 433999
e-mail	info@modelfarm.com
web	www.modelfarm.com

SOMERSET

SOMERSET

Robert, an ex-restaurateur, is a South African and as easy-going as they so often are; Lesley's cooking gets heaps of praise from guests and she runs cookery courses too. It's a perfect Somerset cottage with an apple orchard and views across fields to the lofty church. The interior is utterly in keeping: pine, coir carpets, wooden beams and a warm sense of fun. Bedrooms are light, restful and simple, with white walls and old pine. All this, and with such easy access to the M5. *Children over 10 welcome.*

Extremely pretty with its thatched roof and Strawberry Hill Gothic windows, this house is instantly captivating. You won't find family bustle, but there is immense comfort. Soft, large sofas in the guest sitting room, thick carpeting, easy chairs in the bedrooms and excellent meals at house-party dinners. Carved Tudor oak beams in the sitting room and panelled passages speak of the house's history, and there are French windows from the dining room onto the sweeping lawns. In a tiny conservation hamlet surrounded by farmland, the peace is deep.

rooms	2: 1 double with shower room; 1 twin with bathroom.
room price	£50-£56. Single occ. by arrangement.
meals	Breakfast until 9am. Supper from £15. Dinner from £18.
closed	Christmas.
directions	From M5 junc. 26 take West Buckland road for 0.75 miles. 1st left just before Stone garage. Bear right; 3rd house at end of lane, below church.

rooms	5 twin/doubles, all with bath/shower.
room price	From £80. Single occ. £50.
meals	Dinner, 4 courses, £19.50.
closed	Very occasionally.
directions	At Horton Cross r'bout (junc. A303/A358) A358 for Chard. After Donyatt, left for Ilminster. After 1 mile, right for Cricket Malherbie. House on left after 1 mile, 200 yds past church.

Lesley & Robert Orr
Causeway Cottage,
West Buckland, Wellington,
Somerset TA21 9JZ
tel   01823 663458
fax   01823 663458
e-mail orrs@westbuckland.freeserve.co.uk
web   www.welcome.to/causeway-cottage

Michael & Patricia Fry-Foley
The Old Rectory,
Cricket Malherbie, Ilminster,
Somerset TA19 0PW
tel   01460 54364
fax   01460 57374
e-mail theoldrectory@malherbie.
        freeserve.co.uk
web   www.malherbie.freeserve.co.uk

map: 3 entry: 391

map: 3 entry: 392

Soft hamstone and thatched roofs – the village is a delight. Courtfield, Grade II-listed, hidden in a fine, walled, two-acre garden, is a family home so you'll relax easily. Richard, a keen lepidopterist, is a professional painter and his work is displayed everywhere, as is his daughter's. There is a tennis court and a stunning conservatory, perfect for breakfast or for a candlelit dinner in the summer with views of the floodlit church. Valerie has a real flair for entertaining inherited from her Russian father who was a hotelier in Cairo. The bedrooms are large, unfussy and delightful. *Children over eight welcome.*

So much to delight the eye… elegant Georgian lines, beautiful art, a 19th-century French mirror, French Empire chairs, a mixture of checked, striped and *toile de Jouy* fabrics – all existing in absolute harmony. This is one of the most stylish retreats that you'll find. There's comfort, too… thick bathrobes, warm towels, the fattest pillows. The house, 18th-century, Grade II-listed, has been renovated by the dedicated Deacons. Elizabeth's cooking is sublime and imaginative. You are in the heart of the Somerset Levels, surrounded by mystical views and countryside of huge environmental significance.

rooms	3: 2 doubles, 1 twin, both with private bathroom.
room price	£50-£60. Single occ. £38.
meals	Dinner £18. B.Y.O.
closed	Very occasionally.
directions	From A303, A356 south for Crewkerne. 2nd left to Norton-sub-Hamdon. House in centre of village at foot of Church Lane.

rooms	3: 2 doubles, both with private bathroom; 1 twin with shower room.
room price	From £90. Single occ. £45.
meals	Dinner, 3-4 courses, £20-£25. B.Y.O.
closed	Very occasionally.
directions	From M5, junc. 24. 5 miles via Huntworth & Moorland. 2 miles after Moorland, house on right after sharp right-hand bend.

Richard & Valerie Constable
Courtfield,
Norton-sub-Hamdon,
Stoke-sub-Hamdon,
Somerset TA14 6SG
tel   01935 881246
e-mail   courtfield@hotmail.com

Crispin & Elizabeth Deacon
Saltmoor House,
Saltmoor, Burrowbridge,
Somerset TA7 0RL
tel   01823 698092
e-mail   saltmoorhouse@amserve.net

The harmonious marriage of natural materials with modern and antique furniture makes for a relaxed cosiness. The Burnhams – both of whom worked in fashion – have huge flair and the house and garden have been designed with an excellent eye. Coir matting sits happily with dark, antique furniture; a wrought-iron, real-candle chandelier and high-backed chairs lend the dining room an air of warm, pre-Raphaelite Gothic. Bedrooms are uncluttered with crisp linen and soft robes; the twin is the biggest and its bathroom is very close. Excellent breakfasts include Heal Farm sausages and bacon. *Children by arrangement.*

You'll be delighted whichever room you choose in this listed Regency house; each is decorated with good period furniture, fine bedspreads and elaborate drapes. A flagged hall, high ceilings and long windows give the feel of a small hotel, yet both the grand first-floor rooms and cosier second-floor ones are good value. A stone staircase goes right to the top and the Observatory lets in a cascading light. Roy, a jazz musician and wildlife enthusiast, is charming and excellent company; he's planted 28,000 trees to attract wildlife and stocked the lake with exotic ducks and black swans.

rooms	2: 1 double with shower; 1 twin with private bath.
room price	£50. Single occ. £40.
meals	Dinner from £19.
closed	Christmas.
directions	From Somerton Lake B3153 for Langport. Right after 2 miles for Pitney, just before Halfway Inn. Through Pitney. House last but one on right, with dark green railings.

rooms	9: 2 four-posters, 1 twin, 1 double, 1 family, all with bath; 1 family with private bathroom. 1 twin, 2 doubles in converted Coach House.
room price	£49-£85. Single occ. £45-£60.
meals	Restaurants within walking distance.
closed	Christmas.
directions	From London, M3 junc. 8, A303. At Podimore r'bout A372 to Somerton. House at junction of North Street & Behind Berry.

Peter & Jane Burnham
Estate Farmhouse,
Pitney, Langport,
Somerset TA10 9AL
tel   01458 250210
fax   01458 253227

Mr Roy Copeland
The Lynch Country House,
4 Behind Berry, Somerton,
Somerset TA11 7PD
tel   01458 272316
fax   01458 272590
e-mail   the_lynch@talk21.com
web   www.thelynchcountryhouse.co.uk

Espaliered fruit trees and high walls surround the outdoor pool; you may see badgers and kingfishers and, certainly, ducks waddling to and from the pond. Clanville is a cosy, manageable mini-manor and Sally is the kindest of hosts; she has created an atmosphere in which guests and family co-exist with ease. Bedrooms have solid, traditional furniture; downstairs there are Persian rugs on wooden floors and an old rocking horse in the dining room where local produce is served for breakfast. The family and the current Snooks, who have lived here since 1898, have 200 acres and a dairy herd. You'll like them.

The Good Life in the depths of Somerset: organic vegetables on an organic farm, home-made marmalade and own milk and eggs. The Dowdings have returned from France – they had a Special Place there – and have converted the old stone barn into a super self-contained apartment with a continental feel. Do your own thing – or have Susie cook breakfast and dinner for you (Charles grinds their own wheat for daily bread-making). Central to the oak-floored sitting room is a woodburner and bedrooms have oak floors, exposed beams, lime-washed walls and *toile de Jouy* curtains.

rooms	3: 1 double, 1 single, both with shower room; 1 family/twin with bath/shower.
room price	£50–£60.
meals	Breakfast 8-9am. Good pubs & restaurants 2-4 miles.
closed	Christmas & New Year.
directions	From Wincanton, A371 for Shepton Mallet. After Castle Cary, left on B3153 for Somerton (0.75 miles). Under r'way bridge, white gate & cattle grid immed. on right. Car park up drive, behind house.

rooms	2: 1 double with bathroom; 1 twin with private shower room.
room price	£50–£85.
meals	Breakfast until 9.30am, or you can cook your own. Light supper from £5.
closed	Very occasionally.
directions	From A303 at Wincanton, A371 for Castle Cary. Before Cary, right on A359 for Bruton. 2nd right for S. Montague. Over x-roads by inn. Round sharp bend, church on left. House on right; right into yard.

Sally Snook
Clanville Manor,
Castle Cary,
Somerset BA7 7PJ
tel   01963 350124
fax   01963 350719
e-mail info@clanvillemanor.co.uk
web   www.clanvillemanor.co.uk

Charles & Susie Dowding
Lower Farm,
Shepton Montague, Wincanton,
Somerset BA9 8JG
tel   01749 812253
e-mail lowerfarm@clara.co.uk
web   www.lowerfarm.org.uk

Grand, yes, but without a hint of stuffiness and a terrific place to stay. Pennard has been in Susie's family since the 17th century – the cellars date from then and the superstructure is stately, lofty and Georgian. You have the run of the library, drawing room, magnificent billiard room, 60-acre orchard, meadows, woods, tennis court and six acres of garden with a spring-fed pool where you can swim with the newts. Bedrooms are large and have good views; one is circular with a corner bath in the room. Multi-lingual Martin runs an antiques business from here and he and Susie delight in sharing their house.

rooms	3: 1 twin/double with private bathroom; 1 double, 1 twin, both with bath/shower.
room price	From £60. Single occ. by arrangement.
meals	Good pub 2 miles.
closed	Very occasionally.
directions	From Shepton Mallet south on A37, through Pylle, over hill & next right to East Pennard. After 500 yds, right and on past church to T-junc. at very top. House on left.

Martin & Susie Dearden
Pennard House,
East Pennard, Shepton Mallet,
Somerset BA4 6TP
tel   01749 860266
fax   01749 860266
e-mail   susie.d@ukonline.co.uk

map: 3 entry: 399

Rosalind's enthusiasm for welcoming guests is unstinting; she is cheerful and chatty and, as a geologist and walking enthusiast, is knowledgeable about the area – there are lots of books and maps for you. Pet sheep, goats, chickens, ducks and friendly cats, too. The large Garden Suite has been adapted for wheelchair users; accessible from its pretty secluded walled garden and with an inglenook fireplace in its own sitting room, it retains its 17th-century charm. The other rooms are homely with new pine and white units. Lovely views, and you can walk to Wells Cathedral to hear evensong.

rooms	5: 2 doubles, 1 with bath, 1 with shower; Garden suite: 1 twin/double, single with shower; 1 single, 1 twin/double sharing bathroom & separate wc.
room price	£30–£75.
meals	Packed lunches & light snacks. Good pub food 1 mile.
closed	Occasionally.
directions	From Wells, A371 for Shepton Mallet for 1 mile, then left onto B3139. In Dulcote, left at stone fountain. Farmhouse marked, 4th on right after Manor Barn.

Rosalind Bufton
Manor Farm,
Dulcote, Wells,
Somerset BA5 3PZ
tel   01749 672125
fax   01749 672125
e-mail   rosalind.bufton@ntlworld.com
web   www.wells-accommodation.co.uk

map: 3 entry: 400

An exquisite house: Phoebe, a shepherd, sought the perfect home for her flock and she found it. Terracotta walls, rugs, flagstones and brick – stunning. The antique beds have handmade mattresses, good linen and fat pillows; in the barn you have luxurious privacy. The indoor swimming pool has a breathtaking view through a Gothic, arched window. The house is a treasure box of decorative arts from the carved Dutch fireplaces to the Turkmen rugs, and Phoebe is flexible about arrangements – it's a magnificent place for a house party. *In conjunction with the cottages (right), 11 bedrooms in all. Babies welcome.*

Phoebe returned these Victorian cottages to the estate last year. With wonderful views of Pennard Hill and the Mendips beyond, both self-catering options have been stunningly redesigned. The ground floor of the Golden Fleece is an airy, luxurious living space with a vast kitchen (double Aga, dishwasher, etc) leading to a sunroom and a large drawing room with log fire. The Lamb is a charming cottage for two with kitchen/living room and open fire.

In conjunction with Pennard Hill Farm (left), 11 bedrooms in all.

rooms	6: Barn: 1 double suite with dressing room & kitchen/living area. House: 1 double with bath. 1 double suite with drawing room. 3 singles, usually let to one party.
room price	£100-£180 per room or suite.
meals	Dinner from £25.
closed	Very occasionally.
directions	From Wells, A39 to Glastonbury. 0.5 miles on left for North Wootton, follow for West Pennard. Right onto A361. 1st left. 1 mile up hill. 1st drive to left at top.

rooms	Fleece: 2 doubles, 1 twin, 1 single with 2 bathrooms. Lamb: 1 double with bathroom. Both have living rooms & kitchens.
room price	£90-£160.
meals	Dinner from £25.
closed	Very occasionally.
directions	Directions as for Pennard Hill Farm, left. Do not go to East Pennard.

Phoebe Judah
Pennard Hill Farm,
Stickleball Hill, East Pennard,
Shepton Mallet,
Somerset BA4 6UG
tel 01749 890221
fax 01749 890665
e-mail phebejudah@aol.com
web www.pennardhillfarm.co.uk

Phoebe Judah
Golden Fleece & The Lamb,
Pennard Hill Farm,
Stickleball Hill, East Pennard,
Shepton Mallet, Somerset BA4 6UG
tel 01749 890221
fax 01749 890665
e-mail phebejudah@aol.com
web www.pennardhillfarm.co.uk

map: 3 entry: 401

map: 3 entry: 402

One of our favourites – the cosiest hillside cottage filled with the prettiest things. French-inspired bedheads and wardrobes made by a local craftsman, antique patchwork quilts and jolly china on the old Welsh dresser in the kitchen. And there's Catherine – warm, spirited, cultured; she'll make you fresh coffee, chat about the area, even give you a guided tour of Wells Cathedral, if you wish. The cottage is set in eight acres, with superb walking country all around. You can play tennis or croquet, and have your own pretty sitting room with books and magazines. Excellent value.

The 18th-century farmhouse, with flagstone floors, old beams, pine panelling and country antiques, is sunny and delightful. On the southern slopes of the Mendips, with glorious walks to be walked – if, that is, you're not lying in the garden, dozing under the old apple tree. Wander among the fine old barns and you might almost imagine that you'd stumbled upon a museum: there's an ancient forge, a cider press and a threshing floor – not to mention Tony's collection of classic cars. Cosy, cottagey rooms have a fresh, cared-for feel, and long views to Glastonbury Tor. *Children over 10 welcome.*

rooms	2: 1 twin/double with bath/shower. Further twin available for members of same party.
room price	£50. Single occ. £30.
meals	Good pub 0.25 miles.
closed	Christmas & New Year.
directions	From Wells A371 to middle of Croscombe. Right at red phone box & then immed. right into lane. House up on left after 0.25 miles. Drive straight ahead and park in signed field.

rooms	3: 1 double with shower; 1 twin/double with bath; 1 double with private bathroom.
room price	£52-£58. Single occ. £36.
meals	Breakfast 8-9am. Good pub 0.5 miles.
closed	Christmas Day.
directions	From Wells towards Cheddar on A371. At Westbury-sub-Mendip pass Westbury Inn & Post Office Stores on right. House 200 yds on, on left.

Michael & Catherine Hay
Hillview Cottage,
Paradise Lane, Croscombe, Wells,
Somerset BA5 3RL

tel	01749 343526
fax	01749 676134
e-mail	cathyhay@yahoo.co.uk

Tony & Wendy Thompson
Stoneleigh House,
Westbury-sub-Mendip, Nr. Wells,
Somerset BA5 1HF

tel	01749 870668
fax	01749 870668
e-mail	stoneleigh@dial.pipex.com
web	www.stoneleigh.dial.pipex.com

map: 3 entry: 403

map: 3 entry: 404

STAFFORDSHIRE

The cottage takes its name from the nearby bridge on the Shropshire Union Canal (one of England's prettiest). Bedrooms have floral curtains and covers and all is spotless and cosy with open fire, antique furniture, lovely bathrooms, fresh flowers. Meals can be served outside on the terrace overlooking the canal and dinner can be arranged on board the narrow boat with a delightful trip along the canal. Diana makes her own bread, biscuits, cakes and jams and David provides fresh vegetables and salads from the garden. On a good day there are eggs from the chickens, too.

rooms	2 doubles, both with private bathroom (1 bath, 1 shower).
room price	From £55. Single occ. £35.
meals	Packed lunch £5. Dinner £15.
closed	Christmas & New Year.
directions	From Stafford, A518 for Newport. 4 miles on, left at Haughton (opp. church) for Church Eaton. There, right along Main St. At end of village, left along Little Onn road. Over canal bridge & left after 300 yds. Cottage on left.

Diana Walkerdine
Slab Bridge Cottage,
Little Onn, Church Eaton,
Staffordshire ST20 0AY
tel   01785 840220
fax   01785 840220

map: 9 entry: 405

STAFFORDSHIRE

Mary Queen of Scots was imprisoned in Chartley Castle, opposite this Grade II-listed, half-timbered Elizabethan manor house. Push open the studded oak door to discover panelled walls, a terracotta dining room and a wealth of oak beams. In the Sudbury Yellow drawing room are family portraits and exquisite furniture. The bedrooms are large, airy and flower-filled; the four-poster bedroom is oak-panelled and has a secret door to the bathroom. Uneven floors, hearty breakfasts, family silver and lovely parkland – all close to The Potteries. Jeremy & Sarah are engaging hosts. *Children over 12 welcome.*

rooms	2: 1 four-poster, 1 twin, both with shower.
room price	£60. Single occ. £35-£45.
meals	Breakfast until 9.30am. Good restaurants/pubs 1 mile.
closed	Christmas & New Year.
directions	Halfway between Stafford & Uttoxeter on A518, just past Chartley Castle ruin on left & at top of hill, on right.

Jeremy & Sarah Allen
Chartley Manor Farm,
Chartley, Nr. Stafford,
Staffordshire ST18 0LN
tel   01889 270891
fax   01889 270891
e-mail   jeremy.allen4@btopenworld.com

map: 9 entry: 406

As Stewards of the Countryside, the Balls are restoring wildlife habitats, ponds, hedgerows, wetlands and footpaths on their 105-acre, rare-breed farm. The cosy bedrooms are in Farrier's Cottage and Mews next to the main farmhouse; Diana pops round every morning to serve a good breakfast at separate tables in the beamed dining room. Much of the food is home-produced and Diana can cook dinner for larger parties – just let her know when you book. Set out to discover Croxden Abbey for some 12th-century Cistercian history… or please the children and spend the day at Alton Towers. *Children over five welcome.*

An enchanting, rambling, farmhouse, the kind of time capsule you can't simulate: oak timbers and panelling, stone, tapestry drapes, curios, pewter and books galore. This is a captivating Jacobean gem only two miles from Alton Towers. There are gorgeous, almost grand, lawned grounds full of birdsong, tennis and croquet and a summer house which sports a turret from Leeds Infirmary. Rare-breed (Irish Moiled) cattle graze peacefully. Rooms have majestic four-poster beds (with good mattresses) and great views. Chris and Margaret are busy, informal people and the attitude here is very much 'stay as friends'.

rooms	5: Farrier's Cottage: 2 doubles, 1 family, all with shower room. Mews: 1 double, 1 bunk room, both with shower room.
room price	From £45. Single occ. £35.
meals	Packed lunch £5. Dinner from £12 (minimum 6 people). Good pubs nearby.
closed	Christmas & New Year (self-catering available then).
directions	From A50 take B5030 at Uttoxeter for Rocester. There, left into Hollington Rd. Nabb Lane 1.5 miles on right.

rooms	3 doubles, 1 with shower, 2 with baths.
room price	£46-£52. Single occ. from £26.
meals	Breakfast until 9.30am. Good places to eat within 5 miles.
closed	Christmas.
directions	From Uttoxeter, B5030 for Rocester. Beyond JCB factory, left onto B5031. At T-junc. after church, right onto B5032. 1st left for Prestwood. Farm 0.75 miles on right over crest of hill, through arch.

Diana Ball
Woodhouse Farm,
Nabb Lane, Croxden, Uttoxeter,
Staffordshire ST14 5JB
tel   01889 507507
e-mail   ddeb@lineone.net
web   www.alton-towers.glo.cc

Chris & Margaret Ball
Manor House,
Prestwood, Nr. Denstone, Uttoxeter,
Staffordshire ST14 5DD
tel   01889 590415
fax   01335 342198
e-mail   cm_ball@yahoo.co.uk
web   www.4posteraccom.com

STAFFORDSHIRE

Inigo Jones was commissioned to transform the ancient, crumbling castle into a baronial mansion. The 1270 pink-stone crenellated pile retains its guardhouse, moat and turrets; the stunning interior is Jacobean with vast, oak-panelled drawing and dining rooms and massive carved fireplaces. Upstairs, billiards and pool in an immense room. Bedrooms are panelled and regal, bathrooms excellent. Yvonne travelled much in China and has furnished her new oriental room with eastern antiques and hand-built Chinese furniture. Splendid. You can self-cater in the lovely stone turrets.
Minimum stay two nights.

rooms	5: 3 four-posters, all with bath/shower; 2 self-catering turrets for 2 with living room, dining area, bathroom & kitchenette.
room price	£76-£88. Turrets from £60; £270 p.w.
meals	Breakfast until 9.30am.
closed	November-February. Self-catering always available.
directions	Caverswall is signed, near Blythe Bridge, just off A50. Take M1 junc. 23A, or M6 junc. 14/15. Entrance between 2 churches in village.

Yvonne Sargent
Caverswall Castle,
Caverswall,
Staffordshire ST11 9EA
tel	01782 393239
fax	01782 394590
e-mail	yasargent@hotmail.com
web	www.caverswallcastle.co.uk

SUFFOLK

Energetic Genny's love for her timber-clad home in the heart of flat-racing country is as obvious as her enthusiasm for her garden. She has decorated the big, sunny rooms with thought and care, supplying every treat a guest could want, and books, magazines and an honesty bar for drinks. As you relax in the drawing room by the log fire you will ask, "Why haven't we organised things like this at home?" That's the cake; the icing is the three-acre garden with its sweeping lawns, herbaceous borders, stream, orchard, lily pond and glorious bulbs in spring.

rooms	3: 1 double with shower room; 1 twin with private bathroom; 1 double with bath/shower.
room price	£68. Single occ. £44.
meals	Breakfast 8-9am. Pubs/restaurants, 200 yds-4 miles.
closed	Christmas & New Year.
directions	From A11 (for Thetford/Norwich) B1085 to Red Lodge & Worlington. Right at T-junc. through village; house 200 yds on right.

Genny Jakobson
Brambles,
Worlington, Bury St Edmunds,
Suffolk IP28 8RY
tel	01638 713121
fax	01638 713121
e-mail	genny@trjakobson.freenetname.co.u

SUFFOLK

SUFFOLK

Breakfast, all freshly-squeezed and home-made, is lavish and dinner is a three-course extravaganza. Richard makes the scones for your daily tea; he and Veronica are hugely helpful and kind. The house, begun in 1550, works hard too: beams are exposed, space provided, a stove burns in the inglenook, the library's books are there for you, the cotton is from Egypt and the duvets are of goose down. Play the Steinway or, more energetically, tennis; wander the garden and visit the church dedicated, uniquely in England, to Saint Petronella.

A Suffolk classic, just what you'd expect from an old vicarage: a fine Pembroke table in the flagstoned hall, a large open log fire in the sitting/dining room, a long refectory table covered in magazines such as *The Field*, a come-sit-on-me sofa, a piano and family photos, hunting scenes and silver pheasants. Bedrooms are large, chintzy and handsomely furnished; the double has hill views. Weave your way through the branches of the huge copper beech to the garden that Jane loves; she grows her own vegetables, and keeps hens and house with equal talent. *Children over seven welcome.*

rooms	1 twin/double with shower room.
room price	£70. Single occ. £45.
meals	Dinner, 3 courses, £25. Supper £12.
closed	Very occasionally.
directions	From B. St Edmunds SW on A143 Haverhill road. Left after 30mph zone, for Whepstead 3 miles (B1066). 2 miles on right at dip in road (signed Rede 3 miles). House 1 mile on, past White Horse Inn, on right.

rooms	3: 1 double, 1 twin, both with private bathroom; 1 single off one of the twins.
room price	From £56. Single occ. £32.
meals	Breakfast from 7am. Packed lunch £6. Dinner £18. B.Y.O.
closed	Christmas Day.
directions	From Cambridge, A1307 for Haverhill. Left to Withersfield. At T-junc., left. Almost 3 miles on, high yew hedge & at 'Concealed Entrance' sign on left, sharp turn into drive.

Veronica Hayes
Leaf House,
Rede Road, Whepstead,
Bury St Edmunds,
Suffolk IP29 4SS
tel   01284 735388
e-mail   mail@leafhouse.co.uk
web   www.leafhouse.co.uk

Ms Jane Sheppard
The Old Vicarage,
Great Thurlow, Newmarket,
Suffolk CB9 7LE
tel   01440 783209
fax   01638 667270

map: 11 entry: 411

map: 11 entry: 412

A Queen Anne exterior and a surprising, sumptuous, 1617 oak-panelled Tudor hall. The splendid dining room has massive moulded beams and a fireplace with carved stone pillars and faces. It is a richly interesting, beautiful house, delicate yet lived-in, and with lots of family photos. The double bedroom has an ornate Tudor four-poster, ancient beams, stunning American fabrics at the windows and on the bed, and good views. The twin is in the attic, with uneven oak floors, views and an enchanting garret mood. Diana and her garden are charming.

An immaculate place – gleaming, dark wood antique furniture, fresh flowers and sherry on the oak dresser (17th century, no less). The house is 15th century, timber-framed and thatched and you have your own sitting room with books and an open fire. Home-laid eggs for breakfast, local bacon and home-made bread. A measure of the Oatens' generosity, the bedrooms have goose down duvets, a decanter of Madeira, fresh fruit, sweets and Penhaligon's toiletries, along with co-ordinated furnishings, comfortable beds and good furniture. Bridget and Robin are delightful people who really enjoy having guests.

rooms	2: 1 four-poster, 1 twin, both with private bathroom.
room price	£60-£70. Single occ. from £35.
meals	Breakfast until 9.30am.
closed	Christmas.
directions	From Long Melford on A1092, Clare road. Right to Stanstead on B1066 & right again in village, signed Shimpling. House set back on right 0.5 miles on.

rooms	2: 1 twin/double with bath/shower. 1 double with bathroom & small sitting room.
room price	£60-£70. Single occ. £35-£45.
meals	Excellent local pubs 0.25 miles.
closed	Occasionally.
directions	From Bury St Edmunds, A413 for Haverhill, then B1066 for Glemsford for 6 miles to Hartest. After 30mph signs, on for approx. 0.25 miles; lane on left (signed Cross Green) on sharp double bend.

Diana Banks
Bretteston Hall,
Stanstead, Sudbury,
Suffolk CO10 9AT
tel   01787 280504
fax   01787 280504
e-mail dianabanks@amserve.net

Bridget & Robin Oaten
The Hatch,
Pilgrims Lane, Cross Green, Hartest
Suffolk IP29 4ED
tel   01284 830226
fax   01284 830226

map: 11 entry: 413

map: 11 entry: 414

SUFFOLK

SUFFOLK

Magnificent, Grade I-listed and beautifully restored with respect and sympathy for original fabric and flavour. Built in the 16th and early 18th centuries, the grand house is a paean to architecture – Tudor, Queen Anne, Georgian and Edwardian – with illustrious touches such as Ionic and Corinthian columns on fireplaces. The large bedrooms have beautiful bathrooms, all with original fittings and luxurious towels and linen. Delicious breakfasts are taken at a round table in the oak-panelled breakfast room overlooking the walled garden. The feel of a country house in a town.

Diana was once a stage manager in the London theatre and it shows; she is outgoing, fun, brilliant with people and has a marvellous sense of style. The bedrooms are perfect, with attractive duvets and curtains, pale walls and garden flowers by the beds. On the tea tray are biscuits, proper coffee and a cafetière. The sitting room is a stunning terracotta and a lovely place to be. The garden is surprisingly large, with a terrace, fishpond, lawn and herbaceous borders – very pretty, do sit and enjoy it.

rooms	3: 1 twin/double, 1 double, 1 four-poster, all with bath/shower.
room price	£90-£110. Single occ. £55-£65.
meals	Good pubs/restaurants within walking distance.
closed	Christmas & New Year.
directions	From A14, take Bury Central exit & follow brown signs for Historic City Centre. At r'bout, 1st left into Northgate St. House on right, shortly after lights. Courtyard parking at far end of house.

rooms	3: 2 doubles, 1 twin, all with shower/bath.
room price	From £60. Single occ. from £45.
meals	Pubs/restaurants a short walk away.
closed	Christmas & January; open New Year.
directions	From Sudbury, B1115 to Lavenham. Pass Swan Hotel on right, next right into Market Lane, cross Market Place, right, then left. House on right next to school.

Joy Fiennes
Northgate House,
Northgate Street, Bury St Edmunds,
Suffolk IP33 1HQ
tel 01284 760469
fax 01284 724008
e-mail northgate_hse@hotmail.com
web www.northgatehouse.com

Diana Schofield
The Red House,
29 Bolton Street, Lavenham,
Suffolk CO10 9RG
tel 01787 248074
web www.lavenham.co.uk/redhouse

map: 11 entry: 415

map: 11 entry: 416

Unwind in front of a huge log fire in the Great Hall and soak up the atmosphere of this fascinating place – a Grade I-listed cloth merchant's house in medieval Lavenham. Gilli and Tim have brought old and new together with joyful flamboyance: timber-framed ceilings perfectly restored, slanting oak floors, flagstones heated underfoot. Richly atmospheric bedrooms have handmade mattresses and hand-crafted beds, sumptuous curtains (made by Gilli), flowers, lovely views from mullioned windows. A fabulous house, fully restored to its Elizabethan grandeur. *Children over 10 welcome.*

This little pink cottage was once a pub, but has been tenderly restored to create a pretty, family house; your room, which is in the converted barn, will appeal to the romantic in you. Sue welcomes you with a glass of Madeira by the enormous inglenook fire, then takes you through the neat little garden full of honeysuckle, aqualegia and Canterbury bells to the barn. A stable door opens into the primrose-yellow bedroom with exposed beams and soaring rafters. The chintz-headed, king-size bed is covered in cushions, there are fresh flowers on the table and watercolours of Mauritius on the walls. Stunning!

rooms	6: 1 four-poster suite, 1 double, 3 four-posters, all with bath; 1 twin/double with shower room.
room price	£78-£126. Single occ. £59-£79.
meals	Breakfast 8-9am, Mon-Fri; 8-9.30am Sat & Sun. Restaurants, bistros and pubs within walking distance.
closed	Christmas & New Year.
directions	Turn at The Swan onto Water St, right after 50 yds into private drive.

rooms	1 double with shower room.
room price	£65. Single occ. £37.50.
meals	Packed lunch £3. Dinner available in Lavenham.
closed	Very occasionally.
directions	From Sudbury, B1115 to Lavenham. Pass Swan Hotel on right, next right into Market Lane. Straight across Market Place into Prentice St. Last on right at bottom of hill.

Tim & Gilli Pitt
Lavenham Priory,
Water Street, Lavenham, Sudbury,
Suffolk CO10 9RW

tel	01787 247404
fax	01787 248472
e-mail	mail@lavenhampriory.co.uk
web	www.lavenhampriory.co.uk

Mrs Sue Wade
Anchor House,
Prentice Street, Lavenham,
Suffolk CO10 9RD

tel	01787 249018
fax	01787 249018
e-mail	suewade1@aol.com
web	www.anchorhouse.co.uk

map: 11 entry: 417

map: 11 entry: 418

SUFFOLK

The atmosphere is relaxed and laid-back, yet Juliet has masses of imaginative ideas for making the most of the wonderful countryside: nature trails, local walks, bike rides (you can borrow a bike), tennis and ideas for car-free days out. The house is a glorious unspoiled 16th-century hall farmhouse, lived in and loved by the family for 300 years, with period furniture and lovely bedrooms overlooking a wildflower meadow and walled garden. Home-grown bacon and sausages and bantam eggs for breakfast and equally delicious dinners. Juliet is fun, energetic and a keen conservationist. *Gold award for Green Tourism.*

SUFFOLK

Breakfast on summer mornings on the terrace in the walled garden with home-made marmalade, jams and fruit compotes; in winter, settle beside an arched Tudor brick fireplace in the dining hall. Janus-like, the house looks both ways, Georgian to the front, and richly-beamed, 1485-Tudor behind; Alfred Munnings R.A. was a frequent visitor. The bedrooms one has flower-patterned paper and the other pink sponged walls – are elegant and very English: padded bedheads, thick curtains, armchairs, writing desks, candles, standard lamp, lots of books... pretty and full of thoughtful touches.

rooms	3: 1 double/family with basin, 1 twin, 1 single/twin, all sharing private bathroom.
room price	£55-£70. Single occ. from £35.
meals	Packed lunches available. Supper from £17. B.Y.O. Excellent pub/restaurants 2-3 miles.
closed	Occasionally.
directions	From Lavenham, A1141 for Monks Eleigh. After 2 miles, right to Milden. At x-roads, right to Sudbury on B1115. The Hall's long drive is 0.25 miles on left.

rooms	2: 1 double with shower; 1 twin with bath & separate wc.
room price	£60. Single occ. £30.
meals	Breakfast until 9.30am. Dinner £15 (if staying more than one night). B.Y.O.
closed	Christmas.
directions	From Sudbury B1115 for Lavenham for 3.5 miles. Right to Little Waldingfield. House is on left, 200 yds beyond The Swan.

Juliet & Christopher Hawkins
The Hall,
Milden, Nr. Lavenham,
Suffolk CO10 9NY
tel   01787 247235
fax   01787 247235
e-mail gjb53@dial.pipex.com

Mrs Susan T. del C. Nisbett
Wood Hall,
Little Waldingfield, Nr. Lavenham,
Suffolk CO10 0SY
tel   01787 247362
fax   01787 248326
e-mail susan@woodhallbnb.fsnet.co.uk
web   www.thewoodhall.co.uk

map: 11 entry: 419

map: 11 entry: 420

SUFFOLK

In the heart of Constable country and reached through a web of winding lanes, Sparrows is an idyllic retreat — peaceful, tranquil and homely. You have the run of this gorgeous 15th-century house: a warm, light drawing room with a grand piano, oak beams, open fireplace, a sun room to catch the evening light, a cosy dining room with Suffolk tiles and inglenook fireplace. You also have your own staircase, a king-size bed and a delightful room with many thoughtful touches. Low, leaded windows overlook the peaceful gardens which include a grass tennis court. Rachel is a delight — and a great cook.

SUFFOLK

A lovely early 16th-century house in the River Stour valley made famous by John Constable, now an Area of Outstanding Natural Beauty. The River Box meanders through the delightful garden and numerous old English climbing roses wind through the trees and over the 17th-century barn and stables. Each of the romantically decorated bedrooms is different — some are beamed and all look over the garden, river and fields beyond. There's a charming sitting room with inglenook fireplace. Your hosts are attentive and friendly and your privacy is respected. Hard tennis court available.

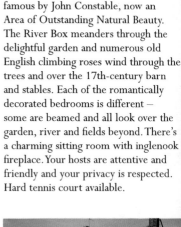

rooms	1 double with private bathroom.
room price	£54-£58. Single occ. £30.
meals	Pub 2 miles.
closed	Christmas & New Year.
directions	Approx. 4 miles between Hadleigh & A12 on country road, 2 miles from Shelley & 1 mile from Polstead. Ring for details as many approaches possible!

rooms	3: 1 double, 1 ground-floor twin/double (with outside access), all with bath; 1 single with private bath.
room price	£60. Single £40.
meals	Breakfast until 9.30am. Dinner available at excellent local pubs.
closed	Christmas & New Year.
directions	3 miles from A12, on B1068 between Higham & Stoke-by-Nayland. On south side of road, 300 yds east of Thorington Street.

	Mrs Rachel Thomas
	Sparrows,
	Shelley, Ipswich,
	Suffolk IP7 5RQ
tel	01206 337381
e-mail	thomas@sparrows.freeserve.co.uk

	Patrick & Jennie Jackson
	Nether Hall,
	Thorington Street,
	Stoke-by-Nayland,
	Suffolk CO6 4ST
tel	01206 337373
fax	01206 337496
e-mail	patrick.jackson@talk21.com

map: 11 entry: 421

map: 11 entry: 422

WE NEED YOU, TOO!

There are three reasons why we need to hear from you, or just like hearing from you.

Firstly – we would end up shouting into the wind if we didn't know what actually happens when you go to one of these places. Most of the letters we get convey tales of kindness and generosity. Occasionally we hear tales of woe – and we always listen carefully, however painfully, to them – and act upon them. We DO drop houses from the book if there are enough complaints (which we follow up with an anonymous inspection).

Secondly – it is fun to learn what goes on out there. We hear some extraordinary stories. An Irish owner, long ago, baffled and bemused a Dutch couple by welcoming them in her bikini and then, thrusting candles into their hands, leading them up the road to attend the funeral of her cat. A Russian asked if he might mow the lawn for he had never seen one before; he came from Siberia. Another guest, whose hosts were puzzled by a strong light near his room, was seen to be collecting moths late into the wee hours with the help of that light.

Thirdly – it is through you, sometimes, that we will hear that owners have decided to sell, convert the barn, lost their marbles or generally 'gone off'. You will tell us if people are exceptionally kind. You will tell us, no doubt, if you got lost following our directions. You will, in other words, keep us up to daste between editions. (We do inspect at least every three years, by the way.)

The beautiful drawing room with carved pine mantelpiece and marble hearth faces south with views of the water meadow and the Rivers Brett and Stour. Blue and white Spode china, silver cutlery, embroidered sheets, fresh fruit and flowers and architectural elegance come with a genuine welcoming feel; Meg really enjoys guests of all ages. You can row, canoe or punt to Stratford St Mary for a pub lunch; or you may fish, play tennis or swim in the pool. This Elizabethan jewel sits snug beside an equally lovely 12th-century church.

Bathe by candlelight in excellent bathrooms. There is more than a touch of theatre about this beautifully proportioned house: the dining room is an opulent, dramatic red, the drawing and sitting rooms are peppered with touches of exotica. Bedrooms have maps (you are near to Sutton Hoo), books, radio, fresh flowers and garden views; one has a four-poster with beautiful embroidered linen. Over seven acres of gardens and woodland include a meadow with orchids and a carpet of wild flowers which has been designated a County Wildlife Site. Cindy and her young family are delightful.

rooms	3: 1 double with bathroom; 1 twin, 1 family for 5, both with private bathroom.
room price	£52-£60. Single occ. £28-£40.
meals	Excellent places for dinner nearby.
closed	Very occasionally.
directions	West off A12 at Stratford St Mary. House on left, opposite church sign, 1 mile down Higham road. House has pink timbers & a sign on wall.

rooms	3: 1 double, 1 single with basin, sharing private bathroom; 1 double with bathroom.
room price	£62-£75 Single occ. £37-£42. Single room, £24.
meals	Dinner, 2/3 courses, £16/£24. B.Y.O.
closed	Very occasionally.
directions	From A12 Woodbridge bypass, exit at r'bout for Melton. Follow for 1 mile to lights; there, right. Immediately on right.

Meg Parker
The Old Vicarage,
Higham, Nr. Colchester,
Suffolk CO7 6JY
tel   01206 337248
e-mail   oldvic.higham@bushinternet.com

Mrs Lucinda de la Rue
Melton Hall,
Woodbridge,
Suffolk IP12 1PF
tel   01394 388138
fax   01394 388982
e-mail   delarue@meltonh.fsnet.co.uk

map: 11 entry: 423

map: 11 entry: 424

SUFFOLK

Wild marshes, deserted beaches – the area is silent but for the call of the birds. Steeped in healing tranquillity, the Augustinian monastery has been brought to life by Frances, an artist and musician. It is undeniably breathtaking and romantic. Decorative stonework clasps the windows, the vaulted dining room soars heavenwards. Forty-seven steps lead to cascades of damask, huge stone-arched windows, beautiful beds with goose down duvets and embroidered linen and invigorating power showers. The magic is all around in seven acres of gardens, lakeside and wooded grounds. Beyond, wonderful walking and seafood restaurants.

rooms	3: 1 double with private bathroom (down small staircase); 1 double with shower room; 1 small double with bath/shower.
room price	£100-£130. Single occ. by arrangement.
meals	Seafood restaurants & pubs nearby.
closed	Occasionally.
directions	From A12 at Woodbridge, B1084 for Orford. In Butley at Oyster Inn, take Hollesley road for 1 mile to x-roads. Private entrance to Priory immed. right after x-roads.

tel	01394 450046
fax	01394 450482
e-mail	cavendish@butleypriory.co.uk
web	www.butleypriory.com

map: 11 entry: 425

SUFFOLK

An estuarine corner of rare loveliness; the views are wide and clean, you can stroll to the river to be among the gulls, avocets and duck. The remote and ancient farmhouse is an aesthetic treat, charmingly scruffy, flagstoned, filled with things that we found beautiful and interesting, surprising, uplifting, fun, exquisitely unmodernised… yet comfortable. The library is crammed with books, the kitchen is a beachcomber's haven. Solitary, winter-bleak splendour with an engagingly relaxed, interesting, artistic and cultured architect. Come if you are easy and open, and do what you want.

rooms	1 four-poster with private bathroom.
room price	£70. Single occ. by arrangement.
meals	Good pubs & restaurants nearby.
closed	Occasionally.
directions	From Orford Market Square, take lane towards castle, & 1st right past castle, marked 'Gedgrave Only, No Through Road'. House on left after 0.5 miles by a lone pine.

tel	01394 450102
fax	01394 450313

map: 11 entry: 426

SUFFOLK

SUFFOLK

Wrap-around sea views – you are almost on the beach. Phil (from Zimbabwe) and Juliet are easy-going hosts, and enjoy sharing this very special place. The furniture is Victorian, some mahogany, some walnut, the colours soft, the bed linen the sort you always meant to buy at home. (White cotton crocheted bedspreads come from the market at Victoria Falls.) Here are old things, good taste, books and magazines galore, fresh milk on the morning tea tray, home-made biscuits, rugs on wooden floors and a special light from every window. You can borrow bikes, play table tennis in the cellar, sail. Perfect.

A dreamy 16th-century Tudor farmhouse – partly moated, with an abundance of beams, original *fleur-de-lys* mouldings, an inglenook fireplace and a thatched summerhouse – yet a real home with a sense of fun and vitality, too. Family photographs, seagrass matting, fresh flowers everywhere, real candles in the candelabra and soft colours: there's a restrained stylishness throughout. Jane and Peter are delightful and will bring you tea in the drawing room or a drink if you arrive a bit later. Jane was a professional cook and can conjure up an inspiring dinner if you give her notice.

rooms	2: 1 double with bathroom; 1 twin with shower room.
room price	£65-£70. Single occ. £55-£60.
meals	Breakfast until 9.30am. Packed lunch £5. Dinner £10-£15. Restaurant 100 yds.
closed	Very occasionally.
directions	From Ipswich A12 north. Right onto A1094 after 20 miles. House in centre of Aldeburgh seafront with parking outside.

rooms	2: 1 double, 1 twin, sharing bathroom.
room price	£60. Single occ. £40.
meals	Dinner £15-£25.
closed	Christmas & New Year.
directions	From A1120 at Earl Soham, take Kenton road & follow signs to Monk Soham for approx. 2 miles. Right fork at top of hill. House 3rd entrance on right.

	Juliet & Phil Brereton
	Ocean House,
	25 Crag Path, Aldeburgh,
	Suffolk IP15 5BS
tel	01728 452094
fax	01728 453909

	Jane & Peter Cazalet
	Monk Soham Hall,
	Monk Soham, Nr. Woodbridge,
	Suffolk IP13 7EN
tel	01728 685178
fax	01728 685944
e-mail	janecaz860@aol.com

The undeniable charms of this mellow red-brick Georgian townhouse lured the Haddons away from London life. Catherine, an interior designer, has poured her considerable energy and talent into its restoration and with a young family *in situ* the whole place feels alive and loved, elegant yet informal. There are lovely fabrics and beautiful colours. Breakfast is served in the panelled dining room and upstairs are a delightful double bedroom, a cottagey twin and, in the attic, a charming family suite. Magnificent gardens, too, with a parterre and rose garden.

A sunken garden and covered terrace lead to a glorious sunroom which is just for you, to read, relax or eat in. Large bedrooms are in the roof of this 1860s converted granary, with high, beamed ceilings and arched windows – they feel very private. Potions for the bath, robes, candlesticks and bottled water are yours, too. All around are impressive medieval churches – why not take off on the bikes with a packed lunch? The beach is only three miles away. Carole, gentle and flexible, is involved in the June Aldeburgh Festival and the year-round Snape Maltings concerts.

rooms	2: 1 double with private bathroom; 1 twin with shower room.
room price	From £65. Single occ. from £35.
meals	Dinner from £15.
closed	Christmas & New Year, unless by arrangement.
directions	Turn off A12 to Saxmundham. Through town & under railway bridge; house 1st on right.

rooms	2: 1 double with private bathroom; 1 twin with shower room.
room price	£53. Single occ. £26.50.
meals	Packed lunch available. Dinner, 3 courses, from £12.
closed	Very occasionally.
directions	From A12, B1119. From Saxmundham to Leiston, left onto B1122 for Yoxford. 2 miles on, left at x-roads just before Theberton (30mph sign). 1st left, then right up 1st driveway.

Catherine & Christopher Haddon
Beech House,
North Entrance, Saxmundham,
Suffolk IP17 1AP
tel   01728 605700
fax   01728 605909

Mrs Carole Bidder
The Granary,
Theberton, Nr. Leiston,
Suffolk IP16 4RR
tel   01728 831633
fax   01728 831633
e-mail granarytheberton@aol.com

map: 11 entry: 429

map: 11 entry: 430

Surrounded by gardens and apple orchards Robin and Patricia are dedicated to the delights of producing their own fruit, veg, free-range eggs, poultry and lamb. Guests wax lyrical about the food. Robin has an artistic streak – a mural is on display over the dining room mantelpiece – and Patricia, a landscape architect, enjoys sharing her garden. The 15th-century, Grade II-listed farmhouse – all beams and open fires – is a haven of peace. Rooms are simply but comfortably furnished and delightfully scattered with books, flowers and the odd patchwork quilt.

Atmosphere and architecture – it's easy to see what seduced Jackum and David into converting this Grade II-listed Victorian chapel into their home. Bedrooms are charming – the Stable Room, with access to the courtyard garden, has cream walls, oak floors and wooden beams; the flag-floored Retreat Room sports bright rugs and bedcovers from far-flung places. An air of tranquillity pervades, from the wind chimes in the peaceful garden to breakfast served by the lovely rose window in the chapel or in the colourful conservatory. Potions and lotions by your bath, books and flowers in every corner, famous bacon from the Peasenhall.

rooms	3: 1 twin/double with bath/shower; 1 double, 1 twin, sharing private bathroom.
room price	£60-£70. Single occ. by arrangement.
meals	Dinner, 3 courses, £20.
closed	Occasionally.
directions	A12 to Yoxford, B1122 to Leiston. After r'way crossing, right by pond down unmarked road. House at end of lane on right.

rooms	2: 1 double with private bathroom & garden access; 1 twin with shower.
room price	£55-£70. Single occ. £32.50-£40.
meals	Good pubs/restaurants within walking distance.
closed	Occasionally.
directions	From A12 in Yoxford, take A1120 (signed Peasenhall & Stowmarket). Chapel 200 yds on right.

	Robin Hare
	Fordley Hall,
	Middleton, Saxmundham,
	Suffolk IP17 3LT
tel	01728 668236
fax	01728 668458
e-mail	robin@fordleyhall.co.uk
web	www.fordleyhall.co.uk

	Jackum & David Brown
	The Old Methodist Chapel,
	High Street, Yoxford,
	Suffolk IP17 3EU
tel	01728 668333
e-mail	browns@chapelsuffolk.co.uk
web	www.chapelsuffolk.co.uk

map: 11 entry: 431

map: 11 entry: 432

The tennis court and large garden are surrounded by the 12th-century listed moat – this is a gorgeous old place with stacks of interest. Ancient stairs rise and fall all over the 13th-century house and there are sloping floors and raw beams. The dining room, for candlelit dinners at the large table, was once the dairy. The family room has a billiard table and toy cupboard and the sitting room a baby grand, open fire, fresh flowers and lots of books. Elizabeth is delightful and generous: home-made cake on arrival, local honey, home-made bread and marmalade for breakfast.

Walberswick is enchanting; artists have congregated here for over a century. Ferry House was built in the 1930s for a playwright, using a butterfly design to catch the light – it has Art Deco touches, hand-painted fireplace tiles, simple but pretty rooms, co-ordinated linens, books and fresh flowers everywhere. There's a warm cloakroom for wet birdwatchers' clothes and a welcoming glass of sherry. You are only 200 yards from the River Blyth and the sea, and there is a self-catering studio for two. *Children over 10 welcome.*

rooms	3: 1 double, 2 twins, sharing bathroom. Extra wc available.
room price	£44. Single occ. £22. Children 10-15 £10-£15.
meals	Breakfast 7.30-9.30am. Supper/dinner £12.50/£14. B.Y.O.
closed	December-February.
directions	A1120 (Yoxford to Stowmarket) to Dennington. B1116 north for approx. 3 miles. Farm on right 0.9 miles north of Owl's Green & red phone box.

rooms	3: 1 double with wc; 2 singles sharing wc. Separate guest bathroom. Self-catering Coach House studio also available.
room price	From £42. Single from £21.
meals	Breakfast until 9.30am. Packed lunch £3.50. Pub/restaurant 150 yds.
closed	Christmas.
directions	From A12, B1387 to Walberswick. House on left at far end of village, near river. Three miles from A12.

	Elizabeth Hickson
	Grange Farm,
	Dennington, Woodbridge,
	Suffolk IP13 8BT
tel	01986 798388

	Cathryn Simpson
	Ferry House,
	Walberswick, Southwold,
	Suffolk IP18 6TH
tel	01502 723384
fax	01502 723384
e-mail	ferryhouse.walberswick@virgin.net
web	www.ferryhouse-walberswick.com

map: 11 entry: 433

map: 11 entry: 434

SUFFOLK

The enchanting Suffolk brick façade hints at the elegance within. Here is a Georgian vicarage in its own tranquil corner with easy access to the heritage coast. Well-proportioned rooms are grand but not too grand – fine old furniture, family portraits in gilded frames, photographs, books. The bedrooms are a treat: four-poster beds, towelling robes and garden views; you have your own delightful sitting room, too. Paula is good company, loves cooking and keeps the flowers fresh. For breakfast expect the best – local sausages and bacon, toasted home-made bread and marmalade, linen napkins in silver rings.

rooms	3: 1 double with private bathroom; 1 double, 1 twin sharing bathroom.
room price	£50-£70. Single occ. £35.
meals	Packed lunch £4. Good pubs 3 miles.
closed	Very occasionally.
directions	From A12, 4 miles north of Yoxford, left for Wenhaston. Pass Star Inn & school on left. After 400 yds, on left is red brick wall around churchyard; drive at far end.

Mrs P. Heycock
The Old Vicarage,
Church Corner, Wenhaston,
Southwold, Suffolk IP19 9EG
tel   01502 478339
fax   01502 478068
e-mail   theycock@aol.com
web   www.southwold.blythweb.co.uk/
       oldvicarage

map: 11 entry: 435

SUFFOLK

Pat, kind and immensely caring, is an experienced B&B-er. The attractive modern house has secluded gardens and is close to a large heath – a lure for early-morning walkers. Pat has filled her new home with lovely family furniture, pictures and many books. Peace and quiet, delicious food, a lovely hostess; and the natural charms of Suffolk (the heritage coast, medieval churches, Southwold) the icing on the cake. Woottens Nursery is nearby too, popular among serious plant collectors.

rooms	2: 1 twin/double with private shower room; 1 twin with shower room.
room price	£36-£50. Single occ. £22-£29.
meals	Breakfast 8-9am. Dinner £12. Good inn very close.
closed	Occasionally.
directions	From A12, 3.3 miles north of Darsham level crossing, left at x-roads for Wenhaston. Left at Star Inn & immed. right into lane. House 2nd on left.

Patricia Kemsley
Rowan House,
Hall Road, Wenhaston, Southwold,
Suffolk IP19 9HF
tel   01502 478407

map: 11 entry: 436

A listed Elizabethan farmhouse with Georgian additions, meticulously restored, with ancient and modern character and in a very quiet hamlet with a 12th-century thatched church. Sarah, well-travelled and entertaining, has created a relaxed atmosphere in which you feel entirely at home. The bedrooms have good fabrics, fresh flowers and cotton sheets; one has a medieval bedstead with carved head- and foot-boards, two have super new bathrooms and all are peaceful. There's a Bechstein to play.

An enchanting, soft, 16th-century Suffolk combination of bricks and beams; enjoy the quietness of the house and garden throughout the day if you wish. It is friendly and handsome, with antique furniture and William Morris-type floral sofas and chairs. The dining room was once a cheese room where 'Suffolk Bang' was made and from here you can wander into the kitchen to chat with Rosemary. You have your own wing; one of the bedrooms is a delightful half-timbered room with sloping ceiling. Four miles away is Wingfield Old College, home of the summer arts festival.

rooms	3: 1 double, 1 twin, 1 single, all with private bathroom.
room price	From £70. Single occ. from £35.
meals	Dinner from £20.
closed	Christmas.
directions	A12 for Wangford. Left signed Uggeshall. Farmhouse is 1 mile on left before church.

rooms	3: 2 doubles, 1 twin, both with private bathroom.
room price	From £54. Single occ. £32.
meals	Good pubs/restaurants 8-minute walk.
closed	Christmas week.
directions	From Scole, A140, right onto A143 for Gt Yarmouth. After 7 miles, right at Harleston. B1116 to Fressingfield. Pass church & Fox & Goose on left. At top of hill, right, then left into Priory Road.

Sarah Jupp
Church Farmhouse,
Uggeshall, Southwold,
Suffolk NR34 8BD
tel   01502 578532
fax   01953 888306
e-mail sarahjupp@compuserve.com

Stephen & Rosemary Willis
Priory House,
Priory Road, Fressingfield, Eye,
Suffolk IP21 5PH
tel   01379 586254
fax   01379 586254

map: 11 entry: 437

map: 11 entry: 438

Originally a 16th-century inn, the farmhouse is now a peaceful haven set in five acres with a small lake that used to form part of a moat; a bridge takes you to a little island. Inside, low beams, wattle-and-daub walls, Jacobean-style furniture, antiques, rugs and log fires. One bedroom has a brass bedstead, another a four-poster; the attic bathroom has a whirlpool. At breakfast you can sit in the conservatory overlooking the lake and be entertained by the ducks. Ann and David are relaxed, unpretentious, easy hosts who are pleased to ferry airport travellers.

It really does ramble – it's 1532 and sits in two and a half acres of smooth lawns beyond which lie the village and Surrey hills. Unlike many houses with masses of beams, low ceilings and dark furniture, this one is light and inviting and it has the sort of family clutter that makes you feel immediately at home. Patrick is enthusiastic and dynamic, Carol makes lovely breakfasts with home-made marmalades; both leave you plenty of space to unfurl at your own pace. The dining room is stone-flagged and there's a snug study just for guests.

rooms	3: 1 double, 1 four-poster, both with bathroom; 1 twin with shower room.
room price	£55-£65. Single occ. £40-£50.
meals	Pub/restaurant 1 mile.
closed	Christmas.
directions	At x-roads in Leigh, follow signs to Charwood. After 1 mile, 1st right (signed Herons Head Farm) after sign to Mynthurst. Continue up drive for 0.5 miles.

rooms	3: 2 doubles, 1 twin, all sharing bathroom.
room price	£50-£60. Single occ. £25-£30.
meals	Breakfast 7-9.30am. Good pubs/restaurants 3-5 miles.
closed	Christmas.
directions	From A3, 1st exit after M25 (for Ripley). Through Ripley & West Clandon, over dual carriageway (A246) onto A25. 3rd right to Shere. There, right to Cranleigh. House 5 miles on left, 1 mile past Windmill pub.

Ms Ann Dale
Herons Head Farm,
Mynthurst, Leigh,
Surrey RH2 8QD
tel   01293 862475
fax   01293 863350
e-mail   heronshead@clara.net
web   www.heronshead.co.uk

Patrick & Carol Franklin Adams
High Edser,
Shere Road, Ewhurst, Cranleigh,
Surrey GU6 7PQ
tel   01483 278214
fax   01483 278200
e-mail   franklinadams@highedser.
          demon.co.uk

This feels as rural as Devon, yet you are (almost) within walking distance of Guildford. It's a gorgeous 16th-century Grade II-listed farmhouse on a country lane beneath the Pilgrim's Way. Beyond the pretty terraced garden – Michael's passion – views of the North Downs and wooded hills stretch out, with hardly a house in sight. Bedrooms have been beautifully furnished by Alison, an interior designer, with lovely fabrics and antique French beds. Log fires are lit in winter when the wind whistles around and there are two friendly dogs to greet you – Herbert and Ha'penny. Perfectly placed for airports and Ascot.

People return time and again – the house, the garden, the countryside and the hosts are exceptional. In a vast sitting room, low-slung beams and striking colours jostle for your attention. A sturdy, turning oak staircase leads to the bedrooms; a peek at them all will only confuse you – each one is gorgeous. There's an ornate bedstead in the Chinese room and, in another, an oak bedstead and beams. A further room has a hint of French decadence: golds, magentas and silks. Sheila knows about antiques and the local antique shops – and day trips to nearby London.

rooms	2 doubles, both with private bathroom.
room price	£70. Single occ. £50.
meals	Good pubs/restaurants 1-2 miles.
closed	Christmas & New Year.
directions	From top of Guildford High St, along Epsom Rd & right into Tangier Rd. At top, bear left into Warren Rd. At sharp r-h bend at top, (One Tree Hill Rd), on for 0.3 miles, bear right into Halfpenny Lane. 0.7 miles down on left.

rooms	3: 1 double with bathroom; 1 twin, 1 single sharing bathroom.
room price	£70-£80. Single occ. from £45.
meals	Breakfast until 9am. Hotel restaurant 0.25 miles.
closed	Very occasionally.
directions	A3 to Milford, then A283 for Petworth. At Chiddingfold, Pickhurst Rd is off green. House 3rd on left, with large black dovecote.

Michael Bennett
Old Great Halfpenny,
Halfpenny Lane, St Martha,
Guildford,
Surrey GU4 8PY
tel   01483 567835
fax   01483 303037
e-mail alisonbird1@btinternet.com

Sheila & John Marsh
Greenaway,
Pickhurst Road, Chiddingfold,
Surrey GU8 4TS
tel   01428 682920
fax   01428 685078
e-mail jfmarsh@nildram.co.uk
web   www.greenaway.nildram.co.uk

map: 5 entry: 441

map: 5 entry: 442

A homely place with a lovely walled garden and super hosts. Gillian welcomes guests from all over the world (she speaks French, German and Spanish), yet she and David will make you feel like their first ever; their conversation is lively and informed. The house, 16th to 19th century, has exposed timber frames and bold colours – like the dining room's red. The guest sitting room, with its log fireplace and piano, is hung with a collection of hats and ethnic treasures. In the walled garden the distant rumble of the A3 reminds you how well placed you are for Gatwick and Heathrow.

It is a surprise to bump along a farm track and find 400 acres of farmland so close to London, but this is Surrey, the most densely wooded and rural home county. The lovely manor has all the impressive features you'd expect. An easy-going John enjoys the higgle and piggle of the 1550s house – wooden floors, big fires, worn carpets and rugs, window seats and church panel doors. Bedrooms and bathrooms are big, with timbered walls and views to a walled rose garden, two acres of lawn, a tree-lined pond and a hillock on which horses graze.

rooms	4: 1 twin/double with bath/shower; 1 twin/double with private bath/shower; 2 singles (1 with basin) sharing shower room.
room price	£60-£75. Singles £35-£42. Single occ. of twin £50.
meals	Breakfast 7.30-9am. Good pub 300 yds.
closed	Christmas & New Year.
directions	A3 south. 5 miles after Guildford, Eashing signed left at service station. House 150 yds on left behind white fence.

rooms	2: 1 twin with bathroom; 1 double with bath.
room price	£60. Single occ. £40.
meals	Supper with wine £25.
closed	Very occasionally.
directions	From M3, A322 to Worplendon; after White Lyon pub, right, down hill to black & white r'bout; right to Aldershot; house signed on left.

David & Gillian Swinburn
Lower Easing Farmhouse,
Eashing, Nr. Godalming,
Surrey GU7 2QF
tel   01483 421436
fax   01483 421436
e-mail   davidswinburn@hotmail.com

John & Pooh Tangye
Littlefield Manor,
Littlefield Common, Guildford,
Surrey GU3 3HJ
tel   01483 233068
fax   01483 233686
e-mail   john.tangye@virgin.net
web   www.littlefieldmanor.co.uk

map: 5 entry: 443

map: 5 entry: 444

It is not easy to get the balance between friendliness and intrusiveness right, but Joan and David have succeeded admirably. Theirs is a converted stables and squash court originally belonging to the next-door manor house; it has a mature charm. There are many trees in the garden, a paddock and a pool. Given the hushed tranquillity you are surprisingly close to the M25 and airports. Bedrooms are not large but one opens onto the garden, one has a balcony and the Applestore is self-contained. There's a self-catering annexe, too. *Children over eight welcome.*

This late-Georgian parsonage, in a pretty village setting, has all the warmth and cosy comfort of a traditional English home plus warm colours, light streaming through French windows, the wrap-around snugness of plump sofas, and those deft touches that make all the difference – like the dark green bathrobes in your room. The en suite shower-rooms are small, but there is sherry in the bedrooms, home-cooked food using free-range meats and local produce, and a chance to chat over dinner with your well-travelled, articulate and relaxed hosts.

rooms	3: 1 double with bathroom & sitting room; 1 twin with shower; 1 twin with private shower.
room price	£75. Single occ. £45. Self-catering annexe, from £400 p.w.
meals	Pub/restaurant 0.75 miles.
closed	Very occasionally.
directions	From M25, exit 11, A319 into Chobham. Left at T-junc., left at mini-r'bout onto A3046. After 0.7 miles, right between street light & postbox. House 2nd on left.

rooms	4: 1 twin/double, 1 twin, 1 double, all with small shower room; 1 double, 1 family, with private bathroom.
room price	£50-£110. Single occ. £38-£55.
meals	Breakfast 7-8.30am, 8-9am Sat-Sun. Dinner, 4 courses, from £20. Light supper £12.50.
closed	Very occasionally.
directions	M25 junc. 13, A30 for Egham. Next r'bout, A30 to Basingstoke. Uphill to lights. Right, then 3rd right, left at T-junc. Immed. on right. Parking is tight, but the Clarks will help.

Joan & David Carey
Swallow Barn,
Milford Green, Chobham, Woking,
Surrey GU24 8AU
tel   01276 856030
fax   01276 856030
e-mail   swallowbarn@compuserve.com
web   www.swallow-barn.co.uk

Sandi & Peter Clark
The Old Parsonage,
Parsonage Road, Englefield Green,
Surrey TW20 0JW
tel   01784 436706
fax   01784 436706
e-mail   the.old.parsonage@talk21.com
web   www.theoldparsonage.com

map: 5 entry: 445

map: 5 entry: 446

SURREY

The two acres of formal rose beds, borders, lawns and orchards sweep down to the Thames: a magical and secluded spot, and so close to London. For garden lovers, Hampton Court Palace (home to the International Flower Show) is next door and Windsor, Wisley and Kew a short drive away. This exceptionally elegant Palladian house has fine moulded ceilings, portraits, books and flowers; bedrooms are sumptuous with fine fabrics, exquisite furniture and lovely views. Sonia serves delicious home-cooking including a fine repertoire of Jewish and continental recipes. French and Italian spoken.
Minimum stay two nights.

rooms	2: 1 double with bath/shower; 1 double with private bathroom.
room price	£90-£100. Single occ. by arrangement.
meals	Breakfast until 9am. Dinner £25.
closed	Occasionally.
directions	From Hampton Court r'bout, A308, west, for 300 yds. Left through wrought-iron gates to house at end of drive. Hampton Court station 5 minutes, 30 minutes Waterloo.

Dr Louis & Sonia Marks
Paddock Lodge,
The Green, Hampton Court,
Surrey KT8 9BW

tel   020 89795254
e-mail   101723.1100@compuserve.com

map: 5 entry: 447

SUSSEX

The gorgeous house has been many things – wool store, school and former home of poet Conrad Aiken; hard to believe the deep red dining room, full of busts and paintings, was an old Baptist chapel. Jenny is engagingly easy-going and has created a lovely atmosphere. Rooms are traditionally furnished, with rich drapes, antique four-posters… there's a large attic room with beams, a library, a book-lined bar, a cosy parlour. A smart retreat among Rye's cobbled streets.

rooms	12: 9 doubles, all with bath/shower; 1 double, 1 single, sharing bathroom; 1 honeymoon suite with bath.
room price	£35-£112.
meals	Breakfast 8-9.30am, 8.30-10am (Sun). Many local restaurants.
closed	Very occasionally.
directions	From London, into centre of Rye on A268, left off High St onto West St, then 1st right into Mermaid St. House on left. Private car park, £3 a day for guests.

Jenny Hadfield
Jeake's House,
Mermaid Street, Rye,
Sussex TN31 7ET

tel   01797 222828
fax   01797 222623
e-mail   jeakeshouse@btinternet.com
web   www.jeakeshouse.com

map: 6 entry: 448

House and owner have a vibrancy that is unique. Sara has created a special atmosphere in her truly welcoming, rule-free townhouse in lovely history-laden Rye. You'll be enchanted by original art, fine antiques and masses of books; attention to detail and many personal touches herald the fact that this is a real home. Super, luxurious bedrooms have views of either a quiet cobbled street or the large, quiet garden (complete with a Smugglers' Watchtower). There is a bookroom for rainy days and a sitting room with open fire, too. Breakfasts are generous and organic/free-range.

Stacks of woody character, with exposed beams and a woodburning stove in an inglenook in the sitting/dining room. Charming views through the lead-latticed windows in the cosy bedrooms and, from the garden room, you can see "the spot where Harold camped before he got it in the eye in 1066". Breakfast and dinner are taken at separate tables and, afterwards, you can walk through the Collins' 40 acres and see the 500 broadleafed trees they've planted. Chickens and geese and 1,000 acres of woodland add to the rural bliss – and Paul and Pauline such nice people.

rooms	2 four-posters, both with bathroom.
room price	£70–£90. Single occ. £45–£65.
meals	Breakfast 8-9.30am. Dinner available nearby.
closed	Very occasionally.
directions	In Rye, follow signs to town centre & enter Old Town through Landgate Arch into High St. West St 3rd on left. House halfway up on left.

rooms	3 doubles, all with bath.
room price	From £54. Single occ. from £33.
meals	Supper around £10.
closed	January.
directions	From Battle on A271, 1st right to Heathfield. After 0.75 miles, right into drive.

Sara Brinkhurst
Little Orchard House,
West Street, Rye,
Sussex TN31 7ES

tel	01797 223831
fax	01797 223831
web	www.littleorchardhouse.com

Paul & Pauline Collins
Fox Hole Farm,
Kane Hythe Road, Battle,
Sussex TN33 9QU

| tel | 01424 772053 |
| fax | 01424 772053 |

map: 6 entry: 449

map: 6 entry: 450

A listed 17th-century house beside the church in the heart of a tiny village, 10 minutes from Glyndebourne. Alison was chef to the Beatles and will not only give you a delicious hamper, but tables and chairs, too. Willie is a former world rackets champion who gives tennis coaching; there's a tennis court in the large, pretty garden, and a swimming pool too. Relax by the inglenook fire in the drawing room after a walk on the Cuckoo Trail or the South Downs; then settle down to a great supper – local fish, maybe, with home-grown vegetables. This is an easy-going, fun and informal household.
Children over 12 welcome.

rooms	2: 1 double, 1 single, sharing bathroom (let only to same party).
room price	£50. Single occ. £30.
meals	Dinner £20. B.Y.O.
closed	Christmas & Easter.
directions	From Boship r'bout on A22, A267. 1st right to Horsebridge & immed. left to Hellingly. House next to church, in Mill Lane.

Alison & Willie Boone
Globe Place,
Hellingly,
Sussex BN27 4EY
tel   01323 844276
fax   01323 844276
e-mail   aliboone@talk21.com

map: 5 entry: 451

Sarah has impeccable taste and is constantly striving to make her thoroughly English 17th-century house even more beautiful. Rich colours, well-chosen fabrics, good oil paintings: it's a perfect escape for cultured sybarites. There's a heated pool, a tennis court and a spectacular garden; she recently planted thousands of Dutch tulip bulbs given to her by a friend. The food is special, too, with an adventurous but always carefully judged menu. She will also prepare you a hamper for Glyndebourne (10 minutes away) and the orange juice for breakfast is freshly squeezed.

rooms	3: 2 twins, 1 with bath, 1 with private bathroom; 1 twin/double with private shower room.
room price	£76-£110. Single occ. by arrangement.
meals	Breakfast until 9.30am. Lunch from £16, hampers £25. Dinner, 3 courses, £24.
closed	Very occasionally.
directions	0.5 miles past Halland on A22, south from Uckfield, 1st left off Shaw r'bout towards E. Hoathly, on for 0.5 miles. Drive on left with postbox. Take central gravel drive.

Sarah Burgoyne
Old Whyly,
East Hoathly,
Sussex BN8 6EL
tel   01825 840216
fax   01825 840738
e-mail   stay@oldwhyly.co.uk
web   www.oldwhyly.co.uk

map: 5 entry: 452

SUSSEX

SUSSEX

A typical 15th-century, beamy, cosy Sussex farmhouse with bags of character. Delightful Celia has filled it with fascinating things; she used to sell antiques and has a good eye. The single rooms are full of charm and style with some interesting pieces of furniture (of course). The double is equally lovely, light and airy and overlooks the garden which has received the same lavish attention as the house. It has been restored to its original layout with two bridged ponds – you could happily spend hours wandering among the colours and scents. Excellent pubs nearby and handy for Glyndebourne.

A thoroughly charming, miniature country house, with a courtyard in front and a walled garden at the back; both a riot of colour in spring and summer. When you arrive you may join Lucy for tea and cakes at the large oak table in the kitchen: a great start. The bedroom is bright and fresh, with Egyptian cotton sheets and home-made biscuits on the tea tray. There are fresh flowers everywhere – it's obvious that Lucy cares – and you'll feel well looked after. Walk through the garden to woodlands behind and yet more peace. Handy for Glyndebourne.

rooms	3: 1 double with private bathroom; 2 singles sharing bathroom.
room price	£58. Singles £29.
meals	Breakfast until 9.30am. Good pub 5 minutes' drive.
closed	Christmas & New Year.
directions	From Uckfield, A26 Lewes road. Right for Isfield & on for 1 mile. Right over level crossing & house on steep left bend with high fence & gate, approx. 0.5 miles on.

rooms	1 twin/double with bath.
room price	£70. Single occ. £45.
meals	Packed lunch £5. Good pub 1 mile.
closed	Christmas & New Year.
directions	A26 for Uckfield; straight at Little Horsted r'bout for Ridgewood. 1st right down New Road; at phone box turn right down concealed drive. Cottage is 2nd on left.

Celia Rigby
The Faulkners,
Isfield,
Sussex TN22 5XG

tel   01825 750344
fax   01825 750577

Mrs Lucy Ann
Park Cottage,
Ridgewood, Nr. Uckfield,
Sussex TN22 5TG

tel   01825 767104
fax   01825 763005
e-mail l.ann@btinternet.com

map: 5 entry: 453

map: 5 entry: 454

Both Graham and Jennifer have travelled extensively in the Army with The King's Own Scottish Borderers; there is a regimental 'museum' in the downstairs cloakroom. They are kind and dedicated hosts happy to help you plan your day or book a table at the village pub for you. Visitors from 55 nations have enjoyed the comforts of this unspoilt, wisteria-clad 1930s bastion of old-Englishness. The garden is beautiful; the fruit and veg plot big enough to feed an army. Log fires in winter. *Children over 10 welcome.*

rooms	3: 1 double, 1 twin, both with private bathroom. Second twin available.
room price	From £62. Single occ. from £42.
meals	Pub in village.
closed	Very occasionally.
directions	From M25, A22 to Maresfield. At mini-r'bout in centre of village, under stone arch opp. church & pub, & over 5 speed bumps. House 1st on left.

Graham & Jennifer Allt
South Paddock,
Maresfield Park, Nr. Uckfield,
Sussex TN22 2HA
tel   01825 762335

All doors lead to the garden, it seems. Wisteria and roses scent the air and you can play croquet amid the beauty; the guest sitting room and the dining room have their own patio, too. You'll feel nurtured in this large, late-Victorian country house: Norma fills the bedrooms with flowers, the bathrooms with soaps and shampoos, and is happy to make restaurant bookings for you. The pretty twin has matching chintz-skirted dressing-table and curtains, the king-size double comes with dressing-gown and slippers. Fine views to Ashdown Forest, too. *Children over 11 welcome.*

rooms	2: 1 twin with shower, 1 double with basin, & private bath/shower.
room price	From £50. Single occ. from £30.
meals	Pubs/restaurants within walking distance.
closed	Occasionally.
directions	A26 from Tunbridge Wells for Uckfield. At Crowborough Cross, take Beacon Rd. 4th right into Warren Rd. Bottom of hill to Rannoch Rd. Right. House on left after 200 yds.

Norma Backhouse
Hope Court,
Rannoch Road, Crowborough,
Sussex TN6 1RA
tel   01892 654017

SUSSEX

Copyhold hides, snugly, behind a 1,000-year-old box hedge, its land delineated by an ancient field boundary. First a farm, then an ale house, the 16th-century building seems small from the outside, but opens into a quirky interior with many exposed timbers. Frances did the renovation herself and landscaped the gardens; nightingales and owls enjoy the woodland parts. The guests' dining room and inglenook sitting room are oak-beamed, uncluttered and cheerful; bedrooms are also beamed, and neat, with views over meadow and woodland. Your lively, independent-minded hostess will happily find time to chat by the fire.

rooms	3: 1 double, 1 twin, both with shower; 1 single with bath.
room price	From £60. Single occ. from £40.
meals	Breakfast 8-9am. Pubs/restaurants 2-3 miles.
closed	Very occasionally.
directions	From Gatwick, M23 south & follow signs to Cuckfield. There, right at 1st mini-r'bout, left at 2nd, right at 3rd. Left at T-junc. Copyhold Lane 1st on right, after entrance to Borde Hill Gardens.

Frances Druce
Copyhold Hollow,
Copyhold Lane, Borde Hill,
Haywards Heath,
Sussex RH16 1XU
tel	01444 413265
e-mail	10@copyholdhollow.freeserve.co.uk
web	www.copyholdhollow.freeserve.co.uk

SUSSEX

Just one ground-floor guest room and a good deal of homely comfort. You are at the opposite end of the house from the owners, so you feel very private and your bathroom is a couple of steps from the bedroom door. Modern pine dressing tables, rattan chairs, co-ordinated curtains and duvet covers and views of the lovely three-acre garden. The Sussex Archeological Society says the house has Elizabethan origins and some of the smaller, mullioned windows bear this out. Old, old timbers in the snug dining room and Jeannie and Nick are charming and easy to talk to.

rooms	1 double with private bathroom.
room price	£50. Single occ. £35.
meals	Pubs 2.5 miles.
closed	Very occasionally.
directions	From Haywards Heath, B2028 to Lindfield. 1.5 miles after passing church at north end of Lindfield, house on left.

Jeannie & Nick Leadsom
Little Lywood,
Ardingly Road, Ardingly, Lindfield,
Sussex RH16 2QX
| tel | 01444 892571 |
| e-mail | nick@littlelywood.freeserve.co.uk |

You'd hesitate to light a match here, lest you set the ancient timbers alight – together with Joy's many paintings, all for sale: land, sea, and other scapes. It is a 15th-century hall house, once one vast room with a central fireplace venting through the roof. Although a 'guesthouse' it only has two rooms and they are comfortable and woody, with Egyptian cotton, power showers and all mod cons. The double is richly beamed and has a padded headboard and opulent bedspread; the twin has velour-padded headboards and fewer beams. Steyning is an ancient market town with a fine 11th-century church worth visiting.

rooms	2: 1 double, 1 twin, both with bath/shower.
room price	£78. Single occ. £49.
meals	Dinner, 3/4 courses £15/£24. Good pubs locally.
closed	Very occasionally.
directions	From A24 take A283 for Shoreham. After 4 miles, right for Steyning through High Street & over mini r'bout. House immed. on left.

Joy & John Turner
30 High Street,
Steyning,
Sussex BN44 3GG

tel	01903 815595
fax	01903 816686
e-mail	johnturner57@aol.com
web	www.artyguesthouse.co.uk

map: 5 entry: 459

Bees buzz contentedly, water bubbles in the fountain and you may swim in the pool. The Sedgwicks – Nigel is studying History of Art and Juliet has a framing business – have created a much-loved haven. Bedrooms are large with generous tea trays; there's a Waring & Gillow bed from which you can gaze across the coastal plain to the South Downs as the sun streams in. This is a sunny spot, hence the many local market gardeners. Juliet frequently travels to London for exhibitions via the excellent rail connection – and, happily, the three-acre garden and double-glazing shield you from train noise.

rooms	3: 1 double with bathroom; 1 double, 1 twin, sharing bathroom.
room price	£60-£80. Single occ. £40-£45.
meals	Packed lunch available. Dinner £15-£25.
closed	Christmas.
directions	From Chichester A27 east (or west from Arundel). South on B2132 for Yapton. Right on Lake Lane just before level crossing. House 0.5 miles on right.

Nigel & Juliet Sedgwick
Todhurst Farm,
Lake Lane, Barnham, Arundel,
Sussex PO22 0AL

tel	01243 551959
e-mail	nigelsedg@aol.com

map: 5 entry: 460

This 1810 flint cottage is prettily and traditionally decorated with chintz and antiques; there's a cosy little sitting room that's all yours and a bedroom with greenfield views. Once a dancer, Lesley now performs – with undimmed vivacity – to the whims of her visitors, and loves having people to stay. Breakfast is served exquisitely, with silver and linen, and locally sourced food. The swimming pool is an added bonus. Peace and quiet, Lesley's easy generosity, delectable Bosham with its harbour and sailing boats – a wonderful place.

Mary is a dear and her 16th-century house equally delightful. Flagstoned floors, beams, a cosily cluttered drawing room filled with Bechstein piano, cello, double bass... and cats: some real, others fashioned from wood and stone. Bedrooms are charming and the house has the feel of a well-loved family home, which it is: Mary has lived here for 30 years. Vast Sussex skies overhead, a short stroll to the water's edge, and 20 minutes to an excellent pub. Perfect.

rooms	1 double with bath.
room price	£55-£65. Single occ. £40.
meals	Breakfast 7.30-9am. Good pubs/restaurants nearby.
closed	Christmas.
directions	From Chichester, A259 west for Bosham; through Fishbourne, past garden centre, left into Walton Lane. After sharp bend, right into Crede Lane; 200 yds to end of drive. On left, with white garage.

rooms	3: 1 twin, 1 double, sharing bathroom; 1 double with private bathroom.
room price	From £44. Single occ. £32.
meals	Excellent pub in village.
closed	Christmas.
directions	From Chichester, head for Portsmouth. Pass Tesco on right. 3rd exit off r'bout, to Bosham & Fishbourne. A259 for 4 miles, pass Saab garage on right. Next left into Chidham Lane. House last on left, 1 mile down.

Mrs Lesley Hankey
Crede Farmhouse,
Crede Lane, Bosham,
Sussex PO18 8NX
tel   01243 574929
e-mail lesley@credefarmhouse.fsnet.co.uk

Mary Hartley
Easton House,
Chidham Lane, Chidham,
Chichester,
Sussex PO18 8TF
tel   01243 572514
fax   01243 573084
e-mail eastonhouse@chidham.fsnet.co.uk

Absolute attention to detail and luxury to revel in; Jeanette has done everything to ensure your comfort. This is olde worlde charm at its most compelling. The Lodge was built in pure neo-Gothic style as the gatehouse to the local manor – its church windows are fascinating. There are ornate mirrors, gold candles, silky curtains, wall sconces and glittering silver and crystal. The conservatory has a woodburner and a mini indoor garden with small fish pond. The garden rambles around the house and is secluded and peaceful. The beds and the linen are sumptuous and Jeanette a delight.

A house has been here since the Bronze Age and the history of Lordington could fill this book. Jacobean, with numerous modifications, it is vast and impressive, with majestic views past clipped yew and box, walled garden and ha-ha, to the Ems Valley. The Hamiltons have brought warmth to the house, yet it remains engagingly old-fashioned. There's a floral double room and the twin, with Windsor bedheads, has *toile de Jouy* wallpaper up and over wardrobe doors; both rooms are large and have magnificent views. There's a lovely panelled drawing room, too. *Children over five welcome.*

rooms	2: 1 double with bathroom, 1 double with shower.
room price	From £50. Single occ. from £35.
meals	Dinner in the village 1 mile away.
closed	Very occasionally.
directions	3 miles west of Chichester on B2178. Lodge 170 yds on left after Salthill Rd. Look for sign for Oakwood School.

rooms	2: 1 double, 1 twin, both with private bathroom.
room price	From £50. Single occ. from £27.50.
meals	Packed lunch and suppers available. Pub 1 mile; restaurants 4-8 miles.
closed	Christmas & New Year.
directions	Lordington (marked on AA road maps) is on B2146 6 miles south of South Harting and 0.5 miles south of Walderton. Enter through white railings by letterbox; fork right after bridge.

Jeanette Dridge
Chichester Lodge,
Oakwood School Drive,
East Ashling, Chichester,
Sussex PO18 9AL
tel   01243 786560

Mr & Mrs John Hamilton
Lordington House,
Lordington, Chichester,
Sussex PO18 9DX
tel   01243 375862
e-mail   audreyhamilton@onetel.net.uk

Vivien is happy for breakfast to turn into an early-morning house-party in her lovely yellow kitchen; you are spoiled with kippers and porridge and, later, home-made cakes for tea. You are close to Goodwood – husband Tim manages a local stud – and the house, built by Napoleonic prisoners of war, was once part of the Goodwood estate. Bedrooms are in the old cattle byres that were originally converted for the Reads' growing family. They are a good size, attractively furnished and decorated and always have fresh flowers. Lovely views from the garden, and there's a tennis court.

Deer come to your window and miles of unspoiled woodland walks start from the door. Not really a B&B, but a tranquil hideaway for independent nature lovers; welcoming hosts live in the listed cottage and lavishly replenish the refrigerator daily with a choice of bread, hams, cheeses, yogurts, real coffee and much more... There are a kettle and a toaster and all mod cons for self-serve, continental-style breakfast. Annabelle prepares your rooms carefully and the feel is simple country style. You have your own front door and terrace and can come and go as you please or stay all day.

rooms	2 twins & doubles, both with bath/shower.
room price	£60-£80. Single occ. £30-£35.
meals	Excellent pubs in village, 1 mile.
closed	Christmas.
directions	A272 to Midhurst, A286 to Singleton. Left for Goodwood: up over Downs, pass racecourse, next right for Lavant. House 1st on right 0.5 miles on.

rooms	2 double studios, both with shower.
room price	From £55. Single occ. by arrangement.
meals	Pubs within walking distance.
closed	Very occasionally.
directions	From Midhurst, A286 for Chichester. After Royal Oak pub on left, Greyhound on right, go 0.5 miles, left to Heyshott. On for 2 miles, do not turn off, look for white posts & house sign on left.

Tim & Vivien Read
The Flint House,
East Lavant, Chichester,
Sussex PO18 0AS
tel   01243 773482
e-mail   theflinthouse@ukonline.co.uk

Alex & Annabelle Costaras
Amberfold,
Heyshott, Midhurst,
Sussex GU29 0DA
tel   01730 812385
fax   01730 812842

A wooded track leads to this beautiful mellow 17th-century farmhouse with tall chimneys and a cluster of overgrown outbuildings. Wood-panelled walls and ancient oak beams, a vast open fireplace, mullioned windows and welcoming sofas create an atmosphere of relaxed, country-house charm. You breakfast in the Aga-warm kitchen; in spring the scent of bluebells reaches you through the open doors. The large, and comfortable, timbered bedrooms (one canopied bed incorporates original oak panelling) overlook fields, rolling lawns and woodland where you can stroll in peace. *Children by arrangement.*

You have the freedom of the place – a rare treat. Much of it has been here for five centuries, as solid and dependable as your welcome. The silence is filled with birdsong, the lawn gives a feeling of endless space and you are in glorious isolation in three acres of the surrounding AONB – don't be surprised if you see deer and pheasant roaming in the garden. The room in the main house is painted magnolia and has flowery curtains and garden access. The Barn has its own sitting room: wooden-floored, rugged and filled with pine and light. The rooms upstairs are cottage-cosy, floral and deeply traditional.

rooms	3: 1 double, 1 twin, sharing bathroom; 1 double/family with bathroom.
room price	£50-£70. Single occ. by arrangement. Advance booking only.
meals	Breakfast 8-9.30am or by arrangement. Excellent pubs/restaurants 2-5 miles.
closed	Christmas.
directions	Given on booking.

rooms	3: 1 double with shower room & sitting room; 1 double with bath/shower; 1 twin/double with shower room.
room price	£75. Suite £80. Single occ. £40-£45.
meals	Good pubs/restaurants nearby.
closed	Christmas.
directions	On old A3, north from Petersfield, at hill brow right for Milland, left after 300 yards. Follow lane through woods for 6 miles, then right for Midhurst and Redford; cottage on right 150 yds beyond Redford sign and pond.

Maggie Paterson
Fitzlea Farmhouse,
Selham, Nr. Petworth,
Sussex GU28 0PS
tel   01798 861429

Caroline & David Angela
Redford Cottage,
Redford, Midhurst,
Sussex GU29 0QF
tel   01428 741242

map: 5 entry: 467

map: 5 entry: 468

WARWICKSHIRE

WARWICKSHIRE

A theatrical home: dark wood, reds and pinks dominate and, in one bedroom – more theatre – plush velvet curtains open to the bathroom. The conversion of the 1737 barn is immaculate: the kitchen, with Aga and stone floors, gives onto a stunning patio, conservatory and drawing room; bedrooms and bathrooms are plush, big and comfortable. Denise, cheerful and kind, runs her B&B with careful attention to detail. Much rural charm, a large garden, excellent value and yet so close to Birmingham and the NEC. *Advance booking essential. Children over 12 welcome.*

Cathy's sense of humour carries her through each gloriously eventful day. This is a paradise for families – there's so much room to play and so much to see: sheep, turkeys, geese and Saddleback pigs. The 1640 farmhouse was extended 25 years ago using old bricks and beams and the bathrooms have recently been upgraded. Tiny timbered corridors lead to large bedrooms with wooden floors and leaded windows; the family room has everything needed for a baby. Next door is the magnificent Big Pool where you can fish with a day ticket.

rooms	3: 1 double, 2 twins, all with bath.
room price	£70. Single occ. £45.
meals	Breakfast until 8.30am. Pub 1 mile.
closed	Occasionally.
directions	At M6 junc. 4, A446 for Lichfield. At sign to Coleshill South, get in right lane & turn off. From High St, turn into Maxstoke Lane. After 4 miles, 4th right. 1st drive on left.

rooms	2: 1 double with single & cot, 1 twin, both with bathroom.
room price	From £50. Single occ. from £32.50.
meals	Breakfast 7-9am. Packed lunch £3. Children's high tea £3. Dinner from £15.
closed	Christmas & New Year.
directions	From M40, junc. 15, A46 for Coventry. Left onto A4177. 4.5 miles to Five Ways r'bout. 1st left, follow for 0.75 miles; signed down track on left.

Mrs Denise Owen
Hardingwood House,
Hardingwood Lane, Fillongley,
Nr. Coventry,
Warwickshire CV7 8EL
tel 01676 542579
fax 01676 541336
e-mail denise@hardingwoodhouse.fsnet.co.uk

Cathy Dodd
Shrewley Pools Farm,
Haseley, Warwick,
Warwickshire CV35 7HB
tel 01926 484315
e-mail cathydodd@hotmail.com

map: 9 entry: 469

map: 9 entry: 470

WARWICKSHIRE

WARWICKSHIRE

Wow! Hot bedroom colours make a change from the usual creams and chintzes – one is vibrant blue with a red ceiling, another yellow with blue and a further one is a super burnt orange, all with contemporary paintings. It's bold and vibrant, 'green' and fun – just like Prue. She's passionate about good food, too – organic and mostly vegetarian. Expect home-made bread, velvety egg puddings, succulent stuffed mushrooms and a fresh fruit platter drizzled with lime and honey dressing. This substantial blue stone 1850s townhouse is right opposite Warwick's park and less than a mile's riverside walk to the castle.

The peace, the views and the greenness will revive flagging spirits and soothe the frazzled; one guest said she'd had "the quietest sleep in years." David and Julia are a generous, well-travelled and unassuming couple devoted to their ancient house and garden. Mallards glide over the pond and a stream runs by the 400-year-old yew. Inside, Cotswold stone walls, comfortable sofas, a beamed dining and drawing room and huge inglenooks complement the bucolic scene, while uneven floors celebrate the appealing character of this 300-year-old house.

rooms	3: 1 twin with bath/shower; 1 double with shower room; 1 double with bath & shower.
room price	£65. Single occ. £40.
meals	Breakfast 6am-12 noon. Restaurants/pubs 0.5 miles.
closed	Occasionally.
directions	On A445, 500 yds past St John's Museum towards Leamington, directly opposite entrance to St Nicholas' Park.

rooms	2: 1 double, 1 twin, sharing bath/shower room.
room price	£54. Single occ. £27.
meals	Restaurant 5 minutes' walk; 3 pubs 1.5 miles.
closed	Christmas & New Year.
directions	From A423, turn to Priors Hardwick 1.8 miles on, left for P. Hardwick. 1st hard left on S-bend ('No Through Road' sign). Down lane & right onto concrete road. On right.

Prue Hardwick
The Hare on the Park,
3 Emscote Road, Warwick,
Warwickshire CV34 4PH

tel	01926 491366
e-mail	prue@thehareonthepark.co.uk
web	www.thehareonthepark.co.uk

Julia & David Gaunt
Hollow Meadow House,
Priors Hardwick, Southam,
Warwickshire CV47 7SP

tel	01327 261540
fax	01327 261540

map: 9 entry: 471

map: 9 entry: 472

# WARWICKSHIRE

Kim has the sort of kitchen that city dwellers dream of: big and welcoming and it really is the hub of the house. She and John fizz with good humour and energy and take pride in those times when family and guests feel easy together. You will be offered tea on arrival, home-made jams for breakfast and perhaps even a guided walk round the fascinating, historic village. The house is large with a wonderful garden, tennis court, terrace and croquet lawn. The rooms are big, soft and supremely comfortable with lovely pieces of furniture. A special place and absolutely genuine people.

rooms	2: 1 double, 1 twin/double, both with private bathroom.
room price	From £54. Single occ. from £35.
meals	Breakfast from 6.45am. Dinner, for 4 only, £22. Good pub 5 minutes' walk.
closed	Very occasionally.
directions	From Banbury, A361 north. At Byfield sign, left into Twistle Lane, straight on to Priors Marston. Fifth on left with cattle grid, after S-bend.

Kim & John Mahon
Marston House,
Priors Marston, Southam,
Warwickshire CV47 7RP
tel   01327 260297
fax   01327 262846
e-mail kim@mahonand.co.uk
web   www.ivabestbandb.co.uk

WARWICKSHIRE

Here's a big house in the country, minus the expected creaks and draughts and plus every mod con. Carpets are thick, beds four-poster and sumptuous; there's a new 'Oriental' room. It feels almost like a small hotel and there's even a helipad. Plush green sofas sit by the stone inglenook and you can have drinks here before eating an organic dinner in the candlelit conservatory. The garden is lush and landscaped and there are fields all around – look out for the fat Hebridean sheep. This is a fully organic, Soil Association registered farm.
Children over 12 welcome.

rooms	3 four-posters, all with bathroom, 1 with dressing room.
room price	From £100. Single occ. from £70.
meals	Dinner, 3 courses, £25.
closed	Very occasionally.
directions	From Stratford, A4200, over Clopton bridge & immed. left onto Tiddington Rd. 1st right onto Loxley Rd. Last on left with white gates.

Ms Kate McGovern
Glebe Farm House,
Loxley, Stratford-upon-Avon,
Warwickshire CV35 9JW
tel   01789 842501
fax   01789 841194
e-mail scorpiolimited@msn.com
web   www.glebefarmhouse.com

You can get from your bath to your seat in the Stratford theatre in 10 minutes, if you hurry. Perfect! This is a Grade II-listed thatched house, of 1501, a house of great and many beams. Even the barn where you sleep is 17th century, also thatched and listed. Each suite is magnificently accoutred, with its own sitting room and kitchenette, so you can peacefully enjoy a glass of wine post-performance. Breakfast – taken in the main house – is the time to be sociable here. Luxurious, beautiful, authentic and slap in the middle of a huge chunk of the best of England.

Spiky plants and driftwood in the garden – a refreshing change from the more familiar herbaceous borders and it would be hard to find a more secluded, peaceful retreat. Carolyn and John could not be nicer and every room feels right; seashell stencils and star-painted ceilings go perfectly with colour-washed walls. Bedrooms have wooden-latched doors to sunny, sky-lit bathrooms. The annexe room has its own entrance and a four-poster iron bedstead. They keep sheep, horses and poultry, and there are plenty of fresh eggs for breakfast. *Children over eight welcome.*

rooms	2 doubles, both with bath/shower.
room price	£64. Single occ. £45.
meals	Pub within 3 minutes' walk for dinner.
closed	1 December-7 January.
directions	From Stratford, A422 Banbury road for 4 miles & turn off for Loxley. Through village & left at bottom of hill. 3rd house on right.

rooms	3: 1 family with bath/shower; 2 doubles, 1 with shower room, 1 with bath/shower.
room price	£44-£52. Single occ. from £28.
meals	Breakfast 7.30-9am. Pubs/restaurants 3 miles away.
closed	Christmas.
directions	From Stratford, A422 to Pillerton Priors, then sign to Pillerton Hersey. There, down Oxhill Bridle Rd, opp. phone box. House at end (1 mile). Or M40 junc. 12, 6 miles on B4451.

Mrs Anne Horton
Loxley Farm,
Loxley, Warwick,
Warwickshire CV35 9JN

tel	01789 840265
fax	01789 840645

Carolyn & John Howard
Dockers Barn Farm,
Oxhill Bridle Road,
Pillerton Hersey, Warwick,
Warwickshire CV35 0QB

tel	01926 640475
fax	01926 641747

Hard to believe the house is so new: with its open-beam ceilings and antiques, it has a perfectly timeless feel. Posy and Graeme, fun and well-travelled, create a mood of warmth and welcome. Pale-walled bedrooms are cheery and fresh with coral checks, soft lighting, excellent beds, top of the range bathroom fittings and lovely long views. Find time to ride locally or play tennis – the court is brand new – or explore the Cotswolds and Shakespeare country: Posy will help you unlock the region's secrets. And watch the setting sun from the patio.

rooms	3: 1 double with shower room; 1 triple with bathroom; 1 twin with bath/shower, available occasionally.
room price	From £58. Single occ. from £34.
meals	Dinner available. Good local pubs.
closed	Very occasionally.
directions	A422 from Stratford-on-Avon for Banbury. After 8 miles, right to Oxhill. Last house on right on Whatcote Road.

Graeme & Posy McDonald
Oxbourne House,
Oxhill, Warwick,
Warwickshire CV35 0RA
tel   01295 688202
e-mail   graememcdonald@msn.com

You'll be in your element if you fish or play tennis, for you can do both from the beautiful, landscaped gardens that slope gently down to the River Stour. Jane, a *Cordon Bleu* cook, runs her 16th- and 17th-century house with huge energy and friendliness. A pretty blue twin bedroom and a single are in a self-contained wing with a large, elegant drawing and dining room; the A-shaped double, with ancient beams and oak furniture, is in the main part of the house, has a lovely bathroom and shares the drawing and dining rooms. It's seductively easy to relax here.

rooms	3: 1 twin, 1 single, sharing bathroom (single let only to members of same party); 1 double with private bathroom.
room price	From £65. Single occ. from £35.
meals	Dinner from £20. Excellent local restaurants.
closed	Very occasionally.
directions	From Stratford, A422 for 4 miles for Banbury. After 4 miles, right at r'bout onto A429 for Halford. There, 1st right. House with black & white timbers straight ahead.

Jane & William Pusey
The Old Manor House,
Halford, Shipston-on-Stour,
Warwickshire CV36 5BT
tel   01789 740264
fax   01789 740609
e-mail   wpusey@st-philips.co.uk

A huge house in 30 acres whose statuettes – atop columned porticoes – overlook an oceanic expanse of mown grass. Vast terraces, cedar tree, oaks, formal garden and an 800-acre farm – a pure English idyll, and the only noise that of passing pheasants. The bedrooms are huge and the bathrooms stately; walls are panelled and floors stripped and embellished with Turkish rugs. You have a formal dining room and a church-sized library littered with armchairs and sofas. Dream of port and cigars – on a pea-green carpet. Kari runs it all without fuss. Unselfconscious and magnificent.

It's smart, stylish and full of personal touches. Angie decorates with strong colours; Chris, an interiors photographer, has an eye for arranging things – and bakes bread most mornings. Flagstones and wooden floors downstairs, and upstairs, one Art Deco-ish bedroom. The other is decorated in lovely warm shades of terracotta and cream, with cream sofa and dramatic canopied bed. The garden reaches out to the River Stour with its waterside willows. Sit on the terrace and watch the sun set over the north Cotswolds, or set off to explore the ancient ridge and furrow meadow.

rooms	3: 1 double, 1 single sharing bathroom (let only to same party); 1 twin with private bathroom.
room price	£90. Single occ. by arrangement.
meals	Plenty of pubs and restaurants within 5 miles.
closed	Christmas & New Year.
directions	From Shipston-on-Stour, turn off B3400 north to Honington. House signed from here. In Idlicote, left at pond & through stone gateposts. House on left.

rooms	2: 1 double, 1 family, both with bath & shower.
room price	£65. Single occ. £39.
meals	Breakfast 8.30am. Good pub 0.5 miles.
closed	Christmas.
directions	From Stratford, south on A3400 towards Shipston. After 3 miles, signed on right.

Kari Dill
Idlicote House,
Idlicote, Shipston-on-Stour,
Warwickshire CV36 5DT

tel	01608 661473
fax	01608 661381
e-mail	dill@idlicote.freeserve.co.uk

Angela & Chris Wright
Alderminster Farm, Alderminster,
Nr. Stratford-upon-Avon,
Warwickshire CV37 8BP

tel	01789 450774
fax	01789 450924
e-mail	angie_wright5@hotmail.com
web	www.b&b@alderminsterfarm.co.uk

map: 9 entry: 479

map: 9 entry: 480

WARWICKSHIRE

WARWICKSHIRE

Admire the Wyandotte bantams strutting across the lawns – they are prize-winners; Liz also keeps quails and you can buy their eggs to take home with you. The garden is pretty with mellow stone, clipped hedges, broad paths, billowing plants and spectacular hostas. There are flagstoned floors, beamed ceilings, deep fireplaces and deep-set mullioned windows. The sitting room has old books and polished furniture and the bedrooms, with low ceilings, are peaceful; two have excellent views. One ground-floor bedroom is ideal for wheelchair users. Home-made marmalade for breakfast and home-grown food at dinner.

An 1856 Victorian farmhouse, with log fires to warm your enthusiasm for a good walk on the Heart of England Way, or maybe a bike ride (cycles available). The views stretch on to folklore-sodden Meon Hill, with its stories of local witchcraft and other spookery. The Angel Room has a pine box bed and a medieval frieze of flying angels. The two other rooms have four-posters with handmade quilts. Healthy and delicious breakfast menus change daily and make imaginative use of organic fruit from the orchard.

rooms	4: 3 twins/doubles, all with bath & shower; 1 single with shower.		rooms	3: 2 four-posters, both with shower room; 1 twin/family with private bathroom.
room price	From £60. Single from £35.		room price	From £65.
meals	Breakfast until 9.30am. Supper, 2 courses, £15.50. B.Y.O. Very good pub 1 mile.		meals	Pub & French café 0.5 miles.
closed	Very occasionally.		closed	Christmas Day.
directions	From Stratford-upon-Avon, A3400 for Oxford. After 5 miles, right by church in Newbold-on-Stour & follow signs to Blackwell. Fork right on entering Blackwell. Entrance beyond thatched barn.		directions	From Stratford, A3400 south, then B4632 (for Broadway & Mickleton) for 6 miles. Left for Upper Quinton. 400 yds on left.

	Liz Vernon Miller		**Mrs Gail Lyon**
	Blackwell Grange,		Winton House,
	Blackwell, Shipston-on-Stour,		The Green, Upper Quinton,
	Warwickshire CV36 4PF		Stratford-upon-Avon,
tel	01608 682357		Warwickshire CV37 8SX
fax	01608 682856	tel	01789 720500
e-mail	sawdays@blackwellgrange.co.uk	e-mail	gail@wintonhouse.com
web	www.blackwellgrange.co.uk	web	www.wintonhouse.com

WARWICKSHIRE

WILTSHIRE

Undeniably beautiful within, solidly handsome without. Jane is a gifted interior decorator; the colours are splendid and nothing looks out of place. Jane and Richard are easy and open: she was a ballet dancer and is refreshingly new to this B&B thing; he has green fingers and grows the fruit that appears in pretty bowls on your breakfast table. The kitchen is engagingly beamed and straight out of a smart magazine. There are some fine pieces of furniture, sofas to sink into and enough comfort to satisfy a pharaoh.

Evidence of artistic flair everywhere – patchwork, tapestries, rush and cane work; Sue, easy-going and articulate, teaches country crafts in her workshop. The fine, George I farmhouse lies in a quiet spot on the edge of the New Forest and has a lovely walled garden with fruit cages, a Wendy house and two Labradors snuffling about. Provençal paintings and fabrics in the breakfast room and orange trees in the beautiful conservatory. Bedrooms are ample and charming with patchwork quilts, brass beds, stencils. Sue, a Blue Badge Guide, can tell you all about things to see and do in the area.

rooms	2: 1 twin/double with bath/shower; 1 twin/double with shower room.
room price	£70-£76. Single occ. £45-£48.
meals	Dinner £20.
closed	Christmas & New Year.
directions	A46 from Evesham or Stratford; exit for Salford Priors. On entering village, right opp. church, for Dunnington. House on right, approx. 1 mile on, after 2nd sign on right for Dunnington.

rooms	4: 1 twin/family, 2 doubles, all with shower; 1 single with private bathroom.
room price	£46-£50. Single occ. £35.
meals	Breakfast 7.30-9.00am. Pub 1 mile.
closed	Christmas & New Year.
directions	From Salisbury, A36 for Southampton. Approx. 5 miles on, Brickworth Lane on left, 200 yds before lights at junction A36/A27. House at top of lane on right.

	Jane Gibson & Richard Beach
	Salford Farm House,
	Salford Priors, Nr. Evesham,
	Warwickshire WR11 8XN
tel	01386 870000
fax	01386 870300
e-mail	salfordfarmhouse@aol.com
web	www.salfordfarmhouse.co.uk

	Sue Barry
	Brickworth Farmhouse,
	Brickworth Lane,
	Whiteparish, Salisbury,
	Wiltshire SP5 2QE
tel	01794 884663
fax	01794 884186
e-mail	susanbarry@brickworthfarmhouse.co.uk
web	www.brickworthfarmhouse.co.uk

Such attention to detail – you couldn't feel anything but thoroughly spoiled. Each bedroom is large and light, with easy chairs or sofas and there's also a separate guest sitting room down the book-lined hall. You could wallow for hours in the roll-topped bath in the splendid oak-panelled bathroom. Watercolours, rich oils, polished antiques and the charm of your hosts fill the family home and a magical garden embraces the Queen Anne farmhouse. Meander down to swans on the river, stride out across the meadows or fish on the farm's lakes. Enchanting. *Children over 12 welcome.*

Immediately impressive – the 15th-century honey stone that lights up in sunlight, the particularly English shade of paintwork, the Jacobean 'extension', the wisteria, the solidness... the feel is engagingly chaotic, natural and family, just the way we like it. If you're travelling with family, or if you want to feel relaxingly away from everybody else, choose the twin that connects with a dear little single; the twin/double, with lily-patterned green-and-white headboard and curtains, is large, too. It's not 'le grand luxe' but there are a pool and a tennis court. A stimulating place.

rooms	3: 2 twins/doubles, 1 with bath & shower, 1 with private bathroom; 1 double with shower room.
room price	£50-£70. Single occ. £35.
meals	Good pub/restaurant nearby.
closed	Christmas.
directions	From Salisbury on A36 for Southampton. After 1 mile right immed. at dual carriageway (no signs). Right at signs to Downton. Farm on right after 2.5 miles.

rooms	3: 1 twin/double with private bathroom; 1 twin/double, 1 single sharing bathroom.
room price	£60. Single occ. £38-£40.
meals	Packed lunch £6.
closed	December & January.
directions	From Salisbury, A36 to Wilton, then A30 (to Shaftesbury). After 3 miles, in Barford St Martin, right onto B3089; after 2 miles, right to Baverstock; after 0.75 mile stone gateway on right, on S-bend.

Ian & Annette Fergie-Woods
Witherington Farm,
Nr. Downton, Salisbury,
Wiltshire SP5 3QT

tel	01722 710222
fax	01722 710405
e-mail	ian@witheringtonfarm.co.uk
web	www.witheringtonfarm.co.uk

Tim & Belinda Hextall
Baverstock Manor,
Dinton, Salisbury,
Wiltshire SP3 5EN

tel	01722 716206
fax	01722 716510
e-mail	hextallbavers@hotmail.com

WILTSHIRE

WILTSHIRE

Toast your toes on a warm stone floor in this quadrangle conversion – what were once Victorian agricultural outbuildings are now a harpsichord workshop and B&B. The geothermal underfloor heating system is just one of the initiatives that has won this environmentally-friendly set-up an award. Bedrooms, which feed off a long corridor, are functionally furnished and perfectly lit. Walls are white or bare brick, ceilings high and beamy: all is simplicity and calm. You'll want for nothing with Gail in charge (her blueberry pancakes are wonderful) and Peter, her harpsichord-maker husband, is charming, too.

You have your own entrance, parking area, terrace and sitting room, freshly decorated and well thought out. Everything is new and cosy and comfortable and just outside your windows is a cottage garden alive with colour. Your hosts are impressively organised – they run a catering business from home – and their breakfasts will set you up for the day. The bathroom is duck egg blue, the bedroom ochre. If you long for your own space and the freedom to come and go as you please, you have it. The family has been here for three generations. *Children over 10 welcome.*

rooms	4: 1 double, 1 twin/double, 2 singles, all with shower.
room price	£35–£70.
meals	Breakfast 7.30-9.30am. Good pubs 1 mile.
closed	December–January.
directions	A354 from Salisbury to Blandford. In Coombe Bissett, right to Broadchalke. House signed 1 mile after White Hart on right behind Stoke Manor.

rooms	1 twin with bath/shower.
room price	£60. Single occ. £40.
meals	Packed lunch £7. Dinner, 3 courses, £20.
closed	Christmas & New Year.
directions	A303 to Wylye, then take road for Dinton. After approx. 4 miles left at x-roads, for Wilton & Salisbury. On for 2 miles, down hill, round sharp bend, signed Sandhills Rd. House is 1st low red brick building on left.

Gail & Peter Smalley
Ebblesway Courtyard,
High Road, Broadchalke, Salisbury,
Wiltshire SP5 5EF
tel 01722 780182
fax 01722 780482
e-mail enquiries@ebbleswaycourtyard.co.uk
web www.ebbleswaycourtyard.co.uk

Harriet & Peter Combes
The Duck Yard,
Sandhills Road, Dinton, Salisbury,
Wiltshire SP3 5ER
tel 01722 716495
fax 01722 716163

Folded into the most stunning countryside, this Grade II-listed, one-time butcher's shop has been in Darea's family for years. Stylishly cluttered, sparkingly clean – and there are beautiful objects and lovely pieces at every turn. Darea's enthusiasm for life, books, travel is infectious: she can identify every rich and rare specimen in her garden, keeps detailed diaries and albums of her many travels and (fortunately) has thrown nothing away. Your chintzy bedrooms are seductively cosy. Stonehenge, Longleat and Stourhead beckon; hostess, home and countryside are a treat.

It is a rare treat to have your milk fresh from the cow – the Helyers have a fine pedigree herd of Holstein Friesians. This rather grand Victorian Gothic farmhouse is a working, tenanted arable and dairy farm. There are very large, pretty bedrooms with crisp linen, period furniture, impressive countryside views, a baby grand and a billiard room. Everything is elegant but cosy and the Helyers are immensely friendly. Terrace doors are thrown open for an *al fresco* summer breakfast. The estate is 1,400 acres and an SSSI, treasured for its wild flowers and butterflies. *Children by arrangement.*

rooms	2: 1 twin with bathroom; 1 twin/double with washbasin & private bath.
room price	£60. Single occ. £35.
meals	Breakfast until 9.30am. Excellent pub 50 yds.
closed	Occasionally.
directions	Leave A303 at junc. with A36 for Wylye. In village, cross river & round sharp left-hand bend. House 25 yds on right.

rooms	3: 1 twin/double with shower room; 1 double with shower room; 1 twin with private shower room.
room price	£54-£60. Single occ. £40-£48.
meals	Pubs within 2 miles.
closed	Christmas & New Year.
directions	Leave A303 at junc. with A36 & follow signs for Salisbury. 2 miles on, right for The Langfords. In Steeple Langford, right for Hanging Langford. At T-junc. opp. village hall, left for Little Langford. House 0.25 miles on left.

Mrs Darea Browne
Perrior House,
Wylye, Warminster,
Wiltshire BA12 0QU

tel	01985 248228
e-mail	darea.browne@amserve.net

Patricia Helyer
Little Langford Farmhouse,
Little Langford, Salisbury,
Wiltshire SP3 4NR

tel	01722 790205
fax	01722 790086
e-mail	bandb@littlelangford.co.uk
web	www.littlelangford.co.uk

In the valley of the Kennet River – which flows briskly past the foot of an immaculate lawn – is this exquisitely decorated home. It looks every inch a doll's house, but Jeremy and Heather, friendly and relaxed, add a deft human touch. The elegance of excellent breakfasts taken in the conservatory is balanced by the comforting hubbub emanating from the family kitchen. There's a sitting room for you with an open fire and, upstairs, the cleverly converted bedrooms are ingeniously clustered around the chimney breast. Time here slips by effortlessly; many people come to visit the crop circles.

You could be a hundred miles from Marlborough, not two. Here is a lovely Queen Anne farmhouse tucked under chalk hills in the middle of the biggest bluebell woods in the country. Elizabeth and Christopher, who have lived here for years, love sharing their home; bedrooms are fresh, white and cosy, with painted pine furniture and modern patchwork quilts, and guests have their own sitting room. The sun-trap garden is full of roses and lavender and views of the surrounding 25 rolling acres – this is marvellous walking country. Your horse is welcome, too.

rooms	3: 1 double with bathroom; 1 twin, 1 single sharing bathroom.
room price	£60. Single £35.
meals	Lunch/packed lunch from £3. Pub 500 yds.
closed	Christmas.
directions	From Hungerford, A4 for Marlborough. After 7 miles, right for Stitchcombe, down hill (bear left at barn) & left at T-junc. On entering village, house 2nd on left.

rooms	2 doubles, 1 with bath, 1 with private bathroom.
room price	£50-£60. Single occ. from £30.
meals	Packed lunch £4. Good restaurants/pubs 2-3 miles.
closed	Christmas & New Year.
directions	From Marlborough, A4 west for 2 miles. 1st left after end of 40mph limit, for Clatford. Over x-roads, farm 1.5 miles on right through 5-bar gate.

	Jeremy & Heather Coulter
	Fisherman's House,
	Mildenhall, Nr. Marlborough,
	Wiltshire SN8 2LZ
tel	01672 515390
fax	01672 519009
e-mail	fishermans.house@virgin.net
web	www.business.virgin.net/ neville.burrell/fishermans.htm

	Elizabeth & Christopher Morgan-Smith
	Clatford Park Farm,
	Marlborough,
	Wiltshire SN8 4DZ
tel	01672 861646
web	www.clatfordparkfarm.co.uk

map: 4 entry: 491

map: 4 entry: 492

SYMBOLS, BATHROOMS AND ECCENTRICS

We'd love to be able to include a symbol for the most eccentric of our owners. But then they'd be **'officially'** eccentric, which isn't quite right. But they are there. Witness the host whose parrot sits over his shoulder during dinner and feeds from an occasionally proffered spoon.

But we do have symbols for other phenomena and **'services'**. Many are the hosts who are potty about children and who will welcome yours. And there are some people who have good reason to prefer keeping them at a distance. Anyway, it is quite helpful for those of you who like to avoid children when travelling to know where you can do so.

The same goes for pets. We have hosts with parrots, hosts with cats, with dogs and with other beasts. Some will give space to your poodle though not to your rottweiler. Others will see off your beloved pooch. We have them all in this book. The symbols are important and are richer than a thousand words.

We also tell you about your bathroom. For some reason we don't like the term 'en suite' (does it remind us of corporate hotel language?) so we say **"WITH bathroom"** or **"WITH shower-room"**. If it is not en suite we say **"with PRIVATE"** or **"with SHARED"** bathroom. The former you will have to yourself, wherever it may be. The latter is unlikely to be shared with more than the owner or one or two other guests.

LASTLY, do use the section at the back that tells you where to find, for example, all the owners who have facilities for wheelchair users, or who are willing to pick you up from the railway station.

Flagstone floors lead you into book-lined rooms scattered with family photographs and fresh flowers – stylishly cluttered, it's an easy place to settle into. Clarissa is a professional cook and looks after you with bundles of energy and enthusiasm. Bedrooms with sprigged papers are bright and fresh; walls and throws are cream, beds are wooden. The sunny yellow ground floor bedroom has garden views and there's a guest sitting room, too. Five acres of gardens include an orchard, vegetable garden, tennis court, pool, and strutting chickens that provide breakfast eggs. You have fresh raspberries in season, too.

Bill – who paints in oils and watercolours – has applied his considerable artistic flair to the renovation of this 17th-century thatched cottage. The A-frame sitting room has bold Chinese yellow walls, three plump sofas, light wooden floor and books – it is unintimidatingly stylish. The bedrooms are in similar vein and Bill and Felicity are easy, cultured hosts. There's a heated swimming pool, which you can use, and a sunken Italianate garden whose borders are edged with clouds of lavender. Shelter on sunny days, colonial style, under a tiled loggia with rattan furniture. Perfect.
Children by arrangement.

rooms	3: 1 double with private bathroom; 1 twin/double with bathroom; 1 twin with shower room.
room price	From £60. Single occ. from £35.
meals	Dinner, 4 courses, £25.
closed	Very occasionally.
directions	From Marlborough, A346 Salisbury road for 3 miles. Right to Wootton Rivers. In village, right (opposite Royal Oak pub) & drive for 0.7 miles. Drive on right after sign for Clench Common.

rooms	3: 1 double with bathroom; 1 double, 1 twin, sharing bathroom.
room price	£50-£56. Single occ. £30-£33.
meals	Dinner £18.
closed	Rarely.
directions	From Marlborough, A346 Salisbury Rd south. At r'bout ending Burbage bypass, take B3087 Pewsey Rd. Right at x-roads 0.3 miles on. 1st house on right.

	Clarissa Roe
	Clench Farmhouse,
	Clench, Nr. Marlborough,
	Wiltshire SN8 4NT
tel	01672 810264
fax	01672 811458
e-mail	clarissaroe@clenchfarmhouse.co.uk
web	www.clenchfarmhouse.co.uk

	Felicity & Bill Mather
	Westcourt Bottom,
	165 Westcourt, Burbage,
	Wiltshire SN8 3BW
tel	01672 810924
fax	01672 810924
e-mail	westcourt.b-and-b@virgin.net
web	www.westcourtbottom.co.uk

WILTSHIRE

A listed Georgian thatched farmhouse and a stylish B&B – Val and David moved out of London in search of peace and found it in the heart of crop circle and Stonehenge country. Val is a talented interior decorator who specialises in paint finishes and has stamped her elegant mark on every room: a gentle terracotta linen-effect in the guest sitting room; big yellow checks in the bathroom. A tranquil atmosphere pervades this home with its old rugs on wooden floors, log fires, crisp white bed linen and plump pillows. The garden is charming too and contains a 16th-century drover's rest – surely the grandest-ever garden shed!

rooms	3: 1 double with bath/shower; 1 twin, 1 single, with private/shared bathroom.
room price	From £60; single occ. from £30.
meals	Dinner available.
closed	Occasionally.
directions	From Marlborough, A345 through Pewsey. 3 miles on, at Woodbridge Inn roundabout, right to Hilcott. House 2nd on left over cattle grid. From M3/A303, Hilcott is 11 miles from Amesbury roundabout via Upavon & Woodbridge roundabout.

Val & David Maclay
Hilcott Farm House,
Hilcott, Marlborough,
Wiltshire SN9 6LE

tel   01672 851372
fax   01672 851192
e-mail   beds@hilcott.com

map: 4 entry: 495

WILTSHIRE

Janet – robust and hardworking – is dedicated to hunting and dressage and runs a thriving livery in the grounds. The presence of the horses and the dogs gives a farming feel and you come not to be feted but to join in with it all. The house's origins lie way back in 1189, bits were added in the 16th century and meals are taken around a monastery refectory table that's as old as the house. Downstairs has a homely, natural feel while the bedrooms, perhaps with patterned carpet and kidney-shaped dressing tables, are comfortable; the double is the prettier, the twin more traditional and formal.

rooms	4: 1 double, 1 twin, both with shower; 2 singles with either private bath or shower.
room price	£48-£56.
meals	Breakfast 7.30-9am. Dinner, 4 courses with wine, £20; reduction for 2 courses.
closed	Christmas & New Year.
directions	From Devizes, A360 to Salisbury or A342 to Andover. After 4 miles right on B3098. House 1 mile west of Urchfont.

Mrs Janet Firth
Eastcott Manor,
Easterton, Devizes,
Wiltshire SN10 4PL

tel   01380 813313

map: 4 entry: 496

According to our inspector, "splendid, sunny and sumptuous" sum up this house. Richard, a wine enthusiast and Pippa, a skilled cook, cosset you in huge style; the whole early Georgian house is elegantly furnished and decorated. Bedrooms are large and luxurious and from the triple-aspect drawing room you look out through French windows onto manicured lawns bordered by mature trees. There's a superb grass tennis court, magnificent walking and two first-class riding stables nearby. In 1643 the Battle of Roundway was fought on the Downs behind the house.
Children over 12 welcome

An impressively handsome medieval manor house. Arched, mullioned windows, jutting gables, tall chimneys and a porticoed entrance raise expectations of an interior which are not disappointed. There's a vast Tudor fireplace (complete with Elizabethan graffiti), a whole gallery of ancestral oil paintings and fascinating historic furniture and artefacts. You dine in spring with the scent of wisteria and lilac wafting through the dining room windows. Bedrooms are sunny and luxurious with big beds, modern touches where they matter and views over the grounds.
Children over nine welcome.

rooms	3: 1 double with private bathroom; 2 twins/doubles, both with bathroom.
room price	£76-£90. Single occ. £50-£60.
meals	Dinner, for 4 or more, £23.50. Pub/restaurant 300 yds.
closed	Christmas & Easter.
directions	West along A4. Left just before Calne for Heddington. 2 miles to Ivy Inn & left at T-junc. House on left opp. church; white gate & cattle grid.

rooms	3: 2 doubles, 1 twin, all with bath/shower.
room price	£85-£100. Single occ. £85-£95.
meals	Breakfast until 9.30am. Dinner for groups only.
closed	Christmas & New Year.
directions	From Bath A36 Warminster road for 5 miles, left onto B3108, under railway bridge & up hill. 1st right, turn off Winsley bypass into old village, then 1st left, into lane marked 'except for access'.

Richard & Pippa Novis
Heddington Manor,
Heddington, Nr. Calne,
Wiltshire SN11 0PN

tel	01380 850240
fax	01380 859176
e-mail	richardnovis@compuserve.com

John & Elizabeth Denning
Burghope Manor,
Winsley, Bradford-on-Avon,
Wiltshire BA15 2LA

tel	01225 723557
fax	01225 723113
e-mail	burghope.manor@virgin.net
web	www.burghope.co.uk

map: 3 entry: 497

map: 3 entry: 498

In an ancient hamlet only a few miles from Bath, this impeccable house was, until 15 years ago, 'just' an early 19th-century barn. Few traces of its workday roots remain – it is a large, light house, carpeted and decorated in pale colours. The huge drawing room, with big dried flower arrangements, ornate frames and chintzy sofa has sliding doors giving onto eight acres of gardens, with tennis and, in summer, croquet. Bedrooms are smaller, with skylights and sloping beamed ceilings, yet beds are big. Helga and David look after their visitors with great care.

Farmyard heaven in the Cotswolds. A 17th-century manor farmhouse in 550 arable acres, with horses in the paddock, dozing dogs in the yard, tumbling blooms outside the door, and a perfectly tended village, with duckpond, a walk away. Here are country antiques and beautiful bedrooms softly lit: colours are muted, linen fine, pillows fat, bathrooms big. At breakfast Victoria treats you to traditional farmhouse fare, or smoked salmon and scrambled eggs, or fresh fruits and home-made breads; and there's a tot of whisky before bed. A perfect setting, and Castle Combe and Lacock so close by. *Children over 12 welcome.*

rooms	2: 1 double, 1 twin/double with private or shared bathroom.
room price	£60. Single occ. £35.
meals	Dinner £15. Also excellent local pubs.
closed	Very occasionally.
directions	From M4 junc. 17, west along A420. Right to Upper Wraxall. 1st left in village opp. village green. House at end of private drive.

rooms	3: 2 doubles, both with bath; 1 twin with private bathroom.
room price	£60. Single occ. £35.
meals	Excellent pubs within walking distance.
closed	Christmas.
directions	From M4 A429 to Cirencester (junc.17). After 200 yds 1st left for Grittleton; there, follow signs to Alderton. Farmhouse near church.

Helga & David Venables
The Coach House,
Upper Wraxall, Nr. Bath,
Wiltshire SN14 7AG

tel	01225 891026
fax	01225 892355
e-mail	venables@compuserve.com
web	www.upperwraxallcoachhouse.co.uk

Victoria Lippiatt
Manor Farm,
Alderton, Malmesbury,
Wiltshire SN14 6NL

tel	01666 840271
fax	01666 840271
e-mail	j.lippiatt@farmline.com
web	www.themanorfarm.co.uk

map: 3 entry: 499

map: 3 entry: 500

The sunken vine-hung, thyme-carpeted arbour and gazebo are magical in summer and there is much in the deliciously walled garden to hold your attention. Doi is relaxed and friendly and does B&B because she loves it; breakfast is cooked just as you want it, when you want it. Gently-decorated bedrooms have space, views, flowers and old photographs; one has a half-tester bed. The dark blue dining room has wooden floors and a solid oak table with tapestry chairs and the drawing room, French windows overlooking the garden and an open fire.

A leafy colonnade leads to the smart, honey-coloured gamekeeper's lodge with mullioned windows, young formal gardens and uninterrupted views. Jenny & Alan are fun-loving, and swapped city jobs for the country life. Your bedroom is immaculate: cream walls, chunky beams, Colefax & Fowler curtains and bedspread, rattan and cream sofas, antiques. Under the eaves is a real discovery: a book-lined staircase that leads to a charming bathroom with views. You are on the edge of ancient forest, carpeted in spring with wild flowers. Sink into the armchair — or the bath — and soak up the peace.

rooms	3: 1 triple with private bathroom; 2 doubles, 1 with bath, 1 with private bath & shower.
room price	£50. Single occ. £30.
meals	Good pubs 1-5 miles.
closed	Christmas.
directions	From Malmesbury B4042 for Wootton Bassett. Left to Lea & Charlton. In Lea, right opp. school. House along drive through fields, 1 mile from road.

rooms	1 double with bath.
room price	£60. Single occ. £35.
meals	Dinner from £15. B.Y.O. Pubs/restaurants 3-7 miles.
closed	Christmas & New Year.
directions	A429 between Malmesbury and Cirencester; from Crudwell take road opp. Plough Inn for Eastcourt, Oaksey & Minety. After 1.5 miles, straight over at x-roads. After 1.2 miles, drive on left, top of hill.

	Tony & Doi Newman
	Winkworth Farm,
	Lea, Nr. Malmesbury,
	Wiltshire SN16 9NH
tel	01666 823267
e-mail	doinewman@winkworth89. freeserve.co.uk

	Jenny Saunders
	Hill House,
	Flistridge, Eastcourt, Malmesbury,
	Wiltshire SN16 9PS
tel	01666 860971
fax	01666 860071
e-mail	hill.house@freeuk.com

WILTSHIRE

WILTSHIRE

Delightful quiet seclusion whatever the season. On colder days, large comfy sofas envelop you and fires warm you; in summer, you eat in the cool shade of the arbour, draped in wisteria and climbing roses. The garden is exceptional. The bright conservatory with its huge oak table is filled with a profusion of flowers and colour. Garden vegetables and herbs (mostly organic) are used to magnificent effect. Bedrooms are quiet with lovely country views and Liz and Colin are so easy and flexible that you quickly feel like a visiting friend. *Children over 12 welcome.*

Lots of thoughtful touches – carefully chosen books in the bedrooms, newspapers at breakfast if you wish, cosy chairs in the guest sitting room, and a fire. Helen makes her own bread and jams and serves breakfast in the dining room where you have views of the vast lawned garden, magnolias, chestnuts and lovely high stone walls that abut All Saints Church. There's a tennis court out there, too. Fine flagstoned floors, little window seats and a carved lintel that dates the house as 1703… it is delightful and very comfortable.

rooms	2: 1 twin with bathroom; 1 twin with private bathroom.
room price	£60-£70. Single occ. £35-£40, by arrangement.
meals	Breakfast until 9.30am. Dinner, 2-3 courses, £14-£18.
closed	Christmas & Easter.
directions	From A429, B4040 through Charlton, past Horse & Groom pub. 0.5 miles on, left signed 'Bullocks Horn – No Through Road'. On to end of lane. Right. 1st on left.

rooms	2 doubles, 1 with bathroom, 1 with private bathroom.
room price	£60. Single occ. £35.
meals	Dinner £18.50.
closed	Christmas & New Year.
directions	A429 Malmesbury to Cirencester. In Crudwell, at Plough, right for Minety & Oaksey. Straight on, then left between church & tithe barn pillars.

Colin & Liz Legge
Bullocks Horn Cottage,
Charlton, Malmesbury,
Wiltshire SN16 9DZ
tel 01666 577600
fax 01666 577905
e-mail legge@bullockshorn.clara.co.uk

Helen & Philip Carter
Manor Farmhouse,
Crudwell, Malmesbury,
Wiltshire SN16 9ER
tel 01666 577375
fax 01666 823523
e-mail user785566@aol.com

map: 9 entry: 503

map: 9 entry: 504

WILTSHIRE

In 100 acres of farmland, the house is sited in the ancient hunting ground of Braden Forest. A fire in the dining room, a sitting room (yours) with floral sofas and matching armchairs, elaborate window treatments and grandfather clock; the look is plushly co-ordinated. Upstairs, dados and prints in spotless rooms and exceptionally comfortable beds – perfect for flopping onto after a day of Cotswold exploration. There's a soft charm to Claire and you'll enjoy chatting over her generous breakfasts. Your hosts can pick you up from the end of the first leg of the Thames Path in Cricklade. Excellent eating places nearby.

rooms	2: 1 double, 1 twin, both with bath/shower.
room price	£60. Single occ. £40.
meals	Breakfast 7-9am. Pub 1 mile.
closed	Occasionally.
directions	From Swindon or Cirencester, A419 to Cricklade, then B4040 for Malmesbury. 3 miles on, sign on left. Go to end of drive (0.5 miles).

Claire Read
Leighfield Lodge Farm,
Malmesbury Road, Leigh, Cricklade,
Wiltshire SN6 6RH
tel 01666 860241
fax 01666 860241
e-mail claireread@leighfieldlodge.fsnet.co.uk

map: 9 entry: 505

WILTSHIRE

Valerie was a student of fashion history and dotted around the Threlfalls' half of the 16th-century manor house are fashion prints, photographs, hatboxes, dressmakers' dummies... William Morris fabrics and paper in the dining room, a cosy sitting room for you in the gabled attic and a grand piano in the ballroom (concerts are held here). The Chinese bedroom has curios brought back from travels; the twin room is smaller. A conservatory looks onto a huge lawn – do look at the small Victorian vegetable garden with gravel walkways and the thatched Wendy house beneath giant copper beeches.

rooms	2: 1 double with bathroom; 1 twin with private shower.
room price	£56-£70. Single occ. £35-£42.
meals	Breakfast until 9.50am.
closed	Christmas & New Year.
directions	From Cirencester, A419 south for 4 miles, leaving dual carriageway on left, for Ashton Keynes. Left immed. after White Hart, 100 yds on, through stone pillars, on right.

Valerie & Roger Threlfall
1 Cove House,
Ashton Keynes,
Wiltshire SN6 6NS
tel 01285 861226
fax 01285 861226
e-mail roger@covehouse.co.uk

map: 9 entry: 506

WORCESTERSHIRE

A 12th-century timber frame house that has been smartly dressed in Georgian attire – it wears it well and surprises you with its beamy interior. The house sits at the foot of the majestic Malvern Hills, so there are fine views; all around the house the Archers have 26 acres and a two-acre trout-stocked lake (you may fly-fish). The dazzling black-and-white floored hall leads to antique-filled dining and drawing rooms. Bedrooms are large and the house Scotch awaits you. Elizabeth breeds and shows miniature horses.

Their cooking, their personality, the welcome and the extensive wine list have guests flocking back time and time again. Maybe grapefruit, home-made marmalade, kedgeree or devilled kidneys for breakfast and rack of lamb or steak for dinner... food lovers will return. Walkers, too, love it here – Ann is happy to lend maps from her collection and there is masses of beautiful countryside very near. Dried flowers, house plants and pastel colours downstairs and, upstairs, large bedrooms are spick and span and have views over the long garden and the Malvern Hills.

rooms	3: 1 twin/double, 1 twin, both with bath/shower; 1 twin with shower room.	rooms	3: 1 twin/double, 1 double, both with bath; 1 double with private bathroom.
room price	£70. Single occ. £45.	room price	£53-£59. Single occ. £35.
meals	Breakfast until 9.30 am. Pubs/restaurants 880 yds & 4 miles.	meals	Dinner, 4 courses, £17.70.
closed	Very occasionally.	closed	Christmas & New Year.
directions	West on A4104 to Upton-upon-Severn. Once there, cross river, left up main street, on for 3 miles until red phone box on left. Left at sign & take left fork.	directions	From M50 junc. 1, A38 for Worcester. After 3 miles, left for Upton-upon-Severn & cross River Severn. At T-junc., right onto B4211. Left onto B4209 for Malvern Wells. 3rd house on right.

Philip & Elizabeth Archer
Welland Court,
Upton-upon-Severn,
Worcestershire WR8 0ST

tel   01684 594426
fax   01684 594426
e-mail   archer@wellandcourt.freeserve.co.uk

Ann & Tony Addison
Old Parsonage Farm,
Hanley Castle, Worcester,
Worcestershire WR8 0BU

tel   01684 310124
fax   01684 310124
e-mail   opwines@aol.com

map: 9 entry: 507

map: 9 entry: 508

WORCESTERSHIRE

The Grade II*-listed part-timbered house, half-moated, peeps through the trees as you approach – a magical spot. Roger and Anne are the nicest of hosts and spoil you at breakfast with local bacon, orchard fruits and home-made jam. Traditional, elegantly manicured bedrooms have glorious views of the Abberley Hills. The log-fired sitting room is yours to share with other guests – so cosy you won't mind if it rains; just snug in for the day. Outside: barns and outbuildings, gorgeous gardens, duck pond, moat, tennis court and, at Great Witley, the finest baroque church in England. *Children over 10 welcome.*

rooms	3: 1 twin with bath; 1 twin with private bathroom, 1 single with private shower room.
room price	Twin: £50-£60. Single: £25-£30. Single occ. £40.
meals	Breakfast served until 9am. Good pub 1 mile.
closed	Christmas & New Year.
directions	A443 from Worcester; 1st left, B4197 to Martley; after 0.25 miles 1st right on sharp left-hand bend; up hill; 1st house on right.

Roger & Anne Kendrick
Home Farm,
Great Witley, Worcester,
Worcestershire WR6 6JJ

tel	01299 896825
fax	01299 896176
e-mail	homefarm@yescomputers.co.uk
web	www.homefarmbandb.com

YORKSHIRE

Gringley Hall was once a children's convalescent home and Dulce and Ian took seven years to restore it to its former beauty – a labour of love. The house now feels like home: big, comfortable bedrooms with armchairs and flowers, and excellent bathrooms in Seventies' style with generous towels. The garden is a gardener's dream: two walled (dog-happy) acres that include a nursery and potager, bright borders and sweeping lawns – a grass tennis court and games room, too.

rooms	4: 2 twins/doubles, both with bath/shower; 1 twin with private shower. Family suite on request.
room price	£60-£70. Single occ. £45-£50.
meals	Breakfast until 9.00am. Dinner, 4 courses, £25.
closed	Very occasionally.
directions	From Bawtry, east on A631. Approaching Gringley, 1st left after school sign. On for 150 yds. House on left with iron gates.

Ian & Dulce Threlfall
Gringley Hall,
Gringley on the Hill,
Yorkshire DN10 4QT

tel	01777 817262
fax	01777 816824
e-mail	dulce@gringleyhall.fsnet.co.uk
web	www.gringleyhall.co.uk

YORKSHIRE

YORKSHIRE

A delightful find – this modern cottage is an excellent city alternative to corporate hotels. Both Stephanie's daughters are designers and a sense of style runs in the family. We loved the strong colours – the tiled hall with Chelsea Green walls, the bold yellow drawing room, the Madder Red room that overlooks the garden, the intense blue single room which has a patchwork throw made from the daughters' childhood dresses. The Hornbys are easy-going and love good food. From here you can catch daily ferries to the continent. You'll want to return. *Children over eight welcome.*

You are in Brontë country and if you're keen to walk, you'll love it here. Step out of the front door, past the walled garden, through the field (horses, Jacob sheep) and into open countryside. Good big bedrooms in the solid, very old listed farmhouse and large bathrooms too, with bright, Seventies' suites full of sudsy things, robes and fluffy towels. Geoff's breakfasts are generous in the finest Yorkshire manner. All is comfortable and homely with open fires and Pat and Geoff love to share their knowledge of walks, golf courses and local history.

rooms	2: 1 double with private bathroom; 1 single available to members of same party.
room price	£30-£60.
meals	Supper/dinner £12/£18, with wine.
closed	Very occasionally.
directions	Where M62 becomes A63, follow Humber Bridge signs. At large r'bout north of bridge, left, A164 to Beverley. 3 miles on, right to Kirk Ella. Pass golf course & immed. after Post Office drive 1st on right after Hogg Lane.

rooms	3: 1 double with bath/shower; 1 twin with shower room; 1 twin with private bath/shower.
room price	£45-£55. Single occ. £25-£35.
meals	Packed lunch available. Dinner from £10. Pub/restaurant 200 yds.
closed	Never.
directions	1 mile from Halifax on A58 Leeds rd. Turn between Stump Cross Inn car park & Rosewood Furniture shop. 100 yds to gates.

Stephanie & Martin Hornby
Box Cottage,
2 Hogg Lane, Kirk Ella, Hull,
Yorkshire HU10 7NU
tel   01482 658852
e-mail boxcottage2@aol.com

Pat & Geoff Horrocks-Taylor
Field House,
Staups Lane, Stump Cross, Halifax,
Yorkshire HX3 6XW
tel   01422 355457
e-mail stayatfieldhouse@yahoo.co.uk
web   www.fieldhouse-bb.co.uk

map: 15 entry: 511

map: 14 entry: 512

It's English to the core – a solid former farmhouse in fine Pennine scenery, its stone mullion windows denoting 17th-century origins. Your gentle, gracious hosts offer guests their own, good-sized sitting room – carpeted and cosy, with flowery curtains, good antiques and, on chilly evenings, an open fire. Bedrooms are generous, and cottagey, with old brass beds and fresh flowers. Home-made muffins for breakfast, and good, traditional English dinners, too – just the thing for walkers who've trekked the Calderdale or the Pennine Way. *Children over eight welcome.*

Come to be truly spoiled – Nigel and Julia's Grade II-listed townhouse is imbued with comfort and easy style. Beds are generous, mostly six foot wide, with large enamel baths or astonishingly powerful showers. For breakfast, free-range eggs, handmade sausages, specially smoked bacon and cafetières of steaming, fresh coffee. Perfect. Gleaming dark wood, pretty fabrics, fresh flowers, fluffy towels… All this in the Duchy, Harrogate's most prestigious area, just yards from the Pump Room Museum and fine antique shops. If you want to be independent, ask about the Garden apartment.

rooms	2: 1 family suite, 1 double, both with shower room.
room price	£60. Single occ. by arrangement.
meals	Packed lunch £4. Dinner £20.
closed	Christmas & New Year.
directions	Ripponden is on A58. Right up Royd Lane 100 yds before lights. Right at T-junc. opp. Beehive Inn. On for 1 mile. House is on right. Gateway on blind bend: reverse in.

rooms	3 doubles, all with bath/shower.
room price	£80. Single occ. £40.
meals	Restaurants within walking distance.
closed	Occasionally.
directions	Take A61 Ripon Road from town centre. 1st left is Swan Road. House is 150 yards in front of you.

	David & Judith Marriott
	Thurst House Farm,
	Soyland, Ripponden,
	Sowerby Bridge,
	Yorkshire HX6 4NN
tel	01422 822820
e-mail	thursthousefarm@bushinternet.com

	Nigel & Julia Macdonald
	Britannia Lodge,
	16 Swan Road, Harrogate,
	Yorkshire HG1 2SA
tel	01423 508482
fax	01423 526840
e-mail	info@britlodge.co.uk
web	www.britlodge.co.uk

YORKSHIRE

Peter and Marion are quiet hosts and their concern is for your rest and well-being. The mill cottage is over 200 years old, a stream runs through the garden and there's wildlife all around. There are oak beams and the breakfast corner has a rounded, stone 'cellar' roof; bedrooms and bathrooms are not large, but modest and cosy and you have your own sitting room. Peter was a professional golfer for 20 years and can arrange for you to play locally. Just one mile from Harrogate, it is an excellent base from which to explore the area. *Children over 12 welcome.*

YORKSHIRE

Garden lovers *have* to visit The Old Vicarage. So should hill-walkers. For teddy-bear-collectors it's optional but a good idea. Judi and Steve make you feel that no part of their much-loved home is out of bounds, and have been known to hold *al fresco* Italian suppers in the courtyard. Start the day with breakfast – and a chat – in the cosy, Aga-warmed kitchen; finish with a soak in a roll-top bath. Over 100 varieties of clematis and rose are to be discovered down cobbled paths past lily pond and willows; trickling waterways, sheep and the odd tractor are all that you will hear.

rooms	3: 1 double, 1 twin, both with shower room; 1 twin with private bathroom.
room price	£50. Single occ. by arrangement.
meals	Breakfast until 9am. Good restaurants 1 mile; pub 0.5 miles.
closed	Occasionally.
directions	Off A61 north of Harrogate, signed on road.

rooms	3: 1 double, 1 twin, sharing bathroom (only let to same party); 1 double with shower room.
room price	£54. Single occ. £32.
meals	Lunches & dinner available. B.Y.O.
closed	Very occasionally.
directions	From Harrogate, A59 (west). Right B6451. Right at Wellington pub. House on right, next to Christ Church.

Peter & Marion Thomson
Knox Mill House,
Knox Mill Lane, Harrogate,
Yorkshire HG3 2AE

tel	01423 560650
fax	01423 560650

Judi Smith
The Old Vicarage,
Darley, Harrogate,
Yorkshire HG3 2QF

tel	01423 780526
fax	01423 780526
e-mail	judi@darley33.freeserve.co.uk
web	www.darley33.freeserve.co.uk

map: 14 entry: 515

map: 14 entry: 516

Chris Knowles-Fitton's father was a devotee of Canada and built this timber-framed house in 1938 in the style of a log cabin. The solitude is restorative and the sitting room gives onto a wooden terrace with stupendous views of the River Wharfe and the Dales Way. There are books, rugs and oak furniture in the sitting room. Bedrooms have pastel colours with splashes of cheerful floral chintz cushions; curtains and bathrooms continue the theme. It is easy to feel at home, and there are great walks all around. You can fish for trout, too.

An air of quiet decency surrounds 17th-century Scar Lodge, reputed to have been a brewery for monks at Fountains Abbey; it's a restful retreat for those intent on sampling a slower pace. Comfortingly traditional bedrooms have valley views, patchwork quilts, fresh fruit, stitched linen, bathrobes; and there's a sitting room and a sunny spot upstairs for reading. Valerie, modest and gentle, is an accomplished artist – she runs courses and holds exhibitions here. Grassington itself is attractive, with cobbled streets, restaurants and interesting shops. *Children by arrangement.*

rooms	3: 2 doubles, 1 twin, all with bath/shower.
room price	£56. Single occ. £33.
meals	Packed lunch £4. Dinner £18.
closed	Very occasionally.
directions	From Skipton A59 to Bolton Abbey. At r'bout, B6160 for Burnall. 3 miles after Devonshire Arms, right immed. after Barden Tower for Appletreewick. Down hill, over bridge, up hill & on for 0.5 miles. Cross bridge; immediately. on left.

rooms	2: 1 double with bath/shower; 1 double with private bathroom.
room price	£50–£55. Single occ. £30–£32.50.
meals	Breakfast from 7am. Packed lunch £3.50. Pubs & restaurants in Grassington.
closed	Occasionally.
directions	B6265 Skipton-Grassington; enter 'main street' Grassington & take right-hand fork past Grassington House Hotel; right again after Folk Museum into Gillsfold; narrow road into Grange; lodge on right.

Pam & Chris Knowles-Fitton
Knowles Lodge,
Appletreewick, Nr. Skipton,
Yorkshire BD23 6DQ

tel	01756 720228
fax	01756 720381
e-mail	pam@knowleslodge.com
web	www.knowleslodge.com

Valerie Emmerson
Scar Lodge,
Hardy Grange, Grassington, Skipton
Yorkshire BD23 5AJ

tel	01756 753388
fax	01756 753388
web	www.scarlodge.co.uk

It is hard to resist Maggie's home-made jams and marmalade, the local home-cured bacon or the sausages from the farm up the road. Harder still to say "no" to her kedgeree. The rambling 16th-century farmhouse, its fireplaces and shutters intact, is cosily furnished with floral fabrics and country antiques. A wonderfully steep stair leads to the main house bedrooms; others are in a converted outbuilding. Maggie's enthusiasm is infectious and her description of Fountains Abbey means a visit there is a must. Remember, this World Heritage Site was the richest area of England when wool was king. *Children over 12 welcome.*

rooms	4: 1 double, 2 twin/doubles, all with shower rooms; 1 double, with bath/shower.
room price	£55-£64. Single occ. from £40.
meals	Breakfast 8-9am. Good pubs & restaurants nearby.
closed	December & New Year.
directions	B6265 from Ripon for Pateley Bridge. Past entrance to Fountains Abbey. House on right.

Maggie Johnson
Mallard Grange,
Aldfield,
Nr. Fountains Abbey, Ripon,
Yorkshire HG4 3BE

tel	01756 620242
fax	01765 620242
e-mail	mallard.grange@btinternet.com.

map: 14 entry: 519

A perfectly proper house run with faultless precision by John and Harriet – former wine importer and interior decorator respectively. The walk to Fountains Abbey and Studley Royal – the most complete remains of a Cistercian abbey in Britain – is a treat; you are spoiled for things to do and see and can consider your options in the manicured garden. Magnificent countryside, with views and deer all around. Two beautifully decorated bedrooms and bathrooms have thoughtful touches such as bathrobes and toiletries. *Golf, riding and clay pigeon shooting can be arranged.*

rooms	2: 1 twin/double, 1 twin, both with bathroom.
room price	£96. Single occ. £63.
meals	Dinner £28.
closed	Christmas & New Year.
directions	A1 to Ripon. B6265/Pateley Bridge road for 2 miles. Left into Studley Roger. House last on right.

John & Harriet Highley
Lawrence House,
Studley Roger, Ripon,
Yorkshire HG4 3AY

tel	01765 600947
fax	01765 609297
e-mail	john@lawrence-house.co.uk
web	www.lawrence-house.co.uk

map: 14 entry: 520

You couldn't fail to have fun here, according to our inspector. These are super folk, genuinely keen to share their home – this is no stifling, set-piece B&B. Dining and drawing rooms are nonetheless smart and bedrooms are traditional with quirky touches. You look out over the Vale of York, yet are only three minutes' walk from the heart of the village and close to York and its Minster. Set in 28 acres that run down to the River Swale (fishing available), it has black sheep, ducks, horses and ponies, a croquet lawn and a tennis court. Hard to believe you are only four miles from the A1.

Gerry is the only person to have won the Grand National (1960 on Merryman II), and started it (in 1996). A portrait of the winning pair hangs in the dining/living room; Gerry is a happy man. The bedrooms differ – one, a twin, sports an exciting cherry-red wall, the second, cream and peppermint colours. A double has a drawn threadwork bedspread. Views are of paddock and moorland. A mecca for real ale enthusiasts, Masham is the home of both Theakston and Black Sheep breweries. It is also boisterous field sports country, so possibly Pasture House is not for objectors.

rooms	3: 1 double with bathroom; 1 twin/double with shower room; 1 four-poster with private bathroom.
room price	£60.
meals	Dinner £25. Good pubs 3-minute walk.
closed	Occasionally in winter.
directions	From A1(M), Boroughbridge exit. At north side of B'bridge follow Easingwold & Helperby sign. In Brafferton-Helperby, right at T-junc., right up Hall Lane. Left in front of school.

rooms	3: 2 doubles, 1 twin with basins, all sharing bathroom & wc.
room price	£36. Single occ. £18.
meals	Dinner, 3 courses, £10. B.Y.O.
closed	Christmas Day.
directions	From A6108 (Ripon to Richmond rd), turn off 0.35 miles north of Masham, for Healey. Through Healey to junction for Colsterdale. Take right fork. House 1st on left.

Sam & Annie Atcherley-Key
Laurel Manor Farm,
Brafferton-Helperby, York,
Yorkshire YO61 2NZ

tel	01423 360436
fax	01423 360437
e-mail	laurelmf@aol.com
web	www.laurelmf.co.uk

Avril & Gerry Scott
Pasture House,
Healey, Masham,
Yorkshire HG4 4LJ

tel	01765 689149
fax	01765 689990

map: 14 entry: 521

map: 14 entry: 522

To the front, the perfect English country village with close-clipped verges; behind, beyond the ancient apple tree and the garden wall, views of the dales. Four 17th-century almshouses have become Rookery Cottage and the oak-panelled dining room was once the village post office. It all feels natural, normal, homely, free of studied co-ordination. That's not to say there aren't spoiling touches – generous baths, pretty basins, Floris soaps, fine food… Breakfast features home-made jams and marmalades and maybe kedgeree made from Ronnie's catch of the day. Dine at the pub opposite – one of the north country's finest.

Oriella goes the extra mile for you and her flamboyancy and style make light of the practicalities of having guests. She is arty, fun-loving and kind and gives you a place to unwind, read, listen to music – you can wander into the totally secluded garden, too, and sit beneath aged copper beeches. There are tapestries, mirrors, thick oak tables and oriental pieces, something to catch the eye at every turn. The bedrooms are big, chintzy/paisley and the suite has a seven-foot square bed with the down of 226 ducks to snuggle under!
A Georgian jewel.

rooms	2: 1 twin, 1 double, both with basin, sharing bathroom.
room price	£48–£58. Single occ. from £34.
meals	Breakfast 8.30–9am. Packed lunch £4.50. Excellent country inn opposite for dinner.
closed	Very occasionally.
directions	From Masham, A6108. Leyburn is 8 miles on. House on left, opp. Blue Lion Country Inn.

rooms	3: 1 double, 1 twin, both with bath; 1 suite with bath/shower.
room price	£90–£100. Single occ. £50–£55.
meals	Dinner, 4 courses, £25. Pub/restaurant 1.5 miles.
closed	Very occasionally.
directions	From A1 at Leeming Bar, A684 to Bedale. 0.5 miles out of town, turn for Newton-Le-Willows. Right at T-junc., left at Wheatsheaf pub, then immed. right through gates.

Mrs Ursula Bussey
Rookery Cottage,
East Witton, Leyburn,
Yorkshire DL8 4SN

tel	01969 622918
fax	01969 622918
e-mail	ursulabussey@aol.com
web	www.rookerycottage.co.uk

Oriella Featherstone
The Hall,
Newton-Le-Willows, Bedale,
Yorkshire DL8 1SW

| tel | 01677 450210 |

map: 14 entry: 523

map: 14 entry: 524

YORKSHIRE

You feel as if you are caught in a tranquil time-warp; no TV, just utter calm and windows that frame beautiful views of Wensleydale. In the heart of the Yorkshire Dales National Park, it's a superb base for walkers. Gail and Ann bake their own bread and make jams and marmalade. Their delicious dinners are prepared with fresh, local produce. Two bedrooms have four-posters and all have those views. If you're arriving by car, take the 'over-the-top' road from Buckden to Hawes for the stunning countryside. Expect a real welcome from their two Labradors.

rooms	4: 1 double, 1 twin, 2 four-posters, all sharing bathroom or shower room.
room price	£40-£42. Single occ. £25-£29.
meals	Breakfast 8.30am. Dinner, 4 courses, £14.50 (not Thurs); good value wine list.
closed	November-mid-February.
directions	Approx. 320 yds off A684, on road north out of Hawes, signed Muker & Hardraw.

Gail Ainley & Ann Macdonald
Brandymires,
Muker Road, Hawes,
Yorkshire DL8 3PR

tel   01969 667482

map: 14 entry: 525

YORKSHIRE

One of our favourites that continues to amaze and captivate guests. In every corner of the breathtakingly romantic garden the marriage of natural beauty and sophistication exists in a state of bliss. The four Doric columns at the entrance draw you through the hall into the dining room and to exquisite views of the Swale Valley. Blissful beds, period furniture, cast-iron baths, myriad paintings – a feast for the senses. Tim and Austin are excellent, engaging hosts.

rooms	3: 1 double, 1 twin, both with bath/shower; 1 double with private bathroom & sitting room.
room price	£70. Single occ. £45.
meals	Breakfast 8.30-9.30am. Pub/restaurant 250 yds.
closed	Very occasionally.
directions	Next door to Halifax Building Society, opposite side of Barclays at bottom of Market Place. Green front door with small brass plaque.

Austin Lynch & Tim Culkin
Millgate House,
Richmond,
Yorkshire DL10 4JN

tel   01748 823571
fax   01748 850701
e-mail   oztim@millgatehouse.demon.co.uk
web   www.millgatehouse.com

map: 14 entry: 526

Persian rugs, *trompe l'oeil* and Farrow & Ball period colours sit beautifully in this elegant Georgian townhouse. A cobbled street leads to the medieval castle and it is a short stroll to the centre of this pretty, old market town with its castle ramparts, Georgian theatre, pubs and Saturday market. There's a sweet country garden with inspirational views of the parish church, Easby Abbey and the Swale Valley and a conservatory to enjoy the setting all year round. Guest rooms are on the ground floor with comfortable beds, pure cotton sheets, quilted bedspreads and a big oak wardrobe.

You have everything Christina's friends would have: biscuits by the bed, magazines, books, bath essences; Christine pampers without being overly solicitous. Her listed limestone farmhouse dates from 1820 and is deceptively big, with a cottagey drawing room and a modern open kitchen with sofa. The bedroom is a suite separated from the house by a latch door, so you're very private. There are panoramic views over rolling countryside, and Newsham is in an AONB: do explore the waterfalls, moorland, castles and exquisite villages. A handy stopover en route to Scotland.

rooms	2: 1 twin with private bathroom; 1 double with shower room.
room price	From £52. Single occ. £32.
meals	Good pubs & restaurants 300 yds.
closed	Christmas.
directions	From Scotch Corner (A1, 30 miles north of Wetherby), to Richmond. There, left at library roundabout & left into Frenchgate. House at top on right with black railings.

rooms	2: 1 twin with bath & shower; 1 twin, for members of same party, willing to share bathroom.
room price	£50. Single occ. £25.
meals	Dinner, 2-3 courses, £12-£15.
closed	Christmas & New Year.
directions	From Scotch Corner west on A66. Approx. 7 miles on, down hill. Left to Newsham. Through village; 2nd left for Helwith. House on right at top, name on gate.

Elizabeth & Ken Parham
58 Frenchgate,
Richmond,
Yorkshire DL10 7AG
tel   01748 823227
e-mail   liz@parham.f9.co.uk

Christina Farmer
Hill Top,
Newsham, Richmond,
Yorkshire DL11 7QX
tel   01833 621513
e-mail   cdfarmer@lineone.net

map: 14 entry: 527

map: 14 entry: 528

The views are over Teesdale and the walking is everywhere; the village, tiny and solid in stone, is perfect. A romantic hideaway in the 18th-century coach house is yours up a steep stone stair: a lofty, cross-beamed ceiling, lemon-yellow fabrics against a cream wall, soft lighting, good linen, and Angela's charming watercolours and pottery adding to the fresh, country feel. Inside the rectory, more rooms in which to linger – here the mood is of a classically English country house. Angela can teach you to fish, is a great cook – salmon fishcakes, own eggs at breakfast – and has green fingers too. The garden is glorious.

The house was once much bigger and what remains is the Victorian section of a Georgian mansion; now a manageable size, it's in tiptop condition and very comfortable. A sense of space remains, with high, plaster-worked ceilings and pale bedrooms. Fireplaces everywhere, big baths, high beds, large windows onto the beautiful grounds and a terraced lawn that runs down to the Tees; there's a book-lined study and a sitting room for you, and you can fish, play tennis or croquet. Both grandeur and a genuine welcome – not to be missed.

rooms	3: 1 double with bath/shower; 1 twin with extra single & bath.
room price	£70. Single occ. from £35.
meals	Breakfast from 7am. Dinner or supper available. Pubs & restaurants 3-10 miles.
closed	Christmas & New Year.
directions	South off A66 for Greta Bridge & Barningham, 10 miles west of Scotch Corner. Immed. left for B'ham for 2 miles. Before entering village through dry stone walls, house 2nd entrance left after village sign.

rooms	2 twins, both with private bathroom.
room price	£60. Single occ. £30.
meals	Good pub 1 mile.
closed	10 December-1 January.
directions	From A1, exit onto B6275. North for 4.2 miles. Turn into drive (on left before Piercebridge) & take 1st right fork.

Angela Delahooke
The Old Rectory,
Barningham, Nr. Richmond,
Yorkshire DL11 7DW
tel   01833 621251
fax   01833 621421
e-mail   jdelahooke@aol.com

Caroline & Richard Wilson
Cliffe Hall,
Piercebridge, Darlington,
Yorkshire DL2 3SR
tel   01325 374322
fax   01325 374947
e-mail   petal@cliffehall.freeserve.co.uk

YORKSHIRE

YORKSHIRE

The look is solid, impressive; within, the feel is warm, family, comfortable, easy. The house was built in 1929 on the site of an 18th-century house, so... masses of architectural history: folly, ice-house, urns and sundials remain from the original estate. A stalwart oak staircase and an inner hall are lit by a glass dome and portraits line the galleried landing. The scale and colour of the gardens are breathtaking, so are the views; there's croquet too and a further, hidden, garden. Sarah always rustles up a fresh coffee or tea to welcome you, and is justifiably proud of the house and its history.

Even in the mayhem of the lambing season they greet you with a smile, tea and biscuits (home-made) — the Pearsons are the nicest, most genuine, straightforward farming folk imaginable. Their farmhouse is as unpretentious as they are; one bedroom is in the house and another three in converted outbuildings away from the homely hub. Rooms have a mixture of antique and modern furniture and views of the garden and of the Hambledon Hills. The road that runs past the house is quiet, yet you are well placed for the dales and the moors. Local sausages, home-made marmalade and home-grown eggs for breakfast.

rooms	2 twins, both with bath.
room price	£70-£80. Single occ. from £45.
meals	Restaurants/pubs 5 miles.
closed	Christmas, New Year and occasionally.
directions	A1 to Scotch Corner, then A66 for Penrith. House 0.25 miles after lay-by on left, lodge & white posts; through gates.

rooms	5: 1 family, 1 twin, 1 double, 1 single, all with shower. Gate Cottage: 1 double with bath.
room price	£44-£50. Single occ. £27-£31. Gate Cottage: £50-£60.
meals	Breakfast until 9.30am. Dinner £16.
closed	December-February.
directions	From Northallerton, A167 north for Darlington for 4 miles. House on right, signed.

Sarah Baker Baker
Sedbury Hall,
Richmond,
Yorkshire DL10 5LQ

tel   01748 822722
e-mail   sarahbakerbaker@hotmail.com

John & Mary Pearson
Lovesome Hill Farm,
Lovesome Hill, Northallerton,
Yorkshire DL6 2PB

tel   01609 772311
fax   01609 774715
e-mail   pearsonlhf@care4free.net

map: 14 entry: 531

map: 14 entry: 532

YORKSHIRE

Over 250 years of family history are modestly displayed and the Kynges have been here that long. The garden and parkland are impressive with a summer house, tennis court, croquet lawn and peaceful spots that trap the sun. Today the farm is fully organic; the Galloway cattle and sheep graze just the other side of the ha-ha. Bedrooms are solidly handsome with oak chests and magnificent wardrobes; one has been freshly decorated in a blue-and-cream *toile de Jouy*. Everywhere there is the nobility of wood and fine furniture. Mrs Kynge's cooking has won many accolades.

rooms	3 + 2: 2 doubles, both with bath; 1 twin with private bathroom & separate shower. Self-catering for 4 also available.
room price	£56. Single occ. £33.
meals	Dinner £20.
closed	December–March.
directions	From A19, A172 for Stokesley for 3 miles. Left & straight over crossroads. Drive is 0.25 miles on, on right.

Major & Mrs Julian Kynge
Potto Grange,
Potto, Nr. Northallerton,
Yorkshire DL6 3HH
tel   01642 700212
fax   01642 701557
e-mail   kynge@btopenworld.com

map: 14 entry: 533

YORKSHIRE

A peaceful spirit, warmth and friendliness pervade this elegant, bay-windowed farmhouse. Anne goes to great lengths to make you comfortable and her cooking is delicious. The house, which incorporates the former cottage and dairy buildings, has pale, fresh colour schemes, an interesting collection of books and superb views. The pretty guest rooms face south and you will be drawn to explore the gentle, rolling dales, the moors and the coastline. York, Durham and other fascinating historic places are nearby. *Children over 12 welcome.*

rooms	2: 1 twin, 1 twin/double, both with private bathroom.
room price	£76. Single occ. £48.
meals	Dinner from £25.
closed	December–January.
directions	North on A19 take A172 for Stokesley. Pass sign on right to Carlton & Busby. House 0.5 miles further on left, with 2 red triangular reflectors at entrance to tree-lined drive.

Anne Gloag
Busby House,
Stokesley,
Yorkshire TS9 5LB
tel   01642 710425
fax   01642 713838

map: 14 entry: 534

The entrance is dramatic – the Cleveland Hills rise up behind and, all around, there are 164 acres of parkland. The views go on forever, the wildlife comes to you. Footpaths lead from the farm to the moors and take you past wild geese and cantering Soay sheep from the Outer Hebrides. Martin and Margaret are interested, involved people: you feel your presence counts. Inside, china knick-knacks and florals contrast with the bright whiteness of the rooms. Guests must take dinner – there are fine wines and you won't mind in the slightest. *Children over 12 welcome.*

Free-range children and dogs scramble and amble around in an atmosphere of happy chaos; Jill is young and energetic and you will immediately warm to her; Andrew is unflappable. You are in a remote valley near the North Yorkshire Moors where the 1800s courtyard is such a rare survivor of local rural architecture that the BBC filmed it for posterity. The rooms, with views to the craggy moor, have been refurbished but this is first and foremost a family home, so don't expect anything designery. Breakfast on home-baked soda bread, farm eggs and proper bacon; for dinner, savour the Kellys' own lamb and beef.

rooms	3: 2 doubles, 1 twin, 1 with bathroom, 2 with private bath/shower.
room price	Half-board £90 per room (£45 p.p.). Single occ. by arrangement.
meals	Breakfast until 9.30am. Dinner, 5 courses, included.
closed	Christmas.
directions	B1257 south from Stokesley to Great Broughton. Left at village hall onto Ingleby road for 2 miles to church at Ingleby Greenhow. Entrance right after church, through pillars.

rooms	3: 1 double, 1 family, 1 twin, all with private bathroom.
room price	£45. Single occ. £25.
meals	Packed lunch available. Dinner, 3 courses, £15.
closed	Very occasionally.
directions	From Malton, A170 Pickering road to Cropton. Through Rosedale Abbey & up onto moor & over cattle grid. Approx 1.5 miles on, right for Fryup. After 2 miles, right at T-junction. Farm 1st on left.

Margaret & Martin Bloom
Manor House Farm,
Ingleby Greenhow, Great Ayton,
Yorkshire TS9 6RB
tel   01642 722384
e-mail mbloom@globalnet.co.uk

Jill Kelly
Stonebeck Gate Farm,
Little Fryup, Danby, Whitby,
Yorkshire YO21 2NS
tel   01287 660363
fax   01287 660363

map: 14 entry: 535

map: 14 entry: 536

YORKSHIRE

L ose yourself in the gardens, dangle your feet in Hutton Beck, which runs through, and feel the history of the place. Settled pre-Roman but rebuilt in Georgian times, the house has a story to tell, having been an 18th-century smithy, a tannery and a fine country house; Kate and Barry have gently coaxed it into a cosseting B&B. Traditional comforts – good beds, fine furniture, log fires, lots of books, deep armchairs – and a modern, multi-cultural twist to the outstanding food, much of which is local or home-grown. The moors and the village – the prettiest in England? – are a fine combination and your hosts great fun.

rooms	3: 1 four-poster, with bath/shower; 1 double, with shower room; 1 twin/double, with bath.
room price	£65. Single occ. £40.
meals	Packed lunches available. Dinner, 3 courses, £18.
closed	Very occasionally.
directions	A170 for Scarborough. Hutton-le-Hole signed left 1 mile east of Kirkbymoorside; house on left before village hall; signed.

Kate Seekings & Barry Jenkinson
Moorlands of Hutton-le-Hole,
Hutton-le-Hole,
North Yorkshire Moors, York,
Yorkshire YO62 6UA
tel 01751 417548
fax 01751 417760
e-mail special@moorlandshouse.com
web www.moorlandshouse.com

YORKSHIRE

A 20-minute stride down the fields to Levisham Station and the start of some wonderful jaunts on the North Yorkshire Moors Steam Railway. Warmth and comfort are the key notes of this family home – log fires on chilly nights, flowers in the rooms, home-made scones for tea. Cheery bedrooms are painted fresh yellow; all are carpeted and cosy. Have a drink at the local pub – a 50-yard stroll – or dine at home on Michael's beef and Yorkshire pudding (Heather does the puds). Superb walks from the doorstep, and excellent riding, too – bring your horse. Very good value.

rooms	3: 1 double, 1 twin/double, both with shower room; 1 twin/double with bath/shower.
room price	£40-£50. Weekly rate: £270-£290. Single occ. £24-£28.
meals	Breakfast 8-9.30am. Packed lunch £3-£5. Dinner £10-£12.
closed	Very occasionally.
directions	From A169 take Lockton/Levisham road. Once through Lockton, look for house sign after 0.75 miles on right, in Levisham.

Mrs Heather Holt
Rectory Farmhouse,
Levisham, Pickering,
Yorkshire YO18 7NL
tel 01751 460491
e-mail stay@levisham.com
web www.levisham.com

YORKSHIRE

YORKSHIRE

The moors lie behind this solid, stone farmhouse, five yards from the National Park, in farmland and woodland with fine views... marvellous walking country. The house is full of light and flowers; bedrooms are pretty and not overly grand. The sitting room has deeply comfortable old sofas, armchairs and fine furniture; rich colours and hunting prints give the dining room a warm and cosy feel. The Orr family has poured affection into this house and the result is a home that's happy and remarkably easy to relax in... wonderful. *Children over 12 welcome.*

An Aga-cooked breakfast and fresh seasonal fruit await you – quantities are generous. The Cravens are equally generous of spirit and we *guarantee* you'll love their Labrador, Barney. The house is of mellow Yorkshire stone, built in 1767 and there is an air of quiet repose – traditional furniture, china in panelled alcoves, lovely prints and watercolours and a drawing room with Delph fire surround. Bedrooms are comfortable and snug and have proper tea trays and fresh flowers; in wintertime there are views to Pickering Vale. A very pretty village and garden enhance the enjoyment.

rooms	2 twins/doubles, 1 with shower, 1 with private bathroom.
room price	£70. Single occ. from £40.
meals	Breakfast until 9.30am. Dinner, 3 courses with wine, from £25.
closed	Very occasionally.
directions	From A170 Kirkbymoorside/Pickering road, turn into Sinnington. On village green, keep river on left & fork right between cottages. Up lane, bearing right up hill. House past church.

rooms	2: 1 twin, 1 double, both with private bathroom.
room price	£60. Single occ. £35.
meals	Breakfast 7.30-9am. Two pubs & 1 bistro in village.
closed	Occasionally.
directions	Through Thornton le Dale on A170 for Scarborough. Road rises after village centre. Pass church on left. Hurrell Lane near top of hill on right. House immediately. on right.

	The Orr Family
	Hunters Hill,
	Sinnington, York,
	Yorkshire YO62 6SF
tel	01751 431196
fax	01751 432976
e-mail	jorr@btclick.com

	Richard & Tuppie Craven
	The High Hall,
	Hurrell Lane, Thornton le Dale,
	Yorkshire YO18 7QR
tel	01751 474371
fax	01751 477701
e-mail	cravengriffin@aol.com

map: 14 entry: 539

map: 15 entry: 540

The Cleveland Way runs along the cliffs a mile away and Christine is keen to help you plan your stay (a trip to the Alan Ayckbourn Theatre, maybe?). Christine loves interior design and bedrooms are carefully co-ordinated: one has a pink, green and floral theme and an original Victorian fireplace, the double has bold blue, gold and deep-rose matching headboard and drapes. Comfort is the thing here: there are bathrobes in fitted wardrobes and big showers. Breakfast either in the south-facing conservatory – there's a huge choice, including kippers – or at the polished mahogany table in the dining room. Billiards, too.

A Regency gem, built in 1735, remodelled in 1810 and re-awoken in 1966 by the neo-Classical architect Francis Johnson, known as "the last of the Georgians". The house sings of the love poured into it and the present owners keep it in the style to which it has become accustomed. There are real working wooden shutters, fine old doors and polished floorboards. In the garden, two sphinxes guard the semicircular Doric-columned entrance and a belvedere with views of Filey Bay. Excellent bedrooms, massively comfortable, perfect peace and setting, and the nicest of hosts.

rooms	2: 1 twin with shower; 1 double with private bath & shower.
room price	From £50. Single occ. from £30.
meals	Pubs 600 yds-2 miles.
closed	Occasionally.
directions	A171 from Scarborough to Whitby; at Scalby x-roads, by tennis courts, take road on right. Signed 500 yds on right.

rooms	3: 1 double with shower room; 1 double & 1 twin, sharing bathroom.
room price	£60-£75. Single occ. £40-£45.
meals	Two restaurants within 5 miles, pub 6 miles.
closed	Christmas & New Year.
directions	A165 Bridlington-Scarborough; into Reighton and take 1st right; house signed just before chevron signs.

John & Christine Goodall
Holly Croft,
28 Station Road, Scalby,
Scarborough,
Yorkshire YO13 0QA
tel   01723 375376
fax   01723 360563
web   www.holly-croft.co.uk

Dawn McKie & Paul Flannigan
Reighton Hall,
Church Hill, Reighton, Filey,
Yorkshire YO14 9RX
tel   01723 890601
e-mail   dawn@reightonhall.com
web   www.reightonhall.com

A book-filled sitting room with brocade sofas, oak furniture, maple floors, dark green walls, shuttered windows – perhaps a coal fire in your room, or a cast-iron bath with Victorian fittings; this is a solidly traditional house set just inland from the drama of Flamborough Head. Geoffrey is a naval historian and the house is stuffed with his books. Lesley keeps alive the craft of Gansey knitting, selling the intricate fishermen's sweaters, along with antiques, in the converted stable block. Take an atmospheric clifftop walk, or a boat trip to see the puffins.

The Woods have spent much of their lives in the East and their Grade II-listed Georgian house has a harmonious mix of oriental and fine English furniture, pictures and fabrics. They look after you well, with plump pillows, flowers and magazines, towelling robes and prettily-decorated bedrooms. The simple elegance is striking. Free-range eggs come from the next-door farm; bread, jams, shortbread and potato scones are home-made; coffee is freshly ground. Colourful lupins stand proud in the garden and masses of roses and dreamy sunsets vie for your attention. *Children over 12 welcome.*

rooms	2: 1 double, 1 twin/double, both with bathroom.
room price	£68–£78. Single occ. £42–£47.
meals	Breakfast 8.30–9.30am. Dinner £24.50.
closed	Christmas.
directions	From Bridlington, B1255 to Flamborough. Follow signs to lighthouse, past church on right. House on next corner (Lighthouse Road/Tower Streer).

rooms	2: 1 twin, 1 double, sharing private bathroom.
room price	£50. Single occ. £25.
meals	Breakfast until 9.30am. Packed lunch £5. Dinner, 4 courses, £17.
closed	Occasionally.
directions	From Malton, B1257 for Helmsley. Through Amotherby then right to Kirkbymoorside. On for 3.25 miles. At Great Barugh, left at T-junction House on right, 50 yds past pub.

	Lesley Berry & Geoffrey Miller
	The Manor House,
	Flamborough,
	Yorkshire YO15 1PD
tel	01262 850943
fax	01262 850943
e-mail	gm@flamboroughmanor.co.uk
web	www.flamboroughmanor.co.uk

	Janie Wood
	Barugh House,
	Great Barugh, Malton,
	Yorkshire YO17 6UZ
tel	01653 668615
e-mail	barughhouse@amserve.net

Each window frames an outstanding view – this spot, on the edge of the North York Moors National Park, was chosen for its views and the house arranged to soak up the scenery, from the Pennines to the Wolds. This is a stylish, elegant and large modern house with a huge mature hillside garden. The generous bedrooms and bathrooms are uncluttered and comfortable; the drawing room has an open fire in winter. Phillip and Anton love what they are doing, so you will be treated like angels and served freshly cooked dinners of outstanding quality.
Children over 12 welcome.

Drive through a stone archway into an old courtyard. A grandfather clock, whose mythological figure blows a furious wind, then greets you. This is a 17th-century, beamed, working farmhouse, once attached to Ampleforth Abbey. The three uncluttered, flowery bedrooms are frilled and co-ordinated and have lovely views. There is a half-tester brass and iron bedstead with a soaring, awning-like canopy in the double. A true, bluff Yorkshire farming welcome from Andrew and graceful efficiency from Margaret.
Children over 10 welcome.

rooms	3: 2 twin/doubles, both with bathroom; 1 double with private bathroom.	
room price	£70-£84. Single occ. £45-£55.	
meals	Breakfast 8-9.30am. Dinner, 4 courses, £22.50.	
closed	Christmas, New Year and very occasionally.	
directions	From Thirsk, A19 south, then 'caravan route' via Coxwold & Byland Abbey. 1st house on left, just before Ampleforth.	

rooms	3: 1 twin, 1 double, both with shower; 1 twin with private bath & shower.
room price	£52-£60. Single occ. £35.
meals	Breakfast 8-9.30am. Excellent pubs & restaurants 1-3 miles.
closed	Christmas & New Year.
directions	A170 from Thirsk for 12 miles. Right onto B1257 1 mile before Helmsley. 50 yds on, left by church. House at end of 'No Through Road'.

	Anton van der Horst & Phillip Gill
	Shallowdale House,
	West End, Ampleforth,
	Yorkshire YO62 4DY
tel	01439 788325
fax	01439 788885
e-mail	stay@shallowdalehouse.demon.co.uk
web	www.shallowdalehouse.demon.co.uk

	Margaret & Andrew Wainwright
	Sproxton Hall,
	Sproxton, Helmsley,
	Yorkshire YO62 5EQ
tel	01439 770225
fax	01439 771373
e-mail	info@sproxtonhall.demon.co.uk
web	www.sproxtonhall.co.uk

map: 14 entry: 545

map: 14 entry: 546

Photography by Michael Busselle

WALES

"The world is like a book and those who
do not travel read only one page."
SAINT AUGUSTINE

ANGLESEY

O ur inspector was blown away by it
– "unbelievable!" An adventure
from the moment you leave your car
and are taken in the 4x4 vehicle along
the cliffs to this isolated outpost on an
RSPB Reserve. The old Fog House (a
former signal station for Trinity House)
is now converted into a bird-watching
observatory. Philippa cares deeply about
guests and is generous with everything,
food included. The dining room and
quiet sitting areas have panoramic
views. The bedrooms, part of the
former keeper's quarters, are simple
and attractive. Don't forget waterproofs
and binoculars. *Advance request for
brochure and booking essential.*

rooms	2: 1 double next to private shower room; 1 twin, with shared/private bathroom.
room price	£54. Single occ. £32.
meals	Dinner, three courses, from £15.
closed	November–March.
directions	On Holyhead seafront, take upper road on left. After 2 bridges, Warden's House at Breakwater Country Park on left. Phone to be collected. If coming by train or ferry, ring from station.

Philippa Jacobs
North Stack,
c/o 4 Lower Park Street, Holyhead,
Anglesey LL65 1DU

tel	01407 761252

BRIDGEND

S quare-on to the seafront and,
indoors, a happy combination of
family comfort and easy elegance.
Bennie ran her own gallery in Ireland
and brought her sense of style and some
great finds (Prunier menus, Bradley
prints) back to Wales in the '80s. She's
in charge of candlelit, Aga-driven four-
course dinners at the big round dining
table. Clark takes care of breakfasts:
home-made soda bread, bacon and eggs
however you want them. Polished
parquet, prettily proportioned rooms
and beautifully clad long windows – it's
tempting to stay in and relax. There's a
heated outdoor pool for summer, and
golf and walking on the doorstep.

rooms	3: 2 doubles, 1 twin, all with shower room.
room price	£70–£80. Single occ. £50–£55.
meals	Dinner £30.
closed	Christmas, New Year & Easter.
directions	From M4, junc. 37; follow signs to Porthcawl seafront. Continue towards Rest Bay; 3rd house after Fairways Hotel.

Clark & Bennie Warren
Michaelston,
11 West Drive, Porthcawl,
Bridgend CF36 3LS

tel	01656 783617
fax	01656 789162
e-mail	clrkbenwar@aol.com
web	www.michaelston.sagenet.co.uk

CARMARTHENSHIRE

CARMARTHENSHIRE

A pure white peacock greets you at this 1708 mansion in the foothills of the Black Mountains. Katy and Carole's work continues on the restoration of both house and beautiful, rambling garden with crumbling dovecote and 25-foot-deep icehouse – you'll forgive the odd unkempt thing. They also produce their own honey, fruit and free-range eggs for breakfast, and informal dinners. Large, simply furnished bedrooms with long country views, an open fire and a baby grand piano in the sitting room. Farmyard doves coo and pot-bellied pigs waffle; wallow in the bucolic sights and sounds of a passing pastoral age. *Six self-catering cottages.*

For 300 years praise has been heaped upon this unique estate overlooking the Towy Valley; Mandinam means 'untouched holy place'. Daniella and Marcus, an artist, are its guardians today: you'll stay as friends and are encouraged to enjoy both garden and house. Stay all day – and Daniella will prepare all your meals. Here are log fires, shutters, rich rugs on wooden floors and, in the woods and fields, wildlife and wild flowers. The twin room in the ancient Coach House has a private terrace and woodburner. As you watch the sun go down before dinner you'll agree this is a magical place.

rooms	3: 1 double, 1 twin/double, both with shower; 1 double sharing bathroom. Self-catering also available.
room price	From £46. Single occ. by arrangement. Self-catering £185-£450 p.w.
meals	Breakfast 8-9.30am. Dinner, 3 courses, from £15.
closed	Very occasionally.
directions	From M4 to Pont Abraham services, 2nd exit marked Ammanford. There, left at 2nd set of lights. After 2 miles, 2nd right after Llandybie sign; house 1 mile up on right.

rooms	3: House: 1 double with private bathroom; 1 single (for same party only); Coach House: 1 twin/double with shower room.
room price	£70. Single £35.
meals	Dinner with wine £15-£25. Lunch or picnic from £7.50. Pub 2.5 miles.
closed	Christmas.
directions	Halfway between Llandeilo and Llandovery on A40, turn off for Llangadog. There, left at Mace foodstore. 50 yds on, right for Myddfai. Past cemetry, 1st right for Llanddeusant. 1.5 miles on, track through woods on left. Signed.

Katy & Carole Jenkins
Glynhir Mansion,
Glynhir Road, Llandybie,
Ammanford,
Carmarthenshire SA18 2TD
tel   01269 850438
fax   01269 851275
e-mail   glynhir@glynhir.demon.co.uk
web   www.theglynhirestate.com

Daniella & Marcus Lampard
Mandinam,
Llangadog,
Carmarthenshire SA19 9LA
tel   01550 777368
e-mail   info@mandinam.co.uk
web   www.mandinam.co.uk

The views to the Black Mountains are breathtaking: "This must be the best view from any bed in the UK," enthused one guest. Generous bedrooms have more than a touch of luxury with lovely deep beds and embroidered sheets. Sue is an interior decorator – and a brilliant cook who uses local lamb, beef and organic veg. Her delicious vegetarian dishes are well worth making a note of. After dinner play a game of billiards or relax in front of a lovely log fire in the sitting room. Aberglasney and the National Botanic Gardens are both nearby.

From the highest point on the Dents' 270 acres you look down the valley to the rushing salmon river and the view takes in long lawns, woodland, bluebell woods, a Norman hill fort and the Towy Valley. The house is Georgian and the flagstones on the ground floor have been lifted to install underfloor heating – it feels luxurious. The drawing room is grand and smart, the dining room has original panelling. Bedrooms are plainer but large, with long windows and lovely views. Big British breakfasts, vegetarian or continental options. *Children over 10 welcome.*

rooms	3: 1 double with bath; 1 twin, 1 single, sharing bathroom (let only to members of same party).
room price	£56. Single occ. £30.
meals	Packed lunch £5. Dinner, 3 courses with wine, £15.
closed	Christmas.
directions	From Llandovery, A40 for Llandeilo. At Llanwrda, right for Lampeter (A482). Out of village, 1st right at large 'To Let' sign. Over bridge & up hill; 1st left. House 1st on right.

rooms	2: 1 twin with shower; 1 twin with bath/shower.
room price	£50. Single occ. £30.
meals	Excellent pubs/restaurants within 2 miles.
closed	Christmas and occasionally.
directions	From Carmarthen A40 east to Pont-ar-gothi. Left before bridge & follow this small lane for approx. 2 miles keeping to the right-hand hedge. House on right. Call for precise details.

Sue & Nick Thompson
Mount Pleasant Farm,
Llanwrda,
Carmarthenshire SA19 8AN

tel 01550 777537
fax 01550 777537
e-mail rivarevival@aol.com

Charlotte & Gerard Dent
Plas Alltyferin,
Pont-ar-gothi, Nantgaredig,
Carmarthenshire SA32 7PF

tel 01267 290662
fax 01267 290662
e-mail dent@alltyferin.fsnet.co.uk

Freddie holds up a standard for B&B – she is dedicated to the comfort of guests without being intrusive. Pilgrims used to stay in this 14th-century chapel high up the River Towy and you'll love the restorative peace. This is a designated SSSI and you can fish on the private stretch of water. Brass beds, chintz, patchwork, terracotta walls and beams and beautifully laid tables for dinner and breakfast. Freddie is planning a new terrace for tea and there will be plants for sale. Her vegetable garden feeds her guests and nearby are Aberglasney and the National Botanic Garden of Wales.

The setting is so deeply rural that this modest Georgian mansion has its own water supply. You can stable your horse, play tennis and revel in 16 acres of beautiful grounds complete with pond and mature woodland; brilliant for bird-watching. Furnishing is traditional; rooms, including bathrooms, are big and light; the oak-floored sitting room has French windows onto the walled garden while the dining room is simpler with separate tables. A hum from the A40 if the wind's from that direction, but this is wonderful value, and 15 minutes from the National Botanic Garden of Wales.

rooms	3 + cottage: 2 doubles, 1 with bath/shower, 1 with shower room; 1 twin with private bathroom. Self-catering cottage for 6.
room price	£60. Single occ. £40. Ask for price.
meals	Breakfast 8-9am. Dinner £25.
closed	Christmas.
directions	B4300 from Carmarthen to Capel Dewi. Leaving village follow sign on left & down drive off main road.

rooms	3: 2 doubles, 1 twin, all with bath/shower.
room price	£45-£55. Single occ. £28-£35.
meals	Dinner, 3 courses, around £18. B.Y.O.
closed	Very occasionally.
directions	From Carmarthen A40 west for 4 miles. Right for Bancyfelin. After 0.5 miles, right into drive on brow of hill.

Fredena Burns
Capel Dewi Uchaf Country House, Capel Dewi Road, Capel Dewi, Carmarthenshire SA32 8AY

tel	01267 290799
fax	01267 290003
e-mail	uchaffarm@aol.com
web	www.walescottageholidays.uk.com

Cynthia & David Fernihough
Sarnau Mansion, Llysonnen Road, Bancyfelin, Carmarthenshire SA33 5DZ

tel	01267 211404
fax	01267 211404
e-mail	fernihough@so1405.force9.co.uk

map: 7 entry: 553

map: 7 entry: 554

CEREDIGION

Carole and Allen, who are devoted to conservation, unfussily draw you into their home, cosy with warm, natural colours in paintings and woollen tapestries; they serve Welsh cakes on your arrival. Their organic farm is Soil Association-registered, so you will eat very well. Plentiful birdlife in their wonderful garden adds an audible welcome to Broniwan: tree-creepers, wrens and redstarts all nest in ivy-covered walls or mature beech trees. Views of the Preseli Hills, and the National Botanic Garden of Wales and Aberglasney to visit.

rooms	2: 1 double with shower room; 1 double with private bathroom.
room price	£50-£54. Single occ. £25-£27.
meals	Breakfast 8-9.30am. Packed lunch from £6. Light supper £11. Dinner £17.
closed	Very occasionally.
directions	From Aberaeron A487 for 6 miles for Brynhoffnant. Left at B4334 to Rhydlewis; left at Post Office & shop, 1st lane on right, then 1st track on right.

Carole & Allen Jacobs
Broniwan,
Rhydlewis, Llandysul,
Ceredigion SA44 5PF

tel	01239 851261
fax	01239 851261
e-mail	broniwan@compuserve.com

map: 7 entry: 555

CONWY

The solid Victorian exterior belies a surprising interior. Patricia, a former restorer, has brought together a fascinating collection of furniture – each piece has a history. Her careful paintwork and use of colour bring light and life to her seaside home. Above you is the Little Orme with stunning views; below, across the main coast road, the sweep of Llandudno Bay. The Marina Room is fresh yellow with a turquoise ceiling and a painted Neptune on the cupboards; all bedrooms – double-glazed and with lovely views – feel special, with crisp white linen and fresh flowers. *Children over 12 welcome.*

rooms	3: 2 doubles, 1 twin, all with bath/shower.
room price	£55-£60. Single occ. £35-£40.
meals	Enjoyable walk to many restaurants.
closed	Mid-December-mid-January.
directions	B5115 Llandudno/Colwyn coast road (sea on left). Pass turn for Bryn Y Bia on right. House on right.

Patricia Richards
Lympley Lodge,
Craigside, Llandudno,
Conwy Ll30 3AL

tel	01492 549304
fax	0870 1383370
e-mail	clive@lympleylodge.co.uk
web	www.lympleylodge.co.uk

map: 12 entry: 556

CONWY

A haven for musicians, walkers and those who love the simple life. Fresh air, birdsong, good conversation and hot scones for breakfast – could you want more? Alan is a pianist who might play after your (excellent) supper; Irish Ger plays the fiddle and the organ. The small bedrooms in this long, low, wonky-floored granite cottage are whitewashed and simple, personalised with cheerful rugs and friends' paintings. The bathroom is overlooked only by sheep – and there's a guests' sitting room with a woodburner. An atmospheric, riverside retreat. *Children over 10 welcome.*

DENBIGHSHIRE

The 15th-century wattle-and-daub house and former cow byre sit in a glorious position. The typical, honey-coloured barn has been sensitively converted for guests, keeping its low sloping ceilings, beams and small windows; you can still see the outlines of the original thick stone walls. The sitting room looks over the Vale of Clwyd and your jolly hosts will drop and collect you from Offa's Dyke walks. Irene runs craft courses – textiles and paper-making, for example: ask for details. Good value. *Self-catering possible. Children over 10 welcome.*

rooms	3: 1 double, 1 twin, 1 single, all sharing bathroom.
room price	£35. Single occ. £17.50.
meals	Packed lunch £4.50. Dinner £10-£12.50. B.Y.O.
closed	November-March.
directions	From A5, B4406 through Penmachno. Left at The Eagles pub. On for 2 miles until 'S' bend sign; cottage on left just before bridge.

rooms	2: 1 double, 1 triple, both with shower.
room price	£40. Single occ. £25.
meals	Packed lunch £3.50. Pub 0.75 miles away.
closed	Very occasionally.
directions	A494 east from Ruthin. Left opp. Griffin Hotel onto B5429. After 0.5 miles, right to Llangynhafal. After 2 miles, Esgairlygain signed on right 100 yds past Plas Draw. House left of courtyard.

Ger Tunstall
Rhyd-y-Grô,
Cwm Penmachno, Betws-y-Coed,
Conwy LL24 0RB

tel	01690 760144
fax	01690 760144
e-mail	afonig@btinternet.com
web	www.afonig.com

Irene Henderson
The Old Barn,
Esgairlygain, Llangynhafal, Ruthin,
Denbighshire LL15 1RT

| tel | 01824 704047 |
| fax | 01824 704047 |

map: 8 entry: 557

map: 8 entry: 558

DENBIGHSHIRE

Welcoming dogs and Welsh air will soothe the weary traveller; so, too, will the mountain and river views and the Harmans who entertain guests without fuss. Rambling, 18th-century, slate-floored, the farm is in the most glorious setting with the River Dee rolling by at the bottom of the valley. Comfortable antique furniture, old beams and simple, good Aga-cooked food. Most vegetables come from the well-tended garden. Guests have two sitting rooms, one upstairs with a lovely view. There is absolutely nothing here to ruffle you.

rooms	3: 1 twin with shower; 1 twin with private bathroom; 1 single sharing bathroom with twin (let only to members of same party).
room price	£46-£50. Single occ. £23-£25.
meals	Breakfast until 9.30am. Packed lunch £3. Supper £11. B.Y.O.. Pub 200 yds.
closed	November-February.
directions	From Shrewsbury, A5, right at lights in Llangollen. Over bridge & left onto A542 for Ruthin. After 1.5 miles onto B5103 to Rhewl. After 2.5 miles farm on left after chapel.

Mary Harman
Dee Farm,
Rhewl, Llangollen,
Denbighshire LL20 7YT

tel	01978 861598
fax	01978 861598
e-mail	harman@deefarm.co.uk

FLINTSHIRE

Church records show that the house was built in Elizabethan times with some later Victorian additions — it is beautiful, surrounded by bluebell woods, and a two-acre terraced garden adds to the magic. Inside, beams everywhere, open fires and lovely views across the valley from every window. The bedding is Egyptian cotton, the duvets are goose down and the towels huge and thick; and there are bathtime goodies. Much of the food is organic and locally-grown and Charmian often adds a Mediterranean touch to her cooking. *Children over eight welcome.*

rooms	2: 1 twin/double, 1 double, both with bath/shower.
room price	£76. Single occ. £55.
meals	Breakfast 8-9.15am. Packed lunch £5. Dinner, 5 courses, £25.
closed	Very occasionally.
directions	From Mold A494 for Ruthin. Past Rainbow Inn & left for Maeshafn. In Maeshafn, past phone box, left fork through woods; follow to end. House on right through gates & courtyard.

Charmian & Ted Spencer
Pentre Cerrig Mawr,
Maeshafn, Nr. Mold,
Flintshire CH7 5LU

tel	01352 810607
fax	01352 810607
e-mail	pentre.cerrig@virgin.net
web	www.pentrecerrigmawr.com

FLINTSHIRE

Climbing the steps to the tower bedrooms you get a real sense of adventure: the age and history permeate your skin as you discover mullioned windows, portraits, antique furniture and big beds. This is the only remaining fortified house on the border and it was built over 500 years ago by the family who occupy it now. The medieval dining hall in the tower displays the coat of arms and the family motto '"without God there is nothing". Breakfast at the library end of the large drawing room. All this, and four acres of formal gardens in which to dream.

FLINTSHIRE

A farmhouse with an Elizabethan panelled drawing room that has been in the family for 500 years. A spring runs beneath the dining room and on a beam above the fireplace is carved *Aelwyd a gymhell* ("a welcoming hearth beckons"). It is a treat to come across a genuine Arts & Crafts interior: good, solid furniture, and not a frill or flounce in sight. Bedrooms have hill views to Offa's Dyke, beds are comfortable, and towels thick. A copper beech rustles in the west wind, and you are six miles from St Asaph with the smallest medieval cathedral in the country.

rooms	3: Tower: 1 double, with bathroom; 1 double with private bathroom. Main house: 1 twin with private bathroom.
room price	£70. Single occ. £50.
meals	Dinner available within 2 miles.
closed	22 December–3 January.
directions	To traffic lights in centre of Mold, turn onto Wrexham road (B5444). After 0.7 miles, fork right into Nercwys. After 0.4 miles, entrance on right, through large black gates.

rooms	2: 1 double, 1 twin, both with shower.
room price	£45–£50. Single occ. £22.50–£25.
meals	Packed lunch £3. Dinner £11.50.
closed	Very occasionally.
directions	From Chester, A55, B5122 left for Caerwys. There, 1st right into High Street. Right at end, on for 0.75 miles to x-roads & left, past camp, straight for 1 mile. House on left, signed.

Charles Wynne-Eyton
Tower,
Nercwys, Mold,
Flintshire CH7 4EW
tel   01352 700220
fax   01352 700220

Mrs Nest Price
Plas Penucha,
Caerwys, Mold,
Flintshire CH7 5BH
tel   01352 720210
fax   01352 720881
e-mail   nest@plaspenucha.freeserve.co.uk
web   www.geocities.com/plaspenucha

map: 8 entry: 561

map: 13 entry: 562

FLINTSHIRE

Pure Elizabethan, magical and intriguing – Golden Grove was built by Sir Edward Morgan in 1580. The Queen Anne dog-leg staircase, oak panelling and furniture are set off beautifully by the rich jewel colour schemes (the breakfast room is red, the dining room a subtle aquamarine). The two Anns are wonderful hosts – they serve breakfast from kitchens at each end of the morning room and the family foursome tend the formal garden, organic vegetable garden and nuttery and run a sheep farm as well as their relaxed B&B. Friendly and worth the trip. *Children over 12 welcome.*

rooms	3: 1 double with bathroom; 1 twin, 1 double, both with private bath & wc.
room price	£76. Single occ. £48.
meals	Breakfast 8-9.30am. Dinner £23.50.
closed	December-January.
directions	Turn off A55 onto A5151 for Prestatyn. At Spar shop before Trelawnyd, right. Branch left immed. over 1st x-roads & right at T-junc. Gates 170 yards on left.

Ann & Mervyn, Ann & Nigel Steele-Mortimer
Golden Grove,
Llanasa, Nr. Holywell,
Flintshire CH8 9NA
tel   01745 854452
fax   01745 854547
e-mail golden.grove@lineone.net

map: 13 entry: 563

GWYNEDD

An immaculate drive leads to the Georgian rectory in three acres of grounds; grand, but not intimidatingly so. The energetic Gabrielle wants guests to relax completely and come and go as they please; she gives you comfortable beds, good linen, luxurious towels and super food and wine. All is harmony and light: seagrass and Persian rugs, big mirrors and family antiques, log fires on chilly evenings, a smart drawing room with paddock views – Gabrielle does dressage and has a horse and pony. So many beaches and mountains to explore, without the traffic and crowds. Guests often book for one night and stay for more.

rooms	4 + cottage: 2 twins, both with bath; 2 doubles, 1 with bath, 1 with shower. Self-catering cottage sleeps 6/7.
room price	£70. Single occ. £40-£50. Cottage £200-£500 p.w.
meals	Breakfast 8-9.30am. Packed lunch £5. Dinner, 3 courses, £22.50. Light supper £17.50.
closed	Christmas.
directions	From Pwllheli, A499 to r'bout. Right onto A497 Nefyn/Boduan road for 3 miles. Left opposite church. House set back, on right.

Gabrielle & Roger Pollard
The Old Rectory,
Boduan, Nr. Pwllheli,
Gwynedd LL53 6DT
tel   01758 721519
fax   01758 721519

map: 7 entry: 564

Trudie's quest for the last word in taste, style and comfort has ended here and bedrooms and bathrooms – with excellent lighting, jumbo towels and organic shampoos – are equally memorable. Edwardian Erw is a fine house that sits in an acre of grounds: gasp as you take in the sea and estuary views. Then take advantage of Trudie's deep knowledge of Snowdonia, enjoy the light, bright atmosphere and her sumptuous organic cookery, and admire the modern art and the way every furnishing has been planned in meticulous detail by a hostess who is larger than life and full of fun. The beaches are glorious.

Watch the waves roll in from your room with the vast four-poster: you feel a million miles from city hustle and bustle. Walkers love Llwyndû; it's warm and earthy, generously simple, with bold colours on ancient stone walls, spiral stone stairways and inglenook fireplaces. Comfy bedrooms are split between the old 16th-century house and the granary. Candlelight and old lamps create their magic in the evening when Peter, a historian turned cook, treats you to casseroled organic Welsh Back beef and other feasts. It's an easy walk down to the beach at Cardigan Bay.

rooms	2 doubles, 1 with shower room, 1 with bath & shower.
room price	£80-£100. Single occ. £65.
meals	Dinner £15-£20.
closed	Very occasionally.
directions	A496 north from Barmouth to Harlech. Through Llanbedr. Past sign to Pensarn station & as road rises, Erw is on left immediately. opposite entrance to Slate Caverns.

rooms	7: 2 doubles, 1 twin, 2 four-posters, 2 family, all with bath/shower.
room price	£64-£76. Single occ. £32-£41.
meals	Packed lunch £4-£5. Dinner, 3 courses, from £17.95.
closed	Christmas Day & Boxing Day.
directions	A496, 2 miles north of Barmouth when street lights stop. Llwyndû signed on right.

Trudie Hunt
Erw,
Llanfair, Harlech,
Gwynedd LL46 2SA
tel 01766 780780
fax 01766 781010

Peter & Paula Thompson
Llwyndû Farmhouse,
Llanaber, Barmouth,
Gwynedd LL42 1RR
tel 01341 280144
fax 01341 281236
e-mail intouch@llwyndu-farmhouse.co.uk
web www.llwyndu-farmhouse.co.uk

map: 7 entry: 565

map: 7 entry: 566

THE LITTLE FOOD BOOK

Whole food, Macrobiotics, Organic food - passion or
fashion? It's a good question. But there is, of course,
far more to food than that, apart from its life-support
role. Food – in the broadest sense of its production,
processing, politics etc - can kill. It can destroy
communities, the environment and hope. It can also
do the opposite.

This little book is written by Craig Sams, founder of
Britain's first macrobiotic shop, Whole Earth Foods
and Green and Black's, famous for its delicious Maya
Gold Organic chocolate. But, more significantly, he is
Chairman of the Soil Association, the UK's main certifier
of organic food and the body responsible for much of
the current interest in organics. He knows his food.

We want to lift the lid off the food industry, much of it
despicable in its cynicism. Much of the food we eat has
more to do with profit than with nutrition and health.
The language used (e.g. 'Farm Fresh' for battery eggs)
can be misleading; the methods used are often
questionable. Contracts between small producers
(such as farmers) and supermarkets are frequently
ignored - if they ever existed. It's a tough – even
brutal - world out there.

We have all been conned into thinking that cheap
food is really cheap. We are, in fact, paying a huge
price in taxes, ill health and a ruined landscape and
environment. And that's just in the UK. The heaviest
price is paid in the developing world. It is, as usual,
the poor who suffer most.

However, there are exciting new developments in the
world of food and we discuss those too. Have you
heard of Slow Food, for example?

It is a fascinating book, a worthy cousin to The Little
Earth Book.

GWYNEDD

The sort of retreat that has city dwellers vowing to leave for the country. There are valleys, mountains and beaches and the pretty terraced garden tumbles down from the house and merges with the scenery. Light-filled bedrooms have long views and there are fresh flowers in each one. There's a guests' sitting room – beamed and warmed by the fire in the inglenook – and you'll be thoroughly spoiled if you decide to eat in. Jane is a professional *Cordon Bleu* chef and uses fresh local produce and home-grown vegetables whenever possible.

rooms	2: 1 double, 1 twin, both with bathroom.
room price	£48-£52. Single occ. negotiable.
meals	Packed lunch from £5. Dinner, 2-4 courses, £13.95-£20.95. B.Y.O.
closed	Very occasionally.
directions	A487 from Machynlleth for Dolgellau. Left onto B4405, through Abergynolwyn. 2nd farmhouse on right after 1 mile.

Mrs J. Howkins
Tan-y-Coed Isaf,
Bryncrug, Tywyn,
Gwynedd LL36 9UP

tel	01654 782639
fax	01654 782639
e-mail	tanhow@supanet.com
web	www.tanycoedisaf.co.uk

map: 8 entry: 567

GWYNEDD

Olwen is the kindest of hosts and will happily drop walkers off at the right spot; or you can catch the steam railway on its way to Bala. This solid, former vicarage has breathtaking views of hills and the lake which lies shimmering below. Olwen loves poetry, people and gardening and has created the cosiest of country homes; waxed pine shutters protect you from the rigours of wind and rain, and bedrooms are bright and modern. One palatial bathroom has pretty stained glass salvaged from a local chapel and there's a sampler detailing the house's owners – from 1318 to Olwen.

rooms	2 + cottage: 1 double with bath; 1 twin with private bathroom. Self-catering cottage for 4.
room price	£48. Single occ. £28. Cottage £150-£390 p.w.
meals	Breakfast 7.30-9.30am. Packed lunch from £3. Pubs/restaurants within 3 miles.
closed	Very occasionally.
directions	On entering Bala on A494, left & drive across head of lake. Right on B4403 to Llangower & cross bridge. Large stone house straight ahead.

Olwen Foreman
Plas Gower,
Llangower, Bala,
Gwynedd LL23 7BY

tel	01678 520431
fax	01678 520431
e-mail	olwen@plasgower.com
web	www.plasgower.com

map: 8 entry: 568

GWYNEDD

Under clear skies there can be few more beautiful views: the long lake and miles of Snowdonia National Park. When not walking, linger on the lawn and over the view, perhaps with a drink as the sun sets beyond the lake. The lawn finishes with a rail before plunging down to the water. All the bedrooms, traditional, modest and big, have the same long views so there's no need to fight over them. Barbara is easy-going and relaxed, willing to give you a key so you can pop in and out... perhaps to the lake to sail, canoe or swim. Bryniau Golau means 'hill of lights', a name given when lime kilns used to glow on the hillside.

rooms	2 doubles, both with bath.
room price	£44-£56. Single occ. £30.
meals	Good bistro & restaurant nearby.
closed	Occasionally.
directions	From Bala B4391 (Ind. Estate). After 1 mile, right on B4403 to Llangower. Pass Bala Lake Hotel; look for sign showing left-hand turn; approx 20 yds after sign; left up hill, over cattle grid. House is 1st on right.

Hugh & Barbara Emsley
Bryniau Golau,
Llangower, Bala,
Gwynedd LL23 7BT
tel   01678 521782
fax   01678 521790
e-mail emsley@bryniau-golau.fsnet.co.uk
web   www.bryniau-golau.fsnet.co.uk

MONMOUTHSHIRE

The approach is majestic and the house, deep in countryside between England and Wales, meets all expectations; the lines of the Welsh longhouse blend beautifully with the Georgian and the Victorian. Surrounded by 140 acres of farmland, with gardens sloping down to a small lake and a stream that meanders through the woodland, there's plenty to explore. Lovely wallpapers and curtains, good linen and antique furniture in the large bedrooms, and you breakfast in an upstairs gallery overlooking that lovely garden. The peace and the seclusion are soothing, and there are a tennis court and a swimming pool, too.

rooms	3: 1 double, 1 twin, 1 family, all with private bathroom.
room price	£70. Single occ: £40.
meals	Dinner £17.50-£20.
closed	December.
directions	Please ask for directions when booking.

Mrs Susan Inkin
Court St Lawrence,
Llangovan, Monmouth,
Monmouthshire NP25 4BT
tel   01291 690279
fax   01291 690279

Rivers rush and castles and Roman ruins stand proud in the magical Usk Valley. In 10 acres of parkland there are rare trees, shady lawns, lofty Wellingtonia, magnificent rhododendrons and a pool. The Countess's home has much to catch the eye: Indian embroidery in carved panels by Flavia's grandmother, sketches by her grandfather (the *Punch* cartoonist) and deep sash windows with seats and lovely views. Bedrooms are large and quiet and the drawing room is Italianate with family portraits. No frills or fussiness, just a timeless, easy elegance that pervades the whole house.

One of very few Grade I-listed buildings in the country – this medieval manor possesses staggeringly ancient beauty. Underfloor heating warms the flagstones, the dining room is lit by candles in Tudor candlesticks and some of the stone window frames retain the original 1600 finger moulding. Bedrooms have dramatic mountain views and there is a fascinating herb and knot garden, plus a yew maze. A truly historic house, and conservation and commitment to the environment are evident everywhere – for example, all the soaps are handmade here to traditional recipes in a medieval still room. *Children over 12 welcome.*

rooms	2: 1 double, 1 twin, both with private bathroom.
room price	£70. Single occ. £35.
meals	Breakfast 8.30-9.30am. Pub 100 yds, restaurant 2 miles.
closed	Christmas & New Year.
directions	On B4233 between Monmouth & Abergavenny. In Llanvapley look for drive with stone gateposts & white railings.

rooms	3: 2 doubles, 1 four-poster, all with bath.
room price	From £80. Single occ. £60.
meals	Excellent pubs and restaurants nearby.
closed	Very occasionally.
directions	From Abergavenny north on A465. 5 miles on, left for Pantygelli. After 0.5 miles, follow signs to B&B Penyclawdd Farm, pass this to buildings at top of track.

	Countess Flavia Stampa Gruss
	Llanvapley Court,
	Llanvapley, Nr. Abergavenny,
	Monmouthshire NP7 8SG
tel	01600 780250
fax	01600 780520

	Julia Horton-McNichol
	Penyclawdd Court,
	Llanfihangel Crucorney,
	Nr. Abergavenny,
	Monmouthshire NP7 7LB
tel	01873 890719
fax	01873 890848
e-mail	pyccourt@hotmail.com
web	www.1stmanorhouse.com

map: 8 entry: 571

map: 8 entry: 572

No wonder this was the Quay Master's house – it has the best views of the Cleddau Estuary. The Wights have decorated boldly, but always with respect for the Georgian interior; in one bathroom there's a ball-and-claw bath and gilt mirror, in others, Philip's fine handmade furniture. The food is memorable – organic and wholesome with a modern twist: their own wild smoked salmon, local fish and much home-grown organic produce. Miles of river footpaths – you may see kingfishers, herons and shell ducks – and a fine inn a minute away. It's fun, vibrant and relaxing and the Wights are brilliant hosts.

An ancient bluebell wood pulsates with colour in the spring; wild flowers of all kinds bloom generously, badgers lumber into the lovely garden to feed. This is an impressive, creeper-clad house, filled with family antiques, candles and crystal; one of the bedrooms has a fine, restored half-tester bed and a giant private bathroom with a big Victorian washstand and wooden floor. There are fluffy bathrobes to envelop you, plus local produce for breakfast with home-made jams and marmalades, fresh fruit and yogurt. The Pembrokeshire coastal path runs through the land.

rooms	3 + cottage: 1 double with shower; 1 four-poster with bath; 1 twin with private bathroom. Self-catering cottage for 4.
room price	£50-£60. Single occ. £35. Cottage from £200 p.w.
meals	Packed lunch from £7.50. Dinner £25.
closed	Christmas.
directions	From A477, right onto A4075. Left at 4x4 garage. House on left after 1.4 miles, just before bridge.

rooms	3: 1 double, 1 twin, both with private bathroom. Further single available for members of the same party.
room price	£50. Single occ. £25-£27.
meals	Packed lunch £5. Pub/restaurant 0.5 miles.
closed	Mid-October-Easter.
directions	B4320 from Pembroke centre for Hundleton. After woods, house 1st on right. House is approx. 1 mile from Pembroke centre.

Philip Wight
Cresswell House,
Cresswell Quay, Nr. Pembroke,
Pembrokeshire SA68 0TE
tel 01646 651435
e-mail phil@cresswellhouse.co.uk
web www.cresswellhouse.co.uk

Mrs Ann Morris
Bowett Farm,
Hundleton, Pembroke,
Pembrokeshire SA71 5QS
tel 01646 683473
fax 01646 683473
e-mail bowett@pembrokeshire.com

PEMBROKESHIRE

PEMBROKESHIRE

A wonderful spot for birdwatchers, fishermen or walkers – the Pembrokeshire Coastal Path runs past the house. Jane and Anthony will give you lifts back from walks and from here it's easy to explore the bird sanctuary islands of Skomer, Skokholm and Ramsey. The setting is breathtaking: you could take your breakfast coffee to the edge of the cliff and still drink it piping hot. Or you could simply admire the views from the sunshiny dining room. The '60s house is formal, traditional, colourful inside and there's *bara brith* and tea on arrival and lots of suggestions for things to do. *Children over eight welcome.*

A country seat in medieval times, this long, white country house has the shingle beaches and clifftop walk s of the Pembrokeshire coast on its doorstep. It is secluded and surrounded by rolling farmland, with horses, peacocks and a croquet lawn. Inside is space without fuss, with antiques and a large orangery which opens onto the walled garden; it is a grand yet modest place. Ben's welcome is wonderfully warm and he can ferry you to or from walks. The air here is so fresh it is a different substance and the sunset views over St Bride's Bay defy all efforts to paint them. *Pets by arrangement.*

rooms	5: 1 twin with conservatory & shower; 1 double, 1 single, both with bath; 1 double, 1 single, both with private bathroom.
room price	£24-£64.
meals	Breakfast 8.30-9.30am. Pubs/restaurants within 1 mile.
closed	November-January.
directions	From Haverfordwest, B4341 for Broad Haven. Right at sea front, then up hill signed Nolton. House 1st on left.

rooms	3: 2 doubles, both with bathroom; 1 twin/double with private bathroom.
room price	£50-£60. Single occ. from £40.
meals	Packed lunch £4. Good pubs & restaurants 1.5-3 miles.
closed	Very occasionally.
directions	B4341 to Broad Haven through Portfield Gate. After 2 miles turn for Timber Hill Holiday Lodges and keep following lodge signs. On right about 0.5 miles after lodges.

Jane & Anthony Main
Lion Rock,
Broad Haven, Haverfordwest,
Pembrokeshire SA62 3JP
tel   01437 781645
fax   01437 781203
e-mail   lion.rock@btinternet.com
web   www.stayatlionrock.co.uk

Ben & Judith Stewart-Thomas
Haroldston Hall,
Portfield Gate, Haverfordwest,
Pembrokeshire SA62 3LZ
tel   01437 781549
e-mail   benjamin@stewart-thomas.fsnet.co.uk
web   www.haroldstonhall.co.uk

map: 7 entry: 575

map: 7 entry: 576

A decanter of port in your room, mints on your pillow: the sort of attention to detail that make a stay here so special. The Swedish-influenced décor echoes the serene west coast light – white floorboards, seagrass matting, pale antiques, original shutters. The Georgian house borders the National Park with its coastal path and all bedrooms have sea views. Hire bikes, play croquet, head off with a picnic (home-made, delicious) to unspoilt beaches. Caroline, a potter, offers tuition in her studio; a further studio for art and craft courses is being planned along with a special garden for guests in wheelchair. A dream of a place.

The guest book is full of praise for the food and the setting. David and Patricia go to great lengths to bring you the freshest, tastiest, most local produce, and there are good wines, too – even Welsh ones, and beer. Britain only has one Coastal National Park and the Old Vicarage is in it; the most challenging section of the path – a stunning bay and great cliffs – is just a mile away. Inland are woodland walks and the Preseli Hills. The Edwardian house, filled with books and family paintings, has an acre of lawned gardens and large bedrooms which drink in the coastal light.

rooms	5: 3 doubles, 2 twins, all with bath/shower.
room price	£60-£85. Single occ. £40-£60.
meals	Packed lunch from £4. Restaurants, pubs and cafe 1.5 miles.
closed	Christmas & very occasionally.
directions	From Fishguard A487. Right at Croesgoch x-roads, 6 miles from St David's. After 1 mile, left at Llanrhian x-roads. House on left, 0.5 miles on.

rooms	3: 2 doubles, 1 twin, all with shower.
room price	£60. Single occ. £40. Special breaks in low season.
meals	Breakfast 8.30-9am. Picnic lunches available. Dinner, 3 courses, £18.
closed	December – February.
directions	From Cardigan bypass for Cardigan at southern r'bout. Left by Eagle Inn to St Dogmaels. Sharp right at end of High Street to Moylegrove. There, 1st left to Glanrhyd, then up hill. House on right, past church.

Caroline Flynn
Trevaccoon,
Llanrhian, St David's,
Haverfordwest,
Pembrokeshire SA62 6DP
tel 01348 831438
fax 01348 831438
e-mail flynn@trevaccoon.co.uk
web www.trevaccoon.co.uk

Patricia & David Phillips
The Old Vicarage,
Moylegrove, Nr. Cardigan,
Pembrokeshire SA43 3BN
tel 01239 881231
fax 0870 1362382
e-mail stay@old-vic.co.uk
web www.old-vic.co.uk

POWYS

POWYS

It's all there: croquet and boules, a piano upon which to tinkle, a jacuzzi for one of the bedrooms, log fires in the sitting rooms and acres of gardens to roam. The Brecon Beacons National Park is close by and there are two huge magnolias, among other ancient trees, to sit and dream under. Inside, all is solid and traditional, rather than informal, and almost luxurious: fitted carpets, antiques and modern furniture, big pelmeted floral curtains and perfect comfort, everything reliable, nothing out of place. It is impressive and terrific value.

Penpont is magnificent in its sweeping grounds on the River Usk and folded into the gentle Brecon Beacons' foothills. It has not a whiff of pretension yet a relaxed stateliness of its own: great one-table dining room, grand oak staircase and an oak-panelled drawing room. Large bedrooms (one with a tapestried wall) have stacks of atmosphere. An early 19th-century conservatory and two Victorian walled gardens are under restoration and a richly imaginative maze is being nurtured. Overflow into tents (£5), show off on the tennis court, fly-fish on the Usk, borrow wellies and just walk – wonderful!

rooms	5: 1 family, 1 twin, both with shower room; 1 master suite, 1 West Wing double, both with bath/shower; 1 twin with jacuzzi.
room price	£54-£70. Single occ. £45-£65.
meals	Packed lunch £3-£5. Dinner £20.
closed	Very occasionally.
directions	From Abergavenny, A40 for Brecon & Crickhowell. Approx. 2 miles on, pass car sales garage on right & 200 yds on, a county sign. Next drive on right with lodge at gate.

rooms	4: 1 double with private shower; 1 twin with bath; 2 family, both with private bathrooms. Self-contained annexe sleeps 14 in 6 bedrooms.
room price	£60-£80. Single occ. by arrangement. Children half price. Cot £5.
meals	Dinner available locally (10 minutes' drive).
closed	Very occasionally.
directions	From Brecon, west on A40 through Llanspyddid. Pass 2nd telephone kiosk on left. Entrance to house on right. (Approx. 4.5 miles from Brecon.)

Mrs Christina Jackson
Glangrwyney Court,
Crickhowell,
Powys NP8 1ES
tel 01873 811288
fax 01873 810317
e-mail glangrwyne@aol.com
web www.walescountryhousebandb.com

Davina & Gavin Hogg
Penpont,
Brecon,
Powys LD3 8EU
tel 01874 636202
e-mail penpont@clara.co.uk
web www.penpont.com

A fascinating, medieval, cruck-built longhouse; it lured the McKays away from the rat race and they've been thankful ever since. Annie and John are knowledgeably restoring this former bishop's summer house to its original state, yet marking it with their distinctive and delightful personalities. Reached by bumpy, private access across farmland, it's utterly quiet. The atmosphere is relaxed, the arrangements flexible. One bedroom has a dramatic half-tester; the other has twin beds with antique patchwork quilts. Chickens, cats, goats, birds. Come once and you'll long to return.

The food is plentiful and truly delicious and the dining room has been created amid corn-milling machinery; B&B guests and campers can eat here together in the evening. The Grade II*-listed watermill has wood, flagstone, terracotta, woodburning stoves, comfortable chairs, simple pine bedrooms and a riverside garden. The bunkhouse and camping facilities in the old cider orchard give the mill an informal mood with a planet-friendly bias. A good base for exploring on foot, horseback, bicycle or canoe – lovers of the outdoors looking for good value will be in heaven.

rooms	3: 1 double, 1 family, both with bath; 1 twin with private shower.
room price	£39–£45. Family room £55. Single occ. from £25.
meals	Dinner £12. B.Y.O.
closed	Christmas.
directions	From Hay-on-Wye, A479 then A470 to Builth Wells. Through Llyswen, past forest on left, down hill. Next left for Trericket Mill, then immediate right & up hill. On right, straight on through gate across track to house.

rooms	3: 1 twin, 1 double, both with continental bath/shower; 1 double with shower.
room price	£44–£50. Single occ. from £32.
meals	Dinner, 3 courses, £12.95. Simple supper £5.75.
closed	Christmas & occasionally.
directions	12 miles north of Brecon on A470. Mill set slightly back from road, on left, between Llyswen & Erwood.

Annie & John McKay
Hafod Y Garreg,
Erwood, Builth Wells,
Powys LD2 3TQ

tel   01982 560400

Alistair & Nicky Legge
Trericket Mill Vegetarian Guesthouse
Erwood, Builth Wells,
Powys LD2 3TQ

tel   01982 560312
fax   01982 560768
e-mail   mail@trericket.co.uk
web   www.trericket.co.uk

map: 8 entry: 581

map: 8 entry: 582

POWYS

There are two donkeys (Coppelia & Ophelia) in the garden, a self-catering cottage and a weeping ash that is over 140 years old. Pistyll Rhaeadr, Wales' highest waterfall, is just up the lane. In this superbly preserved example of neo-Gothic architecture (1861), the hall is dominated by the oak staircase winding to the galleried landing full of pictures, the décor painstakingly restored. Beautiful shower rooms are totally up-to-date and from the bright sunny bedrooms (Sunflower, Orchid and Bluebell) you can see the bracken-gilt Berwyn Mountains. The work on their lovely garden continues.

rooms	3 + cottage: 1 double, 1 twin, 1 family, all with shower room. Self-catering cottage sleeps 2.
room price	£44-£58. Single occ. £27-£34.
meals	Breakfast from 8.30am. Packed lunch on request.
closed	Very occasionally.
directions	12 miles west of Oswestry on B4396. In village, right after HSBC bank into Waterfall Street. 1st large house on right.

Karon & Ken Raines
Bron Heulog,
Waterfall Street,
Llanrhaeadr Y-M Mochnant,
Powys SY10 0JX
tel   01691 780521
e-mail   kraines@enta.net
web   www.kraines.enta.net

map: 8 entry: 583

SWANSEA

Never judge a man by his looks, a building by its roof or a great house by its ability to stand up to a hurricane. Cathedrals have lost spires but nevertheless retain our respect. It seemed churlish to refuse entry to a house that had suffered so much in the storms of the '80s; they had enough troubles without any meanness of spirit on our part and, anyway, it's only the middle that has collapsed. The children won't mind ducking a bit, will they? Such great expanses of authentic tin roof are rare nowadays – noisy and cold but no less rewarding for that.

rooms	All rooms under eaves. Most suitable for short children or small pets.
room price	An hour of effort to push it back up again per night you stay. Bargain!
meals	Taken on the roof terrrace (mind the slope). Army types might like to try frying eggs up there.
closed	Never – but you can try.
directions	From field, pass cherry tree, backflip over fence, leaping on impact to avoid barbed wire reel. The leap should land you on the edge of far side of roof. Slide down to grass at your leisure.

Strut Wanting
The Lean-Too,
Tin Pan Alley, Tin-tagel,
Swansea
tel   01234 567890
e-mail   almost@rightangles.to.us
web   www.topbikeramps.co.uk

map: 7 entry: 584

Photography by Michael Bu

SCOTLAND

"Never take a cross-country trip with
a kid who's just learnt to whistle."

JEAN DEUEL

ABERDEENSHIRE

ABERDEENSHIRE

Great Scottish hospitality from people who care and go the extra mile or 10. Nothing is too much trouble: a superb home-cooked supper, a bottle of wine, delightful conversation and much laughter. Bill gardens and produces much for the table; in summer, they are 95% self-sufficient. Doreen keeps the house spotless and plans culinary feasts for the evening. Bedrooms are delightful, as is the whole house: expect comfy beds, open fires, a baby grand and fine views. Only an hour from Aberdeen airport yet close enough for you to enjoy the little fishing villages of the Moray coast. Exceptional.

Bill and Lois have stripped back the walls of this unusual Gordon castle to their original stone glory, then given the place a 21st-century makeover. Wander around in a world of draped curtains, stripped wooden floors, a faux-leopard skin sofa, lots of tartan, contemporary colours and the odd gilt-framed mirror. The bedrooms are massive and the spiral stone staircase is a 16th-century original. Thirty-five acres of lake, field and walled garden to roam, and the Moray coast to discover: whisky trails, castles, dolphin-spotting, fly-fishing. Fabulous.

rooms	2: 1 double, with shower room; 1 twin with bath.
room price	£55-£60. Single occ. from £30.
meals	Dinner, 3 courses, £20.
closed	Occasionally.
directions	From Keith, A95 for Banff. After 3.5 miles, left signed Grange Church. Left again opposite church.

rooms	5: 2 doubles, 1 four-poster with bath; both with shower room; 1 four-poster, 1 twin, sharing bathroom.
room price	£175. Single occ. £125. Price includes B&B and 5-course dinner with wine.
meals	Dinner, 5 courses, included. Lunch available.
closed	January–February.
directions	On B9023, 0.5 miles south of Cornhill.

Doreen & Bill Blanche
Grange House,
Grange, Keith,
Banffshire AB55 6RY
tel   01542 870206
fax   01542 870206
e-mail   wd.blanche@zetnet.co.uk

Lois & Bill Breckon
Castle of Park,
Cornhill,
Aberdeenshire AB45 2AX
tel   01466 751111
fax   01466 751111
e-mail   booking@castleofpark.net
web   www.castleofpark.net

Veronica's ancestor, William McCrombie, lived here and founded the Aberdeen Angus cattle breed on the farm. The handsome farmhouse has been in the family since 1762 and you can roam in the surrounding 300 acres of rolling hills. Décor is 'traditional country house' with lovely family pieces, hunting prints, Colefax fabrics and Farrow & Ball paints. Guests are treated very much as friends and your *Cordon Bleu*-trained hostess is delightfully easy-going and will set dinner in the dining room or in the Aga-warmed kitchen. On the Aberdeen 'Castle Trail' and totally tranquil.
Fishing and shooting breaks available.

An absolute gem, one of the loveliest places we know. Crystal-clear morning light and views from bedrooms of river, field, forest, hill. Sandpipers and swallows nest, curlew, osprey and lapwing glide. Expect a warm country-house feel and the comfiest beds in Scotland! Your room may be huge – two are – and full of fine furniture, fluffy bathrobes, fresh flowers, maybe even a balcony. Meg picks flowers for your room and her food is delicious; David serves with much good humour. Nearby, golf, hiking, fishing and castles by the hatful. Unmissable.

rooms	3: 1 double, 1 twin, sharing bath/shower; 1 twin with bathroom.
room price	From £60. Single occ. £40.
meals	Dinner, 3 courses, £25.
closed	Occasionally.
directions	20 miles from Aberdeen on A944 (towards Alford); through Tillyfourie, then left for Muir of Fowlis & Tough; after Tough 2nd farm drive on left, signed.

rooms	3: 1 twin/double with bath/shower; 1 twin/double (with balcony & dressing room) with private bath; 1 double with private bath/shower. Extra shower, too.
room price	£70-£80. Single occ. from £35.
meals	Dinner £25. Supper, £15-£18. Local pub/bistro.
closed	Rarely.
directions	From Aboyne, A93 west for Braemar. Just after 50mph sign, left down Rhu-na-Haven Rd. House 400 yds on, 4th gateway on right.

John & Veronica Evans-Freke
Lynturk Home Farm,
Alford,
Aberdeenshire AB33 8DU
tel   01975 562504
fax   01975 563517
e-mail   lynturk@hotmail.com

David & Meg White
Lys-na-Greyne House,
Rhu-na-Haven Road, Aboyne,
Aberdeenshire AB34 5JD
tel   01339 887397
fax   01339 886441
e-mail   dwhite7301@aol.com

ABERDEENSHIRE

At the foot of Glenesk, this 18th-century house has a gorgeous setting. Your hosts are fun; John has a twinkle in his eye and Valerie, lover of Labradors, adores a chat and is charming and kind. Soft sofas, pretty lamps, robes in the bathroom – it's deliciously old-fashioned, stylish and cosy. Family photos sit alongside fine china and prints that hint at John's love of country pursuits. Valerie waves her wand in the kitchen: her fish, meat and game dishes are matched by fine wines (their son is in the trade) served in glasses that sparkle. A delightful place.

rooms	3: 1 twin with shower room; 1 twin with private bathroom; 1 single sharing bathroom if in same party, otherwise private bathroom.
room price	£60. Single occ. £30-£40.
meals	Breakfast until 9.30am. Dinner, 3 courses with wine, £20.
closed	December 14-January 14.
directions	From A90, B966 through Edzell, on towards Fettercairn. House just under 2 miles on, behind a beech hedge; enter 2nd gate on left.

Valerie & John Smart
Woodmyre,
Edzell, Brechin,
Aberdeenshire DD9 7UX
tel   01356 648416
fax   01356 648416
e-mail smart@woodmyre.freeserve.co.uk

map: 23 entry: 589

ARGYLL & BUTE

What views! "The word 'breathtaking' is entirely appropriate," says our inspector. Loch Linnhe is 200 yards away and light floods in; there is wood outside and in, windows everywhere and the walls are white to reflect the sun. The daughter's modern art hangs above a classical marble fireplace in the sitting room. The dining room is open-plan, with a good, simple, long oak table. Bedrooms are done in fresh apple greens, yellows and white with fresh flowers, books and views. The two-acre garden is 100% organic, fertilised by seaweed, the ponies and free-range chickens.

rooms	3: 1 double with shower room; 2 twins sharing bath & shower.
room price	£40-£60. Single occ. by arrangement.
meals	Breakfast until 9.15am. Pub 1 mile.
closed	Christmas & New Year.
directions	From Oban north on A85, then A828. On to village of Duror, then left, for Cuil. On left after 0.5 miles.

Bridget & Hugh Allen
Druimgrianach,
Cuil Bay, Duror,
Argyll & Bute PA38 4DA
tel   01631 740286

map: 21 entry: 590

The road runs out in half a mile, the hills of Glen Creran cradle you, a private loch laps at the end of the garden – this is heaven. Stella and Earle pamper: tea when you arrive, maybe in the garden; delicious food beautifully presented; beds turned down, curtains drawn, bedside lamps on, carafes of water, Roberts radios, hot water bottles, books and flowers…. Nothing is left to chance, everything is a natural response. Absolute peace – and a great place to recharge city-spent batteries. For the more active, Beinn Sguilard is a three-hour climb; the Broadbent young do it before breakfast!

The River Awe roars past the foot of the pretty garden; Robert keeps his rods handy and he can show you where the salmon leap. The 1960s lodge conceals a rich rococo interior of 18th-century style and comfort; a quick tour of his home will net you six busts in the conservatory and an eccentric collection of bric-a-brac. The dining room walls are sponged a pinkish red – very cosy – and a fire crackles on cold nights. Robert entertains easily, turning his gatherings into house parties. Rooms are simply furnished, light and airy and outside the windows are two munros.

rooms	3: 1 twin, 1 double, both with bath; 1 twin with private shower.
room price	£56-£64. Single occ. £28-£32.
meals	Breakfast 8-9am. Dinner, 4 courses, £22.
closed	Very occasionally.
directions	14 miles north of Connel Bridge, 20 miles south of Ballachulish on A828 (Oban/Fort William/Glencoe rd). At north r'bout of new bridge follow Invercreran signs for 2 miles, then straight up glen for 1.5 miles. Cottage on right.

rooms	3; 2 twins/doubles, 1 twin, all with bathroom.
room price	£70. Single occ. by arrangement.
meals	Dinner £25.
closed	Christmas & New Year.
directions	From A85 (Oban road), 23 miles west from Crianlarich. 1.5 miles after Awe Barrage, right signed 'Inverawe Fisheries' just before bridge. House 1st on left after high hedge. If you reach Taynuilt you've travelled 3 miles too far!

Earle & Stella Broadbent
Lochside Cottage,
Fasnacloich, Appin,
Argyll & Bute PA38 4BJ

tel	01631 730216
fax	01631 730216
e-mail	broadbent@lochsidecottage. fsnet.co.uk
web	www.lochsidecottage.fsnet.co.uk

Robert Knight
Bridge of Awe Lodge,
Taynuilt,
Argyll & Bute PA35 1HT

| tel | 01866 822642 |
| fax | 01866 822510 |

map: 21 entry: 591

map: 21 entry: 592

ARGYLL & BUTE

Barbara and Hew are generous, kind people – they run a 400-acre hill farm but find time for real hospitality and delicious food. This includes home baking and local shellfish. The house is elegantly white, the farm definitely working, and the views are stupendous. Wander as you wish and admire; the eye always comes to rest on the water and boats of Loch Craignish and the Sound of Jura. The drawing room is the original 16th-century *bothy* with four-foot-thick walls and log fire. Bedrooms are simple and the downstairs loo doubles as the library.

ARGYLL & BUTE

The view here is stupendous, beyond superlatives, with Mike having dynamited the odd recalcitrant rock in order to open up Loch Crinan and the Western Isles to the eye. Sunsets can be staggering, scarlet skies beyond imagination. And it's not just the view that thrills – Fernfield scoops all the prizes: loveliest house, nicest hosts, finest bath. A friend runs cruises and will take you on magical tours. There's masses to do: castles, Celtic remains, the towpath by the Crinan Canal. The (rare!) horizontal storms are incredible. Don't come for a single night; you'll kick yourself.

rooms	5: 1 double with bathroom & sitting room; 1 suite: 1 double, 2 singles with sitting room & bathroom, let to same party.
room price	£68. Single occ. £34.
meals	Lunch from £10. Dinner £23-£35.
closed	22 December-3 January & 4th week of August.
directions	From A816, B8002 to Ardfern, & through village. 0.75 miles past church, long white house on top of hill on right. Right by Heron's Cottage, up drive to Corranmor.

rooms	3: 1 double with bath; 1 double, 1 single, sharing bathroom (only let to members of same party).
room price	£60-£64. Single occ. £30-£40.
meals	Packed lunch available. Dinner £22.
closed	Christmas & New Year.
directions	From Lochgilphead, A813 for Oban. After 3 miles, B841 west for Crinan. Pass sign to Crinan Harbour and row of cottages. 1st drive on left & fork left between wooden gates.

Hew & Barbara Service
Corranmor House,
Ardfern, By Lochgilphead,
Argyll & Bute PA31 8QN
tel   01852 500609
fax   01852 500609
e-mail   corranmorhouse@aol.com

Michael & Monica Stewart
Fernfield,
Crinan,
Argyll & Bute PA31 8SW
tel   01546 830248
fax   01546 830282
e-mail   fernfield@easynet.co.uk
web   www.fernfield.co.uk

map: 16 entry: 593

map: 16 entry: 594

A 'Wee Free' church used to stand on the site; Rob and Sheila will tell you all about it – history is their delight. This is a delectable place to stay, a 19th-century manse in acres of peaceful woodland garden on the unspoilt Cowal peninsula with the Isle of Bute nearby. Bedrooms have old family pieces and fine views: we liked the twin with the pink French wallpaper, antique brass beds and old desk (complete with writing paper). Your hosts are enormous fun – and very good cooks. The wooden-shuttered, book-lined dining room is an intimate setting for memorable meals. What a treat.

Charm within and without and the Thomsons care for your needs with real ease: you'll quickly feel at home in their unusual, elegant 1930s-style home. The yellow drawing room with an Adam fireplace is smart and large and Felicity, who specialises in Scottish dishes, serves delicious breakfasts at the refectory table in the dark red dining room. Antique furniture, rich, thick curtains, lovely cosy bedrooms – the twin has tartan and thistle motifs – and colour everywhere. A stream runs through the very pretty garden towards 13 acres of woodland and its banks are home to water-loving plants and entertaining ducks.

rooms	3: 1 twin with shower; 1 twin, 1 double, sharing bathroom.
room price	£60. Single occ. £30.
meals	Packed lunch £5. Dinner, 3 courses, £20; 2 courses £15.
closed	Very occasionally.
directions	From Tarbet A83 to Cairndow. Before village, left on A815 to Strachur, then lochside for Dunoon; entrance 75 yds on right signed 'Free Church'. House on brow of hill.

rooms	4: 3 doubles, all with bath/shower; 1 twin with private bathroom.
room price	£90. Single occ. £55.
meals	Excellent pubs, 10-minute drive.
closed	Occasionally.
directions	From Glasgow, A77 for Ayr. Pass Little Chef, left for Underwood & Ladykirk. Left at T-junc., over bridge, past farm on right, down hill and left. Past gates to Underwood House, then immed. left. House signed. At end of lane.

Sheila & Rob Macpherson
The Old Manse,
Strachur,
Argyll & Bute PA27 8DF
tel   01369 860247
e-mail   sheilamacpherson@strachur247.
         freeserve.co.uk

Felicity & Austin Thomson
Nether Underwood,
By Symington, Kilmarnock,
Ayrshire KA1 5NG
tel   01563 830666
fax   01563 830777
e-mail   netherund@aol.com
web   www.netherunderwood.co.uk

AYRSHIRE

W̱ithin and without it is delightful and John and Moira are kind, relaxed and interesting; they have an unfussy manner that makes it easy to relax. The atmospheric drawing room is stately and half-panelled. There are bay windows, oak and oils, and bedrooms are done in fresh colours – blues and whites – with good linen and towels, fine furniture, decorative wash bowls, shutters rather than curtains. It is a fine house, with views to the River Doon flowing past the garden. The sea is only a mile away and Glasgow an hour. *Children over 10 welcome.*

DUMFRIES & GALLOWAY

A̱ comfortable, early-1800s ivy-clad farmhouse, Chlenry stands in its own glen by the Southern Upland Way. Not only are there flowers, fresh fruit, bathrobes and biscuits in your bedroom, but you fall asleep to the sounds of the tumbling burn, retiring pheasants and sheep and the call of the owl. Bathrooms are large with deep old-fashioned tubs and everything that you may have left behind. The dining room is painted deep, warm red – it's flower-filled in summer and firelit in winter. Meals can be simple or elaborate, often with game or fresh salmon. Beautiful gardens to visit nearby.

rooms	2: 1 double with private bath; 1 twin with shower room.
room price	£70. Single occ. £40.
meals	Breakfast until 9.30am. Pub/restaurant 25 yds.
closed	Christmas & New Year.
directions	B7024 into Alloway on south side of Ayr. Follow Burns Heritage Centre signs. House on left, opp. Burns Monument & church.

rooms	2: 1 twin, 1 double, 1 with private bathroom, 1 with shared.
room price	£57. Single occ. £34.
meals	Breakfast until 9.30am. Packed lunch £5. Dinner, 4 courses, £24.50. Supper, 2 courses, £12.50.
closed	Christmas & New Year.
directions	A75 for Stranraer. In Castle Kennedy, right opp. Esso station. Approx. 1.25 miles on, after right bend, right signed Chlenry. Down hill, farmhouse 300 yds on left.

John & Moira Pollok-Morris
Doonbrae,
40 Alloway, Ayr,
Ayrshire KA7 4PQ
tel   01292 442511
fax   01292 442511
e-mail   doonbrae@aol.com

David & Ginny Wolseley Brinton
Chlenry Farmhouse,
Castle Kennedy, Stranraer,
Wigtownshire DG9 8SL
tel   01776 705316
fax   01776 889488
e-mail   wolseleybrinton@aol.com

DUMFRIES & GALLOWAY

DUMFRIES & GALLOWAY

A gorgeous home, run with great charm by Liz and Peter. Chief among its many architectural virtues is the garden room, a spectacular orgy of glass: books and maps, rugs and wall hangings, all the colours of the rainbow. In the dining room ancestors peer down from the walls; in the hall, the art is modern. Georgian windows give country views, there's an open fire in the drawing room, and the odd sloping floor. Bedrooms are just as good, very private (in a different wing). One is huge, with room for a sofa, and an armchair in the bathroom. People who come vow to return.

Sink into the sofas without worrying about creasing them; this is a beautiful, 18th-century, Scottish, Georgian, family home with not a hint of formality. The sociable Dicksons are at ease and so will you be. The sitting and dining rooms connect through a large arch and there are family pictures and rugs on wooden floors. In the bedrooms: a cast-iron bed, excellent furniture, elegant linen and masses of light and good books – this wonderful house gets better and better. There are 200 acres, a dog, cat, donkeys and free-ranging hens, and you can walk, sail or cycle in magnificent countryside.

rooms	2: 1 twin/double with bath/shower; 1 double with bath.
room price	£56. Single occ. £34.
meals	Breakfast 7.30-8.30am. Dinner, 3 courses, £20.
closed	Occasionally.
directions	From Stranraer, A77 for Portpatrick for 1.5 miles. Straight on at A716 for Drummore. Drive on left after approx. 1 mile, at junction with B7077 signed Newton Stewart.

rooms	2: 1 twin with private bathroom; 1 double with bath/shower. Cot etc. available.
room price	£72. Single occ. £36.
meals	Supper may be available, otherwise pub, 3 miles; restaurant, 5 miles.
closed	Christmas.
directions	A75 Dumfries ring road for Stranraer. Approx. 15 miles to Springholm & right to Kirkpatrick Durham. Left at x-roads, after 0.8 miles, up drive on right by white lodge.

Peter & Liz Whitworth
Kildrochet House,
By Stranraer,
Wigtownshire DG9 9BB

tel	01776 820216
fax	01776 820216
e-mail	kildrochet@compuserve.com
web	www.kildrochet.co.uk

Willie & Catriona Dickson
Chipperkyle,
Kirkpatrick Durham, Castle Douglas,
Dumfries & Galloway DG7 3EY

tel	01556 650223
fax	01556 650223
e-mail	dickson@chipperkyle.freeserve.co.uk

map: 17 entry: 599

map: 18 entry: 600

Formal gardens, a small fishing loch, masses of rhododendrons and a large productive vegetable garden within the 20 acres that surround this former Victorian shooting lodge. It is a large, professionally run house – but lots of books, some fine paintings and sculpture, and log fires lit for breakfast demonstrate a personal touch. Christopher is a classic car enthusiast; Mary is an excellent cook, using home produce. Bedrooms are large, bright, and well-furnished, with good rugs and the odd *chaise longue*. A Victorian billiard room with full-size table, too. *Children over 12 welcome.*

Fabulous Knockhill: stunning house, stunning position, a treasure-trove country house full of busts and screens, oils and mirrors, chests and clocks, rugs and fires. Exquisite 'shabby chic' with a lime green drawing room for tea and drinks, floor-to-ceiling windows, and a bohemian feel throughout. Fine stone stairs lead up to country-house bedrooms that are smart yet homely, with great views, loads of books, bathrobes and plush carpets. A grand farming feel, and the Morgans are the easiest of hosts. "These are top people doing B&B in the very best way," says our inspector.

rooms	3 twin/doubles, all with bath/shower.
room price	£62-£66. Single occ. £40.
meals	Breakfast 8.15-9am. Packed lunch from £3.50. Dinner £17.50.
closed	November-Easter.
directions	From Dalbeattie, south-east on B793. House 7 miles down this road on right. Right &, after 30 yds, left through gate posts.

rooms	2 twins, 1 with private bath, 1 with private shower.
room price	£60-£70. Single occ. £30-£35.
meals	Dinner £23. 5 miles to a good pub.
closed	Christmas & New Year.
directions	From M74 junc.19, B725 for Dalton for 1.2 miles. Right at x-roads to Lockerbie, 1 mile on, right at stone lodge. House at top of long drive.

Christopher & Mary Broom-Smith
Auchenskeoch Lodge,
By Dalbeattie,
Dumfries & Galloway DG5 4PG
tel 01387 780277
fax 01387 780277
e-mail brmsmth@aol.com
web www.auchenskeochlodge.com

Yda & Rupert Morgan
Knockhill,
Lockerbie,
Dumfries & Galloway DG11 1AW
tel 01576 300232
fax 01576 300818
e-mail morganbellows@yahoo.co.uk

An old manse at the top of the hill, bang next door to the church, with a 12th-century motte. Views from the garden stretch for miles around. The house is light and airy, with the original varnished pine floors, sweeping stairs and a mellow grandeur throughout. Spotless bedrooms have a simple country elegance, nothing to jar the senses: double-aspect garden views, pretty florals, crisp linen, an old oak dresser, a deep cast-iron bath. Jane loves cooking; you might get pork with plum and sage marinade. Tawny owls in the garden, so music to fall asleep to.

The grandeur may be faded, but this former manse in stunning Border country is holding its own. There's a lovely garden, your own drawing room with old pictures and log fire, comfortable bedrooms and some amazing floral wallpapers. Yours hosts are keen on country sports and, with notice, can arrange hunting or fishing. If you stay for dinner you will have good country food, usually locally raised. This is a smoking household and the bedrooms are only ever let to just you or you and your friends so you can make up your own rules. *Children by arrangement.*

rooms	3: 1 double with private bath; 2 twins, both with bath/shower.
room price	£70–£74. Single occ. from £40.
meals	Dinner £23. B.Y.O.
closed	Very occasionally.
directions	M74 junc. 17 to Lockerbie. B7076 for Johnstonebridge. 1st right after 1.5 miles; after 100 yds left over m'way bridge. After 1 mile, right at T-junc., then 2nd left to church. House next to church.

rooms	3: 2 twins, 1 single sharing private bathroom.
room price	£60. Single occ. £30.
meals	Dinner from £17.50.
closed	Occasionally.
directions	From M74 junc. 20, B722 to Eaglesfield. 2nd left after 350 yds, to Middlebie. House next to church.

Frank & Jane Pearson
Applegarth House,
Lockerbie,
Dumfries & Galloway DG11 1SX
tel 01387 810270
fax 01387 811701
e-mail jane@applegarthtown.demon.co.uk

R. & U. Milne Home
Kirkside of Middlebie,
Lockerbie,
Dumfries & Galloway DG11 3JW
tel 01576 300204

map: 18 entry: 603   map: 18 entry: 604

DUMFRIES & GALLOWAY

An 1800 manse with the village on one side, open country on the other, and the River Esk across the lane. A light and airy home with big rooms, most of which look south to England, two miles away. Drawing room windows frame country views; there are fresh flowers, open fires, rugs on wooden floors and old oils on the walls. Good-sized bedrooms come with crisp linen, patchwork quilts, window seats, maybe a *chaise longue*. Archie and Elisabeth are exceptionally friendly. A three-mile circular walk starts from the door, the local pub does fine food, and Hadrian's Wall beckons.
Children over eight welcome.

rooms	3: 1 double with bath; 1 twin with bath/shower; 1 twin/double with private bath/shower.
room price	£60–£70. Single occ. £30–£35.
meals	Good restaurant 2 minutes' walk.
closed	Occasionally.
directions	M6, junc. 4, then A7 12 miles into Canonbie. Over bridge; immediately right & immediately left into yard.

Elisabeth Findlay
Kirklands,
Church Road, Canonbie,
Dumfries & Galloway DG14 0RA
tel   01387 371769
fax   01387 371784
e-mail   irvineho@aol.com

DUNBARTONSHIRE

Bertie, a navy man, was based in the Falklands for a year; the whole family went, so good tales get told. It also explains the penguins dotted around the 1730s house. Piles of good books in the sitting room, with views out back to the Arrocha Alps rising beyond a hidden Loch Lomond. Bedrooms typically have brass beds, wooden blinds, tartan carpets, pretty pine furniture, fresh flowers, good linen and spotless bathrooms. One room has a distant glimpse of the loch, while triple-glazing assures that the road passes quietly at night. Breakfast? Maybe porridge, kedgeree, oatcakes, bacon, eggs…
Children over 12 welcome.

rooms	3: 2 doubles, 1 twin/double, all with shower room.
room price	£56–£60. Single occ. from £38.
meals	Breakfast 8–9.30am. Dinner, 3 courses, £22.
closed	Christmas & New Year.
directions	A82 north from Glasgow, then A811 east at Alexandria. House signed left 0.75 miles east of Gartocharn.

Bertie & Lizzie Armstrong
The Old School House,
Gartocharn, Loch Lomond,
Dunbartonshire G83 8SB
tel   01389 830373
fax   01389 830373
e-mail   bertiearmstrong@compuserve.com
web   www.the-old-school-house.co.uk

Gwen has lavished a huge amount of time and love on her 1780s Georgian manse — bedrooms are light and airy and hung with generous swathes of fabric; easy chairs have pretty cushions. There are many original features such as fireplaces, arched glass and long, Georgian windows. The sea is two minutes from the house and this is heaven for golfers — there are 18 courses within easy reach. There's also a fascinating sea bird centre close by, and you are only a 30-minute drive from Edinburgh; or regular trains take you to the foot of the castle.

If you fly past in a rush to get to Edinburgh, you're missing a treat: this is a lovely 18th-century family house into which the infectiously vibrant Carina and Jim have poured energy, affection and artistic flair. A comforting hubbub comes from the kitchen — Carina is an excellent cook and you'll be chatting easily before you know it. There's table tennis and snooker and peace for those seeking a country retreat with beaches and traditional pan-tiled villages just a stone's throw away. Bedrooms are well furnished with large, bright and recently decorated bathrooms.

rooms	3: 1 double with shower; 1 twin with private bathroom; 1 four-poster with bath/shower.
room price	£60-£80. Single occ. rate by arrangement.
meals	Restaurants in town.
closed	Christmas & New Year.
directions	From Edinburgh, A1 for Berwick. Left onto A198, follow signs into North Berwick. Right into Station Rd signed 'The Law', to 1st x-roads, left into town centre; house on left behind wall.

rooms	2: 1 double, 1 twin, both with bath/shower.
room price	£70-£90. Single occ. £45.
meals	Lunch from £20. Dinner with wine £25.
closed	20 December-6 January.
directions	From Edinburgh A1 for Berwick-upon-Tweed. Left for East Linton, left under r'way bridge & through village; 0.5 miles on, left for Markle. 1st white house on right.

Gwen & Jake Scott
Glebe House,
Law Road, North Berwick,
East Lothian EH39 4PL

tel   01620 892608
fax   01620 892608
e-mail   j.a.scott@tesco.net

Carina & Jim McGuinness
Markle House,
East Linton,
East Lothian EH40 3EB

tel   01620 860570
fax   01620 860937
e-mail   mcguinness@marklehouse. fsnet.co.uk

EAST LOTHIAN

A Georgian farmhouse surrounded by 350 acres of undulating countryside – and so close to Edinburgh! The farm has won awards for conservation and Michael's commitment to the countryside is wide-ranging. Barbara is a warm and charming hostess. Gardens are informal and pretty, where sometimes pheasants strut; and you may roam on the farm or play tennis. On sunny days, breakfast is served in the lovely conservatory full of climbing geraniums and jasmine. Co-ordinated bedrooms have inspired fabrics and colours, great views and lots of space. The coral drawing room with log fire is particularly striking.

rooms	4: 2 doubles, both with bath/shower; 1 twin with shower room, 1 single with private bathroom.
room price	£50–£60. Single occ. from £25.
meals	Two excellent pubs 1 mile away.
closed	Christmas.
directions	From A1 at Haddington B6368 south for Bolton & Humbie. 2.5 miles on through Bolton, at top of hill, fork left for Eaglescairnie. Entrance 0.5 miles on left.

Barbara Williams
Eaglescairnie Mains,
Gifford, Haddington,
East Lothian EH41 4HN
tel   01620 810491
fax   01620 810491
e-mail   williams.eagles@btinternet.com

map: 18 entry: 609

EDINBURGH

The house is blessed with fine features: a cantilever staircase and cupola, a bow-walled dining room, spiral stairs that lead down to the basement where the guest rooms are. It's a rare find, too – an entire, undivided Georgian house in a lovely terrace (1821) and so close to the city centre. Susie and Andrew have done everything well and the brightly coloured rooms are better kitted out than most poly-starred hotel rooms; the single, however, has no window. But the comfort here comes with a personal touch and with very nice hosts who can give you inside knowledge of this most beautiful of Scottish cities.

rooms	3: 1 double, 1 twin, both with shower room; 1 single with bathroom.
room price	£70–£100.
meals	Breakfast between 8-9am. Huge variety of restaurants close by.
closed	Christmas.
directions	Queensferry Rd out of Edinburgh for Forth Road Bridge. Travel 250 yds along Queensferry St. Before Dean Bridge, bear left.

Andrew & Susie Hamilton
16 Lynedoch Place,
Edinburgh EH3 7PY
tel   0131 225 5507
fax   0131 226 4185
e-mail   susie.lynedoch@btinternet.com

map: 18 entry: 610

EDINBURGH

High on Edinburgh's most exalted Georgian escarpment, this light, bright eyrie mixes 19th-century elegance with Danish and Middle Eastern style. Brass beds, burnished pine floors, a vast hall with a stairway that floats regally above a magnificent sitting room, long views of the Firth of Forth and Fife from the airy twin... Erlend, an award-winning travel writer, creates gourmet feasts at breakfast: oak-smoked salmon, fresh fruits, muffins, home-made Auvergne jam. The Cloustons will meet you from the train, and help you carry your bags up the stairs. It's relaxed, informative, fun.

rooms	2: 1 double with shower room; 1 twin with Victorian bath & shower.
room price	From £95. Single occ. from £70.
meals	Many places within walking distance.
closed	Hardly ever.
directions	Heriot Row is parallel to Princes Street, 3 major blocks north.

Erlend & Hélène Clouston
41 Heriot Row,
Edinburgh EH3 6ES
tel 0131 225 3113
fax 0131 225 3113
e-mail erlendc@lineone.net

map: 18 entry: 611

EDINBURGH

First and foremost it is a home – this Edwardian townhouse certainly feels friendly and easy – but it's big on comfort, too. Barbara goes the extra mile for you: beds are capacious, bathrobes are large and fluffy, curtains and pelmets elaborate, fireplaces are beautifully renovated and there's sherry on the dresser. Barbara is super (so is Poppy, the Cairn terrier!) and you may find it hard to leave. For breakfast, local sausages and bacon, Finnan haddock, kippers or omelette. Regular buses run to the city centre and there are eating places within 10 minutes' walk.

rooms	3: 2 doubles, both with bath/shower; 1 twin/double with shower room.
room price	£75. Single occ. £50.
meals	Many restaurants 10-30 minutes' walk.
closed	Very occasionally.
directions	Leave city bypass at Straiton exit & follow A701 for City Centre until 1st r'bout. Take 2nd exit, Craigmiller Park, then 2nd left, Wilton Road & 2nd right, Granby Road. Free on-street parking.

Barbara Kellett
32 Granby Road,
Edinburgh EH16 5NL
tel 0131 667 9078
fax 0131 668 1051
e-mail barbara.kellett@virgin.net
web www.barbara-kellett.com

map: 18 entry: 612

EDINBURGH

It is a treat to stay in a Victorian Edinburgh townhouse that remains a family home with original fireplaces, cornices and (working) shutters intact. Michele is Australian and a ceramicist – visit her basement studio and enjoy the artistic flair revealed throughout the house and the fascinating collection of antique and modern furniture, art and artefacts collected on her travels. Up the cupola-lit stairs to the guest rooms at the top – we fell for the doubles, with their multi-coloured bedspreads and views to the Pentland Hills. A warm and unintimidatingly stylish city-centre retreat.

rooms	3: 1 double with shower room; 1 double, 1 twin sharing bathroom & separate wc.
room price	£70-£110. Single occ. £45-£60.
meals	Dinner £15-£25.
closed	Very occasionally.
directions	A8 from airport; at Haymarket Terrace, left at lights into Grosvenor St; left into Lansdowne Crescent. Airport bus stops 1 block away. 5-minute walk to Princes St.

Michele Bills
17 Lansdowne Crescent,
Edinburgh EH12 5EH

tel   0131 538 4926
fax   0131 538 4926
e-mail   billsmic@blueyonder.co.uk
web   www.aboutscotland.com/edin/
lansdowne2.html

map: 18 entry: 613

EDINBURGH

The slender glass case, reflected in the gilt mirror, holds just two white lilies, the sea of stripped pine has just one rug. On each soft yellow wall hang just two pictures, such as the two striking charcoal nudes done by their daughter. Big, pure – an aesthetic delight. Breakfast by the white-shuttered window over the gardened square is a lingering pleasure: organic and/or home-made, an imaginative and delicate feast. Sandra is irresistible; John is laconic and interesting. Both are generous with their huge flat. Cars on cobbles are audible, but guests have slept exceptionally well in the antique Georgian brass bed.

rooms	1 double with private bathroom.
room price	£75-£95. Single occ. £50-£55.
meals	Several restaurants within 5-10 minutes.
closed	20-28 December.
directions	In Edinburgh city centre. With castle on left, right off Princes Street for Queen Street (cross 4 streets before crossing Queen Street); left into Heriot Row; last road on right.

Sandra & John Keith
50 India Street,
Edinburgh EH3 6HD

tel   0131 225 3340
e-mail   sandrakeith@brilliantbreakfasts.com
web   www.aboutscotland.com/edin/india

map: 18 entry: 614

Impressive architectural features – cantilevered staircase, marble fireplaces, double-barrelled cupola and soaring ceilings – coupled with Fiona's professional interior design talents make for a luxurious city base. The feel is sumptuous: generous curtains, pretty bedspreads and towels, bathroom goodies that Fiona thoughtfully provides. The chandelier has real candles and the beds are four-poster or canopied. The self-contained flat is equally special, and it's a 10-minute stroll through some of Europe's finest classical architecture to the centre of Edinburgh. *Minimum stay in flat: 3 nights.*

A house of magnificent proportions: a cantilevered staircase with cupola above, lofty ceilings and bedrooms on the expected scale. There are, too, impressive oil paintings, marble mantlepieces, mosaic wall art, elaborate window treatments, antiques and tables set with silver and crystal. You are in New Town, five minutes from the centre, yet rooms at the front overlook acres of private gardens and top-floor rooms at the back have views of the Firth of Forth. Mrs Lloyd is a bright, easy-going hostess and her home one of only 20 complete Georgian houses left in Edinburgh. *Off-street parking available.*

rooms	3 + flat: 2 doubles, 1 single, all with bathroom. Self-catering: 2 doubles in separate flat, both with bath/shower.
room price	£100-£120. Self-catering £100-£150 per night.
meals	Good restaurants 5 minutes' walk.
closed	Christmas Day.
directions	From Edinburgh, Queensferry Road for Forth Road Bridge. 3rd right after Dean Bridge into Dean Park Crescent, then 2nd right into Danube Street.

rooms	9: 1 triple, 1 twin, 3 doubles, 3 twin/doubles, 1 single, all with bath/shower.
room price	£90-£120. Single occ. by arrangement.
meals	Breakfast 8-9am Mon-Fri, 8.30-9.30am Sat-Sun. Restaurants/pubs 2 minutes' walk.
closed	Very occasionally.
directions	Abercromby Place lies parallel to Queen Street, 3 streets north of Princes Street in city centre in 'New Town'. Off-street parking.

Fiona Mitchell-Rose
7 Danube Street,
Edinburgh EH4 1NN
tel 0131 332 2755
fax 0131 343 3648
e-mail seven.danubestreet@virgin.net

Eirlys Lloyd
Abercromby House,
17 Abercromby Place,
Edinburgh EH3 6LB
tel 0131 557 8036
fax 0131 558 3453
e-mail eirlys.lloyd@virgin.net
web www.abercrombyhouse.com

map: 18 entry: 615

map: 18 entry: 616

Catch your breakfast in the river if you will, and Annie will prepare it for you – along with omelettes with fresh herbs, home-made conserves and marmalade: she's a professional cook. Her cosy terraced cottage overlooks the salmon-trout river Esk, and is stylish within. The look is crisp white with dashes of colour: charming. Bedrooms, fresh and airy, are filled with original paintings, fresh flowers, books and magazines; coir carpeting runs throughout. Annie is breezy with a great sense of humour, and there are two gorgeous retrievers to make a fuss of you. *Children over six welcome.*

Vast, high-ceilinged public rooms with a hotchpotch of comfortable furniture, patterned carpeting, artificial flowers and two life-size retrievers that stand sentry by the fireplace! This is a musical household; you may accompany chorister daughter Daisy to performances in St Mary's Cathedral (guests do), or play the grand piano. A superb 19th-century tub adorns the bathroom of the master suite and all the rooms are unfussy and on the expected scale. The house was built on a Roman site and guards a 16th-century secret tunnel; Cromwell plotted his siege of Edinburgh Castle from here.

rooms	2: 1 double with bath/shower; 1 twin with private bathroom (down narrow stairs).
room price	From £40. Single occ. £25.
meals	Breakfast 7-9am. Pubs & restaurants 5-minute drive.
closed	Very occasionally.
directions	From south A1, exit for Musselburgh. Through town & cross bridge. Eskside West 1st left. From Edinburgh, A199 (A1) to Musselburgh bridge. Eskside West on right, just before bridge.

rooms	3: 1 family with bath; 1 double, 1 twin, both with bath.
room price	From £70. Single occ. £40.
meals	Breakfast 8-9am.
closed	Very occasionally.
directions	From Edinburgh, A199 (A1) to Musselburgh. There, follow signs to Inveresk. At top of Inveresk Brae, sharp right into cul-de-sac. 2nd opening on right, opp. gates with GM on them, bear right past cottages to house.

Annie Deacon
53 Eskside West,
Musselburgh,
Edinburgh EH21 6RB
tel   0131 665 2875
e-mail anniedeacon@talk21.com

Alice & John Chute
Inveresk House,
3 Inveresk Village, Musselburgh,
Edinburgh EH21 7UA
tel   0131 665 5855
fax   0131 665 0578
e-mail chute.inveresk@btinternet.com
web   www.btinternet.com/~chute.inveresk

map: 18 entry: 617

map: 18 entry: 618

EDINBURGH

EDINBURGH

Both house and garden are an oasis and American Clarissa has lost none of her enthusiasm for her adopted city. From your own sitting room you look onto pear trees and clematis and, in the distance, the rolling Pentland Hills; snug up in the winter next to the log fire or, in summer, take your morning paper onto the terrace above the south-facing garden. There are books, fresh flowers, interesting art and ceramics and, because you are on an old, quiet street, utter, surprising, peace. One of the bedrooms has a lovely antique American four-poster. Clarissa is involved in the arts and local events and can help plan your day.

Yellow is the keynote here, lending the rooms – including the recently decorated bathroom – a fresh, light, sunny air. Bedrooms, blissfully quiet, come with books and magazines, garden flowers, good linen and pretty china. In the dining room you are treated to the full Scottish breakfast feast, much of it organic; Iola, who is charming, is also a cook, and makes her own bread and jam. There's a peaceful garden with a patio that catches the evening sun: perfect for relaxation after a day of city exploration. The pleasures of Edinburgh lie a bus ride away.

rooms	2: 1 double with bath; 1 double sharing bathroom with owner.
room price	£60-£80. Single occ. £30-£40.
meals	Good restaurants/pubs nearby.
closed	23-29 December.
directions	From centre of Edinburgh, A702 south, for Peebles. Pass Churchill Theatre (on left), to lights. Albert Terrace 1st right after theatre.

rooms	2: 1 twin with private bathroom; 1 double with private shower.
room price	£56-£64. Ask about single occ.
meals	Restaurants within walking distance, more in city centre.
closed	23-28 December.
directions	Enter Edinburgh on A702. 0.5 miles from bypass, fork right down Braid Rd, after pedestrian crossing. House 0.5 miles on left after mini-r'bout. Free on-street parking.

Clarissa Notley
1 Albert Terrace,
Edinburgh EH10 5EA
tel   0131 447 4491
e-mail   canotley@aol.com

Iola & Michael Fass
60 Braid Road,
Morningside,
Edinburgh EH10 6AL
tel   0131 446 9356
fax   0131 447 7367
e-mail   fass@dial.pipex.com
web   www.braidroad.com

map: 18 entry: 619

map: 18 entry: 620

EDINBURGH

Discuss the cultural delights of the city with your friendly, multi-lingual hostess – Gillian is a Blue Badge Guide. Bedrooms (below stairs, looking onto an attractive patio garden) are decorated harmoniously in cerise and cream: Farrow & Ball paints and Nina Campbell fabrics are standard here. Scottish shortbread and books in the bedrooms, local artists' paintings on the walls and from your breakfast table you look onto crocuses, daffodils and cherry blossom. Walk through the Meadows park opposite – from there you can look up to Arthur's Seat. A seductive city base.

FIFE

Borrow a bicycle made for two (or one), take a packed lunch and explore; there are masses of birds and wildlife to spot, or you can wander dreamily amid the glorious profusion of the garden. Rosie, *Cordon Bleu* trained, loves cooking, using produce from her own garden. You eat in the sitting room of this converted 18th-century smithy; it has family paintings, antiques and a real pipe organ. No fear of night starvation, either – in the bedrooms, which have stencilled cornices, there are delicious home-made biscuits.

rooms	2: 1 twin with bath/shower; 1 twin (with single room attached) with bath/shower.
room price	From £65 (from £80 during Edinburgh Festival). Single occ. from £55.
meals	Breakfast until 9am, July-August; flexible rest of the year. Many pubs/restaurants nearby.
closed	22-27 December.
directions	From centre of Edinburgh (West End), Lothian Rd to Tollcross (clock) & Melville Drive. At 2nd major traffic lights, right into Argyle Place & immed. left into Fingal Place.

rooms	2 twins, 1 with shower, 1 with bath/shower.
room price	From £50. Single occ. £30.
meals	Dinner from £15.
closed	Occasionally.
directions	From St Andrews, A917 for Crail. After 4 miles, ignore turning for Boarhills, & continue to small river. Over bridge; house 2nd on left.

Gillian Charlton-Meyrick
2 Fingal Place,
The Meadows,
Edinburgh EH9 1JX

tel	0131 667 4436
fax	0131 667 4436
e-mail	bleish1936@aol.com

Rosie & Keith Birkinshaw
Falside Smiddy,
Boarhills, St Andrews,
Fife KY16 8PT

tel	01334 880479
e-mail	birk@falside.freeserve.co.uk

map: 18 entry: 621

map: 23 entry: 622

An avenue of beech trees patrolled by guinea fowl leads to the house. If the sea views and the salty smack of St Andrew's Bay air don't get you, walk inside and have your senses tickled pink. The double-ended drawing room has two open fires, a grand piano, fine windows and its original pine floor – gorgeous. Great cooking, with maybe crab or pheasant served in the purple dining room; both Sandy and Frippy excel in the kitchen. From the front door head down to the beach, walk the wild coast or jump on a quad in the back field. Exceptional.

Sit on the terrace and listen to numerous songbirds. Surprisingly, you are in the heart of St Andrews, just a 10-minute walk from the Royal and Ancient Golf Club. This tall, terraced house may be grey-stoned and traditional on the outside, but it has been decorated with a contemporary flourish by Jill. Gorgeous mosaic tables and showers, a stunning turquoise kitchen, and a bright conservatory where breakfast can be served. In the bedrooms, antique bedcovers, lovely linen and chintzes. Enchanting. Jill is easy, really friendly and generous. *Children over 12 welcome.*

rooms	3: 1 twin with bath; 1 twin/double with shower; 1 twin/double with private bathroom.
room price	£60–£70. Single occ. from £40.
meals	Dinner £25.
closed	Very occasionally.
directions	From St Andrews, A917 for 2 miles for Crail. Driveway in 1st line of trees on left after St Andrews.

rooms	3: 1 twin, 1 double, both with shower; 1 double with private bathroom.
room price	From £70. Single occ. £42.
meals	Dinner available.
closed	Very occasionally.
directions	Into St Andrews on A917. Past Old Course Hotel. Right at 2nd mini r'bout, left through arch at 2nd mini r'bout. 250 yds on, right into Queens Gardens. Right at T-junc. House on left.

	Sandy & Frippy Fyfe
	Kinkell,
	St Andrews,
	Fife KY16 8PN
tel	01334 472003
fax	01334 475248
e–mail	fyfe@kinkell.com
web	www.kinkell.com

	Jill Hardie
	18 Queen's Terrace,
	St Andrews,
	Fife KY16 9QF
tel	01334 478849
fax	01334 470283
e–mail	jill_hardie@hotmail.com
web	www.aboutscotland.com

map: 23 entry: 623

map: 23 entry: 624

They know the land and its animals, the people and their ways, the geography and the history of their piece of Scotland. Caroline grew up here and Robert, who used to have Les Ambassadeurs, the Park Lane club, has adopted the place as his own; it would be hard to imagine them or their dogs ever leaving. Staying here you will be well cared for yet not fussed over – home-grown veg, home-made bread freshly prepared, extra blankets, torches, wellingtons and rucksacks to borrow. It is one of the homeliest of our houses. *Dogs by arrangement.*

A peaceful, no-smoking home run by Margaret, a professional musician and James, a retired chemical engineer. It is a converted coach house with stables in the beautiful Great Glen that sits among 50 acres of rhododendron, woodland and superb trees in wild lochside grounds. There are lovely views of Loch Lochy and the surrounding mountains from the guest drawing room. Bedrooms are traditional, floral. You can walk to the private shingle beach on the loch – wild roe deer can often be seen. *Children over eight welcome.*

rooms	2 doubles with private bathrooms.
room price	£80. Single occ. £40. 2% credit card charge.
meals	Dinner, 2-4 courses, £14-£25. B.Y.O.
closed	Occasionally.
directions	From Inverness, A9 north. Cross Dornoch bridge. 14 miles on, A839 to Lairg. Cross small bridge in Rogart & sharp right uphill, for St Callan's church. House 1.5 miles on, on right, next to church.

rooms	3: 1 twin with small shower room, 1 twin with bath/shower. Further twin available.
room price	From £50-£52. Single occ. £33-£35.
meals	Breakfast 8.30am. Good restaurants/bistro 2 and 5 miles.
closed	Very occasionally.
directions	From Spean Bridge north on A82. After 5 miles, house signed on left.

	Robert & Caroline Mills
	St Callan's Manse,
	Rogart,
	Sutherland IV28 3XE
tel	01408 641363
fax	01408 641313
e-mail	saintcallan@aol.com
web	www.miltonbankcottages.co.uk

	Margaret & James Cairns
	Invergloy House,
	Spean Bridge,
	Inverness-shire PH34 4DY
tel	01397 712681
fax	01397 712681
e-mail	cairns@invergloy-house.co.uk
web	www.invergloy-house.co.uk

Garramore was one of the Headquarters of Special Operations Executive in World War II. Occasionally, large and aged gentlemen turn up and ask odd questions in strange accents, only to be disarmed by Julia. She runs her home in an easy, slightly irreverent style: throws, rugs, maps, shelves packed with books, and walls stuffed with her mother's exceptional art. Pretty bedrooms come in lilacs, yellows and aquamarines, with tartan woollen blankets on comfy beds. Don't miss the beaches of Morar; when the sun's out you'll think you're in the Caribbean – well, almost!

Staggeringly remote, Skiary is the only surviving house of a 1765 crofting and fishing settlement. A 22-mile roller coaster road ends at Loch Hourn where you decant into a boat, or walk the final mile; no roads lead in and the water laps 20 paces from the front door. No electricity, just oil and paraffin lamps, an open fire, a 'greenhouse' dining room and country cooking to write home about, a swimming hole in the burn, and tame red deer. Stupendous walking either side of the loch (John will ferry you), while snug bedrooms come with wild flowers, fruit, torches and hotties. Incomparable.

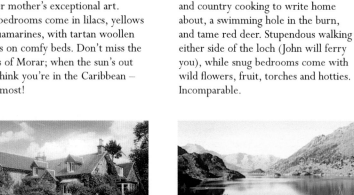

rooms	6: 1 family, 1 double, both with bathroom; 1 twin with private shower; 3 family, sharing separate shower & bathroom.
room price	£40-£56. Single occ. £30.
meals	Dinner, 3 courses, £15-£25, May-Sept; rest of year, supper, £12-£15.
closed	Occasionally.
directions	From Fort William, A830 to Mallaig. Garramore approx. 4 miles past Arisaig & 1 mile before Morar.

rooms	3 twins, all sharing bathroom.
room price	Full-board (B&B, packed lunch & dinner) £160 for two; £80 p.p.
meals	Packed lunch & dinner included. B.Y.O.
closed	Mid-October-mid-March.
directions	From Invergarry, A87 north; left after 5 miles to Kinloch Hourn. On for approx. 22 miles to Kinloch Hourn, at end of road; hosts will meet you with boat.

	Julia & Sophie Moore
	Garramore House,
	South Morar, Nr. Mallaig,
	Inverness-shire PH40 4PD
tel	01687 450268
fax	01687 450268

	John & Christina Everett
	Skiary,
	Loch Hourn, By Invergarry,
	Highland PH35 4HD
tel	01809 511214

HOW TO USE THIS BOOK

sample entry

CORNWALL

Watch the surfers hug the waves, schools of them, all year. Watch the sun, the sand and, it seems, the world. The vastness of the view astonishes. At high tide you are on an island of granite – but not marooned. The bridge, a breathtaking entry, is the only privately owned suspension bridge in the country – but not for those with vertigo. High seas can, spectacularly, wet the house. But all is elegance within: good furniture, deep carpets, family portraits, tradition and luxury with a modern touch. Decking all round for sun bathing, and views to the south, north, east and west. A great escape.

rooms	1 double with private shower room.
room price	£96-£114. Single occ. £48-£57.
meals	Sandwiches & coffee, £5. Excellent pubs/restaurants short walk away.
closed	Very occasionally.
directions	From Treloggen r'bout before Newquay right at Safeways, down hill. Across double r'bout. Left at lights; 1st right Grovesnor Ave. Straight across main road down narrow road, over bridge; 1st left, 1st right down Island Crescent.

Lady Long
The Island,
Newquay,
Cornwall TR7 1EA
tel   01637 879754
e-mail   helen@towanisland.fsnet.co.uk

6
7 map: 1 entry: 53

explanations

❶ rooms
We do not use the words 'en suite'. If a bathroom is 'en suite' we say **with bath** or **with shower**.

If a room is not 'en suite' we say **with private bathroom** or **with shared bathroom**: the former you will have to yourself, the latter may be shared with other guests or family members; both will have a wc, basin and either a bath or a shower.

❷ room price
The price shown is for B&B for two people sharing a room. A price range incorporates room/seasonal differences. We also give single occupancy rates – the amount payable by one person staying in a room for two.

❸ meals
Prices are per person. All meals must be booked in advance. Ask the owner if you may bring your own wine. Some entries say B.Y.O.

❹ closed
When given in months, this means for the whole of the named months and the time in between.

❺ directions
Use as a guide; the owner can give more details.

❻ symbols
see the last page of the book for fuller explanation:

   all children welcome
   wheelchair facilities for one bedroom/bathroom
   step-free access to bathroom/bedroom
   no smoking anywhere
   smoking restrictions exist.
   this house has pets
   pets can sleep in your bedroom
   credit cards accepted
   vegetarians catered for with advance warning
   mostly home-grown/local/organic produce used
   licensed premises
   working farm
   bike
   walk

❼   Map page number; entry number.

A house of windows, an old manse rebuilt in the 1830s to take in the view. And some view: the Five Sisters of Kintail waiting to be scaled six miles distant, and the sea loch sparkling in summer sun; seals, otters, even dolphins, come in. The view is so good they have a painting of it, so if the mist should fall... Big, immaculate bedrooms have Chinese wall hangings, crisp linen and hill views. Bill cooks, maybe sushi or Scottish seafood. Red deer in the garden, eagles and pine martins in the forests and hills. A very spoiling place.

rooms	2 twins/doubles, both with private bathroom.
room price	£68-£76. Single occ. from £46.
meals	Breakfast 8.30-10am. Dinner (not Fridays), 4 courses, from £30. B.Y.O.
closed	November-April. Can open by arrangement.
directions	Down Glenshiel on A87, & left at Shiel Bridge to Letterfearn. Over bridge, & on for 1 mile. Right at next sign for Letterfearn. House 3 miles on left.

Anne Kempthorne
Duich House,
Letterfearn, Glenshiel,
Ross-shire IV40 8HS

tel	01599 555259
fax	01599 555259
e-mail	mail@duichhouse.co.uk
web	www.duichhouse.co.uk

map: 21 entry: 629

A neat, professionally run house that Kate runs with attention to detail and friendliness. Her cooking is good: she places huge importance on presentation and uses whatever is fresh, local and best, and everything, including bread and the cake on your tea tray, is home-made. Bed linens and decor are fully co-ordinated and Kate puts fresh flowers in the rooms and smellies in the bathroom. The whitewashed croft was a blacksmith's until the 50s; the terrace at the back and the conservatory are the places to see the distant An Teallach mountain range; the sea and wonderful beaches are close by.

rooms	3: 1 double with shower; 1 double with bath; 1 double with private shower.
room price	£70-£90. Single occ. £40-£50. Half-board £60-£70 p.p.
meals	Breakfast until 9.30am. Packed lunch £6. Dinner, 4 courses, included (not Sundays).
closed	December-February.
directions	From Inverness on A835 towards Ullapool. Left 12 miles south of Ullapool onto A832 coastal route to Gairloch. 29 miles from this junction, house last on left in Laide.

Kate & Steve Macdonald
The Old Smiddy,
Laide,
Ross-shire IV22 2NB

tel	01445 731425
fax	01445 731696
e-mail	oldsmiddy@aol.com
web	www.oldsmiddy.co.uk

map: 25 entry: 630

|

Yowhave windows for walls in this lovely weatherboard house and stunning views of Loch Broom and the rolling hills beyond. You can scramble around the heather-covered headland, stroll to the private beach and, if you're hardy, swim. Anne is a great cook and she searches out the best local ingredients which she uses in simple, contemporary cooking. The dining room with French windows is connected to a huge sitting room with grand piano, books, CDs, a fire and a hint of the orient. Super bedrooms with rattan furniture, wicker chairs, crisp duvets and great bathrooms.

Joan is lovely, bright and bubbly; she's turned B&B into an art form. Hers is a grand Victorian house, high on the hill with views of Loch Linnhe; whales have been seen from the breakfast table. Bedrooms are tremendous (Jessica Lange stayed while filming *Rob Roy*): a private terrace, a Louis XV walnut bed, crushed velvet window seats, a *chaise longue*, and a marble bathroom with claw-foot bath. Deep greens and reds, decanters of sherry, fresh flowers and an exquisite, carved wood fireplace. Breakfasts are wonderful, so you can stock up, then climb Ben Nevis for the best view in Scotland.

rooms	3: 1 double, 2 twins, all with bath/shower.
room price	£76-£84. Single occ. £58-£62.
meals	Packed lunch from £7.50. Dinner, 4 courses, £28.
closed	Christmas & New Year.
directions	On outskirts of Ullapool from Inverness on A835, left immediately after 4th 40mph sign. Take cattle grid on right & left fork down to house.

rooms	4 doubles, all with bath/shower.
room price	£70-£90. Single occ. £38-£46.
meals	Seafood restaurants 12-minute walk.
closed	Mid-November-Easter.
directions	From Glasgow, A82 to Fort William. There, right up Ashburn Lane, next to Ashburn guesthouse. House on left at top.

	Anne Holloway
	Tanglewood House,
	Ullapool,
	Ross-shire IV26 2TB
tel	01854 612059
fax	01854 612059
e-mail	tanglewoodhouse@ecosse.net
web	www.tanglewoodhouse.co.uk

	Joan & John Campbell
	The Grange,
	Grange Road, Fort William,
	Inverness-shire PH33 6JF
tel	01397 705516
fax	01397 701595
e-mail	jcampbell@grangefortwilliam.com

A stupendous, moated house, in the family since 1780. You get columns, a grand piano, big fireplaces, trophies, a snooker table, massive gilt mirrors, silver candelabras and Elizabeth, who welcomes you in the friendliest way. Beautifully Georgian, the house sits in its own estate; 2.5 lochs to fish, wonderful walks, a boat and 1,000 acres of organically reared cattle. The manor – from the antler-bedecked billiard room to the Italian hand-painted and panelled drawing room to the huge, stately, four-poster room with its bearskin – generates a sense of traditional life lived to the full. Superb.

In the heart of epic Highland countryside, a home much loved by James, Christina and family. They are the third generation to live here and are deeply involved in the local community. The house is comfortable without being imposing, an 1850 original with later add-ons, mostly clad in gleaming white wood. Christina is lively, down-to-earth, a great hostess. Wholesome, whole-hearted hospitality is guaranteed – along with home-produced honey, fruit and veg from the garden. Unexpectedly, three llamas add an exotic touch.

rooms	3: 2 doubles, both with bath/shower; 1 four-poster with shower room.
room price	£70. Single occ. £35.
meals	Dinner, 3 courses, £22.
closed	Occasionally.
directions	From Inverness, A96 for Nairn. After 9.5 miles right on B9090 through Cawdor. B9090 turns left for Nairn, but continue onto B9101. At sign, right up drive.

rooms	2: 1 double (extra single bed), with bath/shower; 1 twin with shower room.
room price	£50. Single occ. £25.
meals	Breakfast until 9.30am. Dinner £15.
closed	Christmas & New Year.
directions	North of Aviemore for 26 miles, left onto B851 for Fort Augustus. Over bridge, through Inverarnie to Farr & past playground on left. House is 2nd gate on left.

Elizabeth & Jamie Mackintosh-Walker
Geddes House,
Nairn,
Highland IV12 5QX
tel   01667 452241
fax   01667 456707
e-mail   elizabeth@geddesonline.co.uk

James & Christina Murray
Farr Mains,
Farr, Inverness,
Inverness-shire IV2 6XB
tel   01808 521205
fax   01808 521466
e-mail   c&tjmurray@farrmains.freeserve.co.uk

map: 22 entry: 633

map: 22 entry: 634

Maureen's gardens (courtyard, heather, woodland, alpine and vegetable) are impressive, particularly given that temperatures fall in mid-winter to minus 17 degrees. An exquisite corner of Scotland, with much to do: bird-watching, hiking, skiing, golf, cycling. Maureen and Paddy have renovated and extended their 1890s stone barn to perfection. A snug sitting room in tartan, a dining room with open fire, and cosy bedrooms with oak bedsteads, pretty fabrics, old pine dressers, lashings of hot water and the morning sun. There's are great Cairngorm views.

Pine martins nested in the hedge recently – rare indeed. This former ferryman's house is small, welcoming, homely, informal, charming and just 50 yards from the River Spey where ospreys and otters fish. Explore the wonderful countryside or relax in the garden with a pot of tea. The sitting room is cosy with a woodburning stove and lots of books (no television). Elizabeth, who lived in the Sudan and is a keen traveller, appreciates delicious food: heathery honeycomb, home-made bread and preserves, herbs from the garden and fresh veg. A superb base for nature lovers. Good value.

rooms	3: 2 doubles, 1 twin, all with bath/shower.
room price	£46-£48. Single occ. £23-£24.
meals	Breakfast 7-9am. Good pubs/restaurants nearby.
closed	November-February.
directions	Leave A9 just past Aviemore for A95. After 4 miles, left opposite junction into village. House 250 yds on left.

rooms	4: 1 double, 1 twin, 2 singles, all sharing 1 bathroom & 2 wcs.
room price	£44. Singles £22.
meals	Packed lunches £5. Dinner £17. B.Y.O.
closed	Occasionally in winter.
directions	From B970 to Boat of Garten, house on left, just before River Spey. From A9, follow main road markings through village, pass golf club & cross river.

Maureen Smyth
Chapelton Steading,
Boat of Garten,
Inverness-shire PH24 3BU
tel   01479 831327
e-mail   chapelton@btinternet.com
web   www.boatofgarten.com/chapelton

Elizabeth Matthews
The Old Ferryman's House,
Boat of Garten,
Inverness-shire PH24 3BY
tel   01479 831370
fax   01479 831370

ISLE OF LEWIS

A cobbled courtyard wall shelters you from blustery winds and, beyond, there's a path to the pebbly Suainboist Sands where, in glorious isolation, you can take in the view to the Butt of Lewis. The modern bedrooms are pinkly squeezed under the eaves, flush with facilities. Downstairs, the sun circles the many-windowed library and its well-stuffed leather suite. John, who was born here, was a motorway cop and now he and Dorothy are Atlantic crofters and run the local post office. "The food is excellent and the people wonderful."

rooms	3: 1 family/double, 2 twins, all with shower room & use of shared bathroom.
room price	From £62-£70. Single occ. £41. Under 4s free, 4s-12s half-price.
meals	Breakfast 8.30am. Dinner £18.
closed	Rarely.
directions	20 miles from Stornoway, on A857 for Port of Ness. House signed left off main road in village, & 0.5 miles on, by sea, on left.

John & Dorothy Russell
Galson Farm,
South Galson,
Isle of Lewis HS2 0SH
tel   01851 850492
fax   01851 850492
e-mail galsonfarm@freeserve.co.uk
web   www.galsonfarm.freeserve.co.uk

map: 24 entry: 637

ISLE OF MULL

Excellent value and marvellous views. Climb up from the rugged coastline of fell and rocky outcrop and watch the sun set over Iona, Coll and Tiree; then turn around and see the heavenly red glow. People sail in just for John's cooking and the cranberry dining room is a welcoming place. The house, warm and simple, is perfect for the setting – the real star of this place. The water is crystal clear, seals – even dolphins or a whale – swim by. Eleanor works in her silversmithing workshop by day; both she and John are free spirits inhabiting a cheerful, cosy and eccentric enclave.

rooms	3: 1 double, 2 twins, sharing 2 bathrooms.
room price	From £33. Single occ. from £16.50.
meals	À la carte dinner in restaurant, from £10.
closed	Rarely. Please check.
directions	4 miles beyond Bunessan on road to Iona ferry, right to Kintra. After 1.5 miles, left down track & through iron gate. Cottage is on shore.

John & Eleanor Wagstaff
Red Bay Cottage,
Deargphort, Fionnphort,
Isle of Mull PA66 6BP
tel   01681 700396

map: 20 entry: 638

ISLE OF RUM

This once-house brings to mind Samuel Johnson's acid remark (about Pepys?): "He's all diary and no entry". But in this case it appears to be all entry and no diary. Heaven knows what this place once was but we thought you'd enjoy the novelty. It is rather like those great blank canvases that masquerade as works of art. The principle is the same: the creativity lies in your own projection, in this case also in your creative 'peopling' (and furnishing) of the house. Pepys would have had no difficulty with that.

rooms	1 'room' only but it stretches out to the horizon & up to the sky.
room price	No worries here; this is priceless freedom.
meals	Barbecues and al fresco eating only.
closed	Never. Nor is it ever open, truth be told.
directions	Follow trench for miles and miles until inadvertently falling into a pronounced dip. Turn around and look for a door.

Gail Blowing
Halfway House,
The Dip, Sunkin Trench, Nr. Kinloch,
Isle of Rum

tel	01234 567890
e-mail	reception@halfwaytonowhere.org
web	www.the-winds-they-do-blow.here

map: 21 entry: 639

ISLE OF SKYE

The sky envelops you; sea, lochs and views surround you. The 300-year-old tacksman's house is hidden down a bluebell-flanked private drive – and with what energy and enthusiasm it has been renovated. Marcus is restoring the 1.5-acre walled garden – it now produces certified organic fruit and vegetables; Linda has created a luxurious retreat. Wrap-around views in your bedroom and sitting room, both bathed in an explosion of golden light at sunset; fresh flowers, bathrobes and a heated floor in the shower room. Popular with honeymooners – but use any excuse to come.

rooms	2: 1 double with shower room; 1 small twin with private bathroom.
room price	From £80. Single occ. £50.
meals	Restaurant 3 miles.
closed	Christmas & New Year.
directions	Cross Skye Bridge; A87 north, through Broadford & Portree. At Borve, A850 (left fork) for Dunvegan. Note Treaslane river & 2.4 miles on, gates & Gate Lodge. House 0.5 miles along drive.

Marcus & Linda Ridsill-Smith
Lyndale House,
Edinbane,
Isle of Skye IV51 9PX

tel	01470 582329
e-mail	linda@lyndale.free-online.co.uk

map: 20 entry: 640

ISLE OF SKYE

Donald looks after the garden, Rosemary cooks fabulously, the loch starts at the end of the garden and the mountains rise beyond. This is Clan MacLeod territory, and MacLeod's Tables, the mountains to the west, are where the chief took the king of Scotland in the 16th century to show him the beauty of Skye. Don't miss the portrait of another ancestor, Colonel Kinnaird, commandant of artillery on St Helena when Napoleon was in exile. They became firm friends… The house is delightful with comfy beds, fine linen, a country-house feel – and tremendously spoiling hosts.

LANARKSHIRE

A 17th-century farmhouse with 1908 restorations and additions and an unusual clapboard extension. The house is imbued with the spirit of the Scottish Arts & Crafts movement: ornate wrought-ironwork and decorative carvings and an amazing 16th-century Florentine ceiling in the drawing room. Great attention to detail here – fruit and flowers in your deeply comfortable rooms, oil lamps on the tables at supper. Bob cooks the freshest ingredients: wild mushrooms, organic hill lamb, garden herbs. Sleep soundly beside the green of the Borders' sheep-farming village, awake to stunning views.

rooms	3: 2 twins/doubles, both with bath/shower; 1 single with private bath/shower.
room price	From £70. Single occ. from £35.
meals	Dinner, 4 courses, £23.
closed	Christmas & New Year.
directions	From Skye Bridge, follow signs for UIG to Sligachan Hotel. Left fork to Dunvegan (22 miles). There, left (just after Health Centre) for Glendale. White house in trees after 0.75 miles.

rooms	5: 2 doubles, 2 twin/doubles, 1 twin, all with bath/shower.
room price	£80. Single occ. £50.
meals	Breakfast 8-9.30am. Dinner £25.
closed	Christmas, January & February.
directions	From Biggar, A702 for Edinburgh. Just outside Biggar, right on A72 for Skirling. Big wooden house on right opp. village green.

Donald & Rosemary MacLeod
Kinlochfollart,
By Dunvegan,
Isle of Skye IV55 8WQ
tel 01470 521470
fax 01470 521740
e-mail klfskye@tiscali.co.uk

Bob & Isobel Hunter
Skirling House,
Skirling, By Biggar,
Lanarkshire ML12 6HD
tel 01899 860274
fax 01899 860255
e-mail enquiry@skirlinghouse.com
web www.skirlinghouse.com

This is the grand home of an illustrious family: Macleans have lived here since 1862, the carpet in the hall is clan tartan, and the solid oak stair is hung with oils, standards and the odd ceremonial sword. John farms 500 acres, Veronica runs a play school and cooks sublimely. You breakfast in the conservatory/kitchen overlooking the walled garden, and feast at night in an immensely smart dining room. A fire crackles in the drawing room, and country-house bedrooms wait upstairs, one decorated eccentrically in electric pink. Peace and quiet surround you, interrupted only by the odd call of the guinea fowl.

rooms	3: 1 twin with bath; 1 twin with private bath & shower; 1 single with private bath.
room price	£60-£70. Single occ. from £30.
meals	Dinner, 3 courses, £20.
closed	Very occasionally.
directions	From Elgin, A96 west for Forres & Inverness. After 2.5 miles, right onto B9013 for Burghead. After 1 mile, signed right at crossroads. Continue to sign 'Westfield House'.

John & Veronica Maclean
Westfield House,
Nr. Elgin,
Moray IV30 8XL
tel   01343 547308
fax   01343 551340

The Meiklejohn coat of arms flies from the flag pole, a mere apple's throw from the orchard in which King Malcolm was murdered 1,000 years ago. This is a small country mansion built in 1776, its huge rooms crammed with beautiful things. A grand double-aspect drawing room, a flower-filled dining room and enormous bedrooms with sofas at the foot of four-posters. Blervie is "a restoration in progress", but much has been accomplished. There are original doors and shutters, antiques, antlers, violins; the stone stairs came from Blervie Castle, the sweet smell of burnt beech from the grand marble fireplaces. Magical.

rooms	2: 1 four-poster with single bed & private bathroom; 1 four-poster with bath.
room price	£60. Single occ. £30.
meals	Breakfast until 9.30am. Dinner, 4 courses, £22.
closed	Christmas & New Year.
directions	From A96 to Forres. South at clocktower, straight across at r'bout & take B9010. Pass hospital & 1 mile on, left at Mains of Blervie sign. Right at farm.

Paddy & Fiona Meiklejohn
Blervie,
By Forres,
Moray IV36 2RH
tel   01309 672358
fax   01309 672358
e-mail   meiklejohn@btinternet.com

PERTH & KINROSS

PERTH & KINROSS

An 18th-century farm building halfway up a mountain: Lindsay has carried out award-winning renovation and is now working on the garden. Inside: patchwork bedspreads, blue-and-white Portuguese tiles, seagrass matting and a woodburning stove. You have your own kitchen, dining and sitting room, so you can self-cater (min. three days, and by arrangement) if you prefer. Lindsay is charming and loves nurturing her garden, her pets and her guests. Sit on the patio as you tuck into her fruitcake, gaze at snow-capped mountain-to-loch views. The sunsets and walks are fabulous. *Children over eight welcome.*

Ancient, historic and packed with interest, the house was begun as a tower in 1585 and added to until Victorian times and into the present century. Inside, it is delightfully old-fashioned, even a little threadbare in places but so much to compensate: beautiful plasterwork, marble busts, antiques, impressive staircase, open fires. Paul is a conservationist and writer and both he and Louise welcome with grace and humour and are generous in a naturally spontaneous way. You can roam freely on the estate with its parkland, woods and heather moorland.

rooms	2: 1 double, 1 twin, sharing private bathroom & sitting room.
room price	£56. Single occ. £40.
meals	Dinner, 3 courses, with wine, £20. Inn 0.75 miles.
closed	Christmas & New Year.
directions	From A9 north of Pitlochry, take Killiecrankie turning. Left onto B8019 for Tummel Bridge & Kinloch Rannoch for 8 miles to Loch Tummel Inn. House up forestry track on right, 0.75 miles on.

rooms	3: 1 double with shared bathroom; 1 four-poster with private bathroom; further single available.
room price	£60-£70. Single occ. £30-£35.
meals	Dinner £15-£20.
closed	Christmas & New Year.
directions	From Blairgowrie, A926 to Kirriemuir. After 5 miles, left to Alyth. Through town on Airlie St. After 2.5 miles, round sharp left bend. Right into drive.

Lindsay Morison
Grenich Steading,
Strathtummel, Pitlochry,
Perth & Kinross PH16 5RT

tel   01882 634332

Paul & Louise Ramsay
Bamff House,
Alyth, Blairgowrie,
Perth & Kinross PH11 8LF

tel   01828 632992
fax   01828 632992
e-mail   louiseramsay@bamff.demon.co.uk
web   www.bamff.co.uk

The view from the circular balcony that rings the drawing room is simply stunning and the deep gorge provides fabulous walks. Nicky and Lachie battle to keep up with the demands of the vast, impressive home which has been in the family for five centuries and you, too, will forgive it any mustiness or dustiness. Staying here is a memorable experience – nothing contrived, sterile or luxurious, but so much drama and intrigue that it could be a film set. Breakfast is served in the 18th-century library and you can use the Regency drawing room.

Historic, traditional, a country house set in lovely gardens and run by delightful people. The bedrooms are big, utterly charming and among the most comfortable that we have stayed in. There's a 170-acre private loch where birds can be watched and pike fished; a great organ halfway up the main stairs with air pumped from a separate building in the grounds; a 16th-century central building with wings added in 1780 to a design filched from Adam. So *much* of interest. Elegant furniture, lovely pictures and excellent bathrooms. *Children over 12 welcome.*

rooms	2: 1 four-poster with bathroom; 1 twin with extra single & private bathroom.
room price	£70. Single occ. £35.
meals	Breakfast 8-9am. Restaurant 3 miles, pub 6 miles.
closed	Christmas & New Year.
directions	From Blairgowrie, A93 for Braemar for 2 miles. Just before end of 30mph limit, sharp right-hand bend, with drive on right. Follow drive for 1 mile.

rooms	3: 1 twin, 1 double, 1 with bathroom, 1 with bath/shower; twin available for children sharing parents' bathroom.
room price	£70-£80. Single occ. from £40.
meals	Pubs/restaurants 2 miles.
closed	Christmas & New Year.
directions	From Blairgowrie, onto A923 for Dunkeld. Look for sign saying 'Kinloch. Drive safely'. 1st entrance on left after sign.

Nicky & Lachie Rattray
Craighall Castle,
Blairgowrie,
Perth & Kinross PH10 7JB
tel   01250 874749
fax   01250 874749
e-mail   lrattray@calinet.co.uk

Kenneth & Nicolette Lumsden
Marlee House,
Kinloch, Blairgowrie,
Perth & Kinross PH10 6SD
tel   01250 884216

map: 22 entry: 647

map: 22 entry: 648

PERTH & KINROSS

Anne clearly has the Midas touch: a traditional Scottish farmhouse outside and, inside, a rainbow of colour and light. Light wooden floors and heapfuls of flowers, a conservatory/dining room overlooking a wonderful garden, and a gate leading out to the hills – the Coronation Way runs through the farm. Big bedrooms are delightful: coral walls, crisp linen, spoiling bathrooms, old rugs, masses of space, windows framing country views. Don't miss Anne's food; it, too, is exceptional. Guests love it here, and even though the A90 (a half mile away) can be busy by day, it passes quietly at night.
Children over 12 welcome.

rooms	3: 1 double with bath/shower; 2 twins, 1 with bath, 1 with shower.
room price	£60-£70. Single occ. from £40.
meals	Dinner £25.
closed	Occasionally.
directions	From A90 Perth to Dundee rd, take Kinfauns exit (not Kinfauns Castle). Drive up hill for 0.25 miles, left, & straight up hill to gates on left.

Anne & David MacLehose
Over Kinfauns,
Perth,
Perth & Kinross PH2 7LD
tel   01738 860538
fax   01738 860803
e-mail b&b@overkinfauns.co.uk
web   www.overkinfauns.co.uk

PERTH & KINROSS

Expensive, but worth it. Here is huge comfort; generously furnished, elegant bedrooms and bathrooms to expand in, beautiful food; you will be spoiled. The approach sets the scene – a mile-long drive through wood and rhododendron leads to formal gardens, exotic trees, ferny burn and waterfall. It is a surprising house (built in 1969) and the third to be built on this historic site; you can see the remains of earlier castles. The interior is magnificent, and your hosts are great fun.
Children over 12 welcome.

rooms	4: 2 twins/doubles, both with bath/shower; 2 twins/doubles, both with bath.
room price	From £140. Single occ. from £85.
meals	Breakfast 8-9.30am. Dinner, 3 courses, £30.
closed	Christmas & New Year.
directions	From M90 Broxden r'bout, A93 for Perth for 1 mile, then sharp right onto B9112 for Dunning. After 2.7 miles, wrought-iron gates on right.

Derek & Angela Straker
Dupplin Castle,
By Aberdalgie, Perth,
Perth & Kinross PH2 0PY
tel   01738 623224
fax   01738 444140
e-mail dupplin@netcomuk.co.uk
web   www.dupplin.co.uk

A lovely Georgian manse tragically burnt down in 1996 but rebuilt with great taste, elegance and style. Light wood predominates and rooms are warm with cornicing, thick carpets, combed ceilings, traditional bedding and lots of space. Joanna and Duncan clearly enjoy doing B&B and the atmosphere is relaxed and informal. Eat in the wonderful country kitchen or in the conservatory overlooking a pretty walled garden with colourful borders. Under five miles from the motorway and 35 from Edinburgh.

It is a delight: now lovingly restored and seamlessly extended, the once-derelict farmhouse has comfortable cottagey bedrooms, pristine shower rooms and an elegant drawing room with a little tower built especially to take in the view that sweeps down the valley to the 'links' of the Forth. Ebullient and enthusiastic hosts – ask Hamish about all things Scottish and try Frances's fragrant jams and jellies. There are books, pictures and family antiques, but a Winnie the Pooh weathervane says it all: this is a fun place to stay. *Children and dogs by arrangement.*

rooms	2: 1 twin with bath/shower; 1 twin with private bathroom.	
room price	£60-£64. Single occ. £30-£32.	
meals	Dinner from £20.	
closed	Christmas & New Year.	
directions	From Edinburgh, cross Forth Road Bridge. Follow M90 to junc. 8. Through Glenfarg, then 1st right, for Arngask. 1st house on right. From north leave M90 at junc. 9 for Glenfarg, then left to Arngask after approx. 6 miles.	

rooms	2: 1 twin, 1 double, both with private shower room.
room price	From £50. Single occ. from £25.
meals	Breakfast 7.30 onwards. Light supper available. Good pub 1 mile.
closed	Very occasionally.
directions	From M90, junc. 6, then A977 to Kincardine Bridge. 1 mile after The Crook of Devon, right to Rumbling Bridge & Crieff (A823). 1 mile on, house signed to right; at end of lane.

Joanna & Duncan Cameron
The Old Manse,
Arngask, Glenfarg,
Perth & Kinross PH2 9QA
tel 01577 830394
fax 01577 830394

Frances & Hamish Lindsay
Caplawhead,
Rumbling Bridge,
By Yetts o' Muckhart, Nr Kinross,
Perth & Kinross KY13 0QD
tel 01259 781556
e-mail hamish-frances@caplawhead.freeserve.co.uk

A grand old country pile set in 200 acres, with its own river in which you may spot the odd commuting salmon. In the house, massive rooms, elegantly proportioned, one with an exceptional 1750s plaster-moulded ceiling. Long shuttered windows give big views across the lawn to an ancient plane tree; its much older sibling blew down in 1868 and was turned into furniture, some of which fills the hall. Bedrooms have old rugs, long curtains, beautiful furniture – just what you'd hope for. Chopin dedicated two nocturnes to Jane Stirling, a former daughter of the house, and probably played here.

The fine, organic garden gives fruit, the river yields salmon, the moors provide game in winter. Likeable and energetic, the Grahams are an exceptionally welcoming family and their house combines informality and luxury in peaceful, rural, central Scotland. There are gigantic beds and generous, sunny bathrooms. Colin, a piper, is a tour guide (juggling a mere three languages) while Fiona is a wine buff and talented cook (shortbread and ice-cream, jam and bread are home-made). Dinners are served in the conservatory with views to a floodlit Stirling Castle. You are 30 minutes from Gleneagles and Loch Lomond.

rooms	2 twins, both with bath/shower.
room price	£76. Single occ. from £48.
meals	Dinner £25.
closed	Very occasionally.
directions	From junc. 11 of M9, B8033 for Dunblane. Get in right hand lane & take 1st right across reservation to lodge. Keep on drive, over bridge, up hill to house.

rooms	2: 1 double, 1 twin/double, both with bath/shower.
room price	£76-£80. Single occ. £53-£55.
meals	Breakfast 8.30-9am. Dinner £25.
closed	Christmas.
directions	From M9, north, junc. 10 onto A84 for Doune. After 5 miles, left on B826 for Thornhill. Drive on left after 2.2 miles, right off farm drive.

Sue & Patrick Stirling-Aird
Kippenross,
Dunblane,
Perth & Kinross FK15 0LQ

tel	01786 824048
fax	01786 824482
e-mail	kippenross@hotmail.com

Fiona & Colin Graham
Mackeanston House,
Doune, Trossachs,
Perth & Kinross FK16 6AX

tel	01786 850213
fax	01786 850414
e-mail	mackeanstonhouse@ btopenworld.com

map: 18 entry: 653

map: 17 entry: 654

RENFREWSHIRE

RENFREWSHIRE

You'd hardly believe that you are 30 minutes from Glasgow. The hamlet used to house the furniture-makers of nearby Beith; each cottage is whitewashed and immaculate and there's absolute peace. Aileen loves her 1800s mini-manor and sharing the house and the garden; she's a Blue Badge guide and full of original travel ideas. The bedroom is under the eaves with chintz poppy curtains and bedspread and views: garden and fields one way, Loch Winnoch the other. Magazines and flowers, conservatory and drawing room, orchards and fields – a special retreat.

Culture seekers, sailors, walkers and cyclists will all be happy here. After such activity, the Andersons' substantial Victorian farmhouse is the ideal place for gentle and cosseting recovery. Large, light bedrooms sport traditional furniture and modern paintings; a warm red sitting room has a wood-burning stove and a huge view over Barr Loch and the Renfrewshire Hills. Linger over a 'Slow Food' dinner of home-grown Jacob lamb or Highland beef with vegetables, salad and herbs from the elegant two-acre garden.

rooms	1 double with bath/shower; child's bed available.	rooms	3: 1 double/family, 1 twin, 1 double, all with shower room.
room price	£60. Single occ. £30. Children £20.	room price	£60-£70. Single occ. from £45.
meals	4 good pubs within 1-2 miles.	meals	Breakfast 7-9am. Packed lunch £7. Dinner £25.
closed	Christmas & New Year.	closed	Very occasionally.
directions	Glasgow-Irvine, A737, bypass village of Howwood, sign on left to riding stables & B&B. Follow road through stables & farm. Signed, 2nd on left.	directions	From Glasgow, M8 west to junc. 28a, A737 to Irvine. After 7 miles, right on A760 to Largs. 2 miles past Lochwinnoch under r'way bridge, 600 yds on left. Brown tourist signs.

Aileen Biggart
Glenshian,
Newton-of-Beltrees,
By Loch Winnoch,
Renfrewshire PA12 4JL
tel   01505 842823
fax   01505 842823
e-mail   sambiggart@aol.com

Janet Anderson
East Lochhead,
Largs Road, Lochwinnoch,
Renfrewshire PA12 4DX
tel   01505 842610
fax   01505 842610
e-mail   eastlochhead@aol.com
web   www.eastlochhead.co.uk

map: 17 entry: 655
map: 17 entry: 656

SCOTTISH BORDERS

Early Victorian and creeper-clad –
the Taylors moved to this old manse
after they retired from farming. The
rooms are large and bright, there is
a fine cantilever staircase up from the
hall, and the dining room's long
windows frame rural views. The big
bedrooms, with shutters and long
curtains, are large and comfortable, the
bathrooms smart. The colourful walled
garden, full of clematis, honeysuckle
and roses, hides a small vegetable
garden, orchard and ornamental pond.
Beyond, fields rise and there is deep
rural seclusion. Genuinely nice people
and good, easy conversation.
Children over 12 welcome.

rooms	2: 1 double, 1 twin/double, both with private bathroom.
room price	From £50. Single occ. from £28.
meals	Dinner from £15.
closed	Christmas & New Year.
directions	From A1 for Duns on B6438 for 5.5 miles. Left at Bonkyl church sign. On for 0.25 miles to church; house 2nd right through black gate.

Libby & Martin Taylor
Kirkside House,
Bonkyl, Nr. Duns,
Berwickshire TD11 3RJ
tel   01361 884340
fax   01361 882273
e-mail e.r.taylor@amserve.net

map: 19 entry: 657

SCOTTISH BORDERS

Lucy's cooking is mouthwatering:
kedgeree and waffles for breakfast,
Cordon Bleu dishes by night, delightfully
served in an elegant, ruby-red dining
room. A sense of solidity pervades this
wide-corridored, high-ceilinged
Victorian home, run by the charmingly
down-to-earth Forrest family who've
been here for years. Bedrooms are
comfortable and full of lovely extras
like fresh flowers, candles and, in one,
an ancient teddy holding the bottled
water. And there's so much to do:
tennis in the garden, golf nearby,
fishing, moorland walks and Edinburgh
less than an hour away.

rooms	3: 1 double, 1 twin, sharing private bathroom; 1 double with extra single bed, with bath/shower.
room price	From £55. Single occ. by arrangement.
meals	Dinner from £15. B.Y.O wine.
closed	Very occasionally.
directions	From A1 north of Berwick, turn off at Grantshouse; A6112 to Duns for 6 miles to village of Preston. House on right, just after sharp bend into village (B&B sign).

Mrs Lucy Forrest
Preston Farmhouse,
Preston Farm, Preston Duns,
Berwickshire TD11 3TQ
tel   01361 882826
fax   01361 882066
e-mail lucy@forrest4.freeserve.co.uk
web   www.forrest-preston.co.uk

map: 19 entry: 658

SCOTTISH BORDERS

SCOTTISH BORDERS

A magical house: a Virginia creeper-clad residence with a turret and a tower in seven acres with views of the Cheviot Hills. But there's no standing on ceremony here – this is a friendly and comfortable place to be and Francis and Elizabeth give a warm welcome. Francis teaches computing so your stay could include a lesson or two. Pastel bedrooms have quilted twin beds, smart dressing-tables and the occasional Scottish touch such as tartan curtains. Walkers and anglers are well catered for – there is a drying room and you can start your day with a full Scottish breakfast to include delicious free-range duck and chicken eggs.

A wonderfully peaceful place in the rolling hills of the Scottish Borders, ideal for families or walkers who want to feel at one with nature. This is an organic farm producing milk from British Friesians and meat and wool from Scottish Mule ewes: a real back-to-nature approach. Simple bedrooms are in traditional farmhouse style; all the nooks and crannies you'd expect to find in a 1700s house, but with rooms brightened by big windows. From the family room you can see the old Border keeps and a spider web of stone walls. Sheila and Martyn have detailed maps with walking routes and points of interest highlighted.

rooms	3 twins, all with private bathroom.
room price	£60. Single occ. £35.
meals	Packed lunch available. Dinner, 3 courses, £22.
closed	Christmas & New Year.
directions	From Coldstream, take Guards Road next to Esso garage for 3 miles until sign on left; drive opposite.

rooms	2: 1 double with shower; 1 family with private bathroom.
room price	£46. Single occ. £28. Family room £55.
meals	Breakfast usually 8.30am. Packed lunch from £4. Dinner from £12.
closed	Very occasionally.
directions	North from Galashiels, A7 past Torwoodlea golf course & right to Langshaw. After 2 miles, right at T-junc., then left at Earlston sign in Langshaw. House is white, in trees, signed at farm road.

Elizabeth & Francis Gradidge
Ruthven House,
Coldstream,
Berwickshire TD12 4JU

tel	01890 840771
fax	01890 840680
e-mail	gradidge@gradidge.worldonline.co.uk
web	www.bordersovernight.co.uk

Sheila & Martyn Bergius
Over Langshaw Farm,
Galashiels,
Selkirkshire TD1 2PE

tel	01896 860244
fax	01896 860244
e-mail	bergius@overlangshaw.fsnet.co.uk
web	www.organicholidays.com

map: 19 entry: 659

map: 18 entry: 660

SCOTTISH BORDERS

SCOTTISH BORDERS

The south-facing front bedrooms have the views – be captivated by the tranquil, rolling Borders at their most romantically beautiful. The house is part 18th-century and dark heavy furniture adds a solid Victorian feel. Bedspreads are patterned, walls pale pink and beige; there's a big log fire in the sitting room to cheer you on chilly days. Johan will tell you all about the best castles and keeps, gardens, walks and rivers, but don't dash off to explore until you've eaten Jill's sustaining Scottish breakfast with haggis; her smoked salmon and scrambled eggs are equally delicious.

Highland cattle graze contentedly as you drive up to the early 17th-century laird's house – you are in the magnificent Borders and Bonchester is a pretty village in the middle of the hills. There are over 140 species of wild flowers in the surrounding countryside and 60 acres of woodland and grazing, so you are undisturbed by 21st-century noise. You breakfast in the big kitchen at one large table and have your own sitting room with woodburner; bedrooms are supremely comfortable and the house filled with lovely things. Before dinner relax with your hosts over a drink – they are super people. *Horse stabling available.*

rooms	3: 2 doubles, 1 twin/double, all with bath/shower.
room price	£50–£54. Single occ. from £37.
meals	Walker's supper from £9. Good food and real ale pub in village.
closed	Christmas.
directions	From Jedburgh, A68 for Edinburgh. Left after 3.5 miles to Ancrum. Fork left to Denholm before village. After 1.75 miles, right, signed Lilliesleaf. Up hill 0.75 miles, then left to Ancrum Craig.

rooms	2: 1 twin, 1 double (with extra bed), both with private bath or shower.
room price	£70–£80. Single occ. from £35.
meals	Dinner with drinks £25.
closed	Very occasionally.
directions	A68 over Border & 1st left onto B6088 for Chesters. Through Chesters; enter Bonchester down hill towards large bridge. Pass The Horse & Hounds. Over small bridge; drive on left.

	Jill & Johan Hensens
	Ancrum Craig,
	Ancrum, By Jedburgh,
	Scottish Borders TD8 6UN
tel	01835 830280
fax	01835 830259
e-mail	acas@ancrumcraig.clara.net
web	www.ancrumcraig.co.uk

	Christopher & Jacqui McLean May
	Hobsburn,
	Bonchester Bridge, Hawick,
	Scottish Borders TD9 8JW
tel	01450 860720
fax	01450 860330
e-mail	b+b@mcleanmay.com
web	www.mcleanmay.com

map: 18 entry: 661

map: 18 entry: 662

SCOTTISH BORDERS

Simple but freshly decorated and comfortable bedrooms, crisp, clean air and a silence disturbed only by wildlife ensure a good night's sleep. Come if you love space, animals and the values of a hard working farm. The views make your heart soar and there are 1,300 acres to roam with sheep, cattle, horses and plenty of wildlife. An excellent place for families: Arran, in spring, encourages children to bottle-feed lambs; she and John are open and friendly, the atmosphere is easy. The walled garden may beckon; or set off to explore the nearby Roman encampment, Lyne Fort. Good value.

rooms	3: 2 doubles, 1 twin, sharing 2 bathrooms.
room price	£40-£44. Single occ. £24.
meals	Breakfast 8-9am. Packed lunch £3-£5. Supper £12. Dinner, 4 courses, £24, by arrangement. B.Y.O.
closed	Christmas Day.
directions	4 miles west of Peebles on A72, signed on right-hand side of main road.

Arran & John Waddell
Lyne Farmhouse,
Lyne Farm, Peebles,
Peeblesshire EH45 8NR

tel	01721 740255
fax	01721 740255
e-mail	awaddell@farming.co.uk
web	www.lynefarm.co.uk

map: 18 entry: 663

STIRLING

A setting that townies dream of – 170 traffic-free acres that wrap around the house, and majestic views. This is an excellent base for families, with sheep, horses and cows and masses of opportunities for fishing, walking, cycling and climbing. You have your own private guest wing with pine-clad, cathedral-roofed sitting room – sunny and south-facing – and double bed, and a gallery landing with a further two single beds. Porridge, cooked overnight on the Aga, is yours for breakfast. Val, generous and enthusiastic, will collect you from the airport or the station; she has cooked professionally, so the food's great.

rooms	Guest wing for 2-4: 1 double, 1 twin on mezzanine, sharing shower room & sitting area.
room price	From £70. Reductions for group bookings. Single occ. £35.
meals	Packed lunch £3-£5. Afternoon tea from £3. Dinner £20-£25.
closed	Rarely.
directions	A81, 3 miles south of Aberfoyle. 0.5 miles north of Gartmore House, over River Forth & 1st private road to right. Look for house sign halfway up. Drive to right of house beside pond.

Val Willis
The Barns of Shannochill,
By Aberfoyle, The Trossachs,
Stirling FK8 3UZ

tel	01877 382878
fax	01877 382964
e-mail	shannochill@aol.com
web	www.thebarnsofshannochill.co.uk

map: 17 entry: 664

STIRLING

A Grade II-listed Georgian country house standing in 28 acres; roe deer 'prune' the roses, pheasants roam, wild flowers flourish. George Buchanan, tutor to James VI of Scotland, was born here. Walking sticks and the bell of HMS Tempest in the porch, long rugs and wooden floors in the hall, an open fire and bay windows in the drawing room. At breakfast, sit at the big oak dining room table and gaze out across open country to the local distillery in the distance! Big bedrooms are excellent: crisp linen, electric blankets, pristine bathrooms, fresh flowers – and a piano on the landing.

rooms	3: 1 twin with bath; 2 doubles, sharing bathroom. Doubles only let to members of same party.
room price	£60. Single occ. £30.
meals	Good pubs/restaurants within 2 miles.
closed	Occasionally.
directions	4 miles west of Blanefield. Left off A81 opp. Cairn Conservatories. After 300 yds, house is 1st entrance on left after bridge.

	Rozie Parker
	The Moss,
	Killearn,
	Stirling G63 9LJ
tel	01360 550053
fax	01360 550053
e-mail	themoss@freeuk.com

WEST LOTHIAN

Some hosts work hard at giving a big welcome; with the Westmacotts it just happens. They are easy-going, entertaining and energetic. You'll enjoy gathering around the fire for a drink before setting off for supper, or lingering over breakfast because conversation is flowing. Family paintings and country views in the dining and drawing rooms; bathrobes and warm comfort in the large bedrooms. Wander in the orchard or pop in and see the working couperage. Ten minutes from Edinburgh airport and from Dalmeny village there are trains to the city every half hour; Louise can meet you at the station.

rooms	4: 2 twins/doubles, 1 double, 1 single, sharing 2 bathrooms & separate wc.
room price	£56-£60. Single occ. from £66.
meals	Good pubs/restaurants 2 miles.
closed	Christmas.
directions	From lights in centre of Kirkliston, follow sign for Forth Rd Bridge (A8000) & on at r'bout. Approx. 0.5 miles on, 1st right after Milton Farm. Down lane, over small bridge & right before cottages.

	Louise & Michael Westmacott
	Craigbrae,
	Kirkliston, By Edinburgh,
	West Lothian EH29 9EL
tel	0131 331 1205
fax	0131 319 1476
e-mail	louise@craigbrae.com

Susan is genetically predisposed to spoiling people rotten. Her home-baking is sinful (expect a feast for breakfast), her green fingers have teased a garden from an awkward field, and she's hot on Scottish history, so can help you plan your day. Her modern house on the edge of a residential estate has lovely big rooms that swim with light. A smart green dining room, a multi-windowed sitting room, and spotless bedrooms, country-cosy, with wicker chairs and crisp linen. The M8 passes within a mile, but triple-glazing soundproofs entirely. *Children over 12 welcome.*

rooms	2: 1 twin with shower; 1 double with private bath/shower.
room price	£60. Single occ. £30.
meals	Packed lunch £5. Pub/restaurants 0.5 miles.
closed	Christmas, New Year & occasionally.
directions	M9, junc. 3, then A803 into Linlithgow. There, right onto A706 for Bo'ness and 0.2 miles on left. Folllow to very end of road.

Mr & Mrs W Denholm
Lochmill House,
3 Lade Court, Linlithgow,
West Lothian EH49 7QF
tel   01506 846682
e-mail   williedenholm@hotmail.com

map: 18 entry: 667

WHAT'S IN THE BACK OF THE BOOK...

WHAT IS ALASTAIR SAWDAY PUBLISHING?

These books owe their style and mood to Alastair's miscellaneous career and his interest in the community and the environment.

A dozen or more of us work in two converted barns on a farm near Bristol, close enough to the city for a bicycle ride and far enough for a silence broken only by horses and the occasional passage of a tractor. Some editors work in the countries they write about, e.g. France; others work from the UK but are based outside the office. We enjoy each other's company, celebrate every event possible, and work in an easy-going but committed environment.

These books owe their style and mood to Alastair's miscellaneous career and his interest in the community and the environment. He has taught overseas, worked with refugees, run development projects abroad, founded a travel company and several environmental organisations. There has been a slightly mad streak evident throughout, not least in his driving of a waste-paper-collection lorry for a year, the manning of stalls at jumble sales and the pursuit of causes long before they were considered sane.

Back to the travel company: trying to take his clients to eat and sleep in places that were not owned by corporations and assorted bandits he found dozens of very special places in France – farms, châteaux etc – a list that grew into the first book, French Bed and Breakfast. It was a celebration of 'real' places to stay and the remarkable people who run them.

The publishing company grew from that first and rather whimsical French book. It started as a mild crusade, and there it stays - full of 'attitude', and the more appealing for it. For we still celebrate the unusual, the beautiful, the individual. We are passionate about rejecting the banal, the ugly, the pompous and the indifferent and we are passionate too about 'real' food. Alastair is a trustee of the Soil Association and keen to promote organic growing and consuming by owners and visitors.

It is a source of deep pleasure to us to know that there are many thousands of people who share our views. We are by no means alone in trumpeting the virtues of resisting the destruction and uniformity of so much of our culture – and the the cultures of other nations, too.

We run a company in which people and values matter. We love to hear of new friendships between those in the book and those using it, and to know that there are many people – among them farmers - who have been enabled to pursue their decent lives thanks to the extra income the book brings them.

WWW.SPECIALPLACESTOSTAY.COM

Britain

France

Ireland

Italy

Portugal

Spain

...all in

one place!

On the unfathomable and often unnavigable sea of internet accommodation pages, those who have discovered **www.specialplacestostay.com** have found it to be an island of reliability. Not only will you find a database full of honest, trustworthy, up-to-date information about Special Places to Stay across Europe, but also:

- Links to the web sites of well over a thousand places from the series

- Colourful, clickable, interactive maps to help you find the right place

- The facility to make most bookings by email –
  even if you don't have email yourself

- Online purchasing of our books, securely and cheaply

- Regular, exclusive special offers on titles from the series

- The latest news about future editions, new titles and new places

The site is constantly evolving and is frequently updated. We've revised our maps, adding more useful and interesting links, providing news, updates and special features that won't appear anywhere else but in our window on the world wide web.

Just as with our printed guides, your feedback counts, so when you've surfed all this and you still want more, let us know – this site has been planted with room to grow.

Russell Wilkinson, Web Producer
website@specialplacestostay.com

If you'd like to receive news and updates about our books by email, send a message to newsletter@specialplacestostay.com

THE LITTLE EARTH BOOK

The Little Earth Book

*Only dead fish float with the current;
live fish swim against it.*

Over 30,000 copies sold.

A fascinating read. The earth is now desperately vulnerable; so are we. Original, stimulating short essays about what is going wrong with our planet, and about the greatest challenge of our century: how to save the Earth for us all. It is pithy, yet intellectually credible, well-referenced, wry yet deadly serious.

Researched and written by a Bristol architect, James Bruges, The Little Earth Book is a clarion call to action, a stimulating collection of short essays on today's most important environmental concerns, from global warming and poisoned food to unfettered economic growth, Third World debt, genes and 'superbugs'. Undogmatic but sure-footed, the style is light, explaining complex issues with easy language, illustrations and cartoons. Ideas are developed chapter by chapter, yet each one stands alone. It is an easy browse.

The Little Earth Book provides hope, with new ideas and examples of people swimming against the current, for bold ideas that work in practice. It is a book as important as it is original. Learn about the issues and join the most important debate of this century.

Did you know…

- If everyone adopted the Western lifestyle we would need five earths to support us?
- In 50 years the US has – with intensive pesticide use – doubled the amount of crops lost to pests?
- Environmental disasters have already created more than 80 MILLION refugees?

www.littleearth.co.uk

And now The Little Food Book! Same style, same purpose: it blows the lid off the food 'industry' – in a concise, entertaining way. Written by Craig Sams, Chairman of the Soil Association, it is pithy, deeply informative and an important contribution to the great food debate.

ALASTAIR SAWDAY'S

French Bed & Breakfast
Edition 7   £14.99

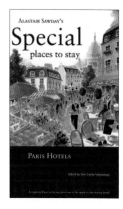

Paris Hotels
Edition 3   £8.95

British Bed & Breakfast
Edition 7   £14.99

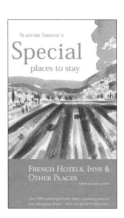

**French Hotels, Inns &
Other Places**
Edition 2   £11.95

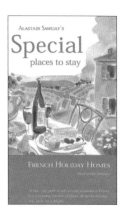

French Holiday Homes
Edition 1   £11.99

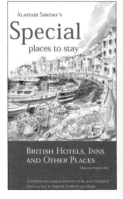

**British Hotels, Inns &
Other Places**
Edition 3   £11.99

www.specialpl

SPECIAL PLACES TO STAY SERIES

Garden Bed & Breakfast
Edition 1   £10.95

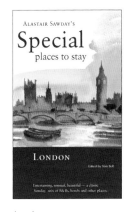

London
Edition 1   £9.99

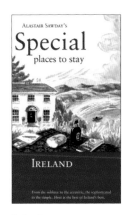

Ireland
Edition 3   £10.95

Spain
Edition 4   £11.95

Italy
Edition 2   £11.95

Portugal
Edition 1   £8.95

estostay.com

REPORT FORM

Comments on existing entries and new discoveries

If you have any comments on entries in this guide, please let us have them. If you have a favourite house, hotel, inn or other new discovery, not just in Britain, please let us know about it.

Book title: _____

Entry no: _____

New recommendation: _____

Country: _____

Name of property: _____

Address: _____

_____

_____

Postcode: _____

Tel: _____

Date of stay: _____

Comments: _____

_____

_____

From: _____

Address: _____

_____

_____

Postcode: _____

Tel: _____

Please send the completed form to:

Alastair Sawday Publishing,
The Home Farm Stables, Barrow Gurney, Bristol BS48 3RW.
or go to www.specialplacestostay.com and click on 'contact'.

Thank you.

ORDER FORM UK

All these Special Places to Stay books are available in major
bookshops or you may order them direct.
Post and packaging are FREE.

		Price	No. copies
French Bed & Breakfast	Edition 7	£14.99	
French Hotels, Inns and other places	Edition 2	£11.99	
French Holiday Homes	Edition 1	£11.99	
Paris Hotels	Edition 3	£ 8.95	
British Bed & Breakfast	Edition 7	£14.99	
British Hotels, Inns and other places	Edition 3	£11.99	
Garden Bed & Breakfast	Edition 1	£10.95	
London	Edition 1	£ 9.99	
Ireland	Edition 3	£10.95	
Spain	Edition 4	£11.95	
Portugal	Edition 1	£ 8.95	
Italy	Edition 2	£11.95	
The Little Earth Book	Edition 2	£ 5.99	

Please make cheques payable to: Total £
Alastair Sawday Publishing

Please send cheques to: Alastair Sawday Publishing,
The Home Farm Stables, Barrow Gurney, Bristol BS48 3RW.
For credit card orders call 01275 464891 or order directly
from our website **www.specialplacestostay.com**

Title   First name

Surname

Address

Postcode

Tel

If you do not wish to receive mail from other
like-minded companies, please tick here. ☐

If you would prefer not to receive information about
special offers on our books, please tick here. ☐   BBB7

ORDER FORM USA

All these books are available at your local bookstore, or you
may order direct. Allow two to three weeks for delivery.

		Price	No. copies
Portugal	Edition 1	$14.95	
Spain	Edition 4	$19.95	
Ireland	Edition 3	$17.95	
Paris Hotels	Edition 3	$14.95	
Garden Bed & Breakfast	Edition 1	$17.95	
French Bed & Breakfast	Edition 8	$19.95	
French Hotels, Inns and other places	Edition 2	$19.95	
British Hotels, Inns and other places	Edition 4	$17.95	
London	Edition 1	$12.95	
Italy	Edition 2	$17.95	
French Holiday Homes	Edition 1	$17.95	
	Total $		

Shipping in the continental USA: $3.95 for one book,
$4.95 for two books, $5.95 for three or more books.
Outside continental USA, call (800) 243-0495 for prices.
For delivery to AK, CA, CO, CT, FL, GA, IL, IN, KS, MI, MN, MO, NE,
NM, NC, OK, SC, TN, TX, VA, and WA, please add appropriate sales tax.

Please make checks payable to: **Total $**
The Globe Pequot Press

To order by phone with MasterCard or Visa: (800) 243-0495,
9am to 5pm EST; by fax: (800) 820-2329, 24 hours;
through our web site: **www.globe-pequot.com**; or by mail:
The Globe Pequot Press, P.O. Box 480, Guilford, CT 06437

Date

Name

Address

Town

State

Zip code

Tel

Fax

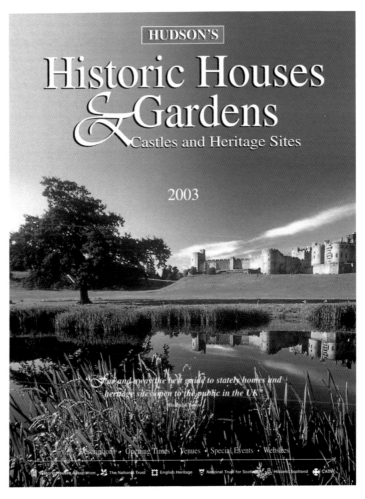

Discover the best-selling, definitive annual heritage guide to Britain's castles, stately homes and gardens open to the public.

600 pages featuring 2000 properties with
more than 1500 colour photographs.
An invaluable reference source <u>and</u> a good read.

Get there by bike!

The National Cycle Network is 10,000 miles of routes throughout the UK due to be completed by 2005. Linking towns and cities with the countryside on quiet roads and traffic-free paths, the Network offers a great way to explore Britain.

Longer-distance sections, ideal for a weekend break or holidays, are covered by an award-winning range of maps.

Alternatively, view the on-line mapping at **www.sustrans.org.uk** or call Sustrans, the charity behind the Network on **0117 929 0888**

sustrans

routes for people

QUICK REFERENCE INDICES

QUICK REFERENCE INDICES

Child friendly

The owners of these houses welcome children of any age but may not have all the equipment you need, so discuss beforehand.

England

Bath & N.E. Somerset • 8 • 9 •11 •13 • Berkshire •18 • Bristol • 21 • 22 • 23 • Cambridgeshire • 27 • 28 • Cheshire • 30 • 31 • Cornwall • 41 • 43 • 47 • 54 • 55 • 58 • 59 • 60 • 61 • 63 • 65 • 68 • 71 • 75 • Cumbria • 83 • 84 • 86 • 88 • 89 • 91 • Derbyshire • 95 • Devon • 108 • 109 • 115 • 116 • 117 • 118 • 119 • 120 • 121 • 122 • 123 • 124 • 129 • 134 • 138 • 139 • 143 • 145 • 146 • 149 • 150 • Dorset • 156 • 157• 161 • 164 • 167 • 169 • 171 • 173 • 177 • Durham • 183 • 185 • Essex • 186 • 187 • 189 • Gloucestershire • 191 • 192 • 193 • 196 • 197 • 199 • 200 • 202 • 204 • 206 • 207 • 208 • 213 • Hampshire • 218 • 221 • Herefordshire • 230 • 231 • 232 • 233 • 235 • 236 • 239 • 240 • 241 • 242 • 243 • 246 • Hertfordshire • 248 • Isle of Wight • 252 • Kent • 256 • 257 • 258 • 261 • 264 • 269 • 270 • Leicestershire • 274 • Lincolnshire • 276 • 279 • 280 • 282 • 283 • London • 284 • 286 • 290 • 291 • 297 • 301 • Norfolk • 304 • 306 • 308 • 309 • 311 • 312 • 313 • 315 • 316 • 318 • 322 • Northamptonshire • 326 • Northumberland • 330 • 331 • 335 • 336 • 338 • 340 • Nottinghamshire • 344 • 345 • 346 • Oxfordshire • 349 • 350 • 352 • 353 • 358 • Shropshire • 361 • 364 • 368 • 371 • 372 • 373 • 377 • Somerset • 388 • 389 • 397 • 398 • 399 • 401 • 402 • 403 • Staffordshire • 405 • 408 • 409 • Suffolk • 416 • 419 • 422 • 423 • 424 • 425 • 426 • 428 • 430 • 431 • 432 • 433 • 436 • Surrey • 439 • 440 • 442 • 443 • 444 • 446 • 447 • Sussex • 452 • 454 • 457 • 460 • 462 • 465 • 468 • Warwickshire • 470 • 471 • 472 • 473 • 475 • 478 • 480 • 482 • Wiltshire • 484 • 492 • 493 • 496 • 501 • 504 • 506 • Yorkshire • 510 • 512 • 514 • 517 • 521 • 522 • 523 • 528 • 529 • 530 • 532 • 533 • 536 • 538 • 542

Wales

Bridgend • 548 • Carmarthenshire • 549 • 553 • 554 • Denbighshire • 559 • Flintshire • 562 • Gwynedd • 564 • 566 • 567 • 568 • Monmouthshire • 570 • Pembrokeshire • 577 • Powys • 579 • 580 • 581 • 583

QUICK REFERENCE INDICES

Scotland
Aberdeenshire • 586 • 587 • 588 • 589 • Argyll & Bute • 590 • 593 • 595 • Dumfries & Galloway • 598 • 599 • 600 • 602 • 605 • East Lothian • 607 • 608 • 609 • Edinburgh • 610 • 611 • 613 • 614 • 615 • 616 • 618 • 619 • 620 • 621 • Fife • 622 • 623 • Highland • 625 • 627 • 633 • 634 • 635 • 636 • Isle of Lewis • 637 • Lanarkshire • 642 • Moray • 643 • 644 • Perth & Kinross • 646 • 647 • 651 • 653 • 654 • Renfrewshire • 655 • 656 • Scottish Borders • 658 • 659 • 660 • 661 • 663 • Stirling • 664 • 665 • West Lothian • 666

No car? These owners have told us that their house can be reached by public transport and that they are happy to collect you from the nearest drop-off point. Check exact details when booking. (Others not on this list may be willing to help, too, so do ask.)

England
Bath & N.E. Somerset • 14 • Bristol • 23 • Cornwall • 38 • 40 • 44 • 53 • 59 • 61 • Cumbria • 86 • 89 • Derbyshire • 93 • Devon • 110 • 112 • 117 • 119 • 146 • 147 • Dorset • 165 • Durham • 184 • Essex • 187 • Gloucestershire • 202 • Hampshire • 214 • 215 • Herefordshire • 226 • 241 • 243 • Kent • 256 • 266 • Leicestershire • 274 • London • 297 • Norfolk • 306 • Northamptonshire • 325 • Shropshire • 363 • 368 • 373 • Somerset • 381 • 388 • 401 • 402 • Suffolk • 411 • 415 • 420 • 431 • 456 • Sussex • 468 • Warwickshire • 474 • Wiltshire • 495 • 500 • 502 • Yorkshire • 518 • 530 • 537 • 542 • 544

Wales
Carmarthenshire • 550 • Conwy • 556 • Flintshire • 560 • Gwynedd • 564 • 565 • 567 • 569 • Pembrokeshire • 573 • 577

Scotland
Aberdeenshire • 586 • Ayrshire • 597 • Dumfries & Galloway • 598 • 601 • 603 • Edinburgh • 614 • Highland • 625 • 627 • 635 • Perth & Kinross • 649 • Renfrewshire • 656 • Scottish Borders • 660 • 663 • West Lothian • 667

QUICK REFERENCE INDICES

Pets welcome

England

At these houses your pet can sleep in your room with you.
Bath & N.E. Somerset • 1 • Cambridgeshire • 27 • 29 •
Cornwall • 37 • 46 • 47 • 55 • 56 • 71 • 72 • Cumbria • 82 •
87 • 90 • Derbyshire • 96 • 98 • Devon • 109 • 115 • 116 • 117
• 118 • 119 • 120 • 122 • 124 • 126 • 127 • 129 • 130 • 138 •
149 • Dorset • 153 • 155 • 158 • 161 • 164 • 167 • 169 • 176 •
Durham • 180 • 181 • 185 • Essex • 186 • Gloucestershire •
193 • 194 • Hampshire • 216 • 218 • Herefordshire • 227 •
231 • 242 • 243 • 244 • 247 • Hertfordshire • 248 • Kent • 266
• 267 • Lincolnshire • 279 • 282 • 283 • Norfolk • 303 • 304 •
306 • 312 • 313 • 314 • 317 • 318 • 321 • 322 •
Northamptonshire • 326 • 329 • 330 • Northumberland • 341
• Nottinghamshire • 345 • Oxfordshire • 349 • Shropshire •
361 • 362 • 364 • 373 • Somerset • 380 • 383 • 388 • 390 •
396 • 398 • 401 • 402 • 403 • Staffordshire • 405 • 406 • 409
• Suffolk • 414 • 416 • 422 • 423 • 424 • 425 • 426 • 430 •
432 • 436 • Sussex • 448 • 450 • 457 • 464 • Warwickshire •
471 • 473 • 475• 476 • 479 • 480 • Wiltshire • 493 • 496 •
Yorkshire • 512 • 517 • 521 • 522 • 523 • 525 • 526 • 528 •
536 • 538 • 544

Wales

Anglesey • 547 • Carmarthenshire • 552 • Ceredigion • 555 •
Denbighshire • 558 • 559 • Flintshire • 562 • Gwynedd • 564 •
566 • Pembrokeshire • 575 • Powys • 579 • 581

Scotland

Argyll & Bute • 591 • Dumfries & Galloway • 601 • 604 • East
Lothian • 608 • 609 • Edinburgh • 611 • 615 • Fife • 622 • 623
• Highland • 627 • 628 • 630 • 633 • 634 • 636 • Isle of Lewis •
637 • Isle of Mull • 638 • Isle of Skye • 641 • Lanarkshire • 642
• Perth & Kinross • 654 • Renfrewshire • 655 • 656 • Scottish
Borders • 660 • 661 • 663 •
West Lothian • 666

At these houses your pet can sleep in the house, but not in your room.
England

Bath & N.E. Somerset • 15 • 17 • Cheshire • 33 • 36 • 41 • 51 •
54 • 63 • Cumbria • 86 • Derbyshire • 101 • 102 • Dorset •
156 • Gloucestershire • 206 • Herefordshire • 243 •
Leicestershire • 274 • Norfolk • 310 • Northamptonshire • 325

At these houses your pet can sleep in kennels or outbuildings.

Tennis   There's a tennis court in the grounds of these houses.

QUICK REFERENCE INDICES

Bikes available | These owners have bikes you can borrow or can organise local hire.
England
Bath & N.E. Somerset • 1 • 13 • Bristol • 24 • Cornwall • 40 •
61 • 68 • Cumbria • 82 • Dorset • 152 • 161 • Durham • 182 •
Gloucestershire • 195 • Isle of Wight • 251 • Kent • 256 • 268
• Leicestershire • 274 • Lincolnshire • 281 • Norfolk • 302 •
313 • 320 • Northamptonshire • 325 • Oxfordshire • 352 •
Shropshire • 366 • 371 • Somerset • 387 • Suffolk • 414 •
419 • 427 • 430 • 434 • Sussex • 461 • Warwickshire • 482 •
Wiltshire • 487 • 490 • 497 • Yorkshire • 537

Wales
Flintshire • 560 • Gwynedd • 567 •

Scotland
Argyll & Bute • 594 • Ayrshire • 597 • Dumfries & Galloway
• 600 • 601 • Fife • 624 • Highland • 636 • Renfrewshire •
656 • West Lothian • 667

Pool | These are houses with a swimming pool in the grounds.
England
Bath & N.E. Somerset • 1 • Berkshire • 18 • Cornwall • 42 •
62 • Devon • 122 • Durham • 180 • Gloucestershire • 192 •
206 • 208 • 210 • 212 • Herefordshire • 227 • Kent • 254 •
264 • Norfolk • 321 • Shropshire • 366 • 371 • 397 • Somerset
• 399 • Suffolk • 423 • Sussex • 451 • 460 • 465 • Wiltshire •
493 • 494

Wales
Monmouthshire • 570 • 571

QUICK REFERENCE INDICES

QUICK REFERENCE INDICES

Horse B&B   Want to travel with your trusty steed? Stabling available here.

INDEX – SURNAME

INDEX – SURNAME

INDEX – SURNAME

INDEX – SURNAME

INDEX – SURNAME

INDEX – SURNAME

INDEX – PLACE NAME

INDEX – PLACE NAME

INDEX – PLACE NAME

INDEX – PLACE NAME

EXCHANGE RATE TABLE

£ Sterling	US$	Euro€
1	1.57	1.56
5	7.83	7.80
7	10.96	10.91
10	15.66	15.59
15	23.48	23.39
17	26.61	26.51
20	31.31	31.18
25	39.14	38.98
30	46.97	46.77
35	54.79	54.57
40	62.62	62.37
45	70.45	70.16
50	78.28	77.96
70	109.58	109.04
90	140.90	140.20

August 2002

EXPLANATION OF SYMBOLS

Treat each one as a guide rather than a statement of fact and check important points when booking:

Children are positively welcomed, with no age restrictions, but cots, high chairs etc are not necessarily available.

Full and approved wheelchair facilities for at least one bedroom and bathroom and access to all ground-floor common areas.

Basic ground-floor access for people of limited mobility and at least one bedroom and bathroom accessible without steps, but not full facilities for wheelchair-users.

No smoking anywhere in the house.

Smoking restrictions exist usually, but not always, in the dining room and some bedrooms. Check when booking.

Pets are welcome but may have to sleep in an outbuilding or your car. Check when booking.

Pets live in the house: dog, cat, duck, parrot…

Credit cards accepted; most commonly Visa and MasterCard.

Vegetarians catered for with advance warning. All hosts can cater for vegetarians at breakfast.

Most, but not necessarily all, ingredients are organic, organically grown, home-grown or locally grown.

The premises are licensed.

Working farm.

You can either borrow or hire bikes here.

Good hiking from house or village.

SSSI   Site of Special Scientific Interest (often rich in flora and fauna).

AONB   Area of Outstanding National Beauty.